WORKSHOP MAINTENANCE MANUAL

FOR THE

Royal Enfield

METEOR 700 1952-1955 and 500 TWIN 1949-1958 MOTOR CYCLES

A Floyd Clymer Publication
This edition published in 2023 by
www.VelocePress.com

All rights reserved. This work may not be reproduced or transmitted in any form without the express written consent of the publisher.

INTRODUCTION

Welcome to the world of digital publishing ~ the book you now hold in your hand was printed using the latest state of the art digital technology. The advent of print-on-demand has forever changed the publishing process, never has information been so accessible and it is our hope that this book serves your informational needs for years to come. If this is your first exposure to digital publishing, we hope that you are pleased with the results. Many more titles of interest to the classic automobile and motorcycle enthusiast, collector and restorer are available via our website at www.VelocePress.com. We hope that you find this title as interesting as we do.

NOTE FROM THE PUBLISHER

The information presented is true and complete to the best of our knowledge. All recommendations are made without any guarantees on the part of the author or the publisher, who also disclaim all liability incurred with the use of this information.

TRADEMARKS

We recognize that some words, model names and designations, for example, mentioned herein are the property of the trademark holder. We use them for identification purposes only. This is not an official publication.

INFORMATION ON THE USE OF THIS PUBLICATION

This manual is an invaluable resource for those interested in performing their own maintenance. However, in today's information age we are constantly subject to changes in common practice, new technology, availability of improved materials and increased awareness of chemical toxicity. As such, it is advised that the user consult with an experienced professional prior to undertaking any procedure described herein. While every care has been taken to ensure correctness of information, it is obviously not possible to guarantee complete freedom from errors or omissions or to accept liability arising from such errors or omissions. Therefore, any individual that uses the information contained within, or elects to perform or participate in do-it-yourself repairs or modifications acknowledges that there is a risk factor involved and that the publisher or its associates cannot be held responsible for personal injury or property damage resulting from the use of the information or the outcome of such procedures.

PAGE NUMBERING

The numbers to the bottom of each page are the page numbers within the book they are not referenced in the index of the individual workshop manuals. However, they may be useful to record and identify any appropriate 'section' when using the 'Notes' pages. The 'Super Meteor' and the 'Constellation' manual begins immediately after the 'Meteor 700' manual at page 113.

WARNING!

One final word of advice, this publication is intended to be used as a reference guide, and when in doubt the reader should consult with a qualified technician.

692 c.c. O.H.V. SPRING FRAME "METEOR 700"

496 c.c. O.H.V. SPRING FRAME "500 TWIN"

Contents

SECTION A1a—TECHNICAL DATA ("METEOR 700" ENGINE)

SECTION A1b—TECHNICAL DATA ("500 TWIN" ENGINE)

SECTION B1—ENGINE SPECIFICATION

	Sub-section	Page
Engine	1	1
Cylinder Heads	2	1
Cylinders	3	1
Pistons	4	1
Connecting Rods	5	1
Crankcase	6	1
Crankshaft and Flywheel	7	1
Main Bearings	8	1
Camshafts	9	1
Valves	10	1
Valve Gear	11	1
Timing Drive	12	1
Ignition and Lighting System	13	2
Carburettor	14	3
Air Filter	15	3
Lubrication System	16	3
Breather	17	3
Gearbox	18	3
Clutch	19	3

SECTION C1—SERVICE OPERATIONS WITH ENGINE IN FRAME

Removal of Timing Cover	1	1
Valve Timing	2	1
Tappet Adjustment	3	1
Ignition Timing	4	1
Primary Chain Adjustment	5	2
Timing Chain Adjustment	6	3
Magneto Chain Adjustment	7	3
Removal of Dual Seat	8	4
Removal of Petrol Tank	9	4

ROYAL ENFIELD WORKSHOP MANUAL

Contents—contd.

SECTION C1—SERVICE OPERATIONS WITH ENGINE IN FRAME

	Sub-section	Page
Removal of Cylinder Heads	10	4
Removal of Valves	11	4
Removal of Rockers	12	4
Removal of Valve Guides	13	5
Renewal of Sparking Plug Inserts	14	5
Removal of Cylinders	15	5
Removal of Pistons	16	6
Decarbonising	17	6
Grinding-in Valves	18	6
Re-assembly after Decarbonising	19	6
Cleaning Oil Filter	20	7
Overhaul of Oil Pumps	21	7
Removal of Timing Chains	22	7
Removal of Pump Worm and Timing Sprocket	23	7
Removal of Camshaft Sprockets	24	7
Removal of Magneto Sprocket	25	7
Removal of Engine and Clutch Sprockets	26	8
Removal of Tappets and Guides	27	8
Dismantling Breather	28	8
Removal of Clutch	29	8
Removal of Final Drive Sprocket	30	8
Removal of Bearing Housing Felt Washer	31	8
Oil Pipe Unions	32	8
Pressure Relief Valves	33	9

SECTION D1—SERVICE OPERATIONS WITH ENGINE REMOVED

Removal of the Engine from the Frame	1	1
Removal of the Gearbox	2	1
Dismantling the Crankcase	3	1
Main Bearings	4	2
Fitting the Connecting Rods	5	2
Re-assembly of the Crankcase	6	2
Pump Worm Locknut	7	3

SECTION E1—GEARBOX AND CLUTCH

Removal of the Gearbox	1	1
To Dismantle the Gearbox	2	1
Removal of the Ball Races	3	3
Change-Gear Mechanism	4	3
Re-assembling the Gearbox	5	3
Dismantling and Re-assembly of the Clutch	6	3
Adjustment of the Clutch Control	7	3
Adjustment of the Neutral Finder	8	4
Gearbox Oil Level	9	4

Contents—contd.

SECTION F1—AMAL NEEDLE TYPE CARBURETTOR

	Sub-section	Page
General Description	1	1
Tuning the Carburettor	2	1
Dismantling Carburettor	3	3
Causes of High Petrol Consumption	4	4

SECTION G1a—LUCAS COIL IGNITION EQUIPMENT

	Sub-section	Page
General	1	1
Ignition Coil	1(a)	1
Distributor	1(b)	1
Routine Maintenance	2	1
Distributor	2(a)	1
High Tension Cables	2(b)	2
Servicing	3	2
Testing in position to locate Ignition Fault	3(a)	2
Dismantling the Distributor	3(b)	2
Bearings	3(c)	3
Contact Breaker	3(d)	3
Reassembly	3(e)	3

SECTION G1b—LUCAS MAGDYNO

	Sub-section	Page
General	1	1
Routine Maintenance	2	1
Lubrication	2(a)	1
Adjustments	2(b)	2
Cleaning	2(c)	2
Renewing High Tension Cables	2(d)	2
Renewing Timing Control Cable	2(e)	2
Contact Breaker Spring	2(f)	3
Testing Magdyno in Position on Engine	3	3

SECTION G2a—LUCAS DYNAMO MODEL C35SD

	Sub-section	Page
General	1	1
Lubrication	2(a)	1
Inspection of Commutator and Brush Gear	2(b)	2
Test Data	3	2
Testing in Position to locate fault in Charging Circuit	4(a)	2
To Dismantle	4(b)	3
Commutator	4(c)	3
Field Coil	4(d)	3
Armature	4(e)	4
Bearings	4(f)	4
Reassembly	4(g)	5
Dynamo Polarity	5	5

Contents—contd.

SECTION G2b—LUCAS DYNAMO MODEL E3LM

	Sub-section	Page
General	1	1
Lubrication	2(a)	1
Inspection of Commutator and Brush Gear	2(b)	1
Test Data	3	1
Testing in Position to Locate Fault in Charging Circuit	4(a)	1
To Dismantle	4(b)	2
Commutator	4(c)	3
Field Coil	4(d)	3
Armature	4(e)	4
Bearings	4(f)	4
Reassembly	4(g)	4
Dynamo Polarity	5	4

SECTION G3a—CONTROL BOX

	Sub-section	Page
General	1	1
Setting Data	2	1
Servicing	3	1

SECTION G4a—BATTERY MODEL PUZ7E

	Sub-section	Page
General	1	1
Preparation for Service	2	1
Routine Maintenance	3	1
Servicing	4	2

SECTION G5a—HEAD AND TAIL LAMPS

	Sub-section	Page
Headlamp	1	1
Lucas Light Unit	2	1
Replacing Light Unit and Bulb	3	2
Parking Light	4	2
Tail Light	5	2

SECTION H1—FRAME

	Sub-section	Page
Description of Frame	1	2
Steering Head Races	2	2
Removal of Rear Suspension Unit	3	2
Servicing Rear Suspension Units	4	2
Removal of Swinging Arm Chain Stays	5	4
Centre Stand	6	4
Wheel Alignment	7	5
Lubrication	8	5

Contents—contd.

SECTION J1—FRONT FORK WITH CASQUETTE, USED ON "METEOR 700" & "500 TWIN," 1954 ONWARDS

	Sub-section	Page
Description	1	1
Operation of the Fork	2	1
Dismantling the Fork to Replace Spring, Oil Seal or Bearing Bushes	3	2
Spring	4	3
Reassembly of Parts	5	3
Steering Head Races	6	3
Removal of Complete Fork	7	3
Lubrication	8	4
Air Vents	9	4

SECTION J3—FRONT FORK WITH FACIA PANEL. USED ON "METEOR 700," 1953

Description	1	1
Operation of Fork	2	1
Dismantling the Fork to Replace Spring, Oil Seal or Bearing Bushes	3	2
Spring	4	2
Steering Head Races	5	3
Removal of Facia Panel Fork Head, Spring, etc.	6	3
Removal of Main Tubes	7	4
Reassembly of Parts	8	4
Lubrication	9	4

SECTION J4—FRONT FORK WITH FACIA PANEL. USED ON "500 TWIN," 1950-53 INCLUSIVE

Description	1	1
Dismantling Fork to Replace Spring, Oil Seal or Bearing Bushes	2	1
Spring	3	1
Steering Head Races	4	1
Removal of Facia Panel Fork Head, Spring, etc.	5	3
Removal of Main Tubes	6	3
Reassembly of Parts	7	3
Lubrication	8	3

SECTION K1—FRONT WHEEL WITH DUAL BRAKE. FITTED TO "METEOR 700," 1953 ONWARDS & "500 TWIN," 1955 ONWARDS

Removal from Fork	1	1
Removal of Brake Cover Plate Assemblies	2	1
Removal of Brake Shoes and Springs	3	1
Replacing Brake Linings	4	2
Removal of Hub Spindle and Bearings	5	2
Hub Bearings	6	2
Fitting Limits for Bearings	7	2
Refitting Ball Bearings	8	2
Reassembly of Brake Shoes on to Cover Plates	9	3
Floating Cam Housings	10	3
Refitting Brake Cover Plates	11	3
Wheel Rim	12	3
Spokes	13	4
Wheel Building and Truing	14	4
Tyre	15	4
Tyre Pressure	16	4
Lubrication	17	4

Contents—contd.

SECTION K2—FRONT WHEEL WITH SINGLE BRAKE. FITTED TO "500 TWIN" UP TO END OF 1954

	Sub-section	Page
Removal from Fork	1	1
Removal of Brake Cover Plate Assembly	2	1
Removal of Brake Shoes and Springs	3	1
Replacing Brake Linings	4	1
Removal of Hub Spindle and Bearings	5	1
Hub Bearings	6	2
Fitting Limits for Bearings	7	2
Refitting Ball Bearings	8	2
Reassembly of Brake Shoes to Cover Plate	9	3
Floating Cam Housing	10	3
Refitting Brake Cover Plate	11	3
Wheel Rims	12	3
Spokes	13	4
Wheel Building and Truing	14	4
Tyres	15	4
Tyre Pressures	16	5
Lubrication	17	5

SECTION L1—REAR WHEEL (DETACHABLE TYPE)

	Sub-section	Page
Description	1	1
Removal and Replacement of Main Portion of Wheel for Tyre Repairs, etc.	2	1
Removal and Replacement of complete Wheel for Access to Brake	3	2
Removal of Brake Shoes for Replacement, Fitting New Linings, etc.	4	3
Replacing Brake Linings	5	3
Removal of Brake Operating Cam and Brake Shoe Pivot Pin	6	3
Cush Drive	7	3
Removal of Ball Bearings	8	4
Hub Bearings	9	4
Fitting Limits for Bearings	10	4
Refitting Ball Bearings	11	4
Reassembly of Brake Shoes, Pivot Pin and Operating Cam into Cover Plate	12	5
Centering Cam Housing	13	5
Final Reassembly of Hub before Replacing Wheel	14	5
Wheel Rim	15	5
Spokes	16	5
Wheel Building and Truing	17	5
Tyre	18	5
Tyre Pressures	19	5
Lubrication	20	6

Contents—contd.

SECTION L2—REAR WHEEL (NON-DETACHABLE TYPE)

	Sub-section	Page
Description	1	1
Removal and Replacement of Wheel	2	1
Removal of Brake Shoes for Replacement, Fitting New Linings, etc.	3	2
Replacing Brake Linings	4	2
Removal of Hub Spindle and Bearings	5	2
Hub Bearings	6	2
Fitting Limits for Bearings	7	2
Refitting Ball Bearings	8	2
Removal of Brake Operating Cam and Brake Shoe Pivot Pin	9	3
Cush Drive	10	3
Reassembly of Brake Shoes, Pivot Pin and Operating Cam into Cover Plate	11	4
Centering Cam Housing	12	4
Final Reassembly of Hub before Replacing Wheel	13	4
Wheel Rims	14	4
Spokes	15	4
Wheel Building and Truing	16	4
Tyre	17	5
Tyre Pressures	18	5
Lubrication	19	5

NOTES

List of Illustrations

FRONTISPIECE
Offside Views of "Meteor 700" and "500 Twin"

SECTION B1—ENGINE SPECIFICATION

			Page
Fig.	1	Exploded "Meteor 700" Engine	*(facing)* 1
Fig.	2	Diagram of Lubrication System	2
Fig.	3A	Diagram of Oil Pump (Feed)	4
Fig.	3B	Diagram of Oil Pump (Return)	4

SECTION C1—SERVICE OPERATIONS WITH ENGINE IN FRAME

Fig.	1	Distributor	2
Fig.	2	Primary Chain Adjustment	2
Fig.	3	Timing Chain Adjustment—"500 Twin"	3
Fig.	4	Ditto	3
Fig.	5	Timing Chain Adjustment—"Meteor 700"	4
Fig.	6	Valve Compressor in Use	4
Fig.	7	Sparking Plug Insert and Special Tool	5
Fig.	8	Removal of Pistons	5

SECTION D1—ENGINE

Fig.	1	Removal of Screws in Crankcase	1
Fig.	2	Pump Worm Locknut	2

SECTION E1—GEARBOX AND CLUTCH

Fig.	1	Front of Gearbox (Cover Removed)	1
Fig.	2	Exploded View of Clutch	1
Fig.	3	Exploded View of Gearbox	2
Fig.	4	Clutch Adjustment (Current Gearboxes)	4
Fig.	5	Ditto (Early Gearboxes)	4

SECTION F1—AMAL STANDARD NEEDLE TYPE CARBURETTOR

Fig.	1	Sectional View showing Air Valve and Throttle Closed	1
Fig.	2	Sequence of Tuning	2
Fig.	3	Exploded View of Carburettor	2

SECTION G1a—LUCAS COIL IGNITION EQUIPMENT

Fig.	1	Detail of High Tension Connector	1
Fig.	2	Distributor	3
Fig.	3	Wiring Diagram	4

SECTION G1b—LUCAS MAGDYNO

Fig.	1	Exploded View of Shock Absorbing Drive	1
Fig.	2	Contact Breaker	1
Fig.	3	Detail of High Tension Connector	2
Fig.	4	Wiring Diagram	4

List of Illustrations—contd.

SECTION G2a—LUCAS DYNAMO MODEL C35SD

Page

Fig.	1	Exploded View of Dynamo	1
Fig.	2	Testing Brush Spring Tension	2
Fig.	3	Undercutting Commutator Insulation	3
Fig.	4	Removing Pole Shoe Retaining Screw	3
Fig.	5	Use of Pole Shoe Expander	4
Fig.	6	Replacing Bearings	4
Fig.	7	Ditto	4

SECTION G2b—LUCAS DYNAMO MODEL E3LM

Fig.	1	Exploded View of Dynamo	1
Fig.	2	Testing Brush Spring Tension	2
Fig.	3	Undercutting Commutator Insulation	3
Fig.	4	Removing Pole Shoe Retaining Screw	3
Fig.	5	Use of Pole Shoe Expander	3
Fig.	6	Dynamo Brush Gear	4

SECTION G3a—CONTROL BOX

Fig.	1	Terminal Connections to Control Box RB107	1
Fig.	2	Internal View of Control Box RB107	2

SECTION G4a—BATTERY MODEL PUZ7E

Fig.	1	Sectioned View of Battery	1
Fig.	2	Topping-Up with Distilled Water	2
Fig.	3	Measuring Specific Gravity	2

SECTION G5a—HEAD AND TAIL LAMPS

Fig.	1	Headlamp with Parking Light in Reflector	1
Fig.	2	Headlamp with Underslung Parking Light	1
Fig.	3	Headlamp Model MCF700	1
Fig.	4	Parking Light 550	2
Fig.	5	Rear Lamp	2
Fig.	6	Tail Lamp 480	2
Fig.	7	Stop-Tail Lamp L.529	3
Fig.	8	Stop-Tail Lamp 525	3
Fig.	9	Stop-Tail Lamp L.564	3

SECTION H1—FRAME

Fig.	1	Exploded View of Frame	1
Fig.	2	Rear Spring Compressor	2
Fig.	3	Rear Suspension Unit. Mark I	3
Fig.	4	Rear Suspension Unit. Mark II	4

SECTION J1—FRONT FORK WITH CASQUETTE

Fig.	1	Section of Fork Leg	1
Fig.	2	Main Tube Spanner	2
Fig.	3	Main Tube Seal Guide	2
Fig.	4	Clamp Bolts securing Steering Stem and Fork Tubes	3
Fig.	5	Outer Cover Centralising Bushes	3

List of Illustrations—contd.

SECTION J3—FRONT FORK WITH FACIA PANEL ("METEOR 700," 1953)

			Page
Fig.	1	Section of Fork Leg	1
Fig.	2	Clamp Bolts securing Steering Stem and Fork Tubes	2
Fig.	3	Outer Cover Centralising Bushes	3
Fig.	4	Drift for Parting Clamp Sleeves	3
Fig.	5	Main Tube Seal Guide	4

SECTION J4—FRONT FORK WITH FACIA PANEL ("500 TWIN," 1950-53)

Fig.	1	Sectioned View	2

SECTION K1—FRONT WHEEL WITH DUAL BRAKE

Fig.	1	Dual Front Brake	1
Fig.	2	Removal of Brake Shoe Assembly	2
Fig.	3	Drift for Refitting Bearings	2

SECTION K2—FRONT WHEEL WITH SINGLE BRAKE

Fig.	1	Front Hub in Exploded View	1
Fig.	2	Removal of Brake Shoe Assembly	2
Fig.	3	Drift for Refitting Bearings	2
Fig.	4A	Wheel Lacing—Dunlop Rim	4
Fig.	4B	Wheel Lacing—Palmer Rim	4

SECTION L1—REAR WHEEL (DETACHABLE TYPE)

Fig.	1	Exploded View of Wheel	1
Fig.	2	Removal of Main Portion of Wheel	2
Fig.	3	Reassembly of Cush Drive	3
Fig.	4	Drift for Refitting Bearing (Fixed Section)	4

SECTION L2—REAR WHEEL (NON-DETACHABLE TYPE)

Fig.	1	Rear Hub in Exploded View	1
Fig.	2	Drift for Refitting Bearings ("500 Twin")	3
Fig.	3	Drift for Refitting Bearings ("Meteor 700")	3
Fig.	4	Reassembly of Cush Drive	3
Fig.	5A	Wheel Lacing—Dunlop Rim	5
Fig.	5B	Wheel Lacing—Palmer Rim	5

NOTES

SECTION A1a

Technical Data

"Meteor 700" Engine

Cubic Capacity	692 c.c.
Stroke	90 m.m.
Bore ... Nominal	70 m.m.
Actual	69·874 m.m./2·751 in.

(Rebore to ·020 in. when wear exceeds ·0065 in. and again to ·040 in. after further ·0065 in. wear).

Compression Ratio	6½ to 1

Piston Diameter—
- Bottom of Skirt—Fore and Aft.   69·811 m.m.
- Top Lands   69·32/69·27 m.m.
- Skirt is tapered and oval-turned.

Piston Rings—
- Width—Plain Rings   ·0625/·0635 in.
- Scraper Ring   ·1550/·1560 in.
- Radial Thickness   2·883/3·085 m.m.
- Gap when in unworn Cylinder   ·011/·015 in.
- Clearance in grooves   ·001/·003 in.

Renew Piston Rings when gap exceeds $\frac{1}{16}$ in.

Oversize Pistons and Rings available ·020 and ·040 in.

Piston Boss Internal Diameter	·7499/·7501 in.
Gudgeon Pin Diameter	·7499/·7501 in.
Con. Rod Small End Internal Diameter	·7507/·7505 in.
Big End Internal Diameter	1·8535/1·8530 in.
Bearing Shell Internal Diameter	1·7515/1·7505 in.
Crank Pin Diameter	1·7500/1·7495 in.

Driving Side Main Ball Bearing—
- Type   S.K.F. 6209 / Hoffman—145 or R and M—LJ 45
- Outside Diameter   85 m.m.
- Inside Diameter   45 m.m.
- Width   19 m.m.

Timing Side Main Roller Bearing—
- Type   S.K.F. N209 / Hoffman—R145 or R and M—LRJ45
- Outside Diameter   85 m.m.
- Inside Diameter   45 m.m.
- Width   19 m.m.

Rocker Inside Diameter	·5627/·5622 in.
Rocker Bearing Inside Diameter	·5622/·5617 in.
Rocker Spindle Diameter	·5617/·5615 in.
Inlet Valve Stem Diameter	·3430/·3425 in.
Exhaust Valve Stem Diameter	·3410/·3405 in.
Valve Guide Internal Diameter	·3437/·3447 in.
Valve Guide External Diameter	·6275/·6270 in.
Valve Guide Hole in Cylinder Head Dia.	·625/·626 in.
Tappet Stem Diameter	·3743/·3740 in.
Tappet Guide Internal Diameter	·3755/·3745 in.
Tappet Guide External Diameter	1·0125/1·0130 in.
Tappet Guide Hole in Crankcase Dia.	1·011/1·010 in.

Tappet Clearance with cold engine—
- Inlet   Nil
- Exhaust   Nil

Valve Spring Free Length—
- Inner $2\frac{1}{32}$ in.
- Outer $2\frac{3}{32}$ in.

(Renew when reduced by $\frac{3}{16}$ in.)

Valve Timing with ·012 in. clearance—
- Exhaust Opens   75° before B.D.C.
- Exhaust Closes   35° after T.D.C.
- Inlet Opens   30° before T.D.C.
- Inlet Closes   60° after B.D.C.

Camshaft Bearing External Diameter	·9095/·9085 in.
Camshaft Bearing Internal Diameter	·7505/·7495 in.

(Bored in position in crankcase)

Cam Lift	·3125 in.
Valve Lift (approx.)	·3125 in.
Timing Sprocket	12 Teeth
Camshaft Sprocket	24 Teeth
Magneto Sprocket	19 Teeth

Timing Chain—
- Type   Single No. 110038 endless
- Length   66 pitches
- Width   ·225 in.
- Pitch   ·375 in.
- Roller   ·250 in.

Magneto Chain—
- Type   Duplex No. 114500 endless
- Length   44 pitches
- Width   8·64 m.m.
- Pitch   8 m.m.
- Roller   5 m.m.

Magneto Speed	Half Engine Speed
Points	·012/·015 in.
Timing Advances	$\frac{3}{8}$ in.—$\frac{7}{16}$ in. before T.D.C.

For Coil Ignition see Section C.4.

Engine Sprocket	32 Teeth
Clutch Sprocket	56 Teeth
Final Drive Sprocket (Solo)	18 Teeth
Final Drive Sprocket (Sidecar)	16 Teeth

Primary Chain Type   Duplex No. 114038 endless
- Length   94 pitches
- Width   ·628 in.
- Pitch   ·375 in.
- Roller   ·250 in.

Feed Oil Pump—
- Speed   1/6 Engine Speed.
- Piston Diameter   ·25 in. (nominal)
- Stroke   ·5 in.

Return Oil Pump—
- Speed   1/6 Engine Speed.
- Piston Diameter   ·375 in. (nominal)
- Stroke   ·5 in.

Sparking Plug.
- Type   Lodge CS14 K.L.G. F.50 Champion L10
- Diameter   14 m.m.

NOTES

ROYAL ENFIELD WORKSHOP MANUAL Section **A1b**

SECTION A1b

Technical Data

"500 Twin" Engine

Cubic Capacity	496 c.c.
Stroke	77 m.m.
Bore — Nominal	64 m.m.
Actual	63·969 m.m./2·585 in.

(Rebore to ·020 in. when wear exceeds ·005 in. and again to ·040 in. after further ·005 in. wear).

Compression Ratio	7½ to 1
Piston Diameter—	
Bottom of Skirt—Fore and Aft.	63·830 m.m.
Top Lands	63·50/63·45 m.m.
Skirt is tapered and oval-turned.	
Piston Rings—	
Width—Plain Rings	·0615/·0625 in.
Scraper Ring	·1552/·1562 in.
Radial Thickness	2·460/2·612 m.m.
Gap when in unworn Cylinder	·011/·015 in.
Clearance in grooves	·0005/·0025 in.

Oversize Pistons and Rings available ·020 and ·040 in.

Piston Boss Internal Diameter	·7500/·7498 in.
Gudgeon Pin Diameter	·7450/·7498 in.
Con. Rod Small End Internal Diameter	·7507/·7505 in.
Big End Internal Diameter	1·8535/1·8530 in.
Bearing Shell Internal Diameter	1·7515/1·7505 in.
Crank Pin Diameter	1·7500/1·7495 in.
Driving Side Main Ball Bearing—	
Type	S.K.F. 6209
	Hoffman—145 or
	R and M—LJ 45
Outside Diameter	85 m.m.
Inside Diameter	45 m.m.
Width	19 m.m.
Timing Side Main Roller Bearings—	
Type	S.K.F. N209
	Hoffman—R145 or
	R and M—LRJ 45
Outside Diameter	85 m.m.
Inside Diameter	45 m.m.
Width	19 m.m.
Rocker Inside Diameter	·5627/·5622 in.
Rocker Bearing Inside Diameter	·5622/·5617 in.
Rocker Spindle Diameter	·5617/·5615 in.
Inlet Valve Stem Diameter	·34275/·34175 in.
Exhaust Valve Stem Diameter	·34175/·34075 in.
Valve Guide Internal Diameter	·3437/·3447 in.
Valve Guide External Diameter	·6245/·6240 in.
Valve Guide Hole in Cylinder Head Diameter	·6230/·6220 in.
Tappet Stem Diameter	·3743/·3740 in.
Tappet Guide Internal Diameter	·3755/·3745 in.
Tappet Guide External Diameter	1·0125/1·0130 in.
Tappet Guide Hole in Crankcase Diameter	1·011/1·010 in.

Tappet Clearance with cold engine—	
Inlet	Nil
Exhaust	Nil
Valve Spring Free Length—	
Inner	2 1/16 in.
Outer	2 3/32 in.
(Renew when reduced by 3/16 in.)	
Valve Timing with ·012 in. clearance—	
Exhaust Opens	75° before B.D.C.
Exhaust Closes	35° after T.D.C.
Inlet Opens	30° before T.D.C.
Inlet Closes	60° after B.D.C.
Camshaft Bearing External Diameter	·9095/·9085 in.
Camshaft Bearing Internal Diameter	·7505/·7495 in.
(Bored in position in crankcase).	
Cam Lift	·3123 in.
Valve Lift (approx.)	·3125 in.
Timing Sprocket	12 Teeth
Camshaft Sprocket	24 Teeth
Magdyno Sprocket	19 Teeth
Timing Chain—Type	Single No. 110038 endless
Length	66 pitches
Width	·225 in.
Pitch	·375 in.
Roller	·250 in.
Magdyno Chain—Type	Duplex No. 114500 endless
Length	44 pitches
Width	8·64 m.m.
Pitch	8 m.m.
Roller	5 m.m.
Magneto Speed	Half Engine Speed
Points	·012/·015 in.
Timing—Advanced	5/16–3/8 in. before T.D.C.

For Coil Ignition, see Section C.4.

Engine Sprocket	25 Teeth
Clutch Sprocket	56 Teeth
Final Drive Sprocket	18 Teeth
Primary Chain Type	Duplex No. 114038 endless
Length	90 pitches
Width	·628 in.
Pitch	·375 in.
Roller	·250 in.
Feed Oil Pump—Speed	1/6 Engine Speed
Piston Diameter	·25 in. (nominal)
Stroke	·5 in.
Return Oil Pump—Speed	1/6 Engine Speed
Piston Diameter	·375 in. (nominal)
Stroke	·5 in.
Sparking Plug—Type	Lodge CS14 K.L.G. F50
	Champion L10
Diameter	14 m.m.

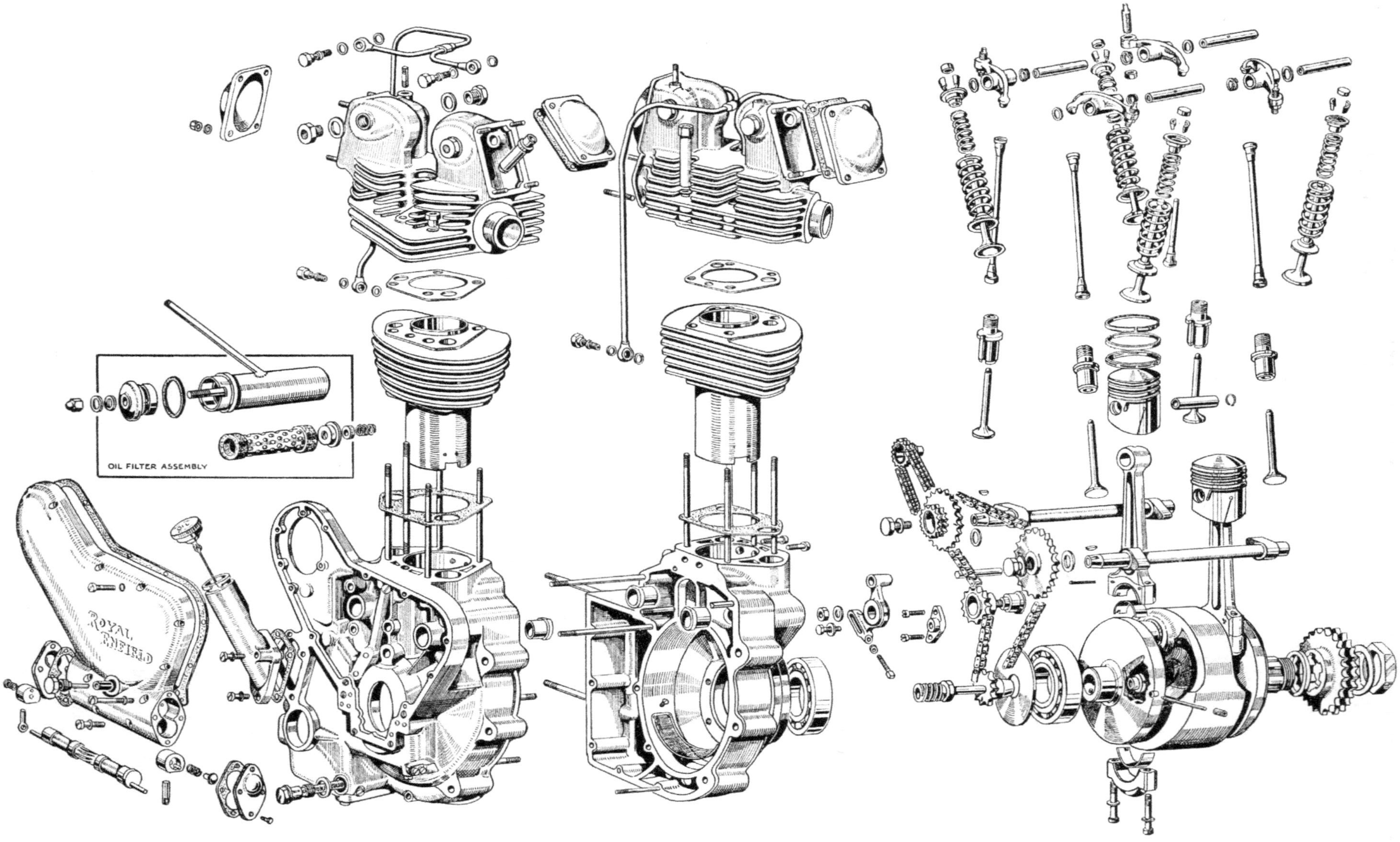

EXPLODED VIEW OF "METEOR 700" ENGINE
Fig. 1

SECTION B1
Engine Specification
"Meteor 700" and "500 Twin"

1. Engine

The engine is an even-firing vertical twin-cylinder, having separate cylinders and heads and fully enclosed pressure-fed overhead valve gear. It has dry sump lubrication with the oil tank integral with the crankcase and a massive one-piece high-strength cast iron crankshaft.

2. Cylinder Heads

The cylinder heads are die-cast from light aluminium alloy with ample finning to ensure adequate cooling. The exhaust pipe inserts are cast in and the valve inserts are of austenitic iron and are shrunk in so that they are replaceable. Steel wire thread inserts which are easily renewable are provided for the sparking plugs to prevent damage to the threads in the heads. The large capacity induction ports are stream-lined and blended to the valve seatings.

On very early models, the cylinder heads were sand castings.

3. Cylinders

The cylinders are separate and of cast iron, with internal tunnels enclosing the push rods. The cylinder heads are located by spigots on the cylinder barrels.

"**Meteor**" **Engine.** The nominal bore is 70 m.m. and the stroke 90 m.m., giving a cubic capacity of 692 c.c.

"**500 c.c. Twin**" **Engine.** The nominal bore is 64 m.m. and the stroke 77 m.m., giving a cubic capacity of 496 c.c.

4. Pistons

The pistons are of low expansion aluminium alloy, heat-treated and form-turned oval and having split skirts. The compression ratio is $6\frac{1}{2}$ to 1 in the "Meteor" engine and $7\frac{1}{2}$ to 1 in the "500 Twin." There are three piston rings, the top two of which are compression rings. Both are taper ground and the top one is chromium plated. The third ring is for oil control and is slotted.

5. Connecting Rods

The connecting rods are produced from stampings of Hiduminium RR56 light alloy. The little end bearings are of alloy direct on to the gudgeon pin. In case of wear after long service the little end can be bored out and fitted with a bush, but this is rarely necessary.

The big end bearings consist of white-metalled steel liners which are renewable. The detachable bearing caps are bolted to the connecting rods by means of high tensile socket screws, secured by cotter pins. Some earlier models have bolts and castle nuts.

6. Crankcase

The combined crankcase and oil tank are die-cast from light alloy in two halves, being split vertically.

7. Crankshaft and Flywheel

The crankshaft is cast in one piece, integral with the massive central flywheel, from high quality cromol or mehanite cast iron. The total weight is 26 lbs. and it is carefully balanced.

The main journals are ground and the big end journals are ground and hand-lapped.

8. Main Bearings

Heavy duty bearings are provided for the crankshaft, the driving side being ball and the timing side roller.

9. Camshafts

The camshafts are machined from drop-forged steel stampings with the cams and bearings hardened and ground. The cam profiles are produced with silencing ramps to ensure quiet running.

10. Valves

The inlet valves are machined from stampings of special Silicon-Chrome Valve Steel and the exhaust valves are of High Nickel-Chromium-Tungsten Steel.

11. Valve Gear

The valves are operated from the camshafts by means of large flat-based guided tappets, alloy push rods and overhead rockers. Two compression springs are fitted to each valve.

On earlier models, steel push rods were used.

12. Timing Drive

The camshafts are located in the crankcase, running in bronze bushes. They are driven by a common, endless chain from the timing sprocket on the crankshaft and the tightness of the chain can be adjusted by means of the chain tensioner in the timing chest.

The magdyno (or dynamo and distributor) is driven by a separate endless chain from the rear camshaft sprocket in the timing chest. The tension of this chain is adjusted by moving the magneto fixing bolts in their slotted holes.

13. Ignition and Lighting System

Lighting and ignition are supplied from a Lucas magdyno, which consists of a magneto running at $\frac{1}{2}$ engine speed and a dynamo running at $1\frac{1}{3}$ engine speed.

The rate at which the dynamo charges the battery is controlled by an automatic regulator which limits the dynamo voltage to approximately 7 volts.

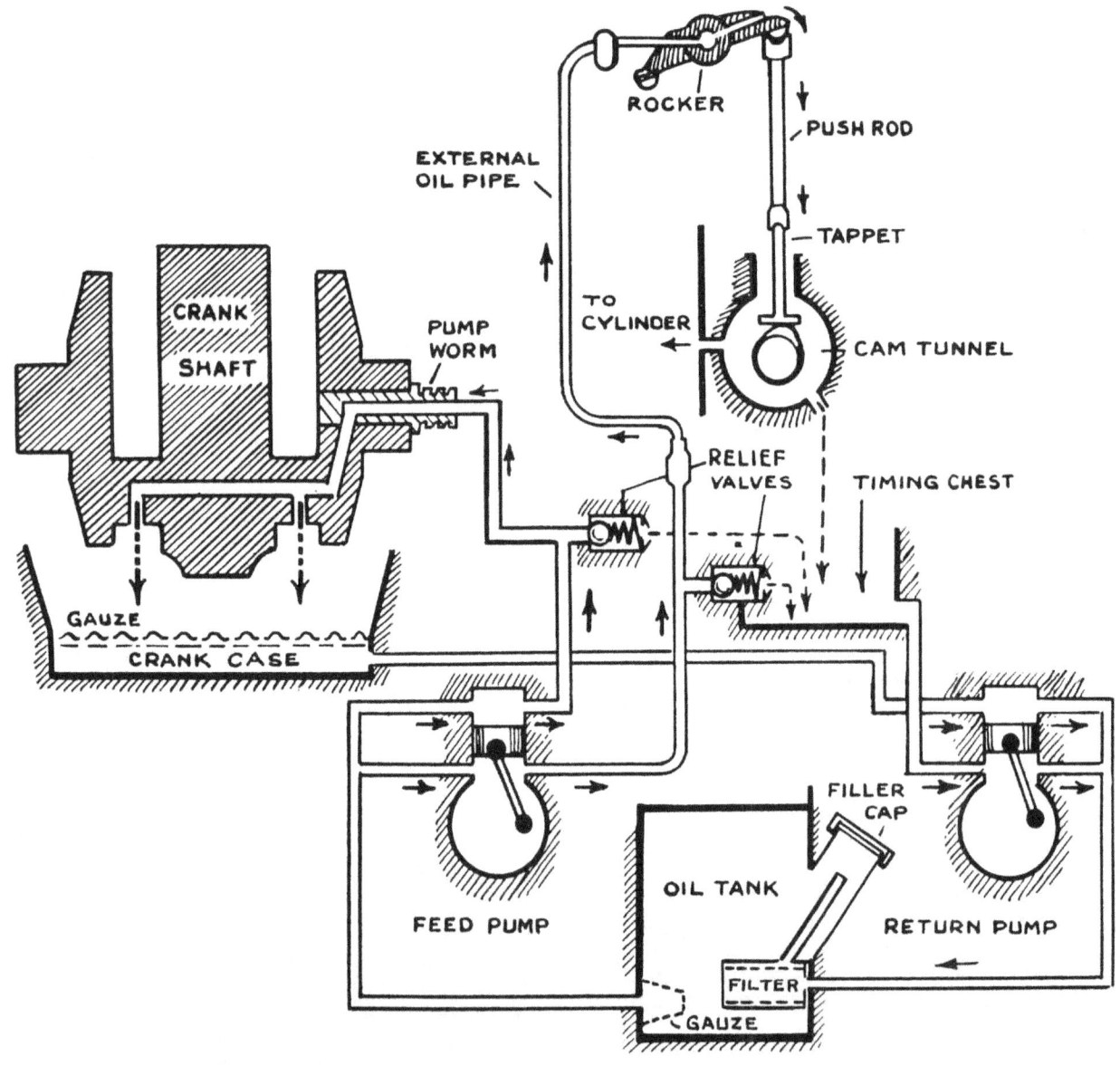

"METEOR 700" and "500 TWIN"
LUBRICATION SYSTEM
DIAGRAMMATIC ARRANGEMENT
Fig. 2

On earlier engines the ignition is provided by a coil energised from the battery and a distributor mounted above the dynamo. The dynamo is driven at engine speed by a chain from the rear camshaft.

14. Carburettor

"Meteor" Amal Type 276 FJ/IAT.
"500 Twin" Amal Type 276 DU/IAT.
Left hand throttle stop and pilot adjuster.
Standard bottom-feed float chamber, cranked at 7°.
Bore: "Meteor 700," $1\frac{1}{16}$ in.; "500 Twin," $\frac{15}{16}$ in.
The correct settings are as follows:—

	"Meteor"	"500 Twin"
Main Jet	No. 170	No. 150
Needle Jet	Standard	No. 109
Throttle Valve	6/4	6/4
Needle Clip	Middle Groove	No. 2 Groove

15. Air Filter

The air filter is a Vokes Micro-Vee felt and gauze dry filter, 5 in. diameter. It is housed in a metal box bolted to the frame.

16. Lubrication System

Lubrication is by the Royal Enfield Dry-Sump system which is entirely automatic and positive in action. The oil tank is integral with the crankcase, ensuring the full rate of circulation immediately the engine is started and rapid heating of the oil in cold weather.

There are two positively driven piston type oil pumps running at 1/6 engine speed,* one at the rear of the timing cover for pumping oil to the bearings under pressure and the other at the front for returning the oil from the crankcase to the tank. The return pump has a capacity approximately double that of the feed pump which ensures that oil does not accumulate in the crankcase.

The oil from the big ends drains into the bottom of the crankcase through a gauze which prevents it being drawn up by the flywheel. On some models the gauze is replaced by a steel deflector plate.

The oil from the rocker bearings is squirted through a small hole in the rocker on to the top end of the push rod. It flows down the push rod into the cam tunnel where it lubricates the cams and tappets and thence into the timing chest, lubricating the timing chains. There are small holes from the cam tunnels through the cylinder walls for the purpose of lubricating the skirts of the pistons.

Both pumps are double acting, one side of the feed pump supplying the big ends only and the other side the rockers and valve gear. In a similar manner one side of the return pump pumps the big end oil back to the tank from the crankcase and the other side the valve gear oil back to the tank from the timing chest.

Separate adjustable spring loaded relief valves control the pressure to the big ends and to the valve gear. The oil supply to the big ends is through internally drilled passages, and that to the valve gear through external pipes.† On some models the oil filter is in the oil feed to the big ends instead of the return circuit and is located in the bottom of the timing cover instead of in the oil tank.

17. Breather

The efficient operation of the breather is of paramount importance to the performance of the engine as it acts as a non-return valve between the crankcase and the outside atmosphere, causing a partial vacuum in the crankcase and rocker boxes which prevents the passage of oil into the cylinder and consequent smoking and oiling of the plugs.

The breather is located on the driving side of the crankcase and consists of a small housing containing two small pen-steel discs covering two holes drilled in the crankcase. Accurate seating of the discs is ensured by a pen-steel plate held between the breather body and the crankcase.

18. Gearbox

The gearbox is bolted on to the back of the crankcase and has four speeds, which are foot controlled, and a patented neutral finder. All gears are in constant mesh, changes being effected by robust dog clutches.

The standard gear ratios are as follows:—
"500 Twin" (solo). 5, 6·5, 9, 13·9 to 1.
"Meteor" (solo). 4·47, 5·8, 8·05, 12·4 to 1.
"Meteor" (sidecar). 5·03, 6·53, 9·05, 13·95 to 1.

19. Clutch

"Meteor" Engine. The clutch has six pressure plates and five friction plates, including the sprocket which is lined on both sides with friction material. The other friction plates have cork or Klinger inserts which give smooth operation and freedom from slipping in the presence of oil. The clutch centre is fitted with shock absorbers consisting of rubber blocks.

"500 Twin" Engine. The clutch is similar to that on the "Meteor" engine except that there are five pressure plates and four friction plates and the clutch centre is solid.

---

*1/12 engine speed on early models. †Early "500 Twins" had internal passages leading to the rocker gear.

OIL PUMP DIAGRAMS

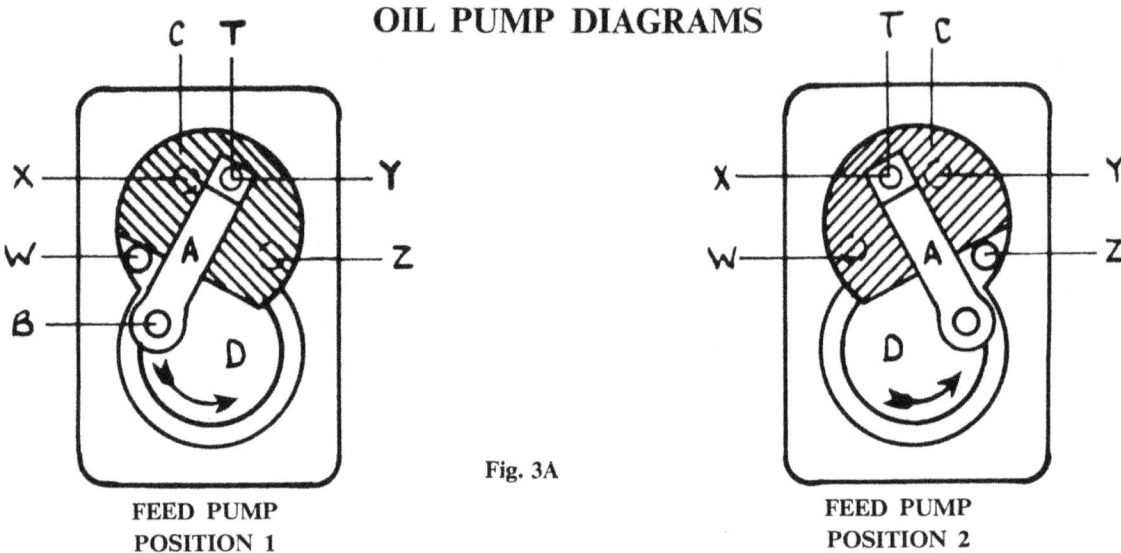

Fig. 3A

FEED PUMP POSITION 1

FEED PUMP POSITION 2

The ports in the housing are connected as follows:

- W — delivery to rocker gear.
- X — delivery to big ends.
- Y — suction from oil tank.
- Z — suction from oil tank.

Position 1. The plunger A is being drawn out of the cylinder hole in the disc C by the action of the peg B on the shaft D. The port T in the disc C registers with the suction port Y in the housing, so that oil is drawn into the cylinder from the oil tank. At the same time the delivery port W in the housing is uncovered and oil below the disc in the housing is forced through W to the rocker Gear.

Position 2. The plunger A is being pushed into the cylinder hole in the disc C. The port T in the disc now registers with the delivery port X in the housing, so that oil is forced out of the cylinder to the big ends. At the same time the suction port Z in the housing is uncovered and oil is drawn into the housing below the disc from the oil tank.

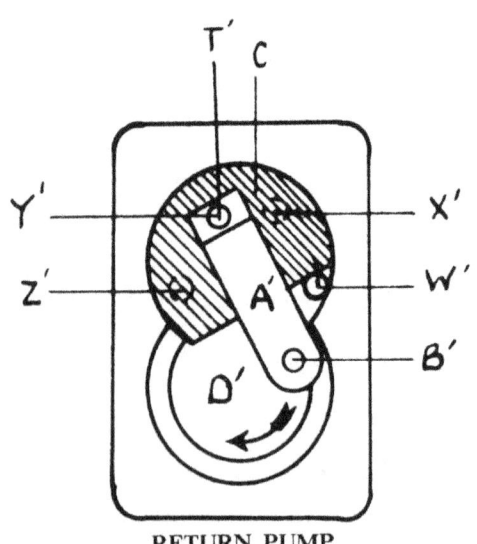
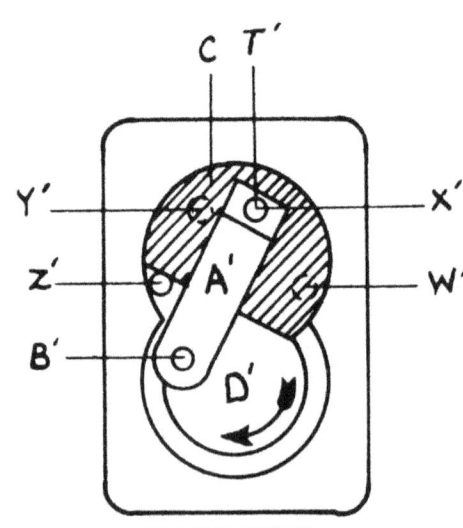

Fig. 3B

RETURN PUMP POSITION 1

RETURN PUMP POSITION 2

The ports in the housing are connected as follows:—

- W' — delivery to oil tank.
- X' — delivery to oil tank.
- Y' — suction from crankcase.
- Z' — suction from timing chest.

(On early models Y' and Z' were reversed)

Position 1. The plunger A' is being drawn out of the cylinder hole in the disc C' by the action of the peg B' on the shaft D'. The port T' in the disc C' registers with the suction port Y' in the housing, so that oil is drawn into the cylinder from the crankcase sump. At the same time the delivery port W' in the housing is uncovered and oil below the disc in the housing is forced through W' back to the oil tank.

Position 2. The plunger A' is being pushed into the cylinder hole in the disc C'. The port T' in the disc now registers with the delivery port X' in the housing, so that oil is forced out of the cylinder back to the oil tank. At the same time the suction port Z' in the housing is uncovered and oil is drawn into the housing below the disc from the timing chest.

SECTION C1

Service Operations with Engine in Frame

"Meteor 700" and "500 Twin"

1. Removal of Timing Cover

First place a tray under the engine to catch the oil which will escape when the cover is removed. Remove the timing side exhaust pipe and the oil filler neck by taking out the three screws fixing it to the crankcase. Remove the timing cover fixing screws. Draw off the timing cover, tapping it lightly if necessary.

In refitting the cover, insert the two long screws through the cover to locate the gasket. See that the thrust washer is on the chain tensioner sprocket spindle and that the rubber plug is in the hole in the oil pump worm. If the plug is damaged it should be renewed to ensure oil pressure to the big end bearings.

When refitting the cover it is important that the engine is turned gently forwards while the cover is being put into place. This will help the engagement of the pump worm with the pump spindle and prevent damage to the gears.

To verify that the oil pumps are working after replacing the timing cover, start the engine up and remove the oil filler cap so that the oil return pipe can be seen.

2. Valve Timing

The camshaft sprockets are keyed to the camshafts so that the valve timing can only be incorrect if the timing chain is maladjusted.

The correct setting is obtained with the marks stamped on the camshaft sprockets facing each other inwards on the centre line and the mark on the crankshaft sprocket pointing vertically downwards (see Fig. 3). If it is necessary to remove the sprockets, see Subsections 23 and 24.

Remember that all three timing sprocket fixing bolts have **Left Hand Threads.** While tightening the camshaft bolts the sprockets should be held.

The correct valve timing at ·012 in. clearance is as follows:—

Exhaust Opens 75° before bottom dead centre.
Exhaust Closes 35° after top dead centre.
Inlet Opens 30° before top dead centre.
Inlet Closes 60° after bottom dead centre.

3. Tappet Adjustment

The tappet clearance is adjusted by means of a screw in the outer end of each rocker. Access to the adjusting screws is obtained by removing the covers of the rocker boxes.

The clearance between the end of the screw and the valve stem cap should be nil or as little as possible with the engine **COLD.**

To adjust the clearance, loosen the locknut beneath the rocker arm, turn the screw with a small spanner and re-tighten the locknut.

The adjustment for each valve should be made with the corresponding valve of the other cylinder fully open. This ensures that the tappet is well clear of the ramp which is located on either side of the cam to reduce valve noise.

If, after long service, the valve stem cap or the rocker adjusting screw is found to be worn, they should be renewed, as uneven thrust, due to the screw being in a different position after adjustment, may cause lateral movement of the rocker, giving rise to a sharp tapping noise.

4. Ignition Timing

Magdyno. The setting of the ignition depends upon the position of the sprocket relative to the magneto shaft.

To obtain access to the magneto sprocket it is necessary to remove the timing cover.

The sprocket is mounted on a smooth taper on the magdyno shaft and is held in position by a nut (**Right Hand Thread**). To remove the sprocket, undo the nut and use a suitable extractor.

Before setting the timing, adjust the contact breaker points to a clearance of ·012/·015 in. when fully opened and put the ignition lever in the full advance position. See that the screw in the magneto ring is in the end of the slot and that it is not sticking.

To set the timing, turn the "Meteor" engine until the left hand piston is $\frac{3}{8}-\frac{7}{16}$ in. before top dead centre on the compression stroke, i.e. with both valves closed.

Insert a piece of thin tissue paper between the points of the contact breaker and turn the magneto forwards until the paper can **just** be pulled out, making sure that the magneto rotor is in the position to cause a spark on the left hand cylinder sparking plug. Give the sprocket a sharp tap to secure it on the shaft and then lock it by tightening the nut.

The 500 c.c. engine has a shorter stroke and the timing should therefore be set at $\frac{5}{16}$—$\frac{3}{8}$ in. before top dead centre.

Coil Ignition. On earlier models a dynamo and distributor were fitted, instead of the magdyno, and coil ignition was used. The distributor includes an automatic advance mechanism which is normally in the "retard" position when the engine is stationary.

The correct setting for the timing is for the contact breaker points to open when the pistons are $\frac{1}{32}$ in. **after** top dead centre.

Before setting the timing, remove the rotor arm of the distributor and adjust the contact breaker points to a clearance of ·014/·016 in.

An approximate setting can be obtained by engaging the most suitable tooth on the dynamo sprocket with the chain when re-assembling the engine or by slackening the screw securing the distributor and replacing it in a different tooth of the skew gear drive. The flat side of the distributor body should be lined fore and aft to avoid the terminal screw fouling the air cleaner.

Make sure that the rotor arm of the distributor is pointing towards the contact connected to the plug lead of the cylinder which is on compression, i.e. with both valves closed.

The fine adjustment of the timing is made by turning the engine until the pistons are $\frac{1}{32}$ in. after top dead centre and then (having slackened the securing screw A) rotating the distributor body until the contact breaker points are just opening. Then tighten the securing screw.

This point can be determined by inserting a thin piece of tissue paper between the contact breaker points and turning the distributor housing until the paper can **just** be drawn out.

An alternative method is to remove the cap from the plug lead and tuck the lead between the fins of the cylinder. Switch on the ignition and rotate the distributor until a spark is seen at the instant the points open. Move the distributor body clockwise to retard the timing and anti-clockwise to advance it.

5. Primary Chain Adjustment

Access to the primary chain adjuster is gained by removing the primary chain cover, which is held in position by a single nut. Before removing the nut, place a tray under the engine to catch the oil from the chain case.

Beneath the bottom run of the chain is a curved slipper on which the chain rests and which may be raised or lowered by turning the adjusting screw after having first slackened the locknut.

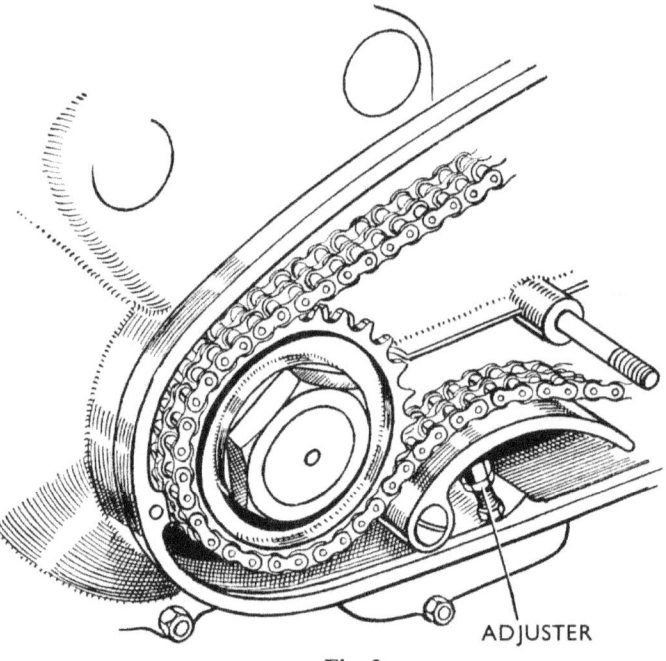

Fig. 2

To take up slack in the primary chain, unscrew the locknut and turn the adjuster beneath the curved slipper until correct chain tension is obtained ; re-tighten the locknut.

On the "Meteor" engine a rubber button is fitted to the end of the adjusting screw to prevent the transmission of chain noise to the chaincase and this is held against the chain case and bouncing is prevented by a hairpin spring. This is not necessary on the "500 Twin" because the chain line is different on account of the smaller sprocket.

After replacing the chain cover, remember to replenish the chain case with oil.

Do not adjust the chain to be dead tight but rotate the engine slowly, and, while doing so, test the tension of the top run of the chain by pressing

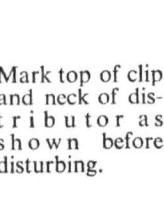

Mark top of clip and neck of distributor as shown before disturbing.

Fig. 1

it up and down with the fingers. Adjust the tension so that there is ¼ in. up and down movement at the tightest spot.

Re-tighten the locknut on the adjusting screw, replace the chain cover and replenish with oil.

6. Timing Chain Adjustment

"**500 Twin.**" Before adjusting the tension of the timing chain, turn the engine until the chain is in its tightest position and any slack is between the rear cam sprocket and the timing sprocket on the engine shaft.

The tension of the timing chain is altered by moving the quadrant after slackening the nut which secures it. This rotates the eccentric spindle on which the chain tensioner jockey sprocket is mounted. Tightening of the chain is effected by moving the quadrant to the left.

It is imperative that the quadrant is fitted the right way round and that the eccentric spindle is fitted correctly in the quadrant fork. If the chain tightens when the quadrant is moved to the right, the tensioner has been wrongly assembled and may cause damage to the quadrant. (See diagram.)

In making the adjustment, care must be taken to see that any backlash in the quadrant is taken up in the "tightening" directions, i.e. do not make the chain too tight and then move the quadrant back slightly, but tighten the chain

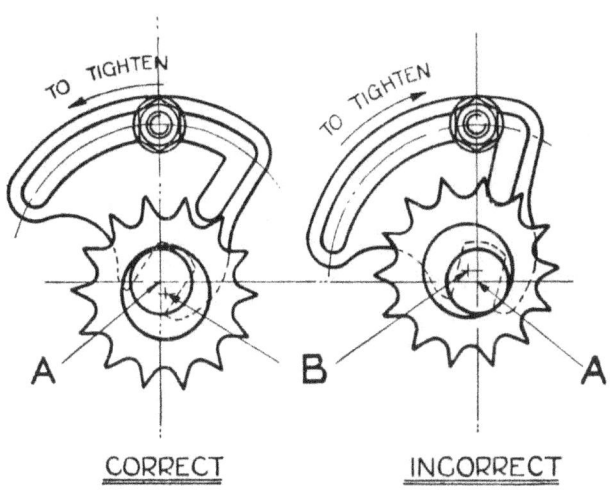

TIMING CHAIN ADJUSTMENT
"500 Twin"
Fig. 4

progressively until the correct tension is obtained and then lock the quadrant. If the chain becomes too tight during adjustment, slacken it right back and make the adjustment again.

After the adjustment has been completed and the quadrant has been locked in position, turn the engine slowly and check the tension at frequent intervals to ensure that excessive tightening does not take place in any one position.

"**Meteor 700.**" Before adjusting the tension of the timing chain, turn the engine until the chain is in its tightest position and any slack is between the rear cam sprocket and the timing sprocket on the engine shaft (see Fig. 5).

Slacken the securing bolt on the chain adjuster and the locknut on the adjusting screw. Turn the adjusting screw until the correct chain tension is obtained and tighten the locknut and securing bolt.

After the adjustment has been completed and the adjusting arm locked in position, turn the engine slowly and check the tension at frequent intervals to ensure that excessive tightening of the chain does not take place in any one position.

On some earlier models the chain tensioner incorporated a spring plunger. This can be replaced, if necessary, by the present design, which is interchangeable.

7. Magneto Chain Adjustment

To adjust the magneto chain tension, remove the timing cover (see Subsection 1), slacken the three magneto fixing bolts and loosen the bolster stud nut. Slide the magneto back until the chain has about 3/16 in. up and down movement, then tighten the fixing bolts.

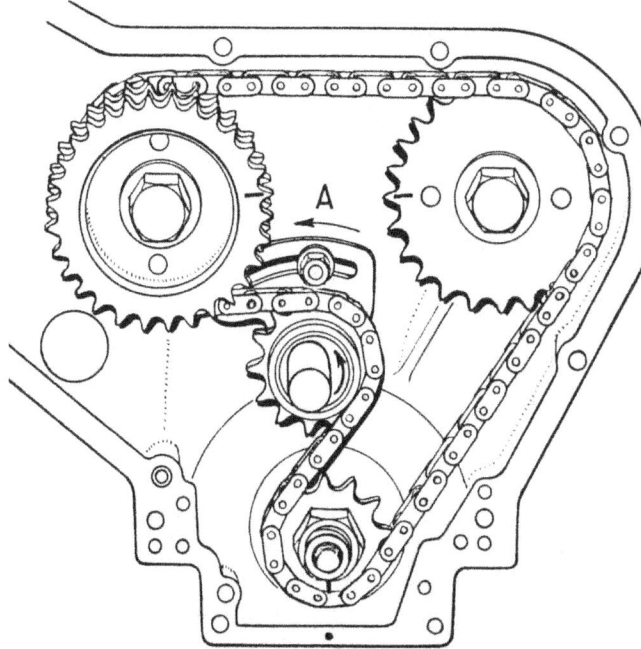

TIMING CHAIN ADJUSTMENT SHOWING TIMING MARKS
"500 Twin"
Fig. 3

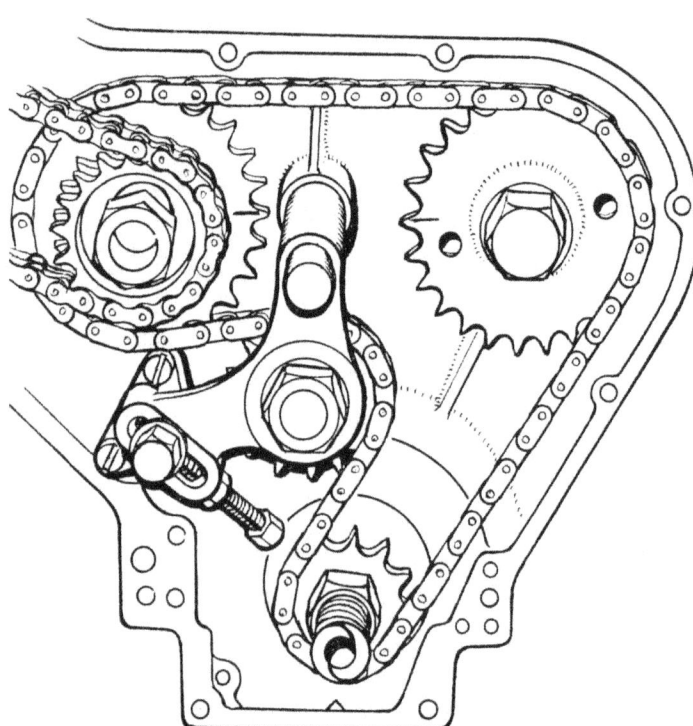

TIMING CHAIN ADJUSTMENT
"Meteor 700"
Fig. 5

On earlier "500 Twin" models no provision was made for adjusting the dynamo chain, but a slipper can now be provided, if necessary.

8. Removal of Dual Seat

Remove the nuts from the two fixing bolts securing the seat which can then be unhooked at the front and lifted off.

9. Removal of Petrol Tank

Turn off the petrol tap.
Disconnect the petrol pipe.
Remove the two bolts which secure the tank to the frame at front and rear and it can then be lifted clear.

10. Removal of Cylinder Head

First remove the petrol tank and petrol pipe. (Subsection 9.)
The dual seat may also be removed if desired. (Subsection 8.) Remove the head steady bolt and bracket or the head steady.
Disconnect the oil pipes and plug leads.
Remove the exhaust pipes and carburettor and induction pipe.
Turn the engine until both valves are closed.
Remove the five cylinder head nuts and lift off the head.

In replacing the head, see that the push rods are the right way up (shallow cups upwards). If steel push rods are fitted, the wide cup should be upwards.

Apply a thin coat of jointing compound to both sides of the gasket and place it in position.

Lower the cylinder head over the push rods, making sure that the rockers locate in the push rod cups.

Fit the head nuts and washers and partially tighten down.

When both heads have reached this stage, fit the induction pipe and tighten the nuts. The cylinder head nuts can now be finally tightened down progressively and diagonally from one side to the other to prevent distortion. After the engine has been run long enough to get thoroughly hot, the tightness of the nuts should be re-checked.

11. Removal of Valves

Remove the rocker box covers, each held by four nuts, swing the rocker clear of the valve and lift or prise away the hardened steel thimble or end cap. If this has stuck, it can be removed by means of a screwdriver. Using a suitable valve spring compressor, compress the valve springs and remove the split conical collets from the end of the valve stem. Slacken back the compressing tool and release the springs. Withdraw the valve and place its springs, top spring collar (and bottom collar if it is loose) and split conical collets together in order that they may be re-assembled with the valve from which they were removed.

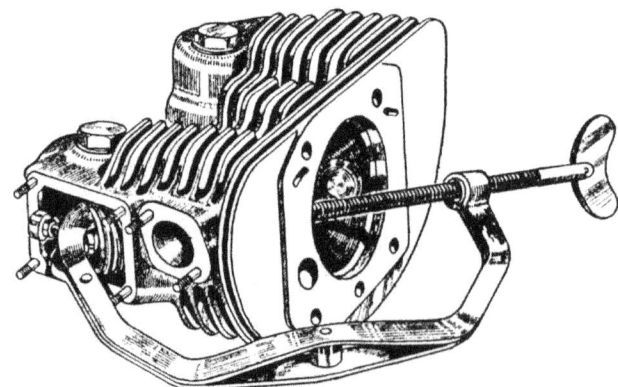

Fig. 6

Deal similarly with the other valves in the heads.
If the valve will not slide easily through the valve guide, remove any slight burrs on the end of the valve stem with a carborundum stone. If the burrs are not removed and the valve is forced out, the guide may be damaged.

12. Removal of Rockers.

Turn the engine so that the valve is closed.

Remove the oil pipe connection and plug from the cylinder head and the rocker spindle can then generally be withdrawn by means of a piece of rod inserted in the central hole.

If this is not successful remove the oil pipe plug on the opposite cylinder head and the two plugs between the heads and drive the rocker spindle out with a piece of rod passing through the rocker spindle in the opposite cylinder head.

On re-assembling, make sure that the spring washers are fitted on the insides of the rockers and the plain thrust washers on the outer sides.

13. Removal of Valve Guides

To remove the valve guides from the heads two special tools are required which can easily be made.

The first is a piece of tube with an internal bore of not less than $\frac{7}{8}$ in.

The second is a mandrel about 4 in. long, made from $\frac{9}{16}$ in. diameter bar with the end turned down to about $\frac{5}{16}$ in. diameter for $\frac{1}{2}$ in.

Support the cylinder head on the tube which fits over the collar of the valve guide. Using the mandrel force the guide out of the head with a hand press or by using a hammer.

To fit a new guide, support the head at the correct angle and use a hand press and the same mandrel. If a hand press is not available and the guide is replaced by a hammer, use a piece of tube of $\frac{9}{16}$ in. internal diameter to prevent damage to the bore of the guide. It is necessary to re-cut the valve seat and grind in the valve after a guide has been replaced.

14. Renewal of Sparking Plug Inserts

A steel thread insert is fitted into each sparking plug bore to prevent damage to the threads in the alloy cylinder heads.

This insert should not normally require renewal but if it does become damaged, for instance by a faulty plug, it can be pulled out with a pair of pliers and a new one fitted.

To fit a new insert a special tool consisting of a piece of $\frac{7}{16}$ in. diameter tube or rod with a slot cut in the end is required.

The new insert is placed over the tool with the tag engaging in the slot and it is screwed into the plug hole in the cylinder head from the outside until the last coil is 1 to $1\frac{1}{2}$ threads below the top face. A reverse twist of the tool will then break off the tag.

If the cylinder head has not been removed from the engine, care must be taken not to drop the end of the tag into the cylinder and in such a case it is better to break off the tag with a pair of long-nosed pliers.

15. Removal of Cylinders

When the cylinder heads have been removed the cylinders can be lifted clear of the studs. This

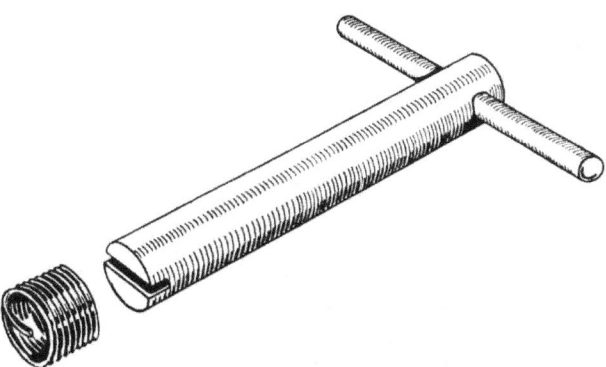

SPARKING PLUG INSERT AND SPECIAL TOOL
Fig. 7

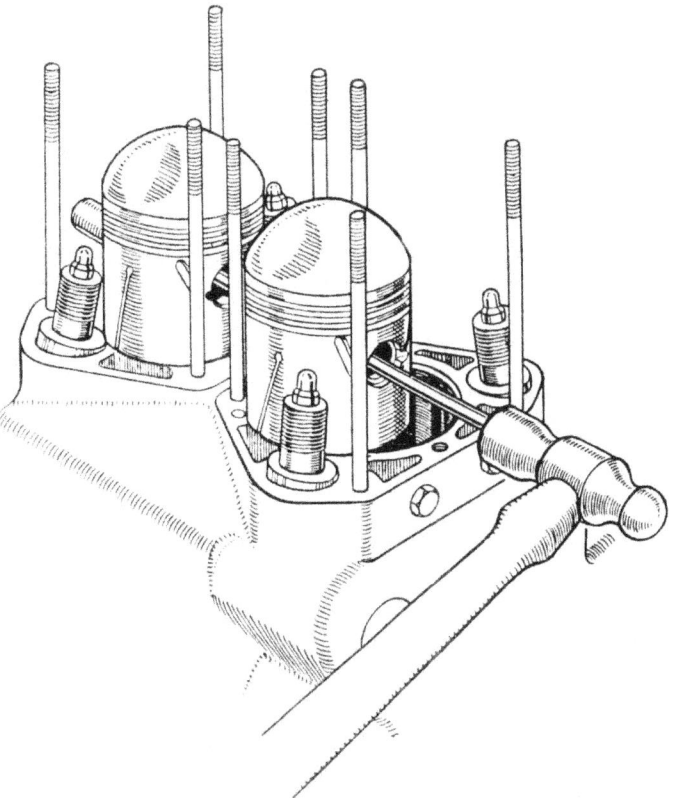

REMOVAL OF PISTON
Fig. 8

should be done with the pistons at bottom dead centre.

When replacing the cylinder, clean off the joint faces and fit new paper joints, two to each cylinder.

In the case of the "500 Twin" engine, see that there are the correct holes in the paper joint for the internal oil passages.

16. Removal of Pistons

Remove the cylinder heads and cylinders.

With the tang of a file remove one of the wire circlips retaining the gudgeon pins. If necessary rotate the engine slightly until the pistons are in such a position that the gudgeon pins will clear the long cylinder studs when being withdrawn.

Use Special Tool No. E.5477 to extract the gudgeon pin or using a rod about $\frac{1}{4}$ in. in diameter, insert this right through one gudgeon pin and drive the other pin out of its piston, supporting the connecting rod substantially meanwhile to prevent distortion.

Having lifted the first piston away, the other one may be readily removed in the same manner. Mark the pistons and gudgeon pins so that they go back into the same pistons the same way round and so that the pistons go back into the same barrels the same way round.

Take care not to drop the gudgeon pin circlip into the crankcase. A clean cloth should be put over the mouth of the crankcase to prevent this.

17. Decarbonising

Having removed the cylinder heads as described in Subsection 10, scrape away all carbon, bearing in mind that you are dealing with aluminium which is easily damaged. Scrape gently and avoid scoring the combustion chamber or the valve seats which are of austenitic iron shrunk into the head. Be careful while performing this work not to injure the joint face which beds down on to the head gaskets.

Do not, in any circumstances, use caustic soda or potash for the removal of carbon from aluminium alloy.

Scrape away all carbon from the valve heads and beneath the heads, being very careful not to cause any damage to the valve faces.

If the piston rings are removed the grooves should be cleaned out and new rings fitted. For cleaning the grooves, a piece of discarded ring thrust into a wooden handle and filed to a chisel point is a useful tool.

If the piston ring gaps exceed $\frac{1}{16}$ in. when the rings are in position in the barrel, new rings should be fitted. The correct gap for new rings is ·011—·015 in. The gap should be measured in the least worn part of the cylinder, which will be found to be the extreme top or bottom of the bore.

While the cylinders and pistons are not in position on the engine, cover the crankcase with a clean cloth to prevent the ingress of dust and dirt of all kinds. Do not, of course, attempt to scrape the carbon from the pistons when the mouths of the crankcase are open.

18. Grinding-in Valves

Wipe the valve faces clean and examine them carefully. If they are at all pitted, have the faces re-cut. Pay similar attention to the valve seats in the head; excessive grinding will form a pocket and the gas flow will be restricted. The angle of the valve face should be 45 degrees to the axis of the valve stem.

To grind a valve, smear the seating with a little grinding-in compound, place a light, short coil spring over the valve stem and beneath the head, insert the valve into its appropriate guide, press it on to the seat using a tool with a suction cup and with a backwards and forwards rotary motion, grind it on to its seat. Frequently lift the valve and move it round so that an even and true seating is obtained. Continue grinding until a bright ring is visible on both valve and seating.

19. Re-assembly after Decarbonising

Before building up the engine, see that all parts are scrupulously clean and place them conveniently to hand on a clean sheet of brown paper.

It is advisable to fit new gaskets to the cylinder base and cylinder head. Two paper gaskets are fitted to the base of each cylinder; in the case of the 500 c.c. engine, make sure that each has two holes which register with the oil passages.

Smear clean oil over the pistons and space the ring gaps, having replaced the rings if these have been removed, lower the piston over the connecting rod and insert the gudgeon pin from the outer side. Fit the circlip and then fit the second piston in a similar manner.

Oil the cylinder bores and lower the barrels over the pistons and seat them gently on their gaskets.

Drop the push rods down their tunnels on to the tappet heads, shallow cups upwards. (Or wide cups upwards in the case of steel rods.)

Fit the copper cylinder head gaskets and replace the cylinder heads as described in Subsection 10.

After the engine has been assembled, run it for a brief period with the ignition fully advanced.

When the engine has been run for some time and has become thoroughly hot, go over all the cylinder head and other nuts to ensure that they are tight.

20. Cleaning the Oil Filters

The oil filter is in the return oil circuit and is located in the oil tank at the back of the crankcase.

The filter element is removed by unscrewing the nut holding the end cap in position. When re-assembling the filter after cleaning, take care that no grit or other foreign matter is sticking to it.

The felt element should be taken out and washed in petrol after the first 500 miles and after every subsequent 2,000 miles. Fit a new element every 5,000 miles.

On some models the oil filter is in the oil feed to the big ends instead of the return circuit and is located in the bottom of the timing cover instead of in the oil tank.

21. Overhaul of Oil Pumps

Remove the timing cover, as described in Subsection 1.

Remove the end plates from both pumps.

Remove the pump discs and plungers.

Remove the pump spindle, which can be pulled out from the front or return pump end.

Check the fit of the plungers in the pump discs; the plungers should have a minimum of clearance but should be able to be moved in and out by hand.

If, when fitting a new disc or plunger, the plunger is found to be too tight a fit, carefully lap with metal polish until it is just free. If the pump disc is not seating properly or if a new pump disc is being fitted, it should be lapped to the seating with special tool No. E.5425, using carborundum 360 fine paste or liquid metal polish, until an even grey surface is obtained.

Wash all passages, etc., thoroughly with petrol after lapping to remove all traces of grinding paste.

Check the pump disc springs for fatigue by assembling in the timing cover and placing the pump covers in position. The latter should be held $\frac{1}{8}$ in. off the timing cover if the springs are correct.

The pump spindle should be renewed if excessive wear has taken place on the teeth.

Re-assemble the oil pumps, replacing the paper cover gaskets if necessary. Before fitting each cover fill the pump chamber with clean oil.

Having assembled the pumps, lay the timing cover flat and fill the oil ports by means of an oilcan. Turn the pump spindle with a screwdriver in a clockwise direction looking on the front and it can then be seen whether the pumps are operating correctly.

When the timing cover has been refitted on the engine, the oil feed to the big ends can be checked by partially unscrewing the feed plug in the timing cover between the oil pumps and the oil return to the tank can be checked by removing the oil filler cap. The feed to the rockers can be observed by removing the rocker box covers, when oil will be seen flowing down the push rods.

The pump drive is by means of a double-start worm so that the pump runs at 1/6 engine speed.

On earlier models a single-start worm was used, giving a pump speed of 1/12 engine speed.

The two are interchangeable but, if a single-start worm is replaced by a double-start worm, the pump spindle must also be changed or damage will be caused.

On the pump spindle mating with the double-start worm the tooth angle is $6\frac{1}{2}°$ to the axis of the shaft, while in the case of the single start it is $3\frac{1}{4}°$.

22. Removal of Timing Chains

"**Meteor.**" Loosen the magdyno fixing bolts. Remove the magneto sprocket. (See Subsection 25.)

Lift the magneto chain off the cam sprocket.

Remove the chain tensioner securing bolt and the anchor plate held by two screws.

Withdraw the chain tensioner fulcrum pin.

Remove the chain tensioner arm and sprocket. Lift the chain off the cam sprockets.

"**500 Twin.**" Loosen the magneto fixing bolts. Remove the magneto sprocket. (See Subsection 25.)

Lift the magneto chain off the cam sprocket.

Loosen the chain tensioner locknut and stud.

Lift the adjusting plate clear of the chain tensioner spindle.

Remove the chain tensioner spindle and sprocket.

Lift the chain off the sprocket.

23. Removal of Pump Worm and Timing Sprocket

Remove the timing chains (Subsection 22).

Unscrew the oil pump worm by means of the hexagon head behind it. This is a **Left Hand Thread**.

Withdraw the timing sprocket using special tool No. E.4869. **Do not attempt to withdraw the sprocket by tapping the worm, as this will dislodge the locking nut in the crankshaft.** (See Section D.1, Subsection 7.)

24. Removal of Camshaft Sprocket

Remove the timing chains (Subsection 22).

Unscrew the camshaft sprocket fixing bolt, **which has a left hand thread,** at the same time holding the sprocket.

Withdraw the sprocket by means of a suitable extractor.

25. Removal of Magneto Sprocket

Magdyno. The sprocket is mounted on a smooth taper on the magneto shaft and is held in position by a nut (**Right Hand Thread**). To remove the sprocket, undo the nut and use a Magdyno sprocket extractor—Special Tool No. 14835.

Dynamo. In the case of engines fitted with coil ignition the sprocket can be withdrawn by means of a dynamo sprocket extractor—Special Tool No. E.5127.

26. Removal of Engine and Clutch Sprockets

The primary chain is endless so that it is necessary to remove both the engine and clutch sprocket simultaneously.

Unscrew the engine sprocket nut using Special Tool No. 4877. The engine sprocket is mounted on splines and can then be removed with the clutch sprocket.

To remove the clutch sprocket unscrew the three clutch spring pins and lift away the spring cap, springs, distance pieces, clutch front plate, centre retaining ring and the assembly of driving and driven clutch plates. The clutch sprocket can then be withdrawn from the centre after removal of the large circlip which secures it.

When replacing the engine sprocket, take care that the felt washer is not nipped behind the sprocket. This would make the engine very stiff to turn over and would damage the washer and allow leakage from the crankcase.

27. Removal of Tappets and Guides

It is only necessary to remove the tappets and guides if they have become worn.

Remove the cylinder heads and barrels. (Subsections 10 and 15.)

Extract the tappet guides using Special Tool No. E.5790.

The guides are made from Nickel Chrome Alloy iron and if a guide should break while removing it, it can be withdrawn with a pair of pliers if the crankcase is heated locally with a blowlamp. Otherwise it is necessary to dismantle the crankcase and drive the tappet and guide out from underneath using a heavy bar in the cam tunnel.

The guide should have an interference of ·0015 to ·0025 ins. in the crankcase and can be driven in with a bronze drift, care being taken when the guide is nearly home to avoid breaking the collar.

If a tappet guide is taken out it should be replaced by an oversize one.

28. Dismantling the Breather

If the breather is not operating efficiently, it may cause pressure in the crankcase, instead of a partial vacuum, giving rise to smoking or over-oiling.

See that the discs and backplate are clean and undamaged and that the discs are seating properly.

When re-assembling the breather, apply jointing compound sparingly to the back of the steel plate taking great care to keep it away from the discs or their seatings.

On earlier models fibre discs were used in the breather, without a backplate. If the fibre discs are re-placed by steel discs, the steel backplate must be fitted to prevent wear on the surface of the alloy casting.

On very early models of the "500 Twin" the breather was located in the end of the crankshaft with a cork seal to prevent breathing into the chaincase.

29. Removal of Clutch

Remove the engine sprocket and clutch sprocket together as described in Subsection 26.

To remove the clutch hub, hold the clutch with Special Tool No. E. 4871 and remove the centre retaining nut and washer with a box spanner.

The hub can then be withdrawn from the shaft with Special Tool No. E.5414.

30. Removal of Final Drive Sprocket

Remove the clutch as described in Subsection 29.

Remove the primary chain tensioner.

Remove the rear half of the primary chain case by taking out three socket screws.

Remove the grub screw locking the final drive sprocket nut.

Hold the sprocket and remove the nut (**Right Hand Thread**). The sprocket can then be withdrawn.

31. Removal of Bearing Housing Felt Washer

Remove the engine sprocket, clutch and rear half of the primary chain case.

The felt washer is located in the steel housing at the back of the chain case.

Great care must be taken not to nip the felt washer behind the sprocket on re-assembly as this would make the engine very stiff to turn over and would damage the washer and allow leakage from the crankcase.

32. Oil Pipe Unions

"**Meteor.**" The oil feed to the rocker gear is through pipes from unions at the back of the crankcase below the cylinder base to unions on the cylinder heads. The unions in the crankcase are fitted with steel wire thread inserts to prevent the threads in the aluminium from stripping.

Those in the cylinder heads are not provided with thread inserts because they are not so liable to damage but, if they should become damaged, the same wire insert that is used in the crankcase can be fitted by cutting a thread with a special tap.

The method of fitting the thread inserts is the same as that used for the sparking plug inserts described in Subsection 14.

"**500 Twin.**" The oil pipe bosses on the "500 Twin" are on the base of the cylinder barrels and not on the crankcase and wire inserts are not therefore necessary.

33. Pressure Relief Valves

There are two pressure relief valves in the oil feeds to the big ends and to the rocker gear respectively. Their function is to prevent excessive pressure and their setting is not critical.

They are set before leaving the Works and should not normally require to be disturbed. If, however, it is found necessary to dismantle either of them, they can be reset as follows:—

Rocker Feed Relief Valve. This is located in the crankcase face behind the timing cover and consists of a $\frac{3}{16}$ in. diameter steel ball held in position by a spring and brass plug. If the plug is screwed in until it is flush with the face of the crankcase, the pressure will be relieved at approximately 10 lbs. per square inch. The plug is prevented from moving by peening over the aluminium into the screwdriver slot with a small centre punch.

Big End Feed Relief Valve. This is located in the inside of the bottom of the timing cover and consists of a $\frac{1}{4}$ in. diameter steel ball and a spring and plug. It should be set to relieve the pressure at approximately 60 lbs. per square inch.

The pressure can be measured by applying an air line with a pressure gauge (or a suitable force feed oil gun) to the oil feed plug in the timing cover which fits into the pump worm.

Rotate the pump spindle by means of a screwdriver until the ports are sealed by the pump disc. The ports are sealed when no leakage occurs on the timing cover face.

Turn the relief valve plug until the pressure at which the valve opens is about 60 lbs. per square inch, then secure the plug by peening as above.

If too high a pressure is applied, the pump disc will be forced off its seating.

On earlier models the pressure relief valve for the oil supply to the big ends was in the crankshaft. Some trouble may be caused by dirt under the ball causing the valve to stick. If so desired, the relief valve can be removed and the oil passage blanked off and the new type of timing cover fitted.

NOTES

SECTION D1

Service Operations with Engine Removed

"Meteor 700" and "500 Twin"

1. Removal of Engine from Frame

Disconnect the battery leads and remove the battery.

Remove the dual seat and petrol tank.
Remove the engine steady brackets.
Remove the air cleaner and battery carrier.
Remove the exhaust pipes.
Disconnect the electric horn leads.
Disconnect the magneto and dynamo leads.
Remove the slides from the carburettor.
Remove the rear chain and chain guard.
Remove the bolts from mudguard bracket at rear of gearbox.

Remove the footrest bar.
Remove the bottom rear engine bolt.
Support the engine on a suitable box or wood block.

Raise the centre stand and remove the spring.
Loosen the bottom gearbox nut and swing the lower engine plate down.
Remove the front engine plates and horn.
Remove the nuts from the top bolt of the rear gearbox plates and then remove the timing side gearbox plate. The engine can then be swung out on the right hand side.

Alternatively, if the engine is to be stripped, remove the primary chain case cover, the engine sprocket and clutch and the back of the primary chaincase. The top rear engine bolt can then be withdrawn without disturbing the rear gearbox plates.

2. Removal of the Gear Box

Remove the engine sprocket (Section C.1, Subsection 26) and clutch (Section C.1, Subsection 29).

Remove the rear half of the primary chain case by removing three socket screws and the chain tensioner pivot.

The gearbox can now be withdrawn from the back of the crankcase after unscrewing the four nuts which secure it.

3. Dismantling the Crankcase

Drain the oil tank by removing the drain plug.

Having removed the engine from the frame as described in Subsection 1, dismantle the heads, barrels, pistons, timing gear, magneto, etc., as described in Section C.1.

Remove the gearbox as described in Subsection 2.

Remove the two hexagon-headed plugs on the driving side of the crankcase just below the cylinder base. (On no account must these plugs be disturbed unless the driving side cylinder has been or is to be lifted because they cannot be tightened without holding the nuts inside).

Access can now be obtained through the plug holes to two screws holding the two halves of the crankcase together which must be removed.

Remove three nuts in the timing chest, two nuts on the driving side crankcase, two loose studs through the bottom of the crankcase and two loose studs through the back of the oil tank.

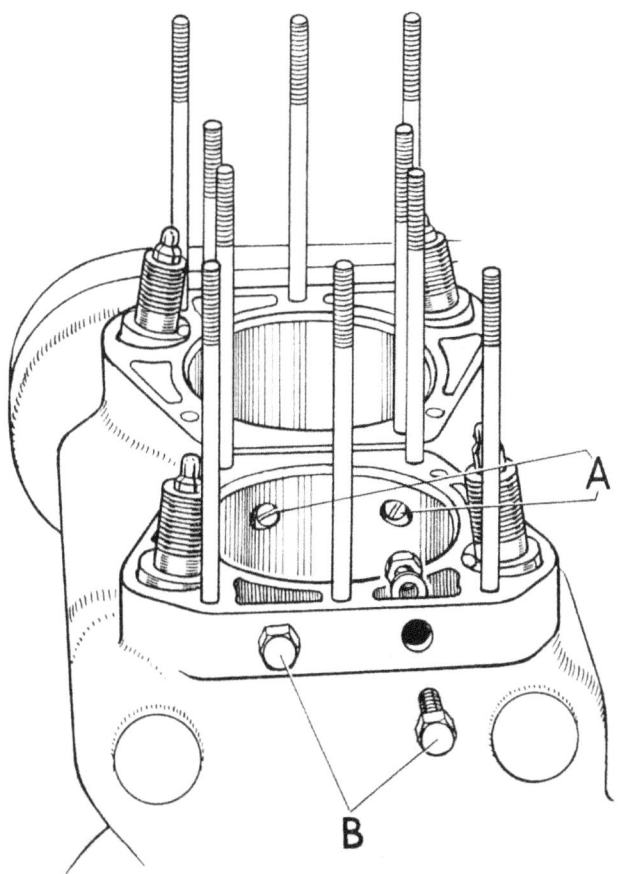

REMOVAL OF SCREWS IN CRANKCASE
Fig. 1

(The other studs have already been removed to take the engine out of the frame.)

The two halves of the crankcase can now be separated.

The inner race of the roller bearing on the timing side will remain on the crankshaft bringing with it the cage and rollers and leaving the outer race fixed to the crankcase.

The inner race of the ball bearing on the driving side is a tight fit on the shaft and can be removed with special tool No. E.5121. If this is not available, the shaft can be driven out with a hide mallet or a soft metal drift.

To avoid damage to the ball bearing the case should be heated to about 100°C. before doing this.

4. Main Bearings

To remove the ball bearing from the driving side crankcase, heat the crankcase to about 100° C., by immersion in hot water or in an oven, after which the bearing can be driven out using a drift **which applies pressure to the outside race only.**

When fitting a new ball bearing, heat the crankcase in the same way and use the same drift, taking great care to keep the bearing square with the bore.

To remove the outer roller race from the timing side crankcase, first heat the crankcase then drive the race out using a small punch through the three holes provided.

The inner race and rollers can be withdrawn from the crankshaft using a claw-type extractor.

When refitting the inner race drive it on to the shaft until just flush with the end **and no further.**

5. Fitting the Connecting Rods.

To remove the connecting rods from the crankshaft, first take out the cotter pins securing the socket screws in the connecting rods and then remove the socket screws themselves.

If the big end bearing caps are removed to examine the condition of the bearings, make sure that the caps are refitted the same way round on the same rods and that the rods themselves are refitted the same way round on the same crank pins.

In refitting the connecting rods, the socket screws should be tightened progressively with a torque wrench set at 200—220 inch-lbs.

If the cotter pins do not come in line remove the socket screws and use a different thickness of washer. A difference of ·005 in. in the washer alters the position of the screw $\frac{1}{8}$ of a turn.

There is a recess in one side of the connecting rod for a cotter pin head and this side must face outwards when the connecting rod is assembled on the crankshaft to avoid fouling between the cotter and the crankshaft web.

White-metalled steel liners are fitted in the connecting rods and these are replaceable.

6. Re-assembly of the Crankcase

Fit the outer roller race in the timing side crankcase, the ball bearing in the driving side crankcase and the inner roller race on to the crankshaft as described in Subsection 4.

Heat the timing side crankcase with the outer roller bearing race in position to about 100°C.

Lay the crankcase flat on the bench and insert the shaft, with the inner roller race in position, arranging the connecting rods so that they do not foul the crankcase.

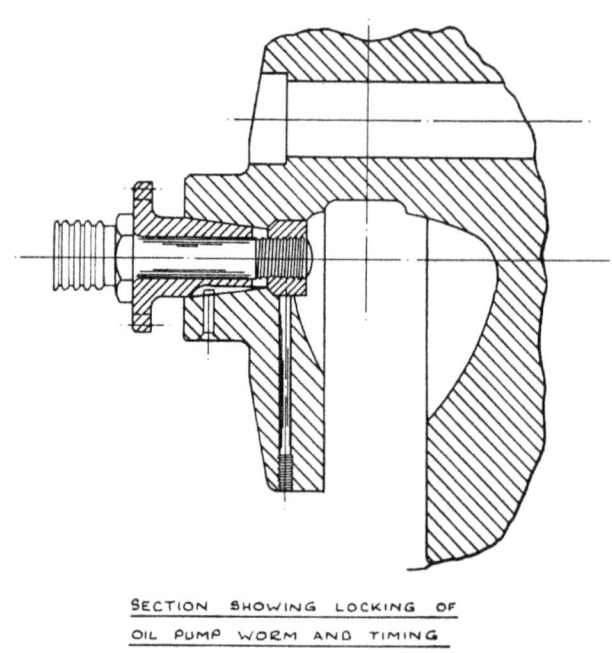

SECTION SHOWING LOCKING OF
OIL PUMP WORM AND TIMING
SPROCKET BY LOCKING ROD.

PUMP WORM LOCKNUT
Fig. 2

Insert the camshafts in their correct position (exhaust front, inlet rear) and see that the filter housing is in position.

Put the distance piece in position on the driving side of the crankshaft.

Apply jointing compound to the timing side crankcase.

Heat the driving side crankcase and bearing to 100°C. and drop it over the crankshaft, **making sure to lift the tappets clear of the cams.**

Bolt the two halves of the crankcase together. The crankcase should now be drawn into its correct position by fitting the engine sprocket temporarily and tightening the nut whilst the crankcase is still hot.

7. Pump Worm Locknut

The pump worm is held in position in the end of the crankshaft by a steel nut which is permanently fixed in the crankshaft and should not be removed.

The nut is fitted in a recess and locked by means of a long peg which in turn is held by a grub screw in the timing side crank web.

If it is necessary to re-fit the nut, assemble the timing sprocket with the pump worm and nut in the crankshaft while out of the crankcase and tighten it up.

By means of a long drill through the hole in the crankshaft web, countersink the nut to about $\frac{1}{8}$ in. Insert the locking rod and grub screw.

Remove the pump worm and sprocket and re-assemble after the shaft has been fitted in the crankcase.

NOTES

SECTION E1
Gearbox and Clutch
"Meteor 700"; "500 Twin"; "500 Bullet"; "350 Bullet."

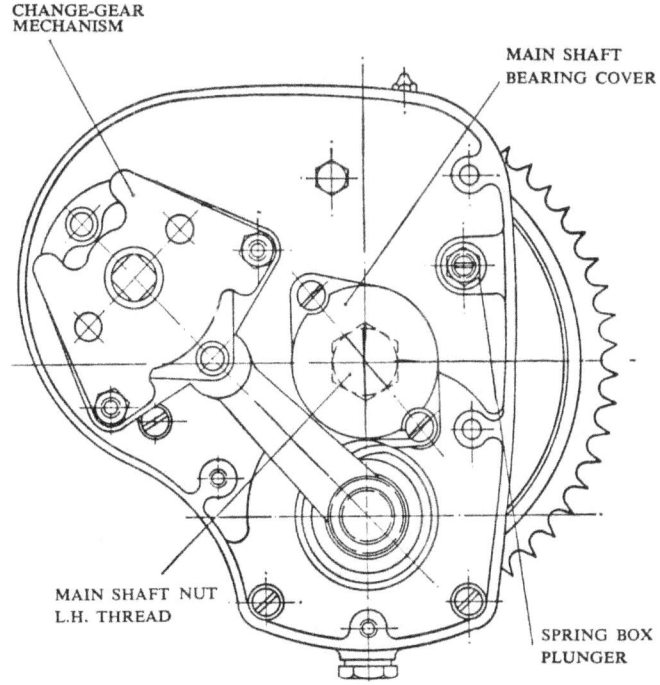

GEARBOX WITH OUTER COVER REMOVED
Fig. 1

1. Removal of Gearbox

This is described in Section D1 or D2.

The gearbox can, however, be completely dismantled with the engine in the frame except for the removal of the inside operator and the bearings in the gearbox shell.

2. To Dismantle the Gearbox

First remove the kickstart crank, the change-gear lever and the neutral finder and pointer.

Remove the top small inspection cover and disconnect the clutch cable.

Remove four screws and the gearbox outer cover can then be detached.

Remove the change-gear mechanism by taking off the two nuts securing it.

Remove the main shaft bearing cover which is attached by two screws.

Remove four cheese-headed screws and one hexagon bolt.

Remove the spring box locating plunger nut and washer.

Remove the main shaft nut (**Left Hand Thread**).

The gearbox inner cover can then be removed.

The mainshaft can be drawn straight out if the clutch has been removed, which, however, should be done before taking off the gearbox inner cover.

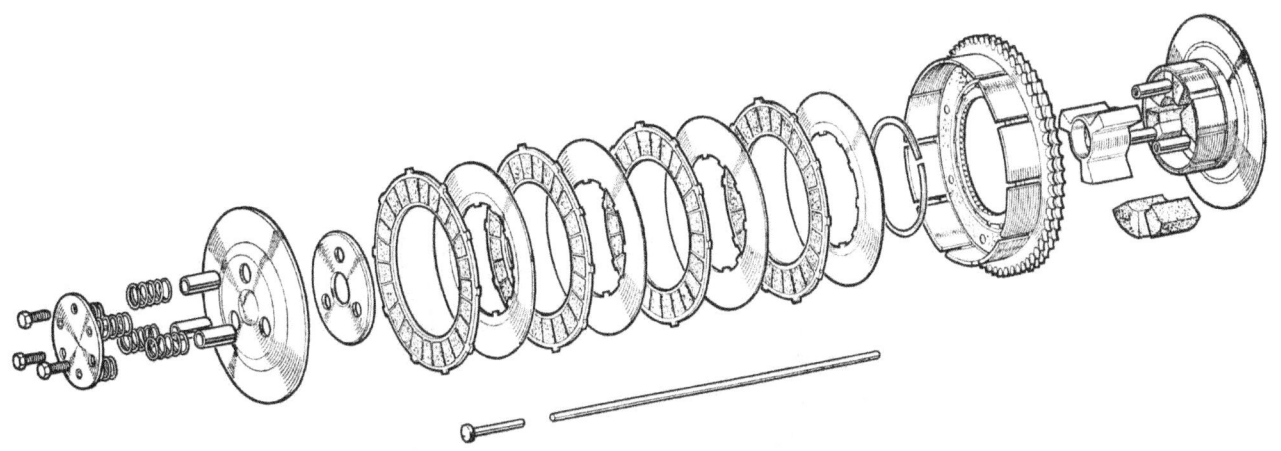

EXPLODED VIEW OF CLUTCH
Fig. 2

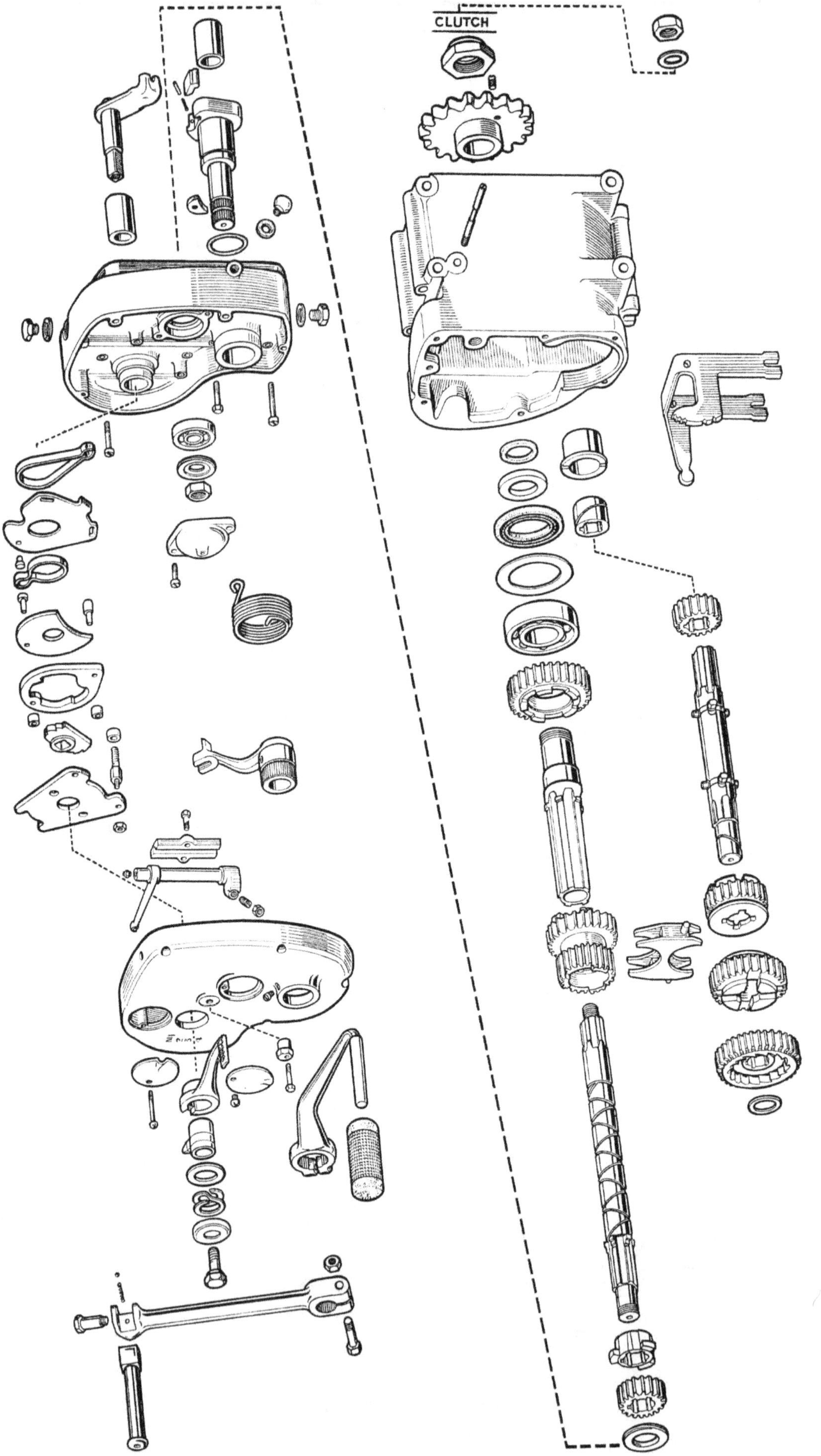

EXPLODED VIEW OF GEARBOX
Fig. 3

(See Section C1 or C2.) The top gear pinion and dog will come away with the mainshaft.

The layshaft can then be removed and the 2nd and 3rd gears drawn off the final drive sleeve together with the operator fork.

To take out the final drive sleeve, the final drive sprocket must be removed and this is preferably done before removing the inner cover. (See Section C1 or C2.)

3. Removal of the Ball Races

The mainshaft ball bearings can be removed by using a stepped drift $1\frac{7}{16}$ in.—$1\frac{11}{64}$ in. diameter for the bearing in the box and $\frac{13}{16}$ in.—$\frac{39}{64}$ in. diameter for the bearing in the cover.

When refitting the bearings stepped drifts of $2\frac{5}{16}$ in.—$1\frac{11}{64}$ in. diameter and $1\frac{1}{16}$ in.—$\frac{39}{64}$ in. diameter must be used for the bearings in the box and cover respectively.

Note the felt washer in the recess behind the larger main shaft bearing and the dished pen-steel washer between the bearing and the felt washer. The second dished pen-steel washer, if fitted, has a smaller central hole and is on the other side of the main shaft bearing and is nipped between the inner face of the bearing and the shoulder on the final drive sleeve. See that both of the dished pen-steel washers have their raised portions facing towards the clutch and final drive sprocket.

4. Change-Gear Mechanism

If the two nuts securing the change-gear ratchet mechanism are slackened, the adjuster plate can be set in the correct position. In this position the movement of the gear lever necessary to engage the ratchet teeth will be approximately the same in each direction.

If the plate is incorrectly adjusted, it may be found that, after moving from top to third or from bottom to second gear, the outer ratchets do not engage the teeth on the inner ratchets correctly.

If, when fitting new parts, it is found that the gears do not engage properly, ascertain whether a little more movement is required or whether there is too much movement so that the gear slips right through second or third gear into neutral. If more movement is required, this can be obtained by filing the adjuster plate very slightly at the points of contact with the pegs on the ratchet ring.

If too much movement is already present, a new adjuster plate giving less movement must be fitted.

5. Re-Assembling the Gearbox

The procedure is the reverse of that given in Subsection 2 but the following points should be noted:—

If the main shaft top gear pinion and dog have been removed, make sure that the dog is replaced the right way round or third and top gears can be engaged simultaneously.

Make sure that the trunnions on the operator fork engage with the slots in the inside operator.

See that the main shaft is pushed right home. (It may tighten in the felt washer inside the final drive shaft nut.)

The layshaft top gear and kickstarter pinion should be assembled on the layshaft and the kickstarter shaft and ratchet assembled on to it before fitting the end cover. Do not forget the washer on the layshaft between the kickstarter pinion and the kickstarter shaft.

The joint between the gearbox and the inner cover should be made with gold size, shellac or a similar jointing compound.

Make sure that all parts are clean before commencing assembly. In normal climates the recesses in the gearbox should be packed with soft grease and the box should be filled up to the correct level with gear oil. (See Subsection 9.) **On no account must heavy yellow grease be used.**

6. Dismantling and Re-assembly of the Clutch

The method of removing the clutch is described in Section C1 or C2.

When re-assembling, note that two of the steel plates are dished and that the other(s) are flat. The correct order of assembly is shown on the exploded drawing.

Do not forget to replace the cush rubber or plate retaining cover before fitting the pressure plate.

Make sure that the distance tubes inside three of the springs pass through the holes in the pressure plate. The other three springs are located by means of bosses on the clutch cap.

Tighten the spring pins as far as they will go.

If the clutch lifts unevenly it is probable that one of the springs has taken a set, in which case new springs should be fitted.

7. Adjustment of the Clutch Control

It is essential that there should be about $\frac{1}{16}$ in. free movement in the clutch cable, to ensure that all the spring pressure is exerted on the plates.

There are two points of adjustment for the clutch cable. The first is at the top of the gearbox just behind the oil filler plug and is provided for taking up any stretch in the cable. The adjustment is made by screwing the collar in or out of the gearbox shell. The connection between the end of the cable and the horizontal lever can be seen if the top small inspection cover on the front of the gearbox is removed. Tighten the locknut on the screwed collar after adjustment has been made.

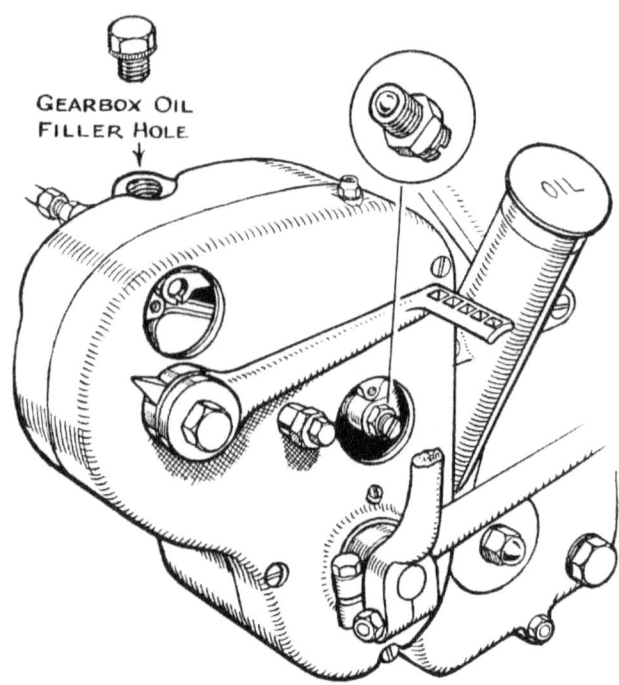

CLUTCH ADJUSTMENT ON CURRENT GEARBOXES
Fig. 4

The other point of adjustment is behind the lower inspection cover on the front of the gearbox and is for compensating for wear on the clutch plate inserts. To make the adjustment, remove the inspection cover, slacken the locknut and turn the central screw. Tighten the locknut after adjustment has been made.

The reason for the two points of adjustment is to enable the lever behind the cover to be kept in its proper position whether the need for adjustment is caused by plate wear or cable stretch.

Owing to initial bedding down of the clutch plate inserts, the clutch control may require adjustment after the first few hundred miles with a new machine. This point should therefore be examined soon after delivery and adjustment made if necessary.

On earlier models the clutch operating mechanism is exposed on the front of the gearbox, but the adjustments are, however, the same in principle as those described above.

The cable adjustment is at the bottom of the front of the gearbox just in front of the kickstart lever. The collar is screwed in or out of a lug on the gearbox cover and is secured by a locknut as before.

The other adjustment is made by slackening the clamping bolt in the horizontal lever and turning the lever on its spindle, which is the end of the operating worm in the gearbox cover.

When correctly adjusted, the lever should be approximately square with the cable when the clutch is fully lifted.

The position of the lever endwise on the worm spindle is important and it should be positioned so that it does not foul the kickstart lever.

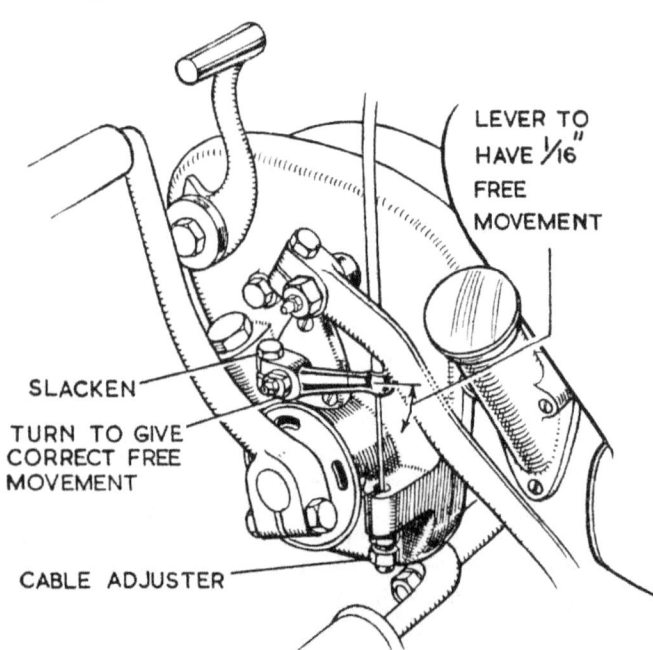

CLUTCH LEVER AND CABLE ADJUSTMENTS ON EARLY GEARBOXES
Fig. 5

8. Adjustment of the Neutral Finder

The neutral finder is adjusted by means of an eccentric stop secured to the front of the gearbox cover by a bolt which limits the travel of the operating pedal. Slacken the bolt and turn the eccentric until the correct movement of the pedal is obtained.

9. Gearbox Oil Level

The gearbox is replenished with oil by removing a plug in the top and the correct level can be checked by removing a second plug lower down on the right hand side looking at the cover.

On earlier models a dip-stick is attached to the filler plug for measuring the level of the oil or was provided loose in the tool kit.

On some models the filler plug is on the side of the gearbox and in such cases the oil should be level with the plug hole and no dip-stick is required. The oil will be found to run into the box more easily on these models if the engine is started up and allowed to tick over so that the gears and shafts rotate.

SECTION F1

Amal Needle Type Carburetter

1. General Description

The Amal Standard Needle Type Carburetter has been in production for many years and has proved itself to be especially suitable for single and twin cylinder motor cycles in which there is a pulsating air flow through the carburetter.

The float chamber is a separate unit bolted on to the base of the mixing chamber and may have either a top or bottom petrol feed.

The supply of air to the engine is controlled by a throttle slide which carries a taper needle operating in the needle jet. The needle is secured to the throttle slide by a spring clip fitting in one of five grooves and the mixture strength throughout a large proportion of the throttle range is controlled by the position of this needle in the slide and by the size of the jet in which it works. There is, however, a restricting or main jet at the bottom of the needle jet and the size of this controls the mixture strength at the largest throttle openings. At very small throttle openings petrol and air are fed to the engine through a separate pilot system which has an outlet at the engine side of the throttle. The air supply to this pilot system is controlled by the pilot air screw and the slow running of the engine can be adjusted by means of this screw and a stop which holds the throttle open a very small amount. The throttle slide is cut away at the back and the shape of this cut-away controls the mixture at throttle openings slightly wider than that required for slow running. There is a compensating system to prevent undue enriching of the mixture with increasing engine speed, this system consisting of a primary choke surrounding the upper end of the needle jet through which air is drawn in increasing quantities as the depression in the main choke increases. This air supply and the supply to the pilot system are taken from a duct in the main air intake to the carburetter so that all the air passing to the engine can be filtered by fitting an air cleaner to the main carburetter air intake. A handlebar controlled air slide is provided to enrich the mixture temporarily when required.

2. Tuning the Carburetter

The throttle opening at which each tuning point is most effective is shown in Fig. 2. It should be remembered, however, that a change of setting at any point will have some effect on the setting required at other points; for instance, a change of main jet will have some effect on the mixture strength at half throttle which, however, is mainly controlled by the needle position. Similarly an alteration to the throttle cut-away may affect both the needle position required and the adjustment of the pilot air screw. For this reason it is necessary to tune the carburetter in a definite sequence, which is as follows :

First—Main Jet. The size should be chosen which gives maximum speed at full throttle with the air control wide open. If two

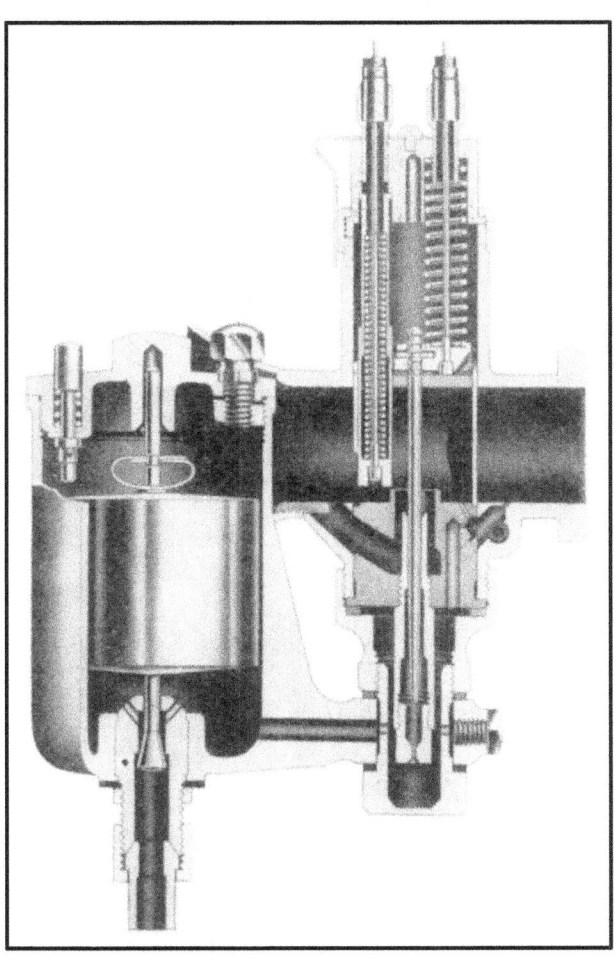

SECTIONAL VIEW SHOWING AIR VALVE AND THROTTLE CLOSED

Fig. 1

different sizes of jet give the same speed the larger should be chosen for safety as it is dangerous to run with too weak a mixture at full throttle.

Second—The pilot air screw should be set to give good idling.

Third—The throttle valve should be selected with the largest amount of cut-away which will prevent spitting or mis-firing when opening the throttle slowly from the idling position.

Fourth—The lowest position of the taper needle should be found consistent with good acceleration with the air slide wide open.

Fifth—The pilot air screw should be checked to improve the idling if possible. When setting the adjustment of the pilot air screw this should be done in conjunction with the throttle stop. Note that the correct setting of the air screw is the one which gives the fastest idling speed for a given position of the throttle stop. If the idling speed is then undesirably fast it can be slowed down by unscrewing the throttle stop a fraction of a turn.

PHASES OF AMAL NEEDLE JET CARBURETTER THROTTLE OPENINGS

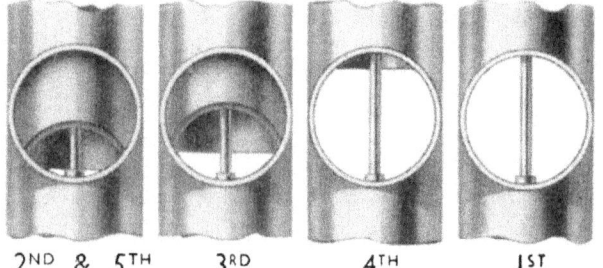

Fig. 2

It will be noted that of the four points at which adjustments are normally made, i.e. pilot air screw, throttle cut-away, needle position and main jet size, the first and third do not require changing of any parts of the carburetter. Assuming that the carburtter has the standard setting to suit the particular model of the motor cycle any small adjustments occasioned by atmospheric conditions, changes in quality of fuel, etc., can usually be covered by adjustment of the pilot air screw and raising or lowering the taper needle one notch. If, however, the machine is used at very high altitudes or with a very restricted air cleaner a smaller main jet will be necessary. The following table gives the reduction in main jet size required at different altitudes:

Altitude Ft.	Reduction %
3,000	5
6,000	9
9,000	13
12,000	17

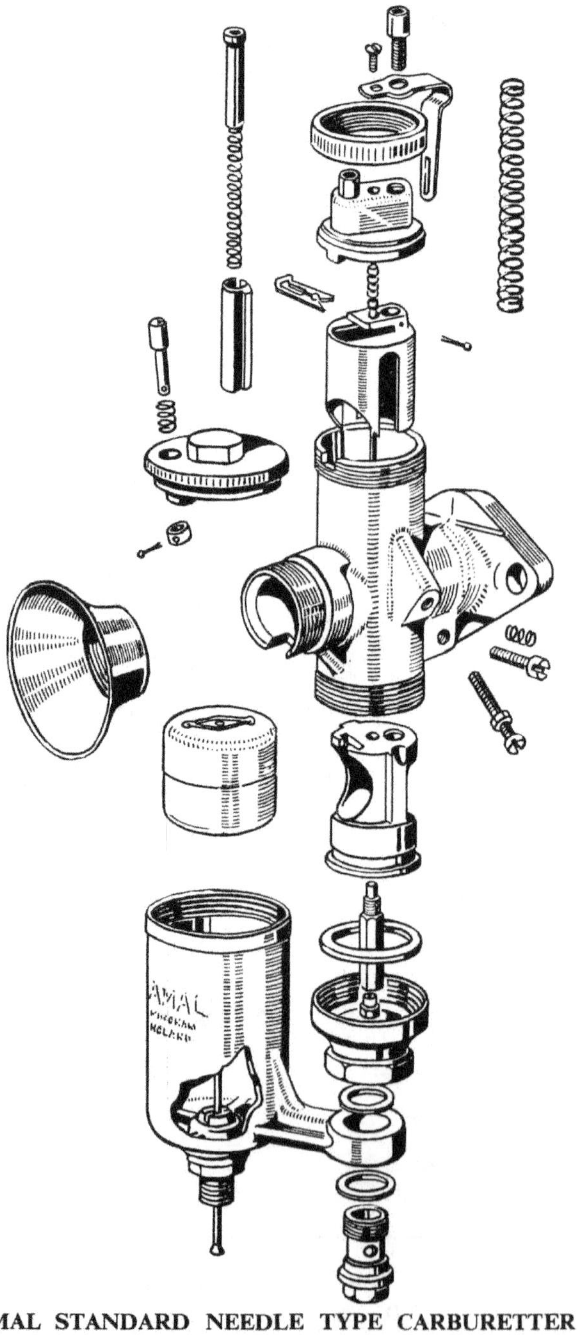

AMAL STANDARD NEEDLE TYPE CARBURETTER
Fig. 3

SETTINGS FOR AMAL STANDARD CARBURETTERS.

MODEL	Carburetter Code No.	Choke Dia. In.	Main Jet	Needle Jet	Needle Position	Throttle Valve	Pilot Outlet In.	REMARKS
"S 250" ohv	274BH/3A	$\frac{25}{32}$	75	Std.	2	4/4	.031	Stub Fitting
"S 250" ohv / "250 Clipper"	274 BS/3A	$\frac{25}{32}$	75	Std.	2	4/4	.031	Flange Fitting
"WD/C 350" sv	274 B/1A	$\frac{25}{32}$	85	Std.	3	4/5	.031	3-gauze Air Intake
"WD/CO 350" ohv	276AC/1A	$\frac{15}{16}$	130	Std.	3	6/4	.037	3-gauze Air Intake, Shallow Mixing Chamber Nut
"G 350" ohv	276BL/1A	$\frac{15}{16}$	130	Std.	3	6/4	.037	Shallow Mixing Chamber Nut
"350 Bullet" Std.	276CX/1A	1	140	Std.	3	6/4	.037	Shallow Mixing Chamber Nut
"350 Bullet" Trials	276EX/1A	$\frac{15}{16}$	140	Std.	3	6/3	.037	Shallow Mixing Chamber Nut
"J 500" ohv 1-Port	276CB/1A, 276CT/1A	1	150	Std.	3	6/4	.031	Stub Fitting / Flange Fitting
"J2 500" ohv 2-Port	276CZ/1A, 276DB/1A	$1\frac{1}{16}$	170	Std.	2	6/4	.031	Reduced O/D Air Intake / Standard Air Intake
"500 Bullet"	289T/1A	$1\frac{1}{8}$	180	Std.	2	29/3	.037	
"500 Twin"	276DU/1AT, 276GQ/1AT	$\frac{15}{16}$	150	109	2	6/4	.025	L.H. Pilot Screw & Throttle Stop / R.H. Pilot Screw & Throttle Stop
"Meteor 700"	276FJ/1AT, 276GR/1AT	$1\frac{1}{16}$	170	Std.	3	6/4	.025	L.H. Pilot Screw & Throttle Stop / R.H. Pilot Screw & Throttle Stop

In the case of carburetters for engines running on alcohol fuel considerably larger jets are needed. In most cases a No. 113 needle jet will be required and the main jet size will require to be increased by an amount varying from 50% to 150% according to the grade of fuel used.

If the engine is run on fuel containing a small proportion of alcohol added to the petrol, a rough and ready guide is that the main jet should be increased by 1% for every 1% of alcohol in the fuel. In most cases alcohol blends available from petrol pumps do not contain sufficient alcohol to require any alteration to the carburetter setting.

The range of adjustment of the taper needle and the pilot air screw are determined by the size of the needle jet and of the pilot outlet respectively. Standard needle jets have a bore at the smallest point of .1065 in. and are not marked for size. Larger needle jets .1075 in., .109 in. and .113 in. bore are available and are marked 107, 109 and 113 respectively.

The standard pilot outlet bore is .031 in. but in some cases larger or smaller size pilot outlets are used. Since the pilot outlet is actually drilled in the body of the carburetter it is necessary to have a carburetter with the correct size pilot outlet if the best results are to be obtained.

The accompanying table shows the standard settings for all Amal standard needle type carburetters used on Royal Enfield machines from 1946 onwards.

3. Dismantling Carburetter

The construction of the carburetter is clearly shown in Fig. 3.

If the float chamber floods first make sure that the float is not punctured and partly filled with petrol, also that the clip on top of the float is engaged correctly with the groove in the fuel needle. If necessary lap the needle into its seating using only liquid metal polish for this purpose.

If it is necessary to remove the jet block do this with great care using a wooden drift and a light hammer to knock it out of the mixing chamber body. A single strand of an inner control cable is useful for clearing the small passages in the jet block and care must be taken not to enlarge these by forcing the wire through them. Compressed air from a pipe line or a tyre pump is preferable. A choked main jet should be cleared only by blowing through it.

4. Causes of High Petrol Consumption

If the petrol consumption is excessive first look for leaks either from the carburetter, petrol pipe, petrol tap(s) or tank. If coloured petrol is in use this will readily indicate the presence of any small leaks which otherwise might pass unnoticed. If the petrol system is free from leaks, carefully set the pilot adjusting screw as described in paragraph 2 to give the correct mixture when idling. Running with the pilot adjusting screw too far in is a common cause of excessive petrol consumption. If the consumption is still heavy, try the effect of lowering the taper needle in the throttle slide by one notch. Do not fit a smaller main jet as this will not affect consumption except when driving on nearly full throttle and may make the mixture too weak at large throttle openings, thus causing overheating.

SECTION G1a

Lucas Coil Ignition Equipment

Used on "Meteor 700" and "500 Twin" up to end of 1954

1. General

The coil ignition equipment comprises an ignition coil, a contact breaker with automatic advance and a high tension distributor.

1 (a). Ignition Coil

The ignition coil consists of a laminated core, around which are wound the primary (or low tension) and the secondary (or high tension) windings. The secondary winding consists of a large number of turns of fine wire and the primary winding of relatively few turns of thicker wire. The primary winding is wound outside the secondary, in order to allow the heat produced to be dissipated more easily.

The coil assembly is mounted on a porcelain insulator within a sealed metal case filled with an insulation compound or oil to prevent the ingress of moisture.

The only maintenance possible is to keep the coil casing clean and free from oil and water, paying especial attention to the moulding at the terminal end and to check the terminal connections for tightness from time to time.

To fit a new H.T. cable to the coil, remove the knurled moulded nut and thread it over the end of the cable. Bare the cable for a length of about ½ in., thread the wire through the brass washer provided and bend back the strands (see Fig. 1). Finally, screw the nut into its terminal.

1 (b). Distributor

Fig. 2 illustrates the distributor model DKX. It has a moulded contact breaker base and the shaft is carried in two porous bronze bushes.* A high-tension distributor rotor is fitted on an extension of the cam spindle, the moulded distributor cover carrying two electrodes and a carbon brush which are connected to the plug leads and the H.T. lead from the ignition coil respectively.

2. Routine Maintenance

2 (a). Distributor

(i) *Lubrication.* To be carried out every 3,000 miles.

Cam. Smear the surface of the cam very lightly with Mobilgrease No. 2 or, if this is not available, clean engine oil may be used.

Cam Bearing. Remove the rotor arm and apply a few drops of thin machine oil to the hollow screw thus exposed. On early models the screw may not be drilled, in which case it should be removed and oil applied to the tapped hole.

Contact breaker pivot. Place a small amount of Mobilgrease No. 2 or clean engine oil on the pivot on which the contact breaker lever turns.

Shaft. When a lubricator is fitted in the shank of the unit add a few drops of thin machine oil. On later models there is a single long bush of

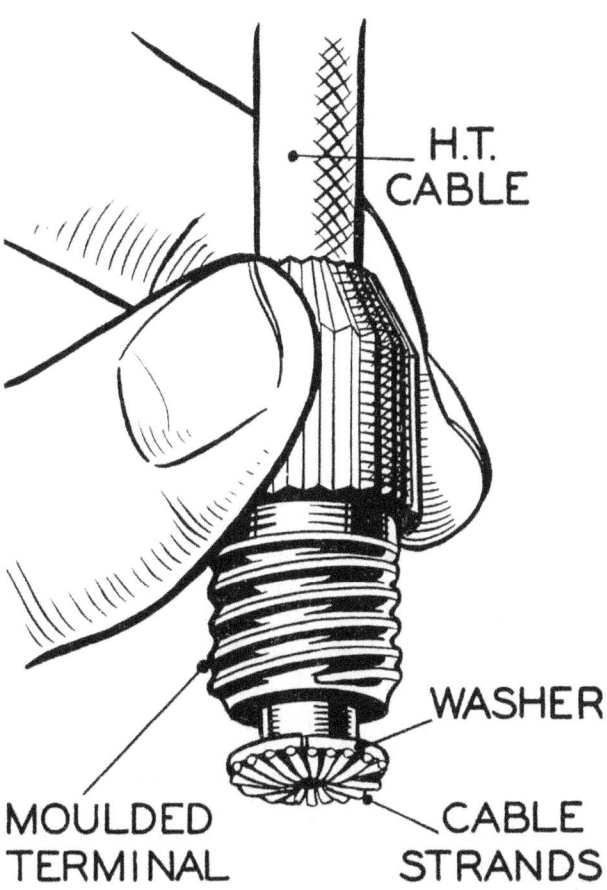

Fig. 1

---

*Later models have a single sintered iron bush.

sintered iron which will absorb sufficient oil from the oil feed to the helical driving pinion.

Automatic timing control. Unscrew the two screws securing the contact breaker base plate to the distributor body and lubricate the timing control mechanism with thin machine oil, paying particular attention to the pivots. Refit the base plate.

No grease or oil must be allowed to get on or near the contacts when carrying out the foregoing procedure.

(ii) *Cleaning.* To be carried out every 6,000 miles. Wipe the inside and the outside of the cover moulding with a soft dry cloth. Pay particular attention to the spaces between the metal electrodes and check that the small carbon brush moves freely in its holder.

Examine the contact breaker. The contacts must be free from grease or oil. If they are burnt or blackened, clean them with a fine carborundum stone or very fine emery cloth, afterwards wiping away any trace of dirt or metal dust with a petrol-moistened cloth. Cleaning of the contacts is made easier if the contact breaker lever carrying the moving contact is removed. To do this, unscrew the nut securing the end of the contact breaker spring and remove the nut, spring washer and bush. Lift the contact breaker lever off its bearing. After cleaning check the contact breaker gap setting.

(iii) *Contact breaker setting.* Contact breaker gaps should be checked every 3,000 miles. If the gap is allowed to decrease below the specified setting, rapid and excessive pitting and piling may occur.

Turn the engine until the contacts are seen to be fully opened and check the gap with a gauge having a thickness of ·014—·016 in. If the gap is correct the gauge should be a sliding fit but if the gap varies from the gauge, the setting must be adjusted.

To do this, keep the engine in the position giving maximum contact opening and slacken the two screws securing the fixed contact plate. Adjust the position of the plate until the gap is set to the thickness of the gauge and tighten the two locking screws.

2 (b). High Tension Cables

Examine the high tension cables. Any which have the insulation cracked or perished, or show signs of damage in any other way, must be renewed, using neoprene covered rubber ignition cable.

3. Servicing

3 (a). Testing in Position to Locate Ignition Fault

If a failure of ignition or misfiring occurs, first make sure that the trouble is not due to defects in the engine, carburetter, petrol supply, sparking plug(s), etc. If necessary adjust the sparking plug gaps to ·018—·020 in. This must be done by bending the earth points only, **not the central electrode.** Ensure also that the battery is not discharged.

(i) *Examine the high tension cables.* If the rubber shows signs of deterioration or cracking the cable should be renewed using neoprene covered high tension cable.

(ii) Test each plug and high tension cable by removing the plug and allowing it to rest on the cylinder head and observing whether a spark occurs at the points when the engine is turned. It should, however, be noted that this is only a rough test, since it is possible that sparking may not take place when the plug is under compression.

(iii) Examine the contact breaker, checking the gap setting and measuring the contact breaker spring tension. This should be 20—24 oz. measured at the contacts.

(iv) Switch on the ignition, turn the engine and observe the ammeter reading. If an ammeter reading is given which rises and falls with the closing and opening of the contacts the low tension wiring is in order. If the reading does not fluctuate in this way a short circuit in the low tension wiring is indicated.

Check the capacitor (condenser) and ignition coil for short circuit by substitution. Examine the insulation of the contact breaker.

When no reading is given a broken or loose connection in the low tension wiring is indicated. Refer to the wiring diagram and examine the connections to the ignition switch. Check the ignition coil by substitution.

Remove the high tension cable from the centre distributor terminal. Switch on the ignition and turn the engine until the contacts close. Flick the contact breaker lever open while the high tension lead from the coil is held about $\frac{3}{16}$ in. away from the cylinder block. If the ignition equipment is in order a strong spark should be obtained. If no spark is given it indicates a fault in the circuit of the secondary winding of the coil and the coil should be replaced.

3 (b). Dismantling the Distributor

Spring back the securing clips and remove the moulded cover (see Fig. 2). Lift the moulded rotor arm off the top of the spindle. Withdraw the two securing screws and lift off the contact breaker base.

Unscrew the nut on the moving contact pillar and remove the spring washer and bush. Lift off the contact breaker spring and contact breaker arm. The fixed contact is secured on a plate by

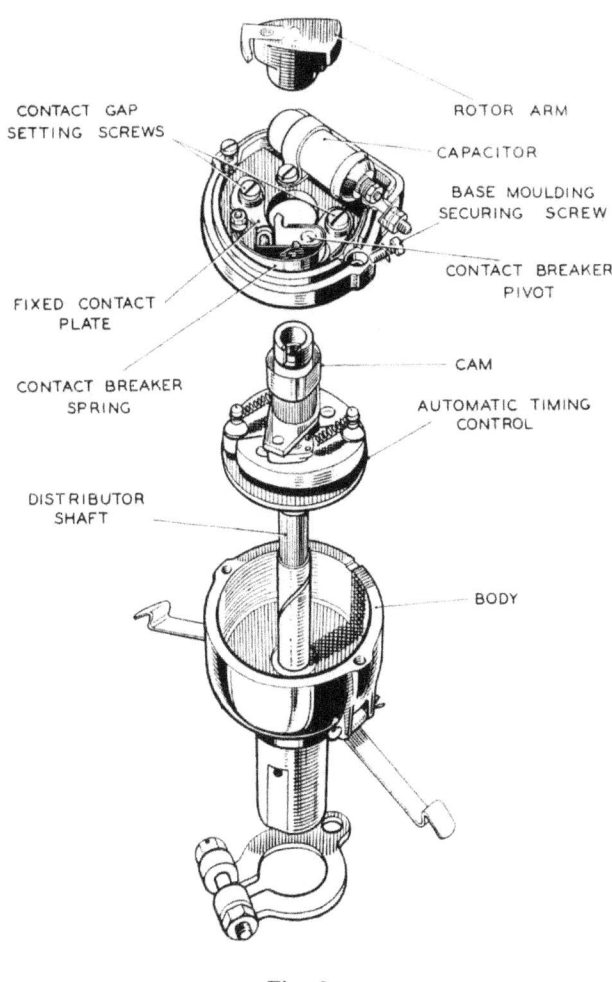

Fig. 2

two screws. Withdraw the two screws and lift off the fixed contact.

Remove the single securing screw and terminal nut on the condenser and lift off the condenser. Withdraw the driving dogs on the shaft carrying the cam and automatic timing control and lift these off the shaft.

The automatic timing control should not be dismantled unnecessarily. If it is desired to dismantle the mechanism, carefully note the position of the various components in order that they may be refitted correctly.

3 (c). Bearings

Badly worn bearings are usually indicated by the maximum opening of the contacts varying considerably as the shaft is slowly rotated by hand while side pressure is applied to the cam. Porous bronze bearing bushes should be inserted in the body on a highly polished shouldered mandrel, which will give the finished bore diameter without machining. Before use, bushes should be stored in a covered container and fully covered with oil of a grade equivalent to Mobiloil Arctic or other good thin mineral oil for a minimum time of 24 hours.

3 (d). Contact Breaker

When trimming a pair of contacts it is not essential to grind down a slightly pitted contact but only to remove excess metal from the piled contact. Should the pitting and piling be found excessive a replacement contact set, comprising both fixed and moving contacts, should be fitted. Before despatch, replacement contacts are given a protective coating of oil, which should be removed with a petrol-moistened cloth before fitting.

3 (e). Reassembly

Reassembly is a reversal of the dismantling procedure described in Subsection 3 (b). Note that an insulating washer must be placed over the contact breaker pivot before the moving contact is fitted.

Section **G1a** *ROYAL ENFIELD WORKSHOP MANUAL* Page 4

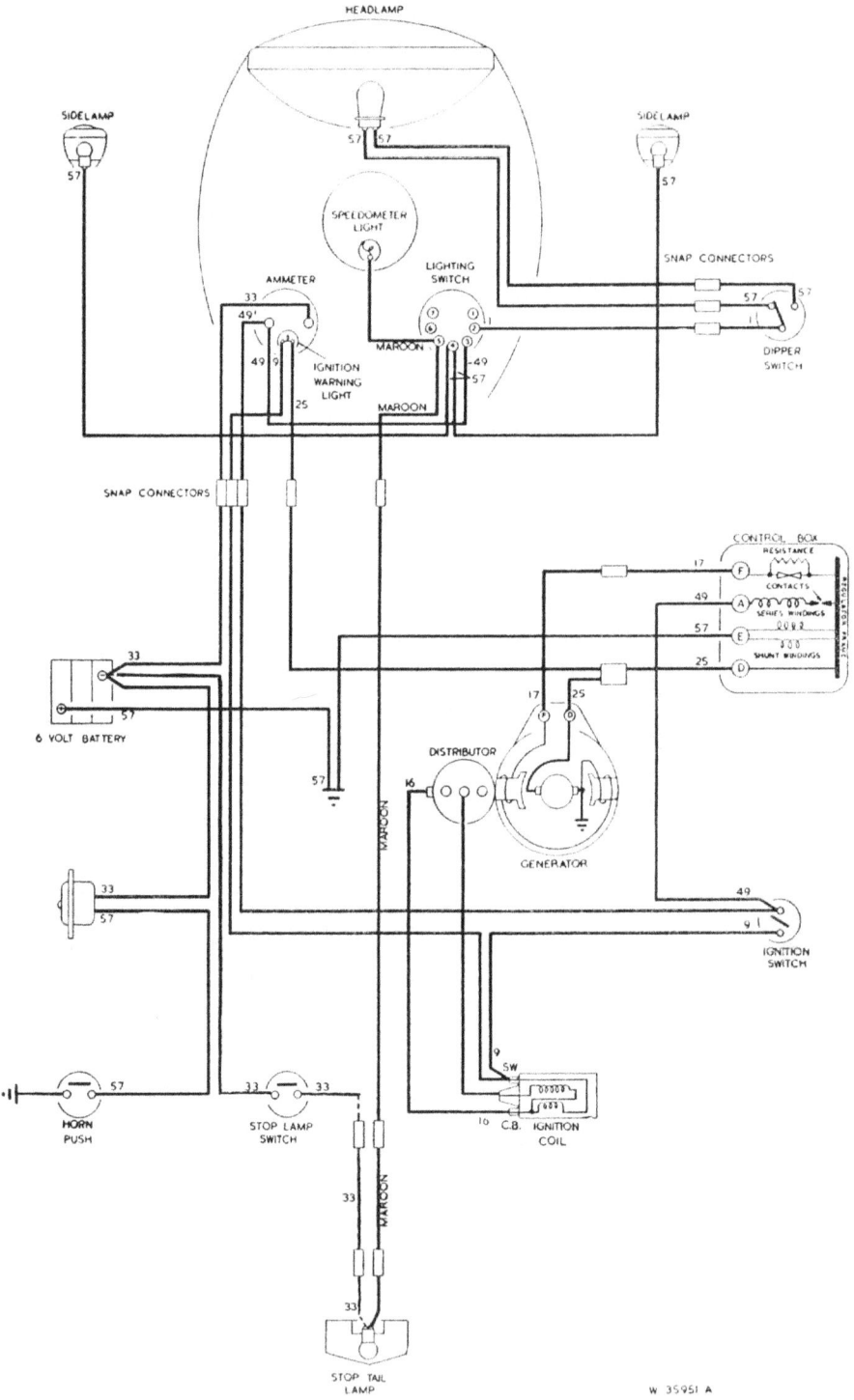

KEY TO CABLE COLOURS

1 BLUE	15 WHITE with BROWN	28 YELLOW with WHITE	41 RED	54 PURPLE with GREEN
2 BLUE with RED	16 WHITE with BLACK	29 YELLOW with GREEN	42 RED with YELLOW	55 PURPLE with BROWN
3 BLUE with YELLOW	17 GREEN	30 YELLOW with PURPLE	43 RED with BLUE	56 PURPLE with BLACK
4 BLUE with WHITE	18 GREEN with RED	31 YELLOW with BROWN	44 RED with WHITE	57 BLACK
5 BLUE with GREEN	19 GREEN with YELLOW	32 YELLOW with BLACK	45 RED with GREEN	58 BLACK with RED
6 BLUE with PURPLE	20 GREEN with BLUE	33 BROWN	46 RED with PURPLE	59 BLACK with YELLOW
7 BLUE with BROWN	21 GREEN with WHITE	34 BROWN with RED	47 RED with BROWN	60 BLACK with BLUE
8 BLUE with BLACK	22 GREEN with PURPLE	35 BROWN with YELLOW	48 RED with BLACK	61 BLACK with WHITE
9 WHITE	23 GREEN with BROWN	36 BROWN with BLUE	49 PURPLE	62 BLACK with GREEN
10 WHITE with RED	24 GREEN with BLACK	37 BROWN with WHITE	50 PURPLE with RED	63 BLACK with PURPLE
11 WHITE with YELLOW	25 YELLOW	38 BROWN with GREEN	51 PURPLE with YELLOW	64 BLACK with BROWN
12 WHITE with BLUE	26 YELLOW with RED	39 BROWN with PURPLE	52 PURPLE with BLUE	65 DARK GREEN
13 WHITE with GREEN	27 YELLOW with BLUE	40 BROWN with BLACK	53 PURPLE with WHITE	66 LIGHT GREEN
14 WHITE with PURPLE				

WIRING DIAGRAM

Fig. 3

SECTION G1b

Lucas Magdyno

Model MN2L for Twin Cylinder Engines used on "500 Twin" and "Meteor 700" 1955 Models

1. General

The magdyno is a base-fixed magneto and dynamo unit, the body of the magneto portion being arranged to carry a standard strap-fixed dynamo. A shock absorbing drive is arranged between the magneto and dynamo portions. The magneto portion has a wound rotating armature and a high-energy magnet case integral with the body.

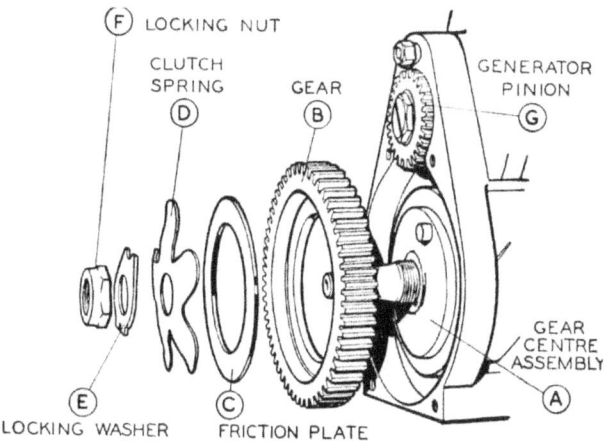

Fig. 1

The shock absorbing drive is incorporated in the larger of the two gears which transmit the drive from the magneto shaft to the dynamo and is shown exploded in Fig. 1. This drive, whilst permitting maximum dynamo output to be obtained, reduces peak shock loadings on the teeth of a bakelised fabric gear to a minimum value. The drive is taken from metal gear centre A, keyed to the magneto shaft, to fabric gear B by means of friction plate C and clutch spring D. A peg projecting from gear centre A prevents relative movement of the gear centre and tension spring D. In the event of a back-fire or an electrical short-circuit, slip will occur between the contacting surfaces of fabric gear B and gear centre A.

2. Routine Maintenance

2 (a). Lubrication

To be carried out every 3,000 miles.

Wipe the outside of the Magdyno to remove dirt or grease, then take off the contact breaker cover (see Fig. 2). Unscrew the hexagon headed screw in the centre of the contact breaker and withdraw the contact breaker from its housing. Push aside the contact breaker arm retaining spring and prise the arm off its pivot. Wipe away any dirt or grease from the contacts with a petrol-moistened cloth.

If necessary, use a very fine carborundum stone to polish the contacts, re-cleaning afterwards with a petrol-moistened cloth. Smear the pivot pin with a little Mobilgrease No. 2 before refitting the contact breaker arm.

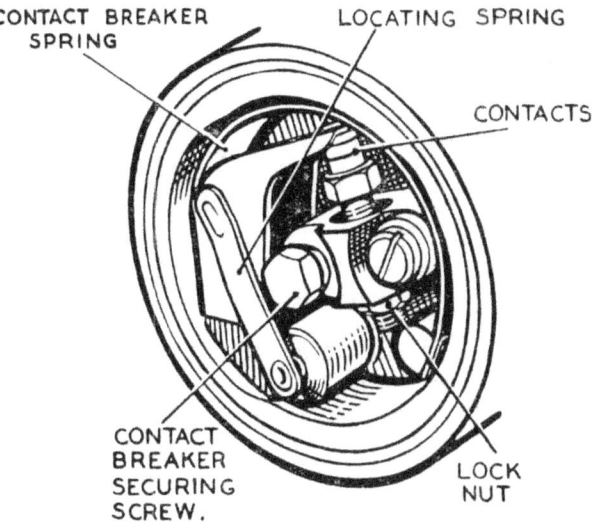

Fig. 2

Remove the cam ring, which is a sliding fit in its housing, and lightly smear inside and outside surfaces with Mobilgrease No. 2. Both removal and refitting of the cam can be made easier if the handlebar control lever is half retarded, thus taking the cam away from its stop pin. Apply one or two drops of thin machine oil to the felt cam lubricator in the housing. Refit the cam, taking care that the stop peg in the housing and the plunger of the timing control engage with their respective slots.

Refit the contact breaker. This can be made easier if the contact breaker heel is away from the cam lobe; turn the engine until this is so. The key on the projecting part of the contact breaker base must engage with the keyway in the armature shaft. Refit the hexagon headed screw and tighten with care. It must not be slack, neither must undue force be used.

The main bearings of the Magdynos are packed with grease during manufacture and need no attention until a general overhaul is undertaken.

2 (b). Adjustments

Check every 3,000 miles.

(i) *Setting contact breaker gap.* The contact breaker gap must be set to 0·012 in.—0·015 in. when the contacts are fully separated. To adjust the gap, turn the engine until the contacts are fully opened. Slacken the locking nut of the adjustable contact and turn the contact by its hexagon head until a feeler gauge of appropriate thickness is a sliding fit in the gap. Tighten the lock nut and re-check the gap.

(ii) *Adjusting the Timing Control Cable.* Any slackness in the cable can be taken up by sliding the waterproofing rubber shroud up the cable and turning the hexagon headed cable adjuster. After adjusting, return shroud to its original position over the adjuster and central barrel.

2 (c). Cleaning

To be carried out every 6,000 miles. Check the contact breaker contacts and, if necessary, clean them as described in Subsection 2 (a). Wipe the outside of the magneto to remove dirt or grease. Check the cable adjuster and control barrel for signs of water ingress.

Remove the high tension pick-ups and polish with soft dry cloth. The carbon brushes must move freely in their holders. If necessary, clean with a petrol-moistened cloth. Should either brush be worn to within $\frac{1}{8}$ in. of the shoulder it must be renewed.

Whilst the pick-up mouldings are removed, clean the slip ring track and flanges by holding a soft dry cloth against them with a suitably-shaped piece of wood while the engine is slowly turned.

The high tension cables must be kept clean and dry.

2 (d). Renewing High Tension Cables

If, on inspection, either high tension cable shows signs of deterioration, it must be replaced, using neoprene covered rubber cable. To fit a new high tension cable, bare the end for about $\frac{3}{8}$ in., thread the knurled moulded nut over the cable, and thread the bared cable through the washer removed from the old cable (see Fig. 3).

Bend back the strands radially and screw the nut into the pick-up moulding.

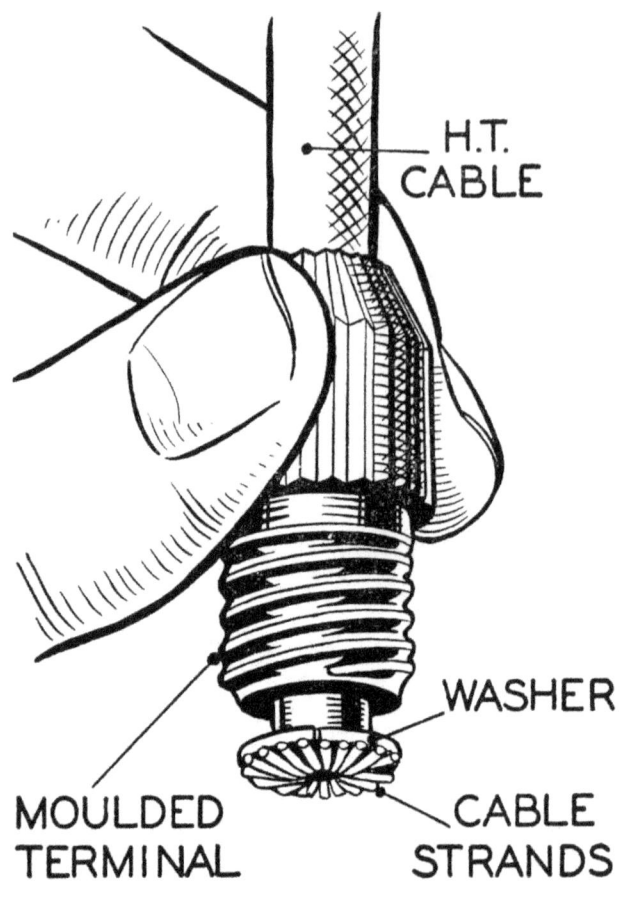

Fig. 3

2 (e). Renewing Timing Control Cable

The Bowden timing control cable should be renewed if it becomes frayed, otherwise moisture may enter the contact breaker housing.

To do this, slip back the rubber shroud and, by means of the hexagon at the base, unscrew the control barrel. If the cable and the plunger to which it is attached are now pulled upwards, the cable nipple can be disengaged from the plunger slot. Soften the solder and remove the nipple.

Thread the new length of cable through the rubber shroud, cable adjuster, control barrel, sealing washer and restoring spring. Solder the nipple to the end of the cable. Engage the nipple with the slot in the plunger and screw the control barrel into the body, ensuring that the sealing washer is correctly fitted between the barrel and the body.

Take up any slackness in the cable by means of the adjuster before refitting the rubber shroud in position.

2 (f). Contact Breaker Spring

The correct contact breaker spring pressure, measured at the contacts, is 18—24 oz.

3. Testing Magdyno in Position on Engine

To locate cause of misfiring or failure of ignition, check as follows:—

(i) Remove the sparking plugs from the engine. Hold the ends of the H.T. cables about $\frac{1}{8}$ in. from the cylinder block and crank the engine. If strong and regular sparking is produced the fault lies with the sparking plug or plugs which must be cleaned and adjusted or renewed.

(ii) If no sparking is produced at either H.T. cable, examine the faulty cable and, if necessary, renew it as described above in Subsection 2 (*d*).

(iii) Very occasionally the fault may be due to a cracked or punctured pick-up moulding. This type of fault is not easily detected by inspection and a check should be made by substitution.

(iv) If an ignition cut-out switch is fitted, disconnect the cable at the magneto and retest. If the Magdyno now functions normally the fault is in either the cable or the cut-out switch. Correct by replacement.

(v) If the Magdyno has recently been replaced or removed, it may be incorrectly timed (see Section C1, Subsection 4.)

(vi) Check the contact breaker for cleanliness and correct contact setting as described in Subsection 2 (*a*).

If the cause of faulty operation cannot be traced from the foregoing checks, the cause may be an internal defect in the Magdyno. The Magdyno should therefore be removed from the engine for attention by a Lucas Agent.

Section **G1b** *ROYAL ENFIELD WORKSHOP MANUAL* Page 4

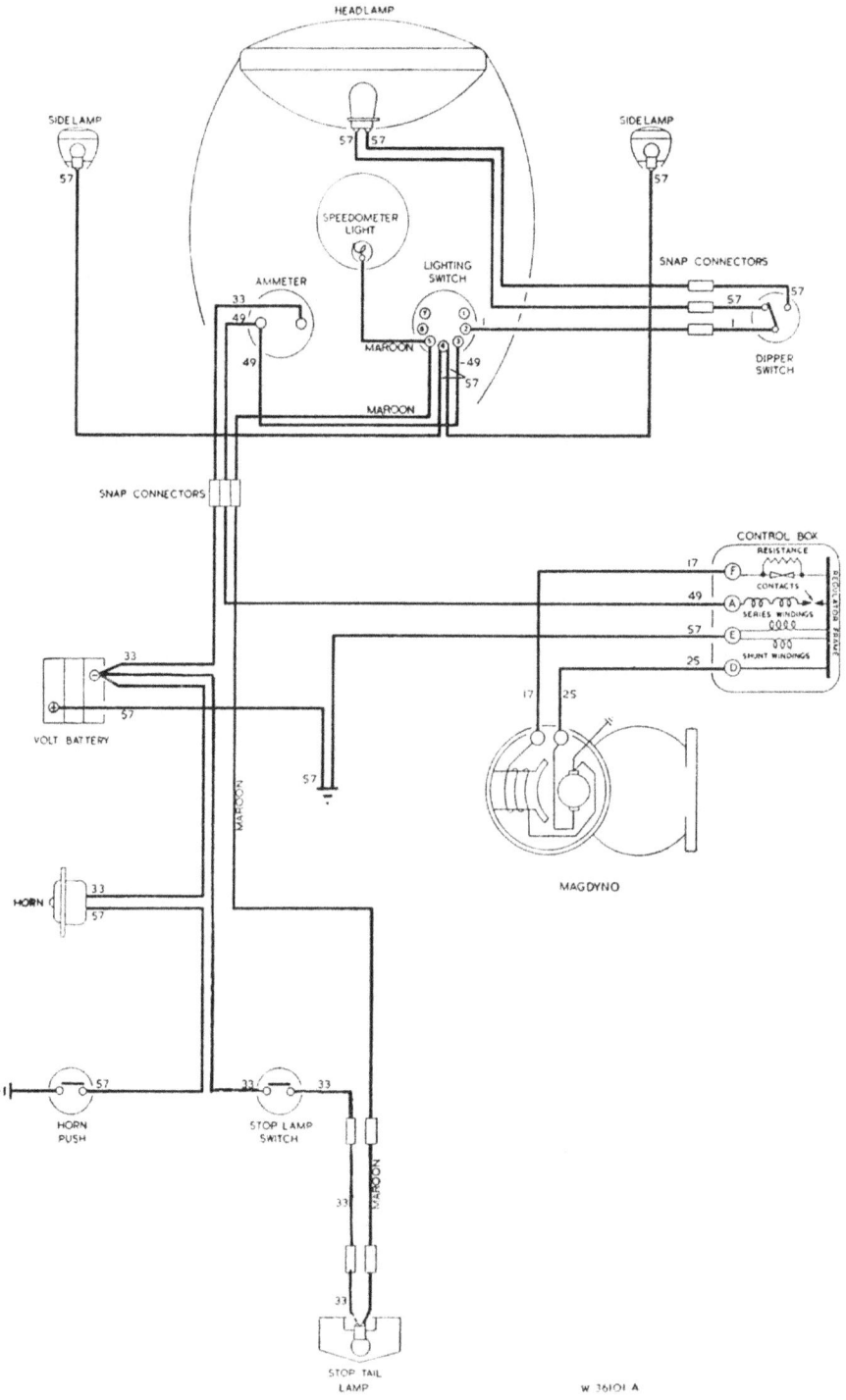

KEY TO CABLE COLOURS

1 BLUE	15 WHITE with BROWN	28 YELLOW with WHITE	41 RED	54 PURPLE with GREEN
2 BLUE with RED	16 WHITE with BLACK	29 YELLOW with GREEN	42 RED with YELLOW	55 PURPLE with BROWN
3 BLUE with YELLOW	17 GREEN	30 YELLOW with PURPLE	43 RED with BLUE	56 PURPLE with BLACK
4 BLUE with WHITE	18 GREEN with RED	31 YELLOW with BROWN	44 RED with WHITE	57 BLACK
5 BLUE with GREEN	19 GREEN with YELLOW	32 YELLOW with BLACK	45 RED with GREEN	58 BLACK with RED
6 BLUE with PURPLE	20 GREEN with BLUE	33 BROWN	46 RED with PURPLE	59 BLACK with YELLOW
7 BLUE with BROWN	21 GREEN with WHITE	34 BROWN with RED	47 RED with BROWN	60 BLACK with BLUE
8 BLUE with BLACK	22 GREEN with PURPLE	35 BROWN with YELLOW	48 RED with BLACK	61 BLACK with WHITE
9 WHITE	23 GREEN with BROWN	36 BROWN with BLUE	49 PURPLE	62 BLACK with GREEN
10 WHITE with RED	24 GREEN with BLACK	37 BROWN with WHITE	50 PURPLE with RED	63 BLACK with PURPLE
11 WHITE with YELLOW	25 YELLOW	38 BROWN with GREEN	51 PURPLE with YELLOW	64 BLACK with BROWN
12 WHITE with BLUE	26 YELLOW with RED	39 BROWN with PURPLE	52 PURPLE with BLUE	65 DARK GREEN
13 WHITE with GREEN	27 YELLOW with BLUE	40 BROWN with BLACK	53 PURPLE with WHITE	66 LIGHT GREEN
14 WHITE with PURPLE				

WIRING DIAGRAM

Fig. 4

SECTION G2a

Lucas Dynamo Model C35SD

Used on "500 Twin," "Meteor 700" up to end of 1954

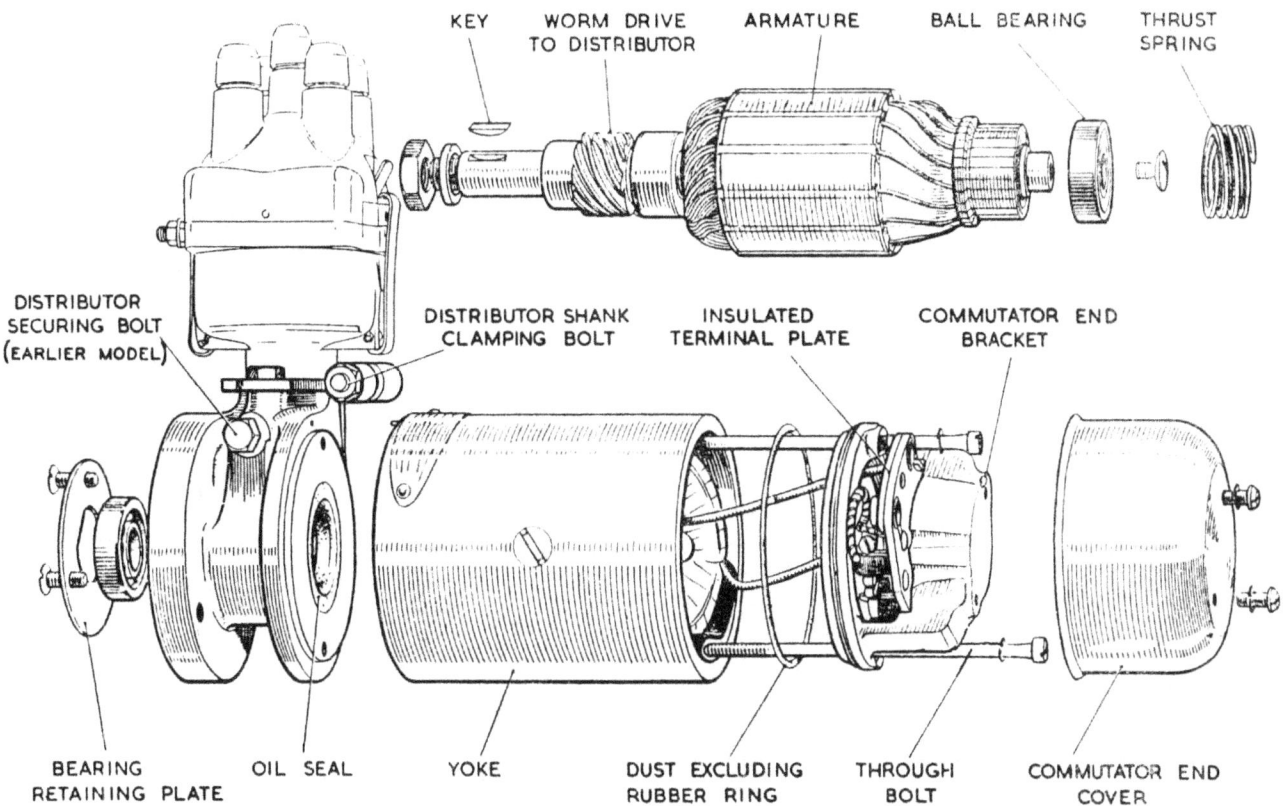

Fig. 1

1. General

The dynamo is a shunt-wound two-pole machine, arranged to work in conjunction with a regulator unit to give an output which is dependent on the state of charge of the battery and the loading of the electrical equipment in use. When the battery is in a low state of charge, the dynamo gives a high output, whereas if the battery is fully charged, the dynamo gives only a trickle charge to keep the battery in a good condition without overcharging. In addition, an increase of output is given to balance the current taken by the lamps when in use.

Model C35SD has both the drive and the commutator ends of the armature supported in ball bearings. The arrangement of the commutator end bearing has been modified on later dynamos. In earlier dynamos a thrust spring was fitted between the commutator and the inner journal of the bearing. In later dynamos (see Fig. 1) the bearing is secured to the armature shaft by a screw and the thrust spring, now loading the outer journal of the bearing, is fitted in the bearing housing in the commutator end bracket. Mounted on the drive end bracket of the dynamo is a distributor (see Section G1a) driven *via* a worm gear and pinion from the armature shaft. The output of the dynamo is 75 watts.

2 (a). Lubrication

No lubrication is necessary as the ball bearings are packed with H.M.P. grease which will last until the machine is taken down for a general overhaul, when the bearings should be repacked.

2 (b). Inspection of Commutator and Brushgear

About once every six months remove the cover band for inspection of commutator and brushes, see Subsection 4 (a) (vi).

3. Test Data

Cutting-in Speed (Dynamo Cold)	Output Test	Field Resistance	Brush Spring Tension
1,000—1,150 r.p.m. at 6·5 volts	10 amps. at 1,700—1,850 r.p.m. at 7 volts*	2·6—2·8 ohms	16—20 oz.

*On resistance load of 0·7 ohm.

4 (a). Testing in Position to Locate Fault in Charging Circuit

In the event of a fault in the charging circuit, adopt the following procedure to locate the cause of the trouble.

(i) Check that the dynamo and regulator units are connected correctly. The dynamo terminal " D " should be connected to the regulator unit terminal " D " and dynamo terminal " F " to regulator terminal " F."

(ii) Remove the cables from the dynamo terminals " D " and " F " and connect the two terminals with a short length of wire.

(iii) Start the engine and set to run at normal idling speed.

(iv) Connect the negative lead of a moving coil voltmeter, calibrated 0—10 volts, to one of the dynamo terminals and connect the positive lead to a good earthing point on the dynamo yoke or engine.

(v) Gradually increase the engine speed, when the voltmeter reading should rise rapidly and without fluctuation. Do not allow the voltmeter reading to rise above 10 volts and do not race the engine in an attempt to increase the voltage. It is sufficient to run the dynamo up to a speed of 1,000 r.p.m. If there is no reading, check the brush gear, as described in (vi) below. If there is a low reading of approximately ½ volt, the field winding may be at fault, see Subsection 4 (d). If there is a reading of approximately 1½ to 2 volts, the armature winding may be at fault, see Subsection 4 (e).

(vi) Remove the cover band and examine the brushes and commutator. Hold back each of the brush springs and move the brush by pulling gently on its flexible connector. If the movement is sluggish, remove the brush from its holder and ease the sides by lightly polishing on a smooth file. Always replace brushes in their original positions.

If the brushes are worn so that they do not bear on the commutator or if the brush flexible is exposed on the running face, new brushes must be fitted.

Test the brush spring tension with a spring scale (see Fig. 2). The correct tension is 16—20 oz. and new springs must be fitted if the tension is low.

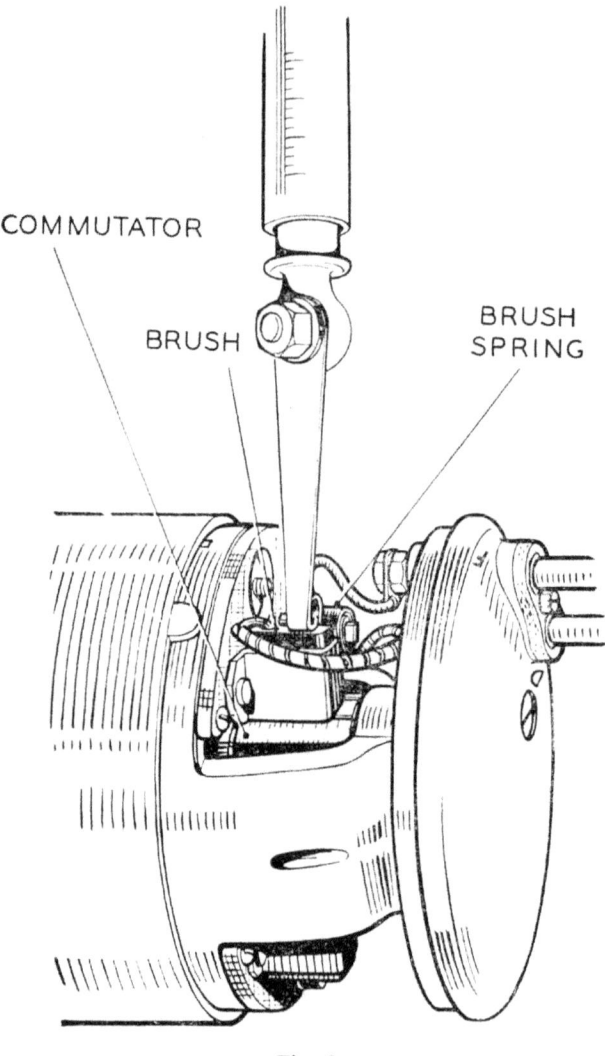

Fig. 2

If the commutator is blackened or dirty, clean it by holding a petrol-moistened cloth against it while the engine is turned slowly by means of the kick start (with sparking plugs removed).

Re-test the dynamo as in (v) above. If there is still no reading on the voltmeter, there is an internal fault and the complete unit should be replaced if a spare is available. Otherwise the unit must be dismantled, see Subsection 4 (b) for internal examination.

(vii) If the dynamo is in good order, restore the original connections. Connect regulator unit terminal " D " to dynamo terminal " D " and regulator terminal " F " to dynamo terminal " F " and check the regulator.

4 (b). To Dismantle

Remove the dynamo and distributor from the motor cycle. To detach the distributor from the dynamo drive end bracket, loosen the distributor shank clamping bolt and withdraw the complete unit from the bracket (see Fig. 1). On earlier models an additional securing bolt is located in the drive end bracket and must be loosened a few turns to allow the distributor to be withdrawn from the bracket. Proceed to dismantle as follows :—

(i) Remove the securing nut from the drive end of the armature shaft and withdraw the sprocket with the aid of an extractor. Knock out the key from the armature shaft.

(ii) Unscrew the two commutator end cover securing screws and remove the cover. Hold back the brush springs and lift the brushes from their holders.

(iii) Disconnect the earthed field connection and unsolder the field connection to terminal " F " on the terminal strip.

(iv) Unscrew and remove from the commutator end bracket the two through bolts securing the end bracket and yoke to the drive end bracket.

(v) Draw the commutator end bracket away from the armature and separate the yoke from the drive end bracket. On earlier models a thrust spring will be found around the armature shaft (on later models it is located between the ball bearing and the housing); take care not to lose this.

(vi) The armature can now be pressed out of the drive end bearing, taking great care not to damage the sealing lip of the rubber oil seal.

(vii) Unscrew the two screws on the inner side of the commutator end bracket which secure the insulated terminal plate carrying the terminals and brushgear. On earlier models removal of the insulating plate will reveal the bearing retaining plate and thrust spring housing.

4. (c) Commutator

Examine the commutator. If it is in good condition, it will be smooth and free from pits or burnt spots. Clean with a petrol-moistened cloth. If this is ineffective, carefully polish with a strip of very fine glass paper while rotating the armature. To remedy a badly worn commutator, mount the armature with or without the drive end bracket in a lathe, rotate at high speed and take a light cut with a very sharp tool. Do not remove more metal than is necessary. Polish the commutator with very fine glass paper.

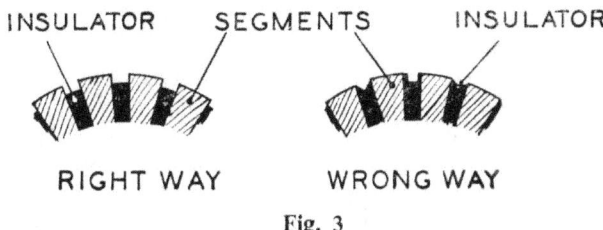

Fig. 3

Undercut the insulation between the segments to a depth of $\frac{1}{32}$ in. with a hacksaw blade ground down until it is only slightly thicker than the insulation (see Fig. 3).

4 (d). Field Coil

Measure the resistance of the field winding by means of an ohm-meter. If this is not available, connect a 6-volt D.C. supply with an ammeter in series with the coil. The ammeter reading should be approximately 2 amps. No reading on the ammeter indicates an open circuit in the field winding.

To check for an earthed coil, connect a mains test lamp between one end of the coil and the yoke. If the bulb lights, there is an earth between coil and yoke.

In either case, unless a replacement dynamo is available, the field coil must be replaced but this should only be attempted if a wheel-operated screwdriver and pole shoe expander are at hand, the latter being especially necessary to ensure that there will be no air gap between the pole shoe and the inner face of the yoke.

To replace the field coil, proceed as follows :—

(i) Unscrew the pole shoe retaining screw by means of the wheel-operated screwdriver (see Fig. 4).

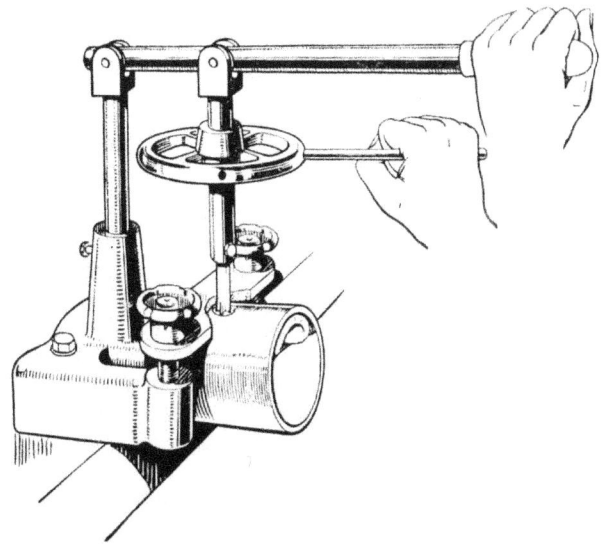

Fig. 4

(ii) Draw the pole shoe and field coil out of the yoke and lift off the coil.

(iii) Fit the new field coil over the pole shoe and place it in position inside the yoke. Take care to ensure that the taping of the field coil is not trapped between the pole shoe and the yoke.

(iv) Locate the pole shoe and field coil by lightly tightening the fixing screw, insert the pole shoe expander (see Fig. 5), open to its fullest extent and tighten the screw. Remove the expander and give the screw a final tightening with the wheel-operated screwdriver. Lock the screw in position by caulking, that is, by tapping some of the metal of the yoke into the slot in the head of the screw.

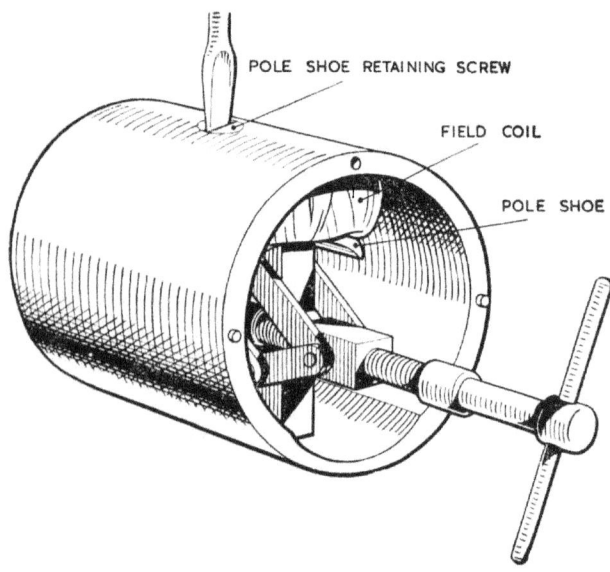

Fig. 5

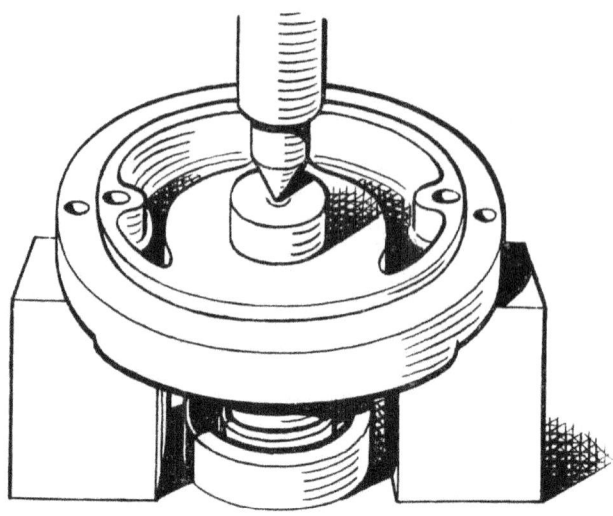

Fig. 6

(ii) Press the defective bearing out of the end bracket. Wipe out the bearing housing and pack the new bearing with H.M.P. grease.

(iii) Position the bearing in its housing and press it squarely home, applying pressure on the outer journal of the bearing.

To replace the ball bearing at the commutator end, proceed as follows :—

Earlier Type

(i) Using an expanding caliper-type extractor, draw the bearing from its housing in the commutator end bracket.

4 (e). Armature

The testing of the armature winding requires the use of a voltdrop test or a growler. If these are not available, the armature should be checked by substitution. No attempt should be made to machine the armature core or to true a distorted armature shaft.

4 (f). Bearings

Ball bearings are fitted to both the commutator and drive end brackets. When the bearings become worn to such an extent that they allow side movement of the armature shaft, they must be replaced (see Figs. 6 and 7). The bearings should not be disturbed except for the purpose of replacement. To replace the ball bearing at the drive end proceed as follows :—

(i) Remove the bearing retaining plate from the drive end bracket by unscrewing the three countersunk screws.

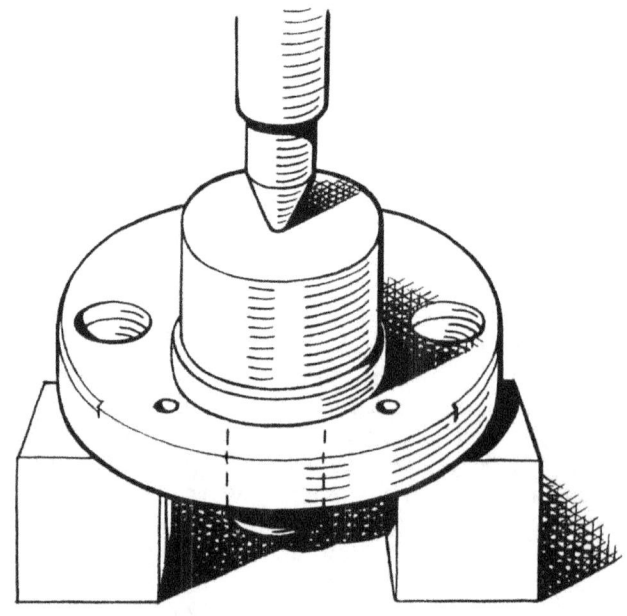

Fig. 7

(ii) Wipe out the bearing housing and pack the new bearing with H.M.P. grease.

(iii) Position the new bearing in its housing and press it squarely home, applying pressure on the outer journal of the bearing.

Later Types

(i) To remove the bearing slacken and withdraw the thrust screw and pull the bearing off the armature shaft with an extractor.

(ii) Wipe out the bearing housing and pack the new bearing with H.M.P. grease.

(iii) Force the new bearing home against the shoulder on the armature shaft. Insert and tighten the thrust screw.

4 (g). Reassembly

In the main the reassembly of the dynamo is a reversal of the operation described in Subsection 4 (b), bearing in mind the following points:—

(i) The field coil lead fitted with the short length of yellow tubing must be connected, together with the eyelet of the earthed brush, to the commutator end bracket by means of the screw provided.

(ii) The second field coil lead must be connected to terminal " F " on the moulded cap.

(iii) The unearthed brush flexible lead must be connected direct to terminal " D " on the moulded end cap.

(iv) Take care to refit the cover band in its original position and make sure that the securing screw, when of flush-fitting pattern, does not "short" on the brushgear.

(v) Take care not to damage the oil seal. If damage is caused a new seal must be fitted.

5. Dynamo Polarity

If a dynamo has been incorrectly connected on the motor cycle and its polarity has become reversed, it must be re-polarised.

To do this, fit the dynamo to the motor cycle but do not at this stage connect the cable to the " D " and " F " terminals. Temporarily connect a length of wire to the battery negative terminal (the positive terminal being earthed) and hold the other end of this wire in contact with dynamo terminal " F " for a few seconds only. This serves to re-polarize the dynamo. The temporary connection can now be removed and the original cables connected to " D " and " F " terminals.

The practice of closing the cut-out points to reverse the dynamo polarity is not recommended, as this method allows a high initial surge of current from the battery to pass through the armature, which can damage the windings, insulation, etc. and result in a decreased service life of the machine.

All Royal Enfield "500 Twin" and "Meteor 700" motor cycles should have the positive terminal of the battery earthed to the frame.

NOTES

SECTION G2b
Lucas Dynamo Model E3LM
Used on all Models fitted with Magdyno

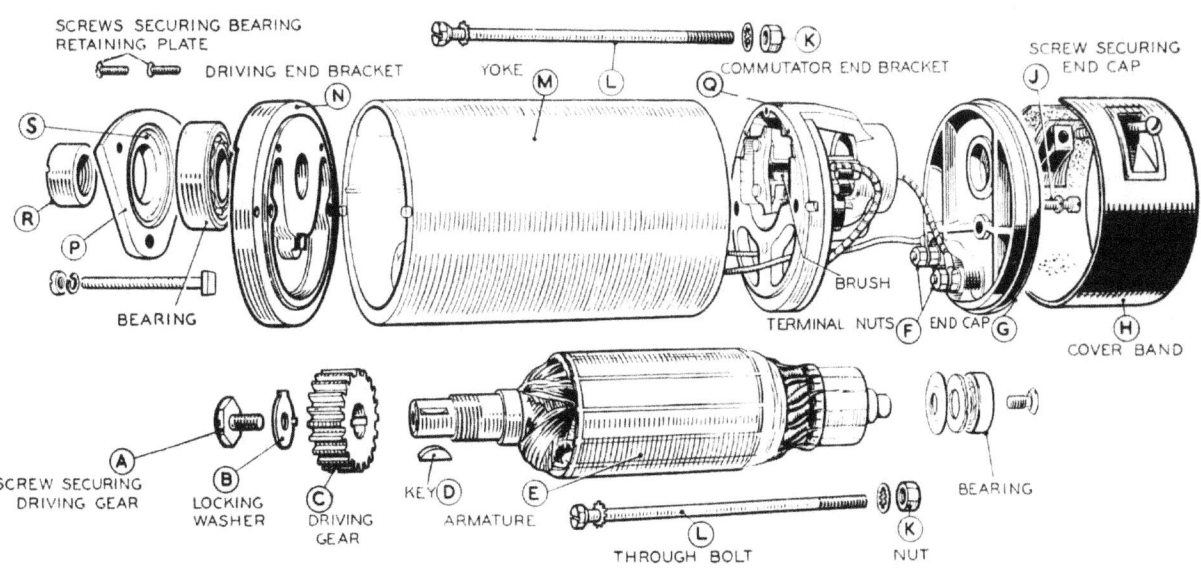

Fig. 1

1. General

The dynamo is a shunt-wound two-pole machine, arranged to work in conjunction with a regulator unit to give an output which is dependent on the state of charge of the battery and the loading of the electrical equipment in use. When the battery is in a low state of charge, the dynamo gives a high output, whereas, if the battery is fully charged, the dynamo gives only a trickle charge to keep the battery in a good condition without overcharging. In addition, an increase of output is given to balance the current taken by the lamps when in use. Model E3LM (see Fig. 1) is designed to be the upper portion of the "Magdyno" and has an output of 60 watts.

2 (a). Lubrication

No lubrication is necessary, as the ball bearings are packed with H.M.P. grease, which will last until the machine is taken down for a general overhaul, when the bearings should be repacked.

2 (b). Inspection of Commutator and Brush Gear

About once every six months remove the cover band for inspection of commutator and brushes, see Subsection 4 (a) (vi).

3. Test Data

Cutting-in Speed (Dynamo Cold)	Output Test	Field Resistance	Brush Spring Tension
1,050—1,200 r.p.m. at 7 volts	8·5 amps. at 1,850—2,000 r.p.m. at 7 volts*	2·8 ohms	16—20 oz.

*On resistance load of 0·82 ohm.

4 (a). Testing in Position to Locate Fault in Charging Circuit

In the event of a fault in the charging circuit, adopt the following procedure to locate the cause of trouble.

(i) Check that the dynamo and regulator units are connected correctly. The dynamo terminal " D " should be connected to the regulator unit terminal " D " and dynamo terminal " F " to regulator terminal " F."

(ii) Remove the cables from the dynamo terminals " D " and " F " and connect the two terminals with a short length of wire.

(iii) Start the engine and set to run at normal idling speed.

(iv) Connect the negative lead of a moving coil voltmeter, calibrated 0—10 volts, to one of the dynamo terminals and connect the positive lead to a good earthing point on the dynamo yoke or engine. Reverse voltmeter connections on negative earth machines.

(v) Gradually increase the engine speed, when the voltmeter reading should rise rapidly and without fluctuation. Do not allow the voltmeter reading to rise above 10 volts and do not race the engine in an attempt to increase the voltage. It is sufficient to run the dynamo up to a speed of 1,000 r.p.m. If there is no reading, check the brush gear, as described in (vi) below. If there is a low reading of approximately ½ volt, the field winding may be at fault, see Subsection 4 (d). If there is a reading of approximately 1½ to 2 volts, the armature winding may be at fault, see Subsection 4 (e).

(vi) Remove the cover band and examine the brushes and commutator. Hold back each of the brush springs and move the brush by pulling gently on its flexible connector. If the movement is sluggish, remove the brush from its holder and ease the sides by lightly polishing on a smooth file. Always replace brushes in their original positions. If the brushes are worn so that they do not bear on the commutator or if the brush flexible is exposed on the running face, new brushes must be fitted.

Test the brush spring tension with a spring scale (see Fig. 2). The correct tension is 16—20 oz. and new springs must be fitted if the tension is low.

If the commutator is blackened or dirty, clean it by holding a petrol-moistened cloth against it while the engine is turned slowly by means of the kick start, with sparking plug(s) removed.

Re-test the dynamo as in (v) above. If there is still no reading on the voltmeter there is an internal fault and the complete unit should be replaced if a spare is available. Otherwise the unit must be dismantled, see Subsection 4 (b) for internal examination.

(vii) If the dynamo is in good order, restore the original connections. Connect regulator unit terminal "D" to dynamo terminal "D" and regulator terminal "F" to dynamo terminal "F" and check the regulator.

4 (b). To Dismantle

Remove the dynamo from the motor cycle. To detach the dynamo from the Magdyno, unscrew the hexagon headed nut from the driving end cover and slacken the screws securing the band clip.

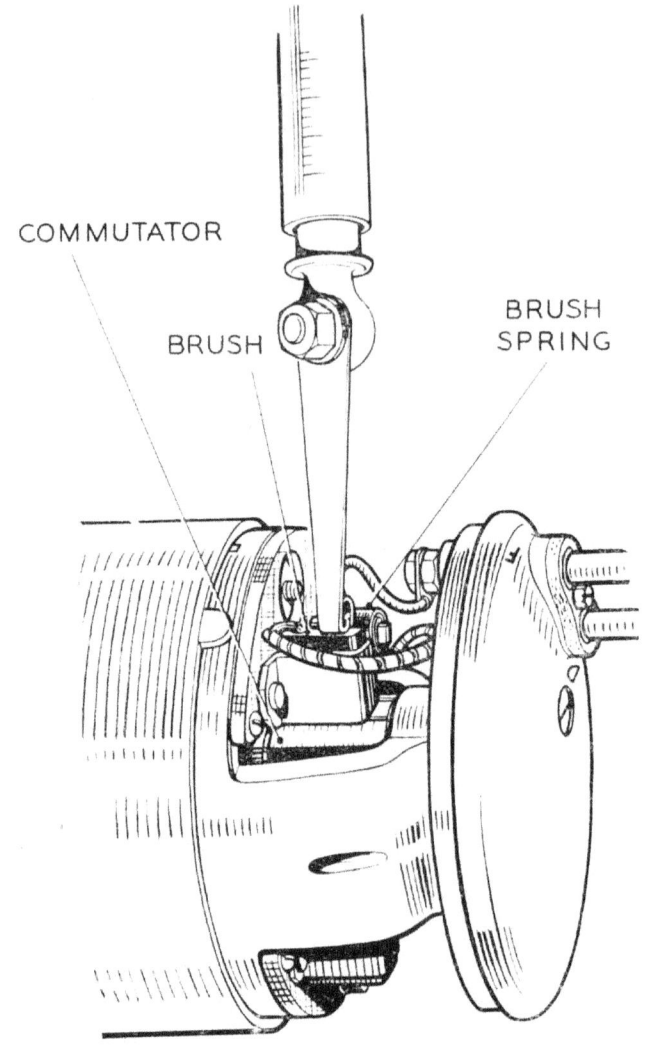

Fig. 2

To dismantle the dynamo proceed as follows :—

(i) Bend back the tag on the washer "B" locking the screw "A" (see Fig. 1). Remove this screw, withdraw the gear "C" from the shaft with the aid of an extractor and remove the key(s) "D" from the shaft.

(ii) Remove the cover band "H," hold back the brush springs and lift the brushes from their holders.

(iii) Take out the screw "J" with spring washer from the centre of the black moulded end cap "G." Draw the cap away from the end bracket, take off terminal nut "F" and spring washer, and lift the connections off the terminals.

(iv) Unscrew and remove from the drive end bracket the two through bolts "L" securing the drive end bracket "N" and commutator end bracket "Q" to the yoke "M." Hold the nuts

"K" at the commutator end while unscrewing the bolts and take care not to lose the nuts.

(v) Draw the drive end bracket complete with armature "E" out of the yoke.

(vi) Remove the nut "R" and press the armature out of the drive end bracket by means of a hand press.

(vii) Remove the bearing retaining plate "P" from the end bracket. This is secured by two screws and a long threaded bolt.

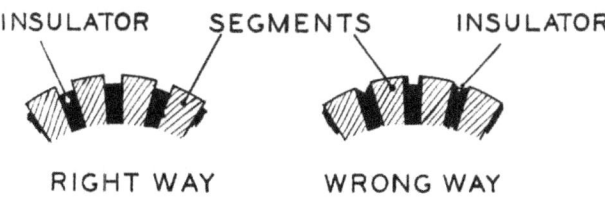

Fig. 3

(viii) Take out the screw securing the green field coil lead with the yellow sleeve to commutator end bracket and remove the end bracket "Q" withdrawing the connectors through the slot in the insulating plate.

(ix) Unscrew the three screws securing the insulating plate to the commutator end bracket and remove the plate with brush gear.

4 (c). Commutator

Examine the commutator. If it is in good condition it will be smooth and free from pits or burnt spots. Clean with a petrol-moistened cloth. If this is ineffective, carefully polish with a strip of very fine glass paper while rotating the armature.

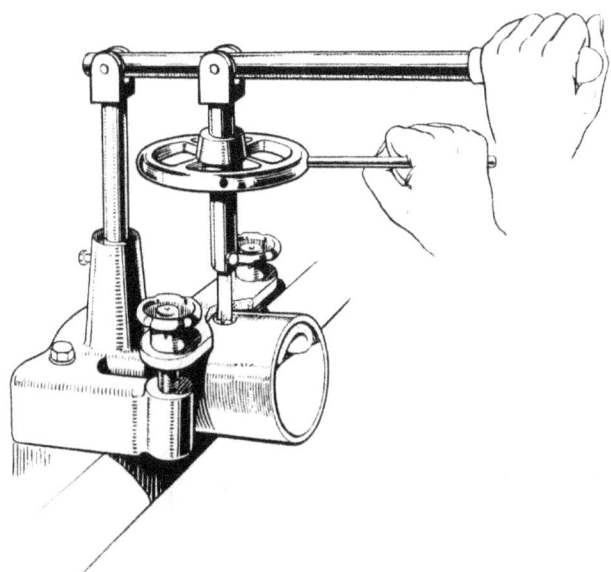

Fig. 4

To remedy a badly worn commutator, mount the armature with or without the drive end bracket in a lathe, rotate at high speed and take a light cut with a very sharp tool. Do not remove more metal than is necessary. Polish the commutator with very fine glass paper.

Undercut the insulation between the segments to a depth of $\frac{1}{32}$ in. with a hacksaw blade ground down until it is only slightly thicker than the insulation (see Fig. 3).

4 (d) Field Coil

Measure the resistance of the field winding by means of an ohm-meter. If this is not available, connect a 6-volt D.C. supply with an ammeter in series with the coil. The ammeter reading should be approximately 2 amps. No reading on the ammeter indicates an open circuit in the field winding.

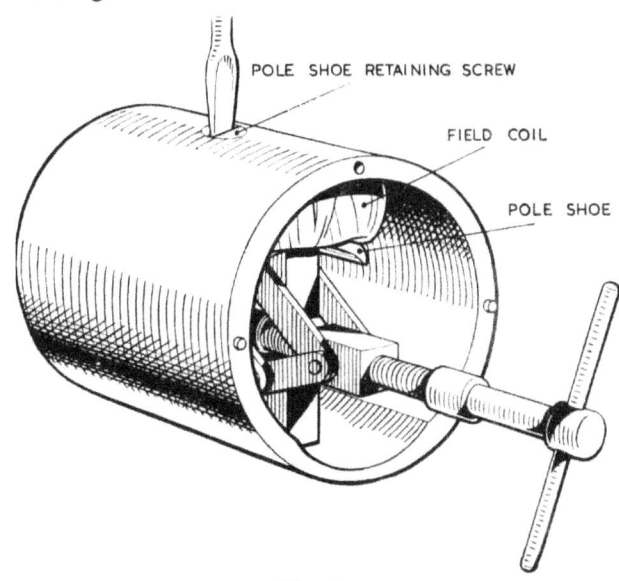

Fig. 5

To check for an earthed coil, connect a mains test lamp between one end of the coil and the yoke. If the bulb lights, there is an earth between coil and yoke.

In either case, unless a replacement dynamo is available, the field coil must be replaced but this should only be attempted if a wheel-operated screwdriver and pole shoe expander are at hand, the latter being especially necessary to ensure that there will be no air gap between the pole shoe and the inner face of the yoke.

To replace the field coil, proceed as follows:—

(i) Unscrew the pole shoe retaining screw by means of the wheel-operated screwdriver (see Fig. 4).

(ii) Draw the pole shoe and field coil out of the yoke and lift off the coil.

(iii) Fit the new field coil over the pole shoe and place it in position inside the yoke. Take care to ensure that the taping of the field coil is not trapped between the pole shoe and the yoke.

(iv) Locate the pole shoe and field coil by lightly tightening the fixing screw, insert the pole shoe expander (see Fig. 5), open to its fullest extent and tighten the screw. Remove the expander and give the screw a final tightening with the wheel-operated screwdriver. Lock the screw in position by caulking, that is, by tapping some of the metal of the yoke into the slot in the head of the screw.

4. (e). Armature

The testing of the armature winding requires the use of a voltdrop test or a growler. If these are not available, the armature should be checked by substitution. No attempt should be made to machine the armature core or to true a distorted armature shaft.

4 (f). Bearings

Ball bearings are fitted to both the commutator and drive end brackets. When the bearings become worn to such an extent that they allow side movement of the armature shaft, they must be replaced. To replace the ball bearing at the commutator end proceed as follows:—

(i) Remove the screw from the end of the armature shaft and, using a caliper type extractor, draw the bearing off the shaft.

(ii) Wipe out the bearing housing and pack the new bearing with H.M.P. grease.

(iii) Position the bearing on the end of the shaft and press it squarely home, applying pressure on the inner journal of the bearing.

To replace the ball bearing at the drive end proceed as follows:—

(i) Remove the bearing retaining plate from the drive end bracket as previously described.

(ii) Press the bearing out of the end bracket, using a metal drift locating on the inner journal of the bearing. Wipe out the bearing housing and pack the new bearing with H.M.P. grease.

(iii) Position the bearing in its housing and press it squarely home, applying pressure on the outer journal of the bearing.

4 (g). Reassembly

In the main, the reassembly of the dynamo is a reversal of the operation described in Subsection 4 (b), bearing in mind the following points:—

(i) The field coil lead fitted with the short length of yellow tubing must be connected, together with the eyelet of the earthed brush, to the commutator end bracket by means of the screw provided.

(ii) The second field coil lead must be con-

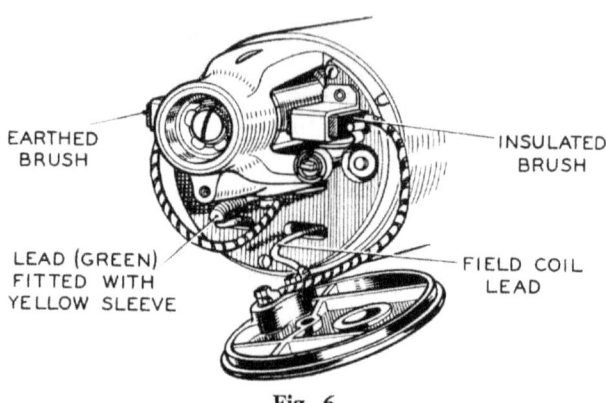

Fig. 6

nected to terminal "F" on the moulded cap (see Fig. 6).

(iii) The unearthed brush flexible lead must be connected direct to terminal "D" on the moulded end cap.

(iv) Take care to refit the cover band in its original position and make sure that the securing screw, when of flush-fitting pattern, does not "short" on the brush gear.

5. Dynamo Polarity

All replacement motor cycle dynamos are despatched from the Works suitable for immediate use on positive earth systems. If the negative terminal of the battery is earthed on the machine for which the replacement dynamo is intended, it will be necessary to re-polarize the dynamo before use to make it suitable for negative earth.

Similarly, if a dynamo has been incorrectly connected on the motor cycle and its polarity has become reversed, then it must be re-polarized.

To do this, fit the dynamo to the motor cycle but do not at this stage connect the cable to the "D" and "F" terminals. Temporarily connect a length of wire to the unearthed terminal of the battery and hold the other end of this wire in contact with dynamo terminal "F" for a few seconds only. This serves to re-polarize the dynamo. The temporary connection can now be removed and the original cables connected to "D" and "F" terminals.

The practice of closing the cut-out points to reverse the dynamo polarity is not recommended, as this method allows a high initial surge of current from the battery to pass through the armature, which can damage the windings, insulation, etc. and result in a decreased service life of the machine.

Generally speaking, motor cycles manufactured up to and including 1951 had the negative terminal of the battery connected to the frame. With a few exceptions, i.e. Miller coil ignition sets and rectifier sets on two-stroke machines, all Royal Enfield machines in current production have the positive terminal earthed.

SECTION G3a

Control Box

Used on Models G, J2, "350 Bullet," "500 Bullet," "500 Twin,"
"Meteor 700," 1950 onwards

MODEL RB107

1. General

In Model RB107 control box, the regulator and cut-out contacts are positioned, for ease of access, above their respective armatures. It will be noticed that some of the internal electrical joints are resistance brazed.

2. Setting Data

(a) Cut-out

Cut-in voltage … …	6·3—6·7 volts
Drop-off voltage … …	4·8—5·3 volts

(b) Regulator

Setting on open circuit relative to ambient temperature :—

10° C. (50° F.) … … …	7·7—8·1 volts
20° C. (68° F.) … … …	7·6—8·0 volts
30° C. (86° F.) … … …	7·5—7·9 volts
40° C (104° F.) … …	7·4—7·8 volts

3. Servicing

Before making any adjustment to the regulator, ensure that the dynamo and battery are in order. When a sound battery does not keep in a charged condition, or if the dynamo output does not fall when the battery is fully charged, the following procedure should be adopted :—

(a) Checking the wiring between battery and regulator

Remove the control box from its mountings and withdraw the cable from terminal "A" (see Fig. 1) and connect it to the negative terminal of a voltmeter.
Connect the positive terminal of the voltmeter to an earthing point on the machine. If a voltmeter reading is given, the circuit from the battery to terminal "A" is in order.
If there is no voltmeter reading, examine the wiring between the battery and the control box for defective cables or loose connections. Re-connect the cable to terminal "A."
Check that the dynamo terminal "D" is connected to control box terminal "D" and

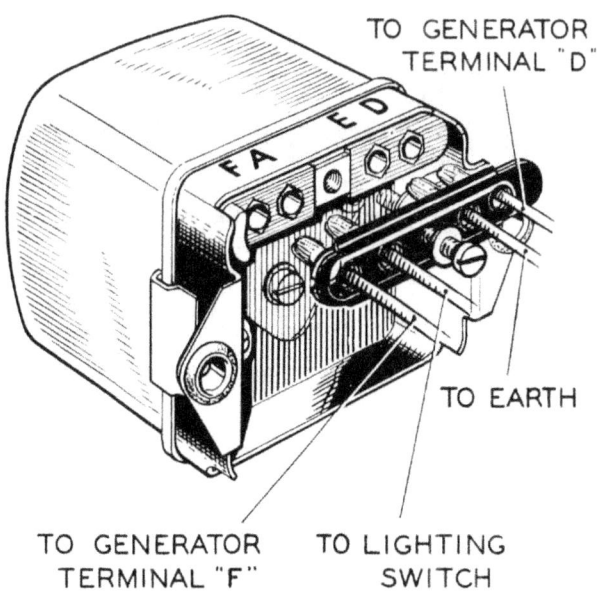

Fig. 1

that the cable is in good condition. Similarly, check the cable between terminals "F" at the dynamo and control box.

(b) Checking the electrical setting of the regulator

The regulator is carefully set during manufacture and, in general, it should not be necessary to make further adjustment. If, however, the charging system is suspected it is important that only a good-quality **moving coil voltmeter** (0—20 volts) is used to check the system. The electrical setting of the regulator can be checked without removing the cover from the control box.
Withdraw the plug-in connectors a small distance, so that a voltmeter connection can be made to terminals "D" and "E."
Connect the negative lead of the voltmeter to control box terminal "D" and the positive lead to terminal "E."
Remove the negative terminal from the battery. If coil ignition is fitted, run a temporary connection from the negative terminal of the battery to the "SW" terminal of the coil.

With the ignition switch in the "OFF" position, start the engine.

Slowly increase the speed of the engine until the voltmeter needle "flicks" and then steadies. Note this value and stop the engine.

If this value lies outside the limits given in para. 2 (b), the regulator setting must be adjusted.

If the value is within the limits, examine the cut-out as described in para 3 (c).

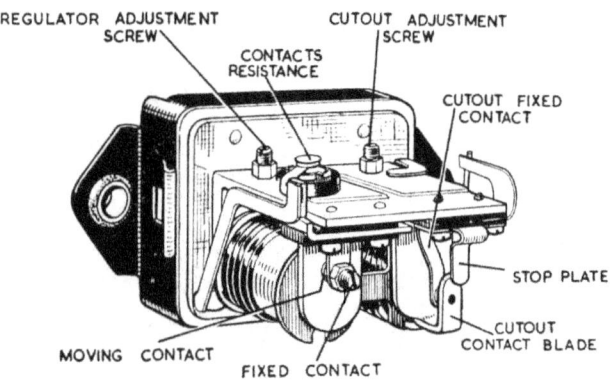

Fig. 2

(c) Adjusting the electrical setting of the regulator

Adjustment of the regulator requires removal of the control box cover. This is facilitated by removing the control box from the machine and providing temporary connections. Loosen the control box cover securing clips by slackening the securing screws set in the base of the control box, and lift off the cover.

It is important that regulator adjustments are carried out with the control box supported in a similar position to that on the machine.

Restart the engine.

Slacken the locknut of the regulator adjusting screw (see Fig. 2) and turn the screw in a clockwise direction to raise the setting or an anti-clockwise direction to lower the setting. Turn the screw only a fraction of a turn at a time and then tighten the locknut. Repeat as above until the correct setting is obtained.

Adjustment of regulator open-circuit voltage should be completed within 30 seconds, otherwise heating of the shunt winding will cause false settings to be made.

Stop the engine.

Remake the original connections and replace the cover. Ensure that the cover seats correctly on the sealing washer.

N.B.—A dynamo run at high speed on open circuit will build up a high voltage. Therefore, when adjusting the regulator, do not run the engine up to more than half throttle or a false setting will be made.

(d) Checking the electrical setting of the cut-out

If the regulator is correctly set but the battery is still not being charged, the cut-out may be out of adjustment.

Replace the control box in the testing position, remake the temporary connections and remove the control box cover. Connect a voltmeter between terminals "D" and "E."

Start the engine and slowly increase the speed until the cut-out contacts close. Note the voltage at which this occurs and stop the engine. This should be 6·3—6·7 volts. If operation of the cut-out takes place outside these limits, it will be necessary to adjust.

(e) Adjusting the electrical setting of the cut-out

Restart the engine.

Slacken the locknut securing the cut-out adjusting screw and turn the adjusting screw in a clockwise direction to raise the voltage setting or in an anti-clockwise direction to reduce the setting.

Turn the screw only a fraction of a turn at a time and then tighten the locknut. Test after each adjustment by increasing the engine speed and noting the voltmeter reading at the instant of contact closure.

Stop the engine.

Electrical setting of the cut-out, like the regulator, must be made as quickly as possible because of temperature-rise effects. Tighten the locknut after making the adjustment.

N.B.—If the cut-out does not operate, there may be an open-circuit in the wiring of the cut-out and regulator unit, in which case the unit should be removed for examination or replacement.

SECTION G4a
Battery Model PUZ7E

1. General

The model PUZ7E (see Fig. 1) is a "dry-charged" battery and is supplied without electrolyte but with its plates in a charged condition. When the battery is required for service it is only necessary to fill each cell with sulphuric acid of the correct specific gravity. No initial charging is required.

Fig. 1

2. Preparation for Service

The electrolyte is prepared by mixing together distilled water and concentrated sulphuric acid, using lead-lined tanks or suitable glass or earthenware vessels. Slowly add the acid to the water, stirring with a glass rod. Never add water to the acid, as this causes dangerous spurting of the concentrated acid. The specific gravity of the filling electrolyte depends on the climate in which the battery is to be used.

Specific gravity of electrolyte for filling "dry-charged" batteries:

Climates below 90°F. (32°C.)	Climates above 90°F. (32°C.)
Filling, 1·270	Filling, 1·210

The approximate proportions of acid and water to obtain these specific gravities:

To obtain specific gravity (corrected to 60°F.) of :	Add 1 vol. of 1·835 S.G. acid (corrected to 60°F.) to :
1·270	2·9 vols. of water.
1·210	4·0 vols. of water.

Heat is produced by the mixture of acid and water, the electrolyte should be allowed to cool before pouring it into the battery.

The specific gravity of the electrolyte varies with the temperature. For convenience in comparing specific gravities, they are always corrected to 60°F, which is adopted as a reference temperature.

The method of correction is as follows :—

For every 5°F. below 60°F., deduct ·002 from the observed reading to obtain the true specific gravity at 60°F. For every 5°F. above 60°F. add ·002 to the observed reading to obtain the true specific gravity at 60°F.

The temperature must be that indicated by a thermometer having its bulb actually immersed in the electrolyte and not the ambient temperature.

Fill the cells to the tops of the separators, in one operation. The battery filled in this way is 90% charged. When time permits, a short freshening charge for no more than four hours at the normal recharge rate of 1·5 amp. should be made.

3. Routine Maintenance

Fortnightly (or more frequently in hot climates) examine the level of electrolyte in the cells and if necessary add distilled water to bring the level up to the tops of the separators. The use of a Lucas Battery Filler will be found helpful, as it ensures that the correct electrolyte level is automatically maintained and also prevents distilled water from being spilled on the top of the battery (see Fig. 2).

Occasionally examine the terminals, clean and coat them with petroleum jelly. Wipe away all

The following table shows the state of charge at different values of specific gravities:

State of Charge	Temperature under 90°F.	Temperature over 90°F.
Battery fully charged ...	1·270—1·290	1·210—1·230
Battery about half charged ...	1·190—1·210	1·130—1·150
Battery fully discharged ...	1·110—1·130	1·050—1·070

If the battery is discharged, it must be recharged, either on the motor cycle by a period of daytime running or from an external D.C. supply at the normal recharge rate of 1·5 amp.

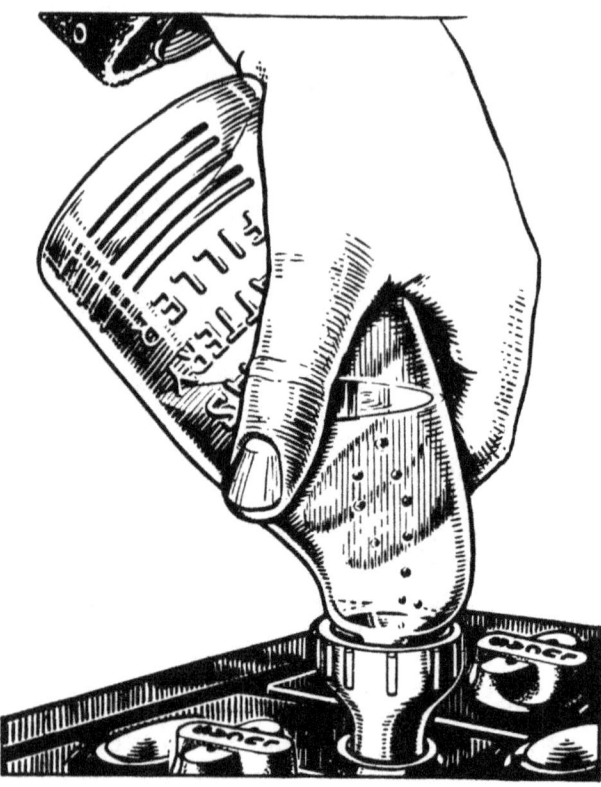

Fig. 2

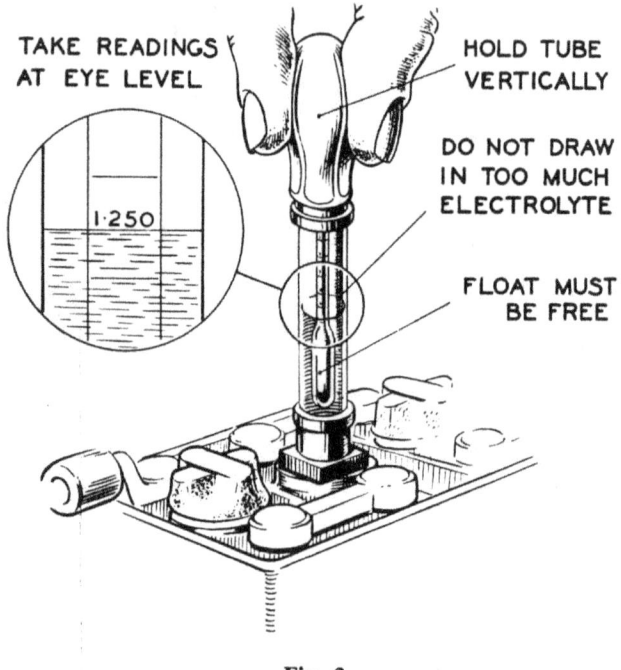

Fig. 3

dirt and moisture from the top of the battery and ensure that the connections are clean and tight.

4. Servicing

If the battery is subjected to long periods of night parking with the lights on, without suitable opportunities for recharging, a low state of charge is to be expected.

Measure the specific gravity of the acid of each cell in turn with a hydrometer (see Fig. 3).

SECTION G5a

Head and Tail Lamps

Used on Models G, J2, "350 Bullet," "500 Bullet," "500 Twin," "Meteor 700," 1950 onwards

1. Headlamp

In all the above Models the headlamp incorporates the Lucas Light Unit MCF700. This is either fitted into a lamp shell (see Figs. 1 and 2) carried on brackets in front of the facia panel type of fork head and housing a switch, ammeter and parking lamp, or, on later models, is built into the Casquette fork head which contains twin parking lamps as well as the ammeter and switch. On machines fitted with coil ignition the ammeter has a red central window with the ignition warning light beneath.

2. Lucas Light Unit

The unit incorporates a combined reflector and front lens assembly (see Fig. 3). This construction ensures that the reflector and lenses are permanently protected, thus the unit keeps its high efficiency over a long period. A "prefocus" bulb is used, the filaments of which are accurately positioned with respect to the reflector, thus no focusing device is necessary.

The bulb has a large cap and a flange, which has been accurately positioned with relation to the bulb filaments during manufacture. A slot in the flange engages with a projection on the inside of the bulb holder positioned at the back of the reflector.

A bayonet-fitting adaptor with spring-loaded contacts secures the bulb firmly in position and carries the supply to the bulb contacts.

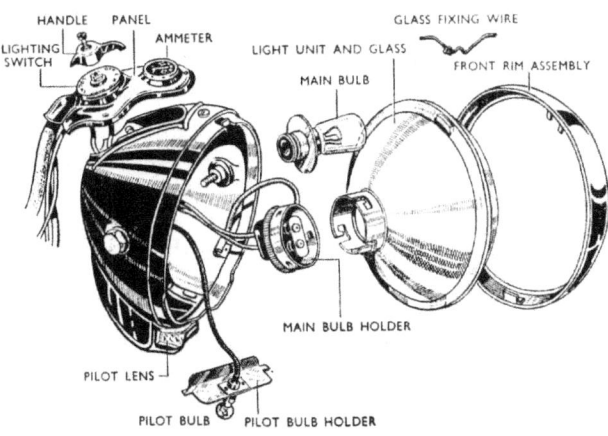

Fig. 1

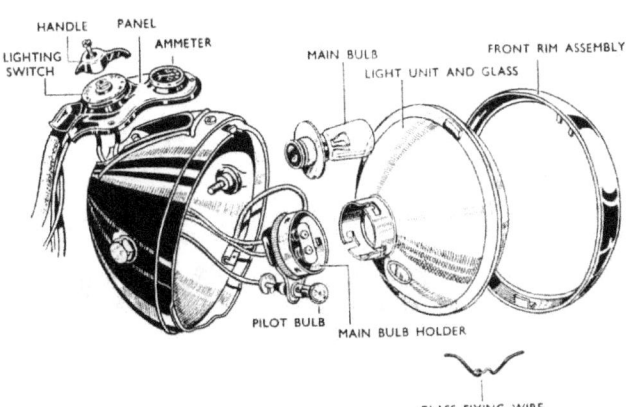

Fig. 2

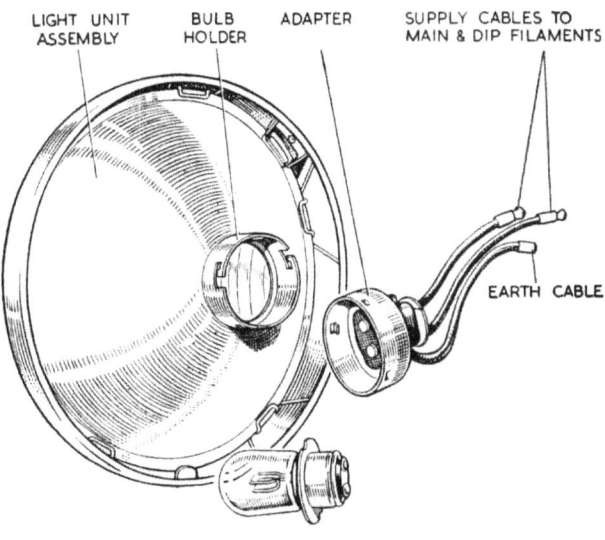

Fig. 3

The outer surface of the lens is smooth to facilitate cleaning. The inner surface is formed of a series of lenses which determine the spread and pattern of the light beams.

In the event of damage to either the lens or reflector a replacement light unit must be fitted.

3. Replacing the Light Unit and Bulb

Slacken the securing screw at the top of the headlamp rim. Remove the front rim and Light Unit assembly.

Withdraw the adaptor from the Light Unit by twisting it in an anti-clockwise direction and pulling it off. Remove the bulb from its locating sleeve at the rear of the reflector.

Disengage the Light Unit securing springs from the rim and lift out the Light Unit.

Position the new unit in the rim so that the word "TOP" on the lens is correctly located when the assembly is mounted on the headlamp. Refit the securing springs ensuring that they are equally spaced around the rim.

Replace the bulb and adaptor. The bulb must be the Lucas "prefocus" type—6 v. 30/24 watt Lucas No. 312.

Locate the bottom of the Light Unit and front rim assembly in the headlamp shell or in the fixing rim attached to the Casquette fork head. Press the front on and tighten the securing screw at the top of the headlamp.

4. Parking Lights

In the case of lamps having separate shells the parking bulb may be mounted either to show through a hole in the back of the main reflector (Fig. 1) or may be mounted in a separate housing beneath the lamp shell (Fig. 2). In the case of lamps fitted into a Casquette fork head twin parking lights are provided. In all cases the bulb is the same, i.e. 6 v. 3 watt M.B.C. Lucas Part No. 988.

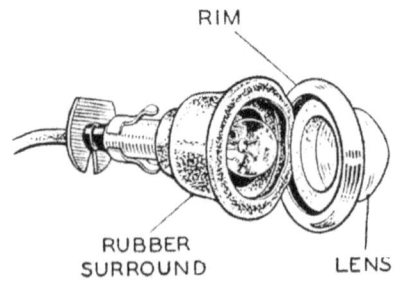

Fig. 4

Access to the parking bulb in the case of lamps with separate shells is obtained by removing the light unit as described in Subsection 2. In the case of lamps in which the parking bulb shows through a hole in the main reflector the bulb holder assembly should be removed. This will come away bringing with it the parking bulb which will then be readily accessible.

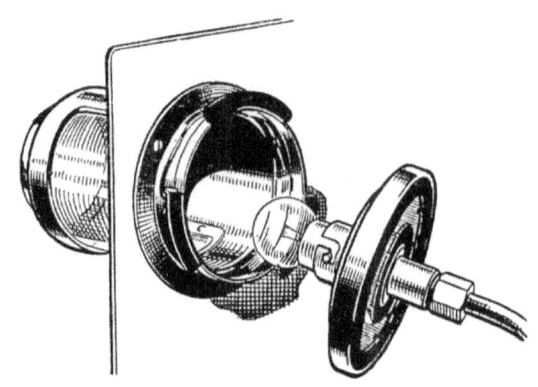

Fig. 5

In the case of lamps having the underslung parking light the parking bulb holder can be lifted out of the lamp shell after removal of the Light Unit.

In the case of lamps fitted into Casquette fork heads access to the parking bulbs is obtained by removing the parking lamp rim (see Fig. 4). This may merely be forced over the edge of the rubber lamp body or in the case of later machines is additionally secured by means of a small fixing screw. After removal of the lamp rim the parking lamp lens can be pulled out of the rubber body, after which the bulb will be accessible.

5. Tail Light

Earlier machines used a circular metal-bodied tail light, either Lucas No. MT110 (Fig. 5) or No. 480 (Fig. 6). In the former case, access to the bulb is obtained by removing the back of the lamp, which will come away bringing the bulb with it. In the latter case, the front of the lamp is removed, leaving the bulb carrier in position. In either case the bulb is the same, that originally fitted being 6 volt 3 watt S.B.C., Lucas Part No. 200, which, however, on machines of over 250 c.c. should now be replaced by 6 volt 6 watt S.B.C. Lucas No. 205.

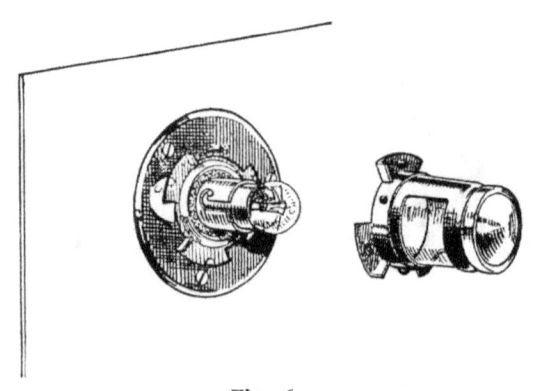

Fig. 6

Recent machines use lamps with red plastic covers, either Type 529 (Fig. 7), which is a tail lamp only; 525 (Fig. 8), which is a combined stop and tail lamp; or 564 (Fig. 9), which is a combined stop and tail lamp and reflector.

Access to the bulb is obtained by removing the two screws which secure the plastic cover.

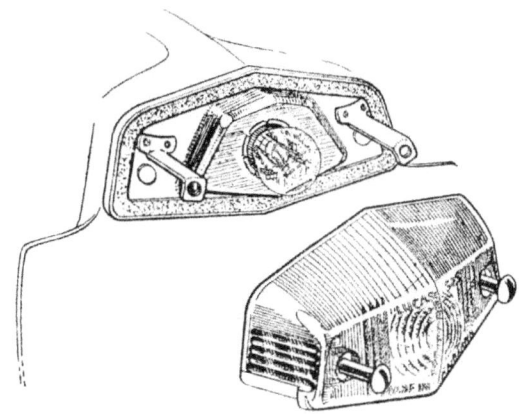

Fig. 8

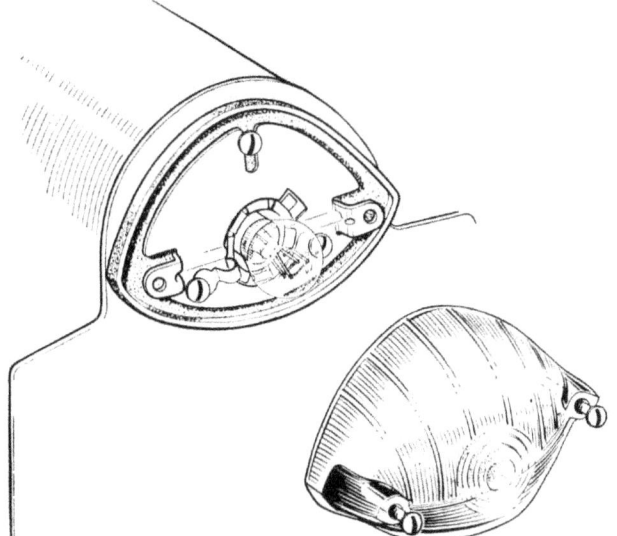

Fig. 7

Care must be taken that the leads to the stop tail lamp are correctly connected, as the use of the 18 watt filament on the normal tail light will not only discharge the battery but could cause trouble from excessive heat affecting the plastic cover. At the same time, the 3 or 6 watt filament, if used as a stop-tail light will be ineffective in bright sunlight.

The correct bulb for the 529 lamp is either Lucas No. 988 6 volt 3 watt M.B.C. or No. 951 6 volt 6 watt M.B.C.

The correct bulb for the stop tail lights 525 and 564 is either Lucas No. 352 6 volt 3/18 watt or Lucas No. 384 6 volt 6/18 watt. The 3 watt or 6 watt filament provides the normal tail light, while the 18 watt filament is illuminated on movement of the brake pedal.

6 watt bulbs are now required by law in Great Britain on machines of more than 250 c.c. capacity.

Fig. 9

NOTES

SECTION H1

Frame

"Meteor 700"; "500 Twin"; "500 Bullet"; "350 Bullet"; "250 Clipper"

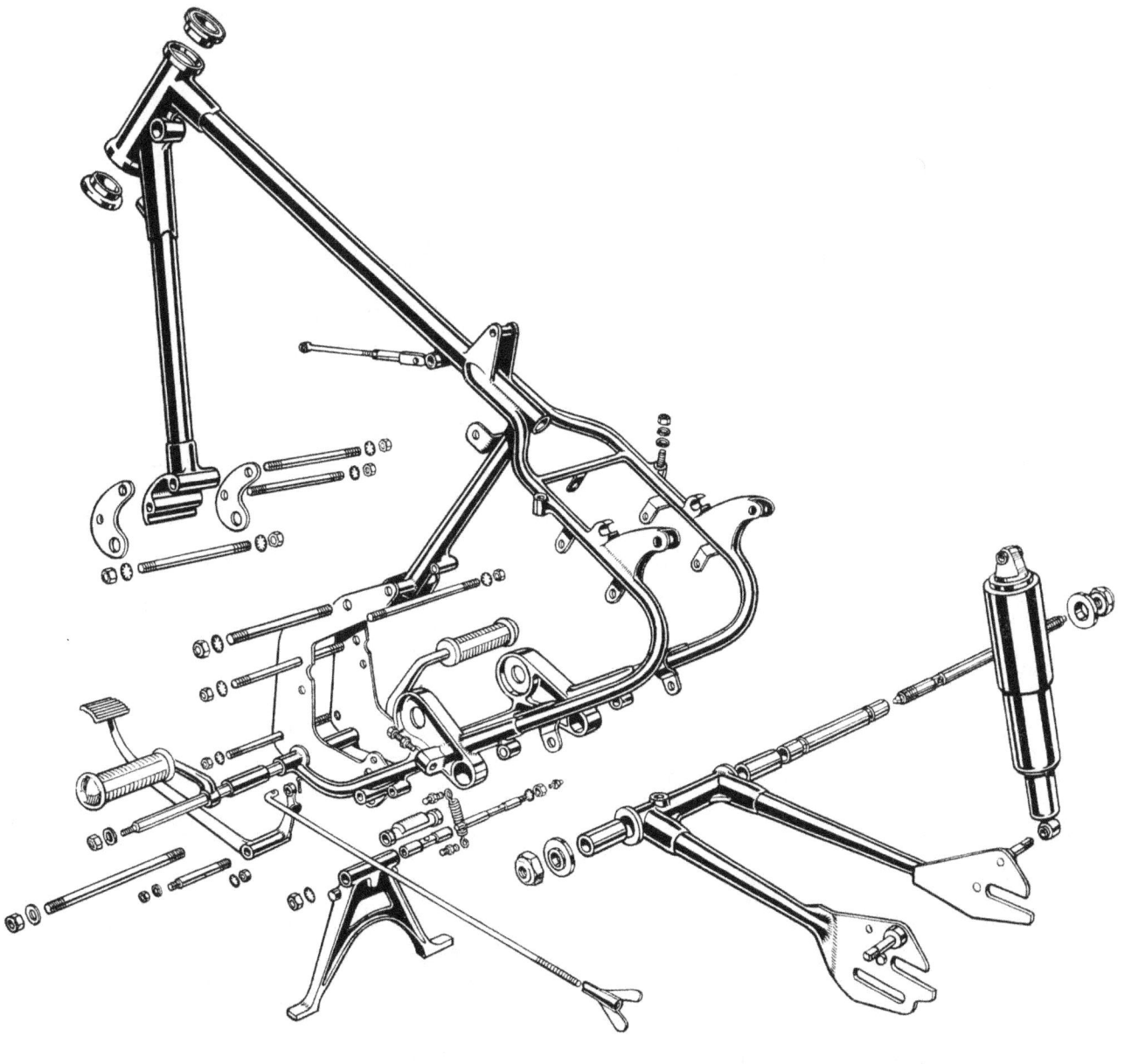

EXPLODED VIEW OF "250 CLIPPER" FRAME
Fig. 1

1. Description of Frame

The frames used on the above models are basically identical, with swinging arm rear suspension, but there are some small differences in the lugs for engine attachment, the method of attachment of the pivot point for the swinging arm and in the width between the brackets supporting the upper ends of the rear suspension units. For part numbers of frames see appropriate spares lists.

The frame is built throughout of cold drawn weldless steel tubing with brazed or welded joints, liners being fitted where necessary for extra strength. All the main frame members are made of chrome-molybdenum alloy steel tubing which retains its strength and resistance to fatigue after brazing or welding.

The swinging arm unit which forms the chain stays is provided with large diameter phosphor bronze bushes and pivots on a stout steel tube which is secured to the main frame by a long bolt passing through the pivot lugs. Hardened steel thrust washers are provided to deal with side thrust. The torsional rigidity of the swinging arm unit helps to maintain the rear wheel upright in the frame and thus relieves the wheel spindle of bending stresses to which it is subject with other types of rear suspension.

2. Steering Head Races

The steering head races, 34085, are the same at the top and bottom of the head lug and are the same for all models. They are easily removed by knocking them out with a hammer and drift and new races can be fitted either under a press or by means of a hammer and a wooden drift.

3. Removal of Rear Suspension Unit

The rear suspension units are readily removed by undoing the top pivot pin nut, driving out the pivot pin, then hinging the suspension unit back on the lower pivot pin, removing the lower nut and pushing the suspension unit off the pivot pin welded to the fork end.

4. Servicing Rear Suspension Units

(a) Proprietary Units. The proprietary units fitted to most 1954 and all 1955 models are sealed and servicing of the internal mechanism can be carried out only by the manufacturers.

The rubber bushes in the top and bottom eyes can easily be renewed and the spring can be removed by pushing down on the top spring cover so as to release the split collar above it. After removal of the split collar the top cover and spring can be lifted off. When reassembling, the spring should be greased to prevent rust and

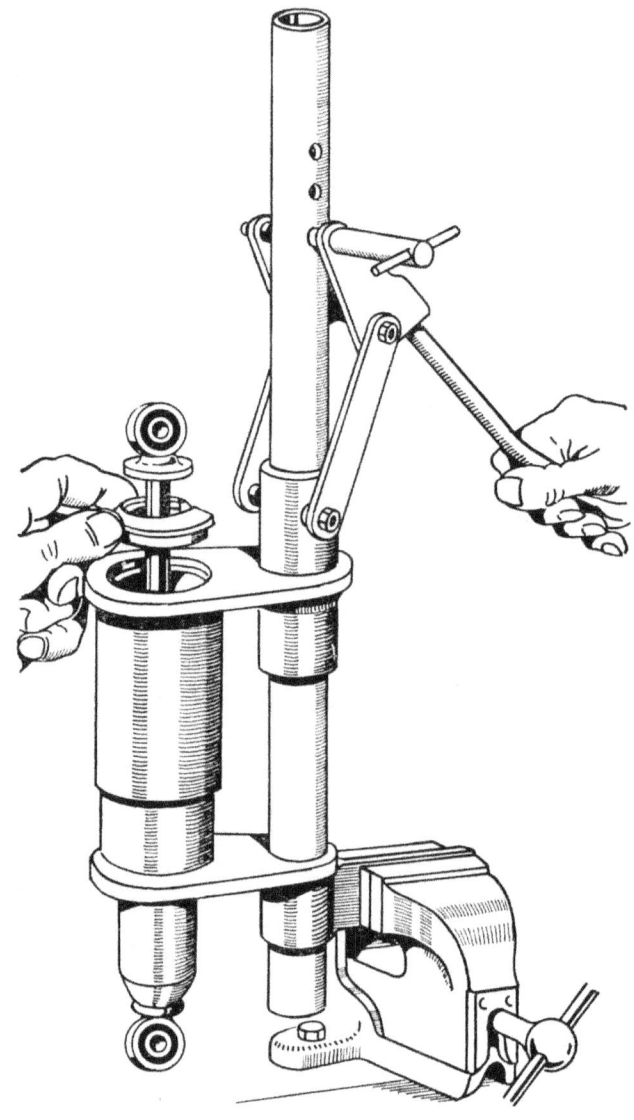

REAR SPRING COMPRESSOR
Fig. 2

squeaking if it should come into contact with either of the covers.

The standard solo springs have a rate of 100—105 lb. per inch and it is not difficult to compress these by hand. Heavier springs having a rate of 130 lb. per inch are available which may require the use of a spring compressor, as shown in Fig. 2.

(b) Royal Enfield Units. Mark I. Enfield rear suspension units, Part Number 34276 or 36451, are shown in Fig. 3. Units having Part No. 34276 are fitted with springs of ·252 in. diameter wire (Part No. 34284) having a rating of approximately 200 lb. per inch (when fitted on the scrolls). Units having Part No. 36451 have a spring of ·264 in. diameter wire (Part No. 35494) having a rating of approximately 250 lb. per inch. The free overall length of both types of spring is $7\frac{3}{4}$ in. New springs should be fitted if they have set more than $\frac{1}{8}$ in.

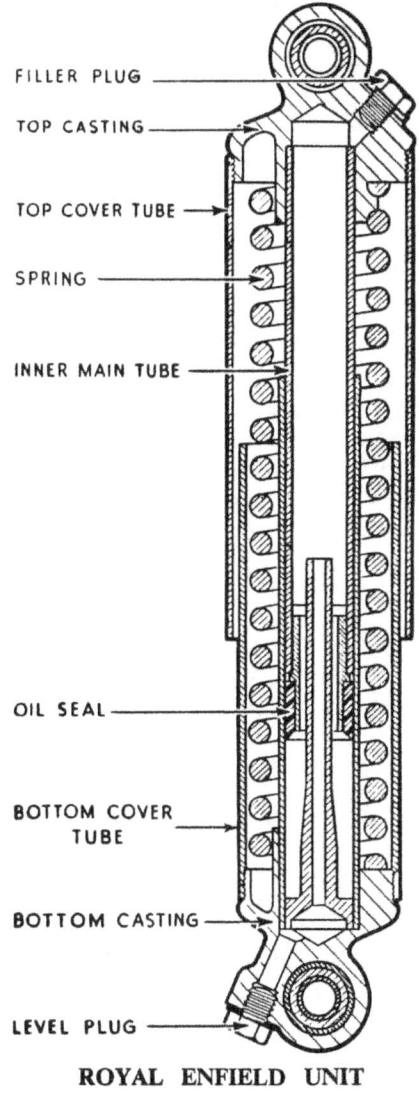

ROYAL ENFIELD UNIT
MARK I
Fig. 3

This type of suspension unit was fitted on "350 Bullet" and "500 Twin" Models up to the early part of the 1954 season, and on the "250 Clipper" Model up to the later part of the 1954 season.

To dismantle the unit, remove it from the machine, grip the lower end of the bottom casting in a vice, unscrew the top cover tube, place a suitable bar through the Silentbloc bush in the top casting and turn so as to unscrew the spring from the scroll on either the top or bottom casting.

The top casting with the inner main tube (which is brazed into it) and the oil seal can now be withdrawn from the outer main tube and bottom casting. If the spring has remained attached to the bottom casting unscrew the bottom cover tube and unscrew the spring from the scroll on the bottom casting, if necessary tapping it with a hammer and a blunt chisel. The outer main tube is brazed into the bottom casting and the hollow damper post is brazed into the main tube.

Oil tightness of these units depends on the condition of the edge of the oil seal which must be handled with great care. The synthetic rubber seal is bonded to a hollow metal plug which forms the valve port in the hydraulic damping system. If the oil seal needs renewing the easiest way to remove it from the inner main tube is to pass a $\frac{13}{32}$ in. diameter bar through the hollow plug to prevent it closing in, then grip the oil seal in a vice, pass a bar through the eye in the top casting and pull and twist to withdraw the hollow metal plug from the end of the main tube. Take care not to damage the new seal when fitting it.

After reassembling, remove the oil filler and level plugs and fill with one of the following oils until it runs out through the level plug orifice:—
Castrolite;   Vacuum Arctic;
Shell X-100. 20/20w;   Essolube 20;
B.P. Energol S.A.E. 20.

Wait till the oil has ceased running, then replace the oil filler and level plugs.

(c) **Royal Enfield Units. Mark II.** Enfield rear suspension units, Part No. 38109, are shown in Fig. 4. This type provides positive damping on the rebound stroke and in consequence does not need the spring to be anchored on scrolls. The range of movement is greater than the Mark I dampers and on account of this and the improved damping the ride is better, particularly on extended rough sections. The spring rate is 150 lb. per inch.

This type of unit was fitted on the "Meteor 700" model up to the early part of the 1954 season and on the "500 Bullet" model up to the later part of the 1954 season.

The Plunger Head contains a disc valve which on the bump stroke provides only a slight restriction to passage of oil between the inside of the Bottom Bearing Tube and the Damper Chamber which is bounded by the inside wall of the upper end of the bottom bearing tube, the outer wall of the lower end of the top bearing tube, the upper surface of the plunger head and the lower end of the bearing bush. Since there is not room in the damper chamber for all the oil displaced on the bump stroke, provision is made for the surplus to pass up the inside of the top bearing tube and into the hollow top end casting.

On the rebound stroke the disc valve in the plunger head closes under pressure in the damper chamber, so that the oil is forced past the clearance between the plunger head and the inside wall of the bottom bearing tube, thus providing positive damping on the rebound stroke.

At the end of the bump stroke the Oil Damping Post enters the open end of the top bearing tube thus providing a hydraulic cushion to prevent bottoming.

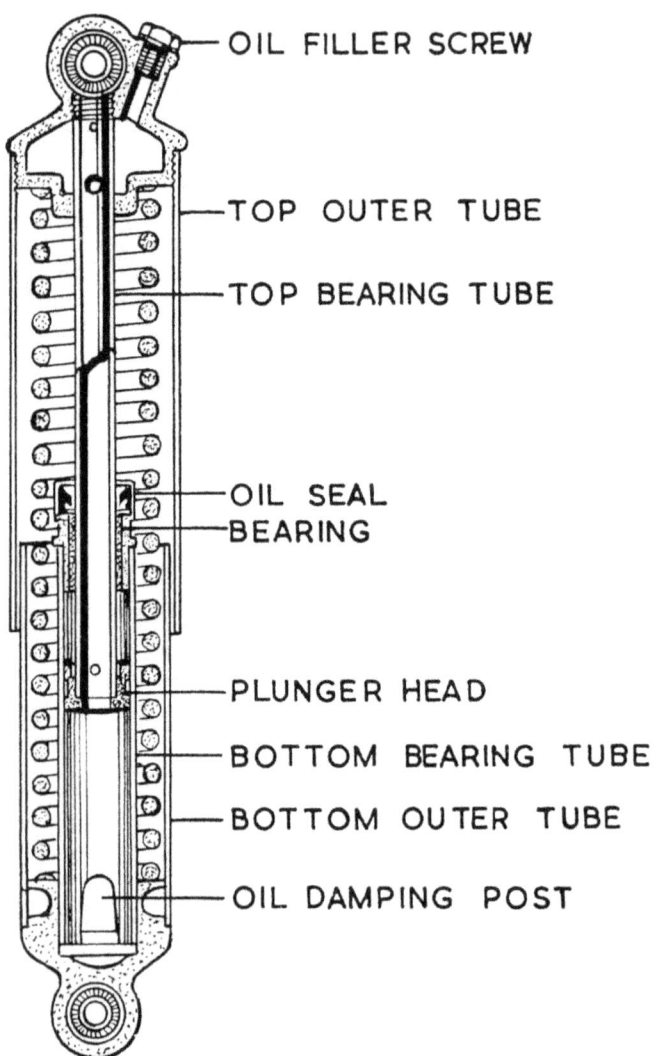

**ROYAL ENFIELD UNIT
MARK II
Fig. 4.**

To dismantle the unit, remove it from the machine, grip the lower end of the bottom casting in a vice and unscrew the top outer tube. Now insert a thin spanner ·820 in. across flats between the coils of the spring to engage the flats on the top bearing and oil seal assembly, unscrew this and withdraw the top casting, top bearing tube and plunger head from the bottom bearing tube, bottom casting and outer tube assembly.

The spring can now be lifted away. Its original free length is $8\frac{3}{4}$ in. If it has closed more than $\frac{1}{8}-\frac{3}{16}$ in. a new spring should be fitted.

If it is required to renew the bearing bush or oil seal, the plunger head must be dismantled by unscrewing it from the top bearing tube and then lifting away the Oil Control Valve and circlip. The top bearing assembly comprising the oil seal and bearing bush in a housing can now be withdrawn from the lower end of the top bearing tube. The oil seal and bearing bush are secured in the housing by spinning over the end of the latter. A new assembly must therefore be fitted if either oil seal or bearing require renewing.

After reassembly of the plunger head, fill the bottom bearing tube with oil of one of the grades given below. Remove the oil filler screw from the top casting, replace the spring, and carefully insert the plunger head into the bottom bearing tube, pushing it down slowly so as to spill as little oil as possible and allow time for oil to enter the damper chamber and pass up the inside of the top bearing tube. Tighten down the top bearing and oil seal assembly with a thin spanner inserted between the coils of the spring.

Now use a mandrel press or a vertical drilling machine to compress the damper unit fully and carefully insert oil through the filling orifice until the unit is completely full. Slightly release the pressure and then compress again fully several times to remove air bubbles. Release the pressure to allow the spring to expand about 1 in. before replacing the oil filler plug.

Use one of the following grades of oil:—
Castrolite;   Vacuum Arctic;
Shell X-100 20/20w;   Essolube 20;
B.P. Energol S.A.E. 20.

5. Removal of Swinging Arm Chain Stays

First remove one of the pivot pin nuts and pull the pivot pin out from the other end. To release the pivot bearing it is necessary to spread the rear portion of the frame, using the frame expander E.5431, which will spread the frame sufficiently to enable the spigots on the thrust washers to clear the recesses in the pivot lugs forming part of the frame.

If it is necessary to remove the bronze bushes these can be driven out by means of a hammer and a suitable drift and new bushes can be fitted under a press without difficulty. After fitting the bushes they must be reamed to ·844/·843 in.

6. Centre Stand

To remove the centre stand unscrew the nut from one end of the stand spindle, knock out the latter and withdraw the stand complete with its bearing sleeve after disconnecting one end of the stand spring. Note that the position of the stand when raised is controlled by the stop on the rear engine plate spacer, Part No. 35060. This should be adjusted so that the stand is as high as possible without actually hitting the exhaust pipe.

7. Wheel Alignment

Note that it is not possible to guarantee that the wheels are correctly aligned when the same notch position is used on both adjuster cams. It is therefore not sufficient to count the notches and use the same position on both sides of the machine. The only way to guarantee that the wheels are in line is to check the alignment from front wheel to back using either a straight edge or a piece of taut string. The alignment should be checked on both sides of the machine and if the front and rear tyres are of different section allowance must be made for this.

It is usual to check the alignment of the wheels at a point about six inches above the ground but, if the alignment is checked also towards the top of the wheels, it will be possible to ascertain whether or not the frame is twisted so as to cause one wheel to be leaning while the other is vertical. To do this it is always necessary to remove the mudguards and, unless a straight edge cut away in its centre portion is available, it will be necessary also to remove the cylinder, toolboxes, battery, etc., in order to allow an unbroken straight edge or a piece of taut string to contact the front and rear tyres.

8. Lubrication

The steering head races, swinging arm pivot bearing and stand pivot bearing should be well greased on assembly. The swinging arm pivot and stand pivot are provided with grease nipples but no nipples are provided for the steering head as experience has shown that the provision of nipples at this point causes trouble through chafing and cutting of control and lighting cables. If the steering head bearings are well packed they will last for several years or many thousands of miles.

Recommended greases are Castrolease (Heavy), Mobilgrease (No. 4), Esso Grease, Energrease C.3 or Shell Retinax A.

NOTES

SECTION J1

Front Fork

With Casquette and Aluminium Alloy Bottom Tubes

Used on "Meteor 700," "500 Twin," "500 Bullet," "350 Bullet," 1954 onwards

1. Description

The telescopic fork consists of two legs each of which comprises a main tube of chrome molybdenum alloy steel tubing which is screwed into the Casquette fork head at the upper end and securely clamped to the fork crown. Fitted over the lower end of the main tube is the bottom tube made of high strength aluminium alloy with an integral lug which carries the wheel spindle. Fitted on the lower end of the main tube is a steel bush which is a close fit in the bore of the bottom tube. The upper end of the bottom tube carries a bronze bush which is a close fit over the outside diameter of the main tube. The bush is secured to the bottom tube by means of a threaded housing which contains an oil seal. A stud known as the "spring stud" is fitted in the lower end of the bottom tube and a valve port is secured to the lower end of the main tube. As the fork operates oil is forced between the spring stud and the bore of the valve port forming a hydraulic damping system. A compression spring is fitted inside the main tube between the upper end of the spring stud and the upper end of the main tube. The lower end of the main tube and upper end of the bottom tube are protected by a cover secured to the fork crown.

A special fork is available for sidecar machines. This has bottom tubes with extended wheel lugs giving less trail and is fitted with stronger springs and a steering damper.

2. Operation of the Fork

The fork provides a range of movement of 6 in. from the fully extended to the fully compressed position. The movement is controlled by the compression spring and by the hydraulic damping system. The hydraulic damping is light on the bump stroke and heavier on the rebound stroke, thus damping out any tendency to pitching or oscillation without interfering unduly with the free movement of the fork when the wheel encounters an obstacle.

The fork is filled with a light oil (S.A.E. 20) to a point above the lower end of the spring so that the damper chamber "B" is always kept

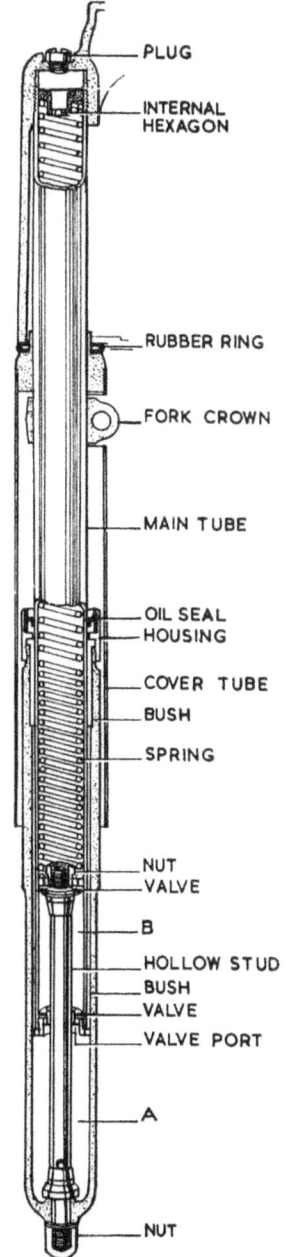

SECTION OF FORK LEG

Fig. 1

full of oil. Upward movement of the wheel spindle forces oil from the lower chamber "A" through the annular space between the spring stud (38067) and the bore of the main tube valve port (38138) into the damper chamber "B." During this stroke the pressure on the underside of the valve plate (38073) causes this to lift so that oil can also pass from "A" to "B" through the eight holes in the valve body. Since, however, the diameter of chamber "B" is less than that of chamber "A" there is not room in "B" to receive all the oil which must be displaced from "A" as the fork operates. The surplus oil passes through the cross hole in the spring stud and up the centre hole in the stud, spilling out through the nut (38076) which secures the upper end of the spring stud to the bronze guide at the lower end of the fork spring.

On the rebound stroke the oil in the damper chamber "B" is forced through the annular space between the spring stud and the bore of the main tube valve port. During this stroke pressure in chamber "B" closes the two disc valves at the upper and lower ends of the chamber so that the only path through which the oil can escape is the annular space between the spring stud and the port. Damping on the rebound stroke is therefore heavier than on the bump stroke. At the extreme end of either bump or rebound stroke a small taper portion on the spring stud enters the bore

MAIN TUBE SPANNER

Fig. 2

of the valve port, thus restricting the annular space and increasing the amount of damping. At the extreme end of the bump stroke the larger diameter taper on the oil control collar (38075) enters the main counterbore of the valve port thus forming a hydraulic cushion to prevent metal to metal contact.

3. Dismantling the Fork to Replace Spring, Oil Seal or Bearing Bushes

Place the machine on the centre stand, disconnect the front brake control and remove the front wheel and mudguard complete with stays. Unscrew the bottom spring stud nut (38080) which will allow oil to run out of the fork down to

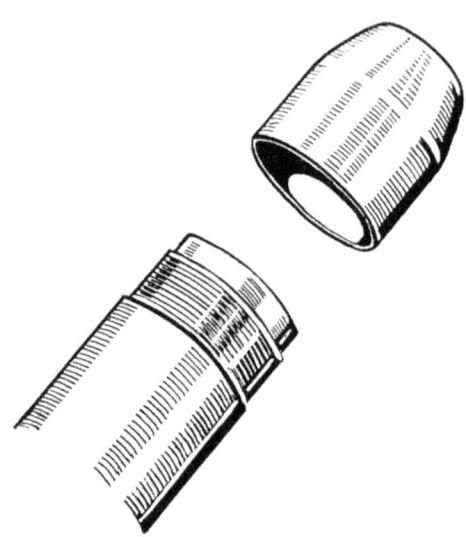

MAIN TUBE SEAL GUIDE

Fig. 3

the level of the cross hole in the spring stud. Now knock the spring stud upwards into the fork with a soft mallet, thus allowing the remainder of the oil to escape. Pull the fork bottom tube down as far as possible, thus exposing the oil seal housing (38157). Unscrew this housing either by means of a spanner on the flats with which it is provided or using the gland nut hand grips (E.4912).* The bottom tube can now be withdrawn completely from the main tube, leaving the bottom tube bush, oil seal housing and oil seal in position on the main tube.

Now unscrew the main tube valve port using "C" spanner (E5418).* The spring stud and spring can now be withdrawn from the lower end of the main tube.

The steel main tube bush (38156) can now be tapped off the lower end of the tube, if necessary using the bottom tube bush for this purpose. Before doing this, however, it is advisable to mark the position of the bush with a pencil line so as to ensure reassembling it in the same position on the main tube. The reason for this is that these bushes are finish ground to size after fitting on to the tubes so as to ensure concentricity. After

*See Manual of Workshop Tools.

removal of the main tube bush the bottom tube bush, oil seal housing and oil seal can be removed.

In case of difficulty in removing the main tube bush it is possible to withdraw the oil seal housing after loosening the crown clip bolt 39038, removing the plug screw 38968 and unscrewing the main tube from the fork head by means of a hexagon bar ·500 in. across flats (Unbrako wrench W.11) or the special tool shown in Fig. 2.

4. Spring

Solo and Sidecar springs are available. The free length of each is 20½ ins. The spring should be replaced if it has closed by more than 1 inch.

5. Reassembly of Parts

When refitting the oil seal, or fitting a new one, great care must be exercised not to damage the synthetic rubber lip which forms the actual seal. If the seal has been removed from the upper end of the main tube and is refitted from this end a special nose piece (Fig. 3) must be fitted over the end of the tube to prevent the thread from damaging the oil seal.

The spring stud is a tight fit in the hole at the lower end of the bottom tube. Once the stud has been entered in the hole push the bottom tube up sharply against the spring until two or three threads on the stud project beneath the end of the bottom tube. Now fit the nut and washer and pull the stud into position by tightening the nut. If necessary fit the nut first without the washer until sufficient thread is projecting to enable the washer to be fitted.

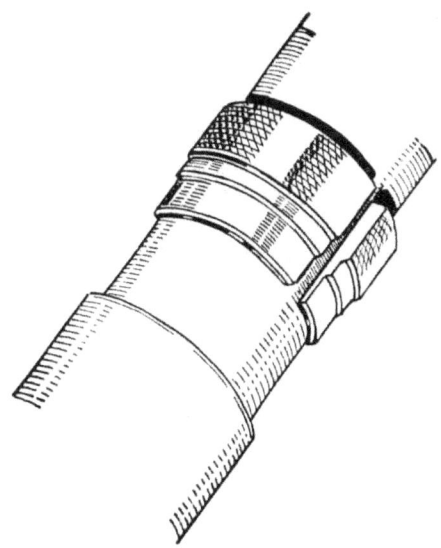

OUTER COVER CENTRALISING BUSHES

Fig. 5

6. Steering Head Races.

The steering head bearing consists of two deep groove thrust races each containing nineteen ¼ in. diameter balls. The bearing is adjusted by tightening the steering stem locknut after loosening the ball head clip screw and both the fork crown clamp bolts. The head should be adjusted so that, when the front wheel is lifted clear of the ground, a light tap on the handlebars will cause the steering to swing to full lock in either direction, while at the same time there should be only the slightest trace of play in the bearings. When testing for freedom of movement the steering damper, if fitted, should be disconnected by unscrewing the anchor plate pin. Do not forget to tighten the ball head clip screw and fork crown clamp bolts. Before tightening the latter make sure that the cover tubes are located centrally round the main tubes so that the bottom tube does not rub inside the cover tube. A pair of split bushes (Fig. 5) is useful to ensure centralisation of the cover tubes.

7. Removal of Complete Fork

The fork complete with front wheel and mudguard can be removed from the machine if necessary by adopting the following procedure.

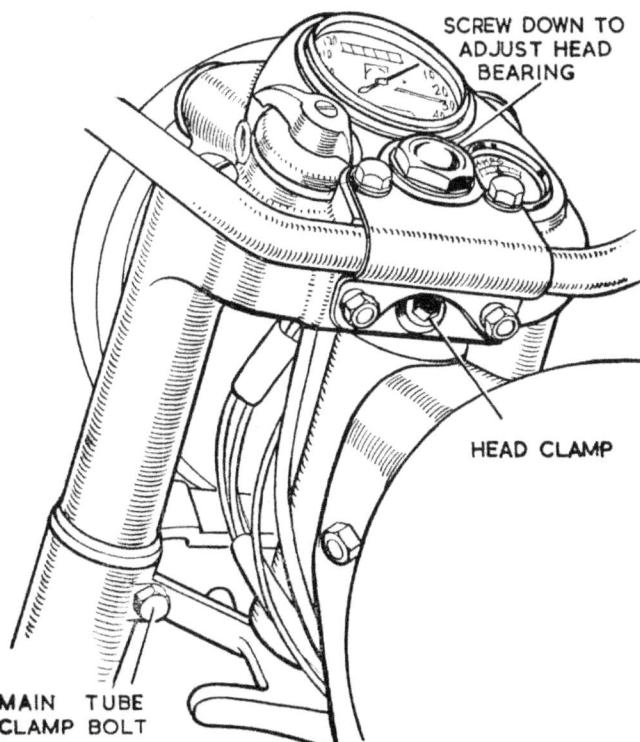

SHOWING THE POSITIONS OF THE CLAMP BOLTS SECURING THE STEERING STEM AND FORK TUBES

Fig. 4

The leads to the lighting switch and ammeter should be disconnected from the battery, regulator, tail lamp, etc. at their lower ends or by means of the plug and socket connectors when these are provided. The switch and ammeter are push fits into the rubber bushes in the fork head.

Disconnect the speedometer drive from the speedometer head and unscrew the steering damper knob and rod (on sidecar forks) after removal of the split pin through the lower end of the rod. Undo the steering damper anchor plate pin so as to disconnect the damper from the frame of the machine.

Remove the two plug screws (38968) and loosen the steering head clip bolt and the two fork crown clamp bolts.

Now unscrew the fork main tubes from the fork head and the steering stem locknut from the top of the steering stem, turning each tube and the nut a turn or two at a time. When the nut has been removed from the steering stem and the main tubes have been completely unscrewed from the fork head the complete fork and wheel with steering stem can be lifted out of the head lug of the frame.

8. Lubrication

The lubrication of the fork bearings is effected by the oil which forms the hydraulic damping medium. All that is necessary is to keep sufficient oil in the fork to ensure that the top end of the bottom spring stud is never uncovered even in the full rebound position. The level of oil in the fork can be gauged by removing the top plug screw and inserting a long rod about $\frac{3}{8}$ in. diameter. If slightly tilted this will ledge against the nut at the upper end of the bottom spring stud and indicate the level of oil above the stud. If the fork is empty to start with the quantity required is approximately $7\frac{1}{2}$ fluid ounces in each leg. Recommended grades of oil are Castrolite, Mobiloil Arctic, Essolube 20, B.P. Energol S.A.E. 20 and Shell X-100 20/20W.

9. Air Vents

The earlier forks of this type were provided with holes at the upper end of each main tube communicating with small vent holes in the Casquette head. Experience has shown that on rough roads oil may escape through these air vents which in consequence are now omitted. Escape of oil from the earlier forks can be largely eliminated by fitting specially long plug screws which are available. The Part Number is 40118. If these are fitted and the final vent hole is stopped up with a wooden plug leakage at this point is impossible. Fitting the special plug screws alone is sufficient in most instances.

SECTION J3

Front Fork

With Facia Panel and Aluminium Alloy Bottom Tubes

Used on "500 Bullet," 1953; "Meteor 700," 1953

1. Description

The telescopic fork consists of two legs each of which comprises a main tube of chrome molybdenum alloy steel tubing which is securely clamped to the Facia Panel Fork Head and to the fork crown. Fitted over the lower end of the main tube is the bottom tube made of high strength aluminium alloy with an integral lug which carries the wheel spindle. Fitted on the lower end of the main tube is a steel bush which is a close fit in the bore of the bottom tube. The upper end of the bottom tube carries a bronze bush which is a close fit over the outside diameter of the main tube. The bush is secured to the bottom tube by means of a threaded housing which contains an oil seal. A stud, known as the "spring stud," is fitted in the lower end of the bottom tube and a valve port is secured to the lower end of the main tube. As the fork operates oil is forced between the spring stud and the bore of the valve port forming a hydraulic damping system. A compression spring is fitted inside the main tube between the upper end of the spring stud and the upper end of the main tube. The main tube and upper end of the bottom tube are protected by a one-piece cover secured to the fork crown and carrying a pressed steel lamp bracket welded to it.

A special version of the fork is available for sidecar use. This has a modified fork head and fork crown setting the main tubes $1\frac{1}{2}$ in. further forward thus giving less trail and providing lighter steering when used with a sidecar. These sidecar forks also are fitted with a steering damper and have stronger springs.

2. Operation of Fork

The fork provides a range of movement of 6 in. from the fully extended to the fully compressed position. The movement is controlled by the compression spring and by the hydraulic damping system. The hydraulic damping is light on the bump stroke and heavier on the rebound stroke, thus damping out any tendency to pitching or oscillation without interfering unduly with the free movement of the fork when the wheel encounters an obstacle.

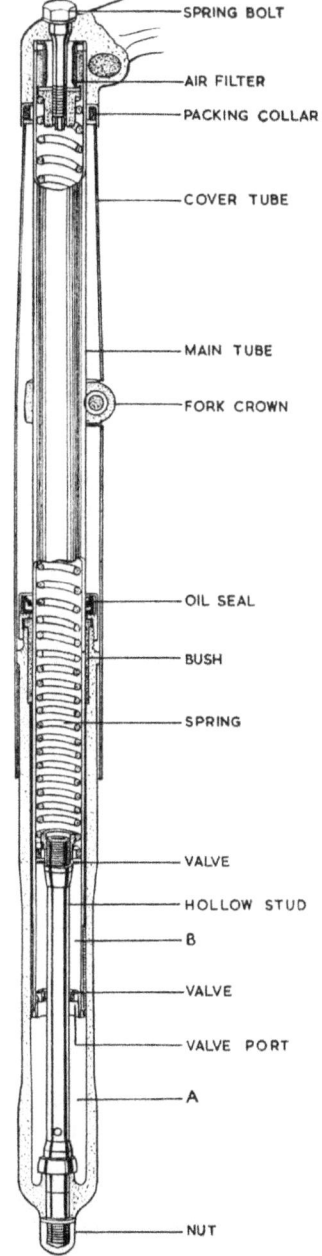

SECTION OF LEG

Fig. 1

The fork is filled with a light oil (S.A.E. 20) to a point above the lower end of the spring so that the damper chamber "B" is always kept full of oil. Upward movement of the wheel spindle forces oil from the lower chamber "A" through the annular space between the spring stud (38067) and the bore of the main tube valve port (38138) into the damper chamber "B." During this stroke the pressure on the underside of the valve plate (38073) causes this to lift so that oil can also pass from "A" to "B" through the eight holes in the valve body. Since, however, the diameter of chamber "B" is less than that of chamber "A" there is not room in "B" to receive all the oil which must be displaced from "A" as the fork operates. The surplus oil passes through the cross hole in the spring stud and up the centre hole in the stud, spilling out through the nut (38076) which secures the upper end of the spring stud to the bronze guide at the lower end of the fork spring.

On the rebound stroke the oil in the damper chamber "B" is forced through the annular space between the spring stud and the bore of the main tube valve port. During this stroke pressure in chamber "B" closes the two disc valves at the upper and lower ends of the chamber so that the only path through which the oil can escape is the annular space between the spring stud and the port. Damping on the rebound stroke is therefore heavier than on the bump stroke. At the extreme end of either bump or rebound stroke a small taper portion on the spring stud enters the bore of the valve port thus restricting the annular space and increasing the amount of damping. At the extreme end of the bump stroke the larger diameter taper on the oil control collar (38075) enters the main counterbore of the valve port thus forming a hydraulic cushion to prevent metal to metal contact.

3. Dismantling the Fork to Replace Spring, Oil Seal or Bearing Bushes

Place the machine on the centre stand, disconnect the front brake control and remove the front wheel and mudguard complete with stays. Unscrew the bottom spring stud nut (38080) which will allow oil to run out of the fork down to the level of the cross hole in the spring stud. Now knock the spring stud upwards into the fork with a soft mallet, thus allowing the remainder of the oil to escape. Pull the fork bottom tube down as far as possible, thus exposing the oil seal housing (38157). Unscrew this housing either by means of a spanner on the flats with which it is provided or by using the gland nut hand grips (E4912).* The bottom tube can now be withdrawn completely from the main tube, leaving the bottom tube bush, oil seal housing and oil seal in position on the main tube.

Now unscrew the main tube valve port using "C" spanner (E5418).* The spring stud and spring can now be withdrawn from the lower end of the main tube.

The steel main tube bush (38156) can now be tapped off the lower end of the tube, if necessary using the bottom tube bush for this purpose. Before doing this, however, it is advisable to mark the position of the bush with a pencil line so as to ensure reassembling it in the same position on the main tube. The reason for this is that these bushes are finish ground to size after fitting on to the tubes so as to ensure concentricity. After removal of the main tube bush the bottom tube bush, oil seal housing and oil seal can be removed.

In case of difficulty in removing the main tube bush it is possible to withdraw the oil seal housing from the upper end after removal of the main tube from the fork head and fork crown as described in paragraphs 6 and 7.

4. Spring

Solo and sidecar springs are available. The free length of each is 20½ in. The spring should be replaced if it has closed by more than 1 inch.

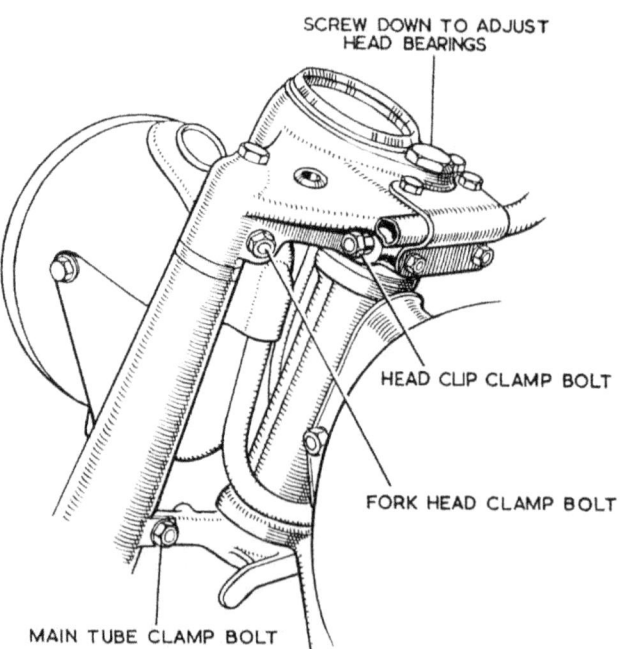

SHOWING THE POSITIONS OF THE CLAMP BOLTS SECURING THE STEERING STEM AND FORK TUBES

Fig. 2

*See Manual of Workshop Tools.

5. Steering Head Races

The steering head bearing consists of two deep groove thrust races each containing nineteen $\frac{1}{4}$ in. diameter balls. The bearing is adjusted by tightening the steering stem locknut after loosening the nuts on the three pinch bolts which secure the fork head to the steering stem and to the two main tubes. The head should be adjusted so that when the front wheel is lifted clear of the ground a

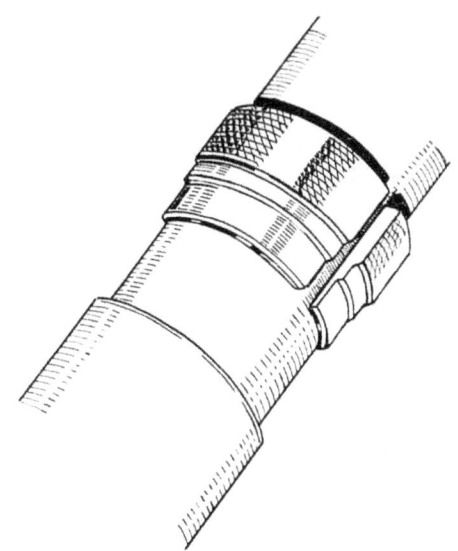

OUTER COVER CENTRALISING BUSHES

Fig. 3

light tap on the handlebars will cause the steering to swing to full lock in either direction, while at the same time there should be only the slightest trace of play in the bearings. When testing for freedom of movement the steering damper, if fitted, should be disconnected by unscrewing the anchor plate pin.

Adjustment of the steering head depends on the ability of the fork head to slide on the steering stem and on the fork main tubes. A rubber washer is interposed between the fork head and the top of the lamp bracket tube to permit the necessary movement. If this rubber washer is fully compressed while there is still some play in the steering head it will be necessary to remove the fork head (see paragraph 6) and shorten the lamp bracket tube by, say, $\frac{1}{32}$ in. Alternatively, if the lamp bracket tube is loose when the steering head is correctly adjusted, it can be tightened by fitting an additional steel washer (Part No. 35974) beneath the rubber washer.

It is also possible that the steering head cannot be adjusted because the main tube is bottoming in the recess in the fork head in which it fits. In this case the nuts on the fork crown clamp studs must be loosened and the sleeves separated (see paragraph 7) thus permitting the main tubes to slide through the fork crown. Do not forget to tighten the fork head pinch bolts and the nuts on the fork crown clamp studs after adjusting the steering head. Before tightening the latter make sure that the cover tubes are located centrally round the main tubes so that the bottom tube does not rub inside the lower end of the cover tube. A pair of split bushes (Fig. 3) is useful to ensure centralisation of the cover tubes.

6. Removal of Facia Panel Fork Head, Spring, etc.

To remove the Facia Panel Fork Head for access to the lamp bracket tubes (or to change the fork spring without disturbing the bearings) proceed as follows—disconnect all control cables at the handlebar end and remove the headlamp from the lamp brackets. The switch panel can conveniently be removed from the back of the lamp so that the body of the lamp can be removed completely.

Now remove the two Fork Spring Guide Bolts from the fork head, unscrew the nuts on the fork head clip bolt and the two main tube clip bolts, remove the three clip bolt sleeves and knock out the three clip bolts. The facia panel fork head can now be tapped gently upwards with a hide mallet or a hammer and a wooden drift but care must be taken to hit only the more solid parts of the fork head, i.e. beneath the handlebar clip and at the back of the main tubes, avoiding the underside of the comparatively thin portion in front of the speedometer.

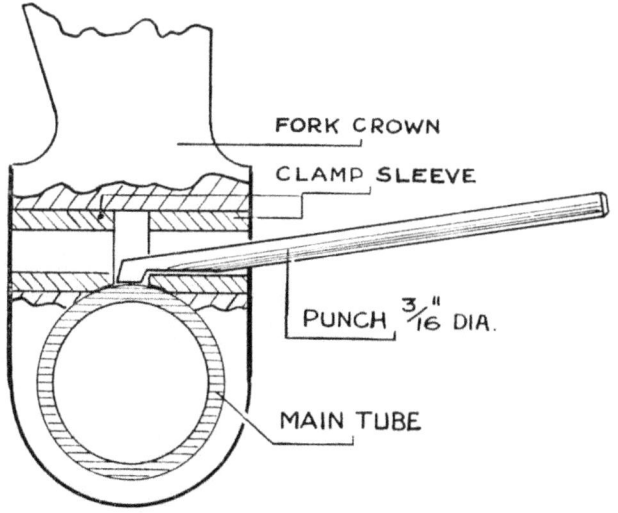

DRIFT FOR PARTING CLAMP SLEEVES

Fig. 4

After removal of the fork head the lamp bracket tubes can be lifted straight off and the springs can be withdrawn from the upper end of the main tubes.

7. Removal of Main Tubes

To remove the main tubes first dismantle the fork as described in paragraph 3 then remove the facia panel fork head and lamp bracket tubes as described in paragraph 6. Now remove one nut from each of the fork crown clamp studs, remove the studs and separate the clamp sleeves with a drift of the form shown in Fig. 4. Now knock the main tubes out of the fork crown either upwards or downwards as may be most convenient. If the machine has been in an accident and the tube is badly bent both above and below the fork crown, it may be necessary to cut through the tube with a hacksaw before it can be withdrawn.

8. Reassembly of Parts

No difficulty should be experienced with this. When refitting the main tube use the lamp bracket tube as a guide to its correct position in the fork crown. The small shoulder some $1\frac{1}{2}$ in. from the upper end of the tube should be $\frac{1}{8}$ in. above the top of the lamp bracket tube when the latter is in position on the fork crown. With the main tube in this position tighten the fork crown clamp screws before fitting the facia panel fork head.

The cover tube must be fitted in position on the fork crown and the clamp sleeves placed in position before the main tube is fitted. To keep the clamp sleeves in position it is convenient to insert a short piece of tube or bar in the eye of the fork crown before putting the cover tube in position. The short piece of tube will be pushed out when inserting the main tube. Before tightening the nuts on the three fork head clip bolts make sure that the bolt heads and the sleeves are correctly positioned with the cut-away portion engaging the main tube or steering stem. Failure to do this may result in a cracked fork head.

When refitting the oil seal or fitting a new one great care must be exercised not to damage the synthetic rubber lip which forms the actual seal. If the seal has been removed from the upper end of the main tube and is refitted from this end a special nose piece (Fig. 5) must be fitted over the end of the tube to prevent the thread from damaging the oil seal.

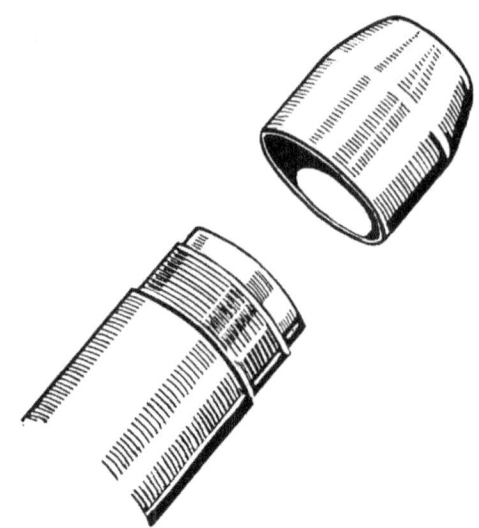

MAIN TUBE SEAL GUIDE

Fig. 5

The spring stud is a tight fit in the hole at the lower end of the bottom tube. Once the stud has been entered in the hole push the bottom tube up sharply against the spring until two or three threads on the stud project beneath the end of the bottom tube. Now fit the nut and washer and pull the stud into position by tightening the nut. If necessary fit the nut first without the washer until sufficient thread is projecting to enable the washer to be fitted.

9. Lubrication

The lubrication of the fork bearings is effected by the oil which forms the hydraulic damping medium. All that is necessary is to keep sufficient oil in the fork to ensure that the top end of the bottom spring stud is never uncovered even in the full rebound position. The level of oil in the fork can be gauged by removing the top plug screw and inserting a long rod about $\frac{3}{8}$ in. diameter. If slightly tilted this will ledge against the nut at the upper end of the bottom spring stud and indicate the level of oil above the stud. If the fork is empty to start with the quantity required is approximately $7\frac{1}{2}$ fluid ounces in each leg. Recommended grades of oil are Castrolite, Mobiloil Arctic, Essolube 20, **B.P. Energol S.A.E. 20 and Shell X-100 20/20 w.**

SECTION J4

Front Fork

With Facia Panel and Steel Bottom Tubes

Used on "350 Model G," "500 Model J2," 1951 onward;
"350 Bullet," "500 Twin," 1950-53 inclusive

1. Description

The telescopic fork consists of two legs each of which comprises a main tube of chrome molybdenum alloy steel tubing which is securely clamped to the facia panel fork head at the upper end and to the fork crown. Fitted over the lower end of the main tube is the bottom tube made of steel tubing with a forged steel fork end flash-welded to it.* Fitted on the lower end of the main tube is a bronze bush which is a close fit in the bore of the bottom tube. The upper end of the bottom tube carries a bronze bush which is a close fit over the outside diameter of the main tube. The bush is secured to the bottom tube by means of a gland nut with an oil seal fitted inside it. A stud, known as the "spring stud," is fitted in the lower end of the bottom tube and a valve port is secured to the lower end of the main tube. As the fork operates oil is forced through the annular space between the bore of the valve port and the outside diameter of the "spring stud," which is formed with a double taper. Thus hydraulic damping is provided which is light at the normal position of the fork and becomes increasingly effective towards each end of the fork's travel. A compression spring is fitted inside the main tube and is secured by scrolls so that it is in tension on the rebound. The lower end of the main tube and upper end of the bottom tube are protected by a cover tube screwed to the fork crown. The upper end of the main tube is covered by a tube with a pressed steel lamp bracket welded to it.

The fork is filled with a light oil (S.A.E. 20) up to a level above the valve port, this oil providing both the damping medium and the lubricant for the bearings.

A special version of the fork is available for sidecar use. This has a modified fork head and fork crown setting the main tubes $1\frac{1}{2}$ in. further forward, thus giving less trail and providing lighter steering when used with a sidecar. These sidecar forks also are fitted with a steering damper and have stronger springs.

2. Dismantling Fork to Replace Spring, Oil Seal or Bearing Bushes

Place the machine on the stand and in the case of Model "G" or "J2" place a box beneath the crankcase to raise the front wheel from the ground. Disconnect the front brake control and remove the front wheel and mudguard complete with stays. Unscrew the oil level plug after placing a tray to catch any oil which may run out. Undo the nut which secures the spring stud to the fork end and knock the spring stud upwards into the fork with a soft mallet, thus allowing the remainder of the oil to escape.

Unscrew the outer cover tube using the hand grips E4912† thus exposing the gland nut which can be unscrewed with the hand grips E5417,† using a bar through the bracket for the wheel spindle to prevent the bottom tube from turning. The bottom tube can now be withdrawn completely from the main tube leaving the bottom tube bush, oil seal and gland nut on the main tube.

Now unscrew the main tube valve port using "C" spanner E5418.† The spring stud and spring can now be withdrawn from the lower end of the main tube.

The bronze main tube bush can be now tapped off the lower end of the tube using the bottom tube bush for this purpose. The bottom tube bush, oil seal and gland nut can then be withdrawn.

3. Spring

The original length of the spring is 19 in. overall. A new spring should be fitted if the old one has set by more than 1 inch.

4. Steering Head Races

The steering head bearing consists of two deep groove thrust races each containing nineteen

---

*On early models the fork end was made of aluminium alloy screwed on to the bottom tube.

† See Manual of Service Tools.

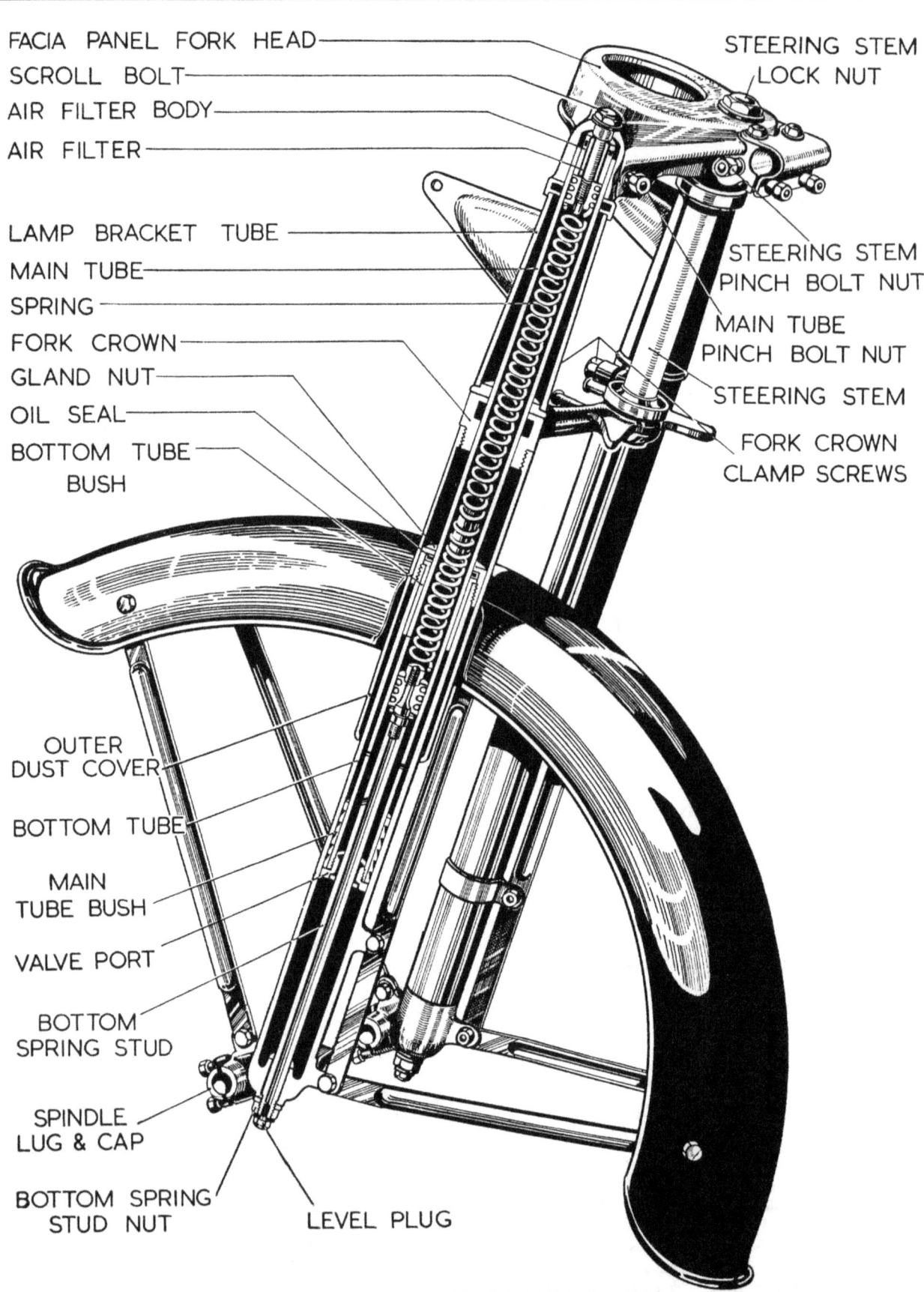

SECTIONED VIEW OF TELESCOPIC FORK
Fig. 1

$\frac{1}{4}$ in. diameter balls. The bearing is adjusted by tightening the steering stem locknut after loosening the nuts on the three pinch bolts which secure the fork head to the steering stem and to the two main tubes. The head should be adjusted so that when the front wheel is lifted clear of the ground a light tap on the handlebars will cause the steering to swing to full lock in either direction, while at the same time there should be only the slightest trace of play in the bearings. When testing for freedom of movement the steering damper, if fitted, should be disconnected by unscrewing the anchor plate pin.

Adjustment of the steering head depends on the ability of the fork head to slide on the steering stem and on the fork main tubes. A rubber washer is interposed between the fork head and the top of the lamp bracket tube to permit the necessary movement. If this rubber washer is fully compressed while there is still some play in the steering head it will be necessary to remove the fork head (see paragraph 5) and shorten the lamp bracket tube by, say, $\frac{1}{32}$ in. Alternatively, if the lamp bracket tube is loose when the steering head is correctly adjusted, it can be tightened by fitting an additional steel washer (Part No. 35974) beneath the rubber washer.

It is also possible that the steering head cannot be adjusted because the main tube is bottoming in the recess in the fork head in which it fits. In this case the fork crown clamp screws must be loosened, thus permitting the main tubes to slide through the fork crown. Do no forget to tighten the fork head pinch bolts and the fork crown clamp screws after adjusting the steering head.

5. Removal of Facia Panel Fork Head, Spring, etc.

To remove the Facia Panel Fork Head for access to the lamp bracket tubes (or to change the fork spring without disturbing the bearings) proceed as follows—disconnect all control cables at the handlebar end and remove the headlamp from the lamp brackets. The switch panel can conveniently be removed from the back of the lamp so that the body of the lamp can be removed completely.

Now unscrew the two Fork Spring Scroll Bolts from the fork head, unscrew the nuts on the fork head clip bolt and the two main tube clip bolts, remove the three clip bolt sleeves and knock out the three clip bolts. The facia panel fork head can now be tapped gently upwards with a hide mallet or a hammer and a wooden drift but care must be taken to hit only the more solid parts of the fork head, i.e. beneath the handlebar clip and at the back of the main tubes, avoiding the underside of the comparatively thin portion in front of the speedometer.

After removal of the fork head the lamp bracket tubes can be lifted straight off and the springs can be withdrawn from the upper end of the main tubes after unscrewing the oil level plug and the nut which secures the spring stud to the fork end and knocking the spring stud upwards.

6. Removal of Main Tubes

To remove the main tubes first dismantle the fork as described in paragraph 2 then remove the facia panel fork head and lamp bracket tubes as described in paragraph 5. Now loosen the fork crown clamp screws and knock the main tubes out of the fork crown either upwards or downwards as may be most convenient. If the machine has been in an accident and the tube is badly bent both above and below the fork crown, it may be necessary to cut through the tube with a hacksaw before it can be withdrawn.

7. Reassembly of Parts

No difficulty should be experienced with this. When refitting the main tube use the lamp bracket tube as a guide to its correct position in the fork crown. The small shoulder some $1\frac{1}{2}$ in. from the upper end of the tube should be flush with the top of the lamp bracket tube when the latter is in position on the fork crown. With the main tube in this position tighten the fork crown clamp screws before fitting the facia panel fork head.

If new oil seals have been fitted it may be found that the action of the fork is very stiff when the gland nuts are tightened down fully. In this case the nuts may be left half a turn or so slack until the seals have freed off, after which they should be tightened down. Note that the seals must be fitted with the larger bore uppermost, i.e. with the scraping edges facing downwards.

When refitting the three clip bolts, which secure the fork head to the main tubes and steering stem, make sure that the clip bolts and their sleeves are correctly fitted so that the cut-away portions of them bear against the tubes. Any attempt to tighten the nuts with the bolts or sleeves incorrectly fitted may result in cracking the facia panel fork head.

8. Lubrication

The lubrication of the fork bearings is effected by the oil which forms the hydraulic damping medium. The oil level is fixed by a cross hole in the spring stud leading to a drilled passage terminating in the oil level plug. To fill each fork leg to the correct level remove the plug screws from the fork head and the oil level plugs from the fork ends. Pour oil in at the top until it runs out at the bottom of the fork. Wait till oil has stopped running and replace level plugs and plug screws.

Recommended grades of oil are Castrolite, Mobiloil Arctic, Essolube 20, B.P. Energol S.A.E. 20, Shell X-100 20/20 w.

NOTES

SECTION K1

Front Wheel

With Dual 6 in. Brake

Fitted to "Meteor 700," 1953 onwards;
"500 Twin," "500 Bullet," "350 Bullet," 1955 onwards

1. Removal from Fork

To remove the front wheel from the fork place the machine on the centre stand and front stand, if fitted, or alternatively with sufficient packing (about 2 in.) beneath each side of the stand to lift the wheel clear of the ground when tilted back on to the rear wheel. Slacken brake cable adjustments and disconnect cables from handlebar lever and from operating cam levers on hub. Unscrew the four nuts securing the fork bottom tube lug caps (Part No. 38593) and allow the wheel to drop forwards out of the front fork. Make sure that the machine stands securely on the rear wheel and centre stand—if necessary place a weight on the saddle or a strut beneath the fork to ensure this.

2. Removal of Brake Cover Plate Assemblies

Lock the brake "on" by pressure on the operating lever, 38905 (R.H.) or 38906 (L.H.), and unscrew the cover plate nuts 31347. The right and left hand cover plate assemblies can then be withdrawn from the respective brake drums.

3. Removal of Brake Shoes and Springs

This is best done by unscrewing the pivot pin locknuts, 28715, and the operating lever nuts, 10314, after which the assembly of brake shoes, return springs, pivot pin and operating cam can be removed from the cover plate by light blows with a hammer and drift on the ends of the pivot pin and the operating cam. The return springs, 29236, can then be unhooked from the spring posts

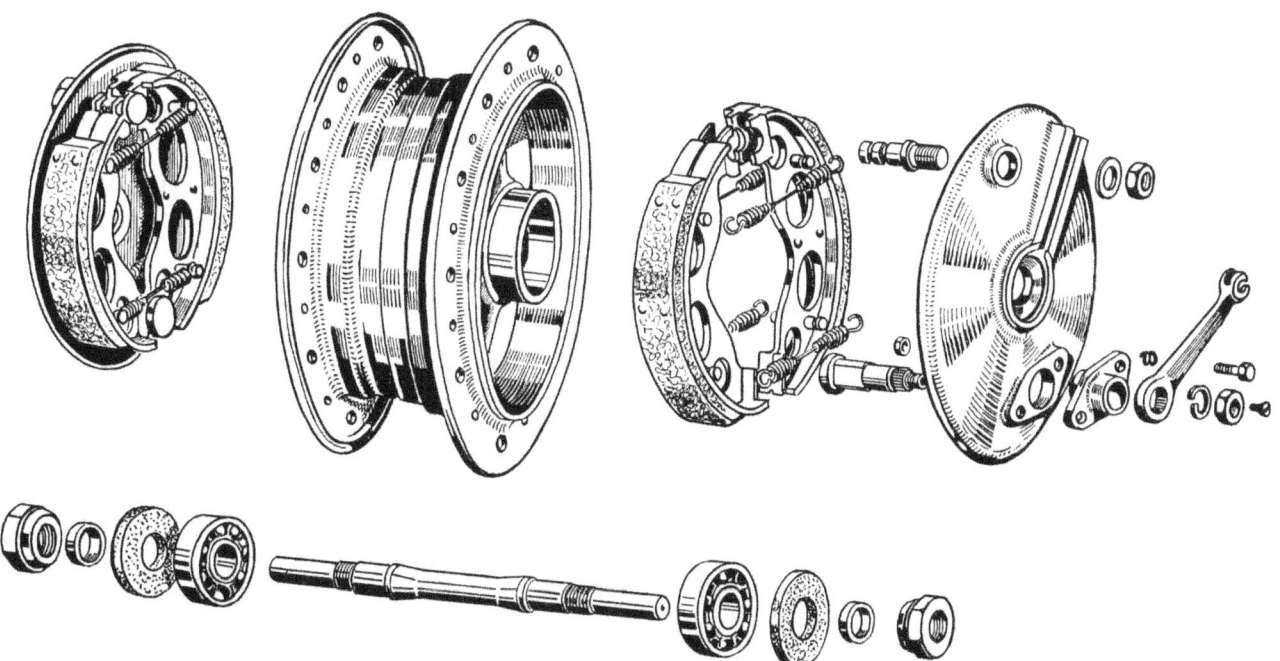

DUAL FRONT BRAKE
Fig. 1

in the brake shoes thus allowing the whole assembly to fall apart.

4. Replacing Brake Linings

Brake linings are supplied either in pairs ready drilled complete with rivets (Part No. 37786BX) or ready fitted to service replacement brake shoes (Part No. 38042). When riveting linings to shoes secure the two centre rivets first so as to ensure that the lining lies flat against the shoe. Standard linings are Ferodo MR41, which are drilled to receive cheese headed rivets.

5. Removal of Hub Spindle and Bearings

To remove the hub spindle and bearings having already removed the brake cover plate assemblies, lift out the felt washers, Part No. 21466, and distance washers, Part No. 30538. Now hit one end of the wheel spindle with a copper hammer or mallet, thus driving it out of the hub bringing one bearing with it and leaving the other in position in the hub. Drive the bearing off the spindle and insert the latter once more in the hub at the end from which it was removed. Now drive the spindle through the hub the other way, when it will bring out the remaining bearing.

6. Hub Bearings

These are deep groove single row journal ball bearings $\frac{5}{8}$ in. i/d by $1\frac{9}{16}$ in. o/d by $\frac{7}{16}$ in. wide. The Skefko Part No. is RLS5. Equivalent bearings of other makes are Hoffmann LS7, Ransome and Marles LJ$\frac{5}{8}$ in., Fischer LS7.

7. Fitting Limits for Bearings

The fit of the bearings in the hub barrel is important. The bearings are locked on the spindle between shoulders and the distance pieces, 30538, which in turn are held up by the cover plate nuts 31347. In order to prevent endways pre-loading of the bearings it is essential that there is a small clearance between the inner edge of the outer race of the bearing and the back of the recess in either end of the hub barrel. To prevent any possibility of sideways movement of the hub barrel on the bearings it is, therefore, necessary for the bearings to be a tight fit in the barrel but this fit must not be so tight as to close down the outer race of the bearing and thus overload the balls. The following are the manufacturing tolerances which control the fit of the bearings. The figures for the bearings themselves are for SKF bearings but other manufacturers' tolerances are similar.

Bearing o/d	1·5622/1·5617 in.
Housing bore	1·5620/1·5616 in.
Bearing bore	·6252/·6247 in.
Shaft diameter	·6252/·6248 in.

8. Refitting Ball Bearings

To refit the bearings in the hub two hollow drifts are required, as shown in Fig. 3. One

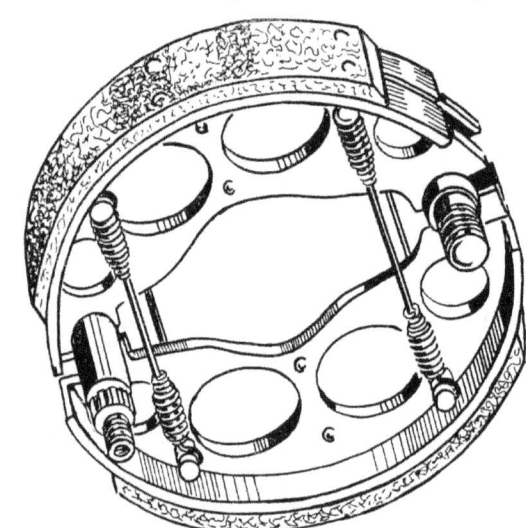

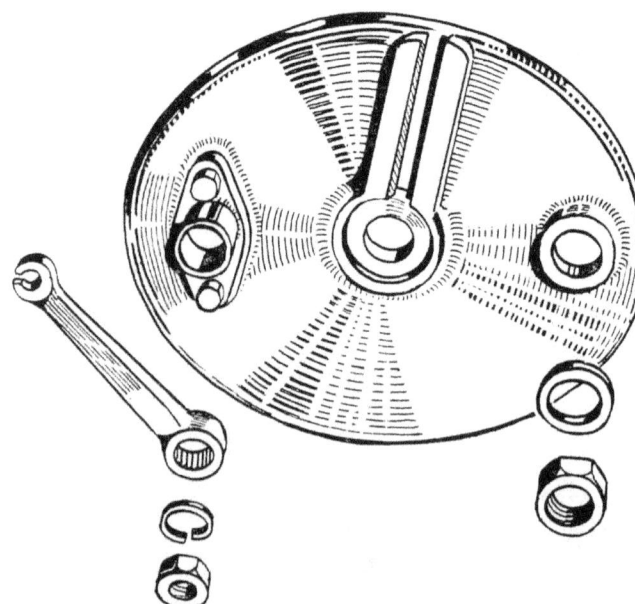

REMOVAL OF BRAKE SHOE ASSEMBLY
Fig. 2

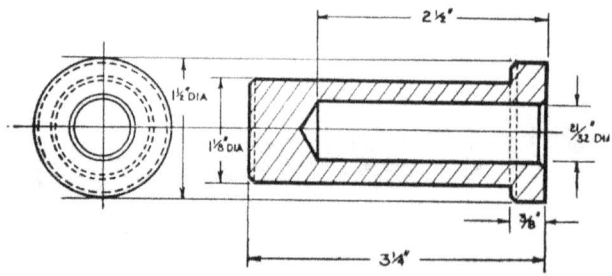

DRIFT FOR REFITTING BEARINGS
Fig. 3

bearing is first fitted to one end of the spindle by means of the hollow drift; the spindle and bearing are then entered into one end of the hub barrel which is then supported on one of the hollow drifts. The other bearing is then threaded over the upper end of the spindle and driven home by means of the second hollow drift either under a press or by means of a hammer which will thus drive both bearings into position simultaneously. In order to make quite sure that there is clearance between the inner faces of the outer bearing races and the bottom of the recesses, fit the distance washers, 30538, and the cover plate nuts, 31347, with either the cover plates themselves or additional packing washers behind the nuts. Tightening the nuts should not have any effect on the ease with which the spindle can be turned. If tightening the nuts makes the spindle hard to turn this may be taken as proof that the bearings are bottoming in the recesses in the hub barrel before they are solid against the shoulders on the spindle. In this case the bearing should be removed and a thin packing shim fitted between the inner race and the shoulder on the spindle.

9. Reassembly of Brake Shoes on to Cover Plates

Assemble each pair of shoes with their return springs on to the pivot pin and operating cam, putting a smear of grease in the grooves of the pivot pin and on the operating faces of the cam. Now fit the assembly into the cover plate, putting a smear of grease on to the cylindrical bearing surface of the operating cam and secure with the pivot pin locknut, 28715, and washer, 17551. Fit the operating lever, 38905 or 38906, on its splines in a position to suit the extent of wear on the linings and secure with the nut, 10314, and washer, 14613. Note that the position of the operating levers may have to be corrected when adjusting the brake after refitting the wheel. The range of adjustment can be extended by moving these levers on to different splines. Limit of wear is reached when the cam is turned through nearly 90° with the brake hard on so that there is a danger that the operating springs cannot return the brake to the off position.

10. Floating Cam Housings

Note that the cam housings, Part No. 26836, are intended to be left free to float. The bolt holes in the cam housings are slotted and the securing pins, Part No. 252, are provided with double coil spring washers beneath their heads to enable them to be tightened sufficiently to prevent the cam housings moving under the influence of road shocks, while at the same time they can be, and should be, left free enough to be capable of being moved by hand in the direction of the slots.

The pins, 252, are secured by locknuts, 7916, which are centre punched as an additional precaution.

The leading shoes (i.e. those towards the rear of the machine) have a servo action which render them more effective than the trailing shoes. This servo action causes the linings on the leading shoes to wear more quickly than those on the trailing shoes and at the same time tends to lift the leading shoes off the cams and press the trailing shoes harder on to the cams. With a fixed cam housing the result is that the majority of the cam pressure is applied to the less efficient trailing shoe. By leaving the housing free to float the cam can follow up the leading shoe thus maintaining equal pressure between the cam and the two shoes and so making full use of the more efficient leading shoe. Owing to the servo action the wear on the leading shoe with a floating cam housing is greater than that of the trailing shoe and in time the limit of float of the cam housing will be reached, after which the brake will continue to function as a fixed cam brake with some loss of efficiency. This can be restored by removing the shoes and fitting them in the opposite positions. Floating cam brakes are self-centering and there is no need to take any special precautions to see that the two linings are of equal thickness or that the brake shoe assembly is centered in the drum.

11. Refitting Brake Cover Plates

After assembling the brake shoe pivot pins and operating cams into the cover plates repack the hub bearings with grease. The recommended greases are Castrolease (Heavy), Mobilgrease (No. 4), Esso Grease, Energrease C3 or Shell Retinax A. These are all medium heavy lime soap or aluminium soap greases. The use of H.M.P. greases which have a soda soap base is not recommended as these tend to be slightly corrosive if any damp finds its way into the hubs.

Before fitting the distance washers and felt washers make sure that the inside of the brake drums are quite clean and free from oil or grease, damp, etc., and replace the brake cover plate assemblies. Securely tighten the cover plate nuts, 31347.

12. Wheel Rim

The rim is Type WM2—19 in. plunged and pierced with forty holes for spoke nipples. The spoke holes are symmetrical, i.e. the rim can be assembled to the hub either way round. Rim diameter after building is 19·062 in., tolerances on the circumference of the rim shoulders where the tyre fits being 59·930/59·870 in. The standard steel measuring tape for checking rims is $\frac{5}{16}$ in. wide, ·011 in. thick and its length is 59·964/59·904 in.

13. Spokes

The spokes are of the single butted type 8—10 gauge with 90° countersunk heads, angle of bend 95°—100°, length $6\frac{5}{8}$ in., thread diameter ·144 in., 40 threads per inch, thread form British Standard Cycle.

14. Wheel Building and Truing

The spokes are laced one over two and the wheel rim must be built central in relation to the nuts which secure the brake cover plates. The rim should be trued as accurately as possible, the maximum permissible run-out both sideways and radially being plus or minus $\frac{1}{32}$ in.

15. Tyre

The standard tyre is Dunlop 3·25—19 in. Ribbed tread.

When removing the tyre always start close to the valve and see that the edge of the cover at the other side of the wheel is pushed down into the well in the rim.

When replacing the tyre fit the part by the valve last, also with the edge of the cover at the other side of the wheel pushed down into the well.

If the correct method of fitting and removal of the tyre is adopted it will be found that the covers can be manipulated quite easily with the small levers supplied in the toolkit. The use of long levers and/or excessive force is liable to damage the walls of the tyre. After inflation make sure that the tyre is fitting evenly all the way round the rim. A line moulded on the wall of the tyre indicates whether or not the tyre is correctly fitted. If the tyre has a white mark, indicating a balance point, this should be fitted near the valve.

16. Tyre Pressure

The recommended pressure for the front tyre is 18 lb. per square inch for wheel loads up to 240 lb.

17. Lubrication

Two greasing points are provided both of which lead grease to the centre of the hub barrel. Unless the barrel is packed full with grease on assembly (which is apt to lead to trouble through grease finding its way past the felt seals on to the brake linings) these greasing points are of little value and the best way to grease the bearings is by packing them with grease after dismantling the hub as described above.

Note that the brake cams are drilled for grease passages but the ends of these are stopped up with countersunk screws instead of being fitted with grease nipples. This is done to prevent excessive greasing by over-enthusiastic owners. If the cams are smeared with grease on assembly they should require no further attention but in case of necessity it is possible to remove the screws, fit grease nipples in their place and grease the cams by this means.

SECTION K2

Front Wheel

With Single 6 in. Brake

Fitted to "250 Clipper," Model "S," Model "G" and Model "J2."
Also "350 Bullet," "500 Bullet," and "500 Twin" up to the end of 1954.

1. Removal from Fork

To remove the front wheel from the fork place the machine on the centre stand (in the case of the spring frame models) with sufficient packing (about 2 in.) beneath each side of the stand to lift the wheel clear of the ground when tilted back on to the rear wheel. In the case of Models G and J2 place the machine on the rear stand and place a suitable box or block beneath the crankcase to lift the front wheel clear of the ground. Slacken the brake cable adjustment and disconnect the cable from the handlebar lever and from the operating cam lever on the hub. Unscrew the four nuts securing the fork bottom tube lug caps (Part No. 38593) and allow the wheel to drop forwards out of the front fork. Make sure that the machine stands securely on the rear wheel and centre stand—if necessary place a weight on the saddle or a strut beneath the fork to ensure this.

2. Removal of Brake Cover Plate Assembly

Lock the brake "on" by pressure on the operating lever and unscrew the cover plate nut. The cover plate assembly can then be withdrawn from the brake drum.

3. Removal of Brake Shoes and Springs

This is best done by unscrewing the pivot pin locknuts and the operating lever nuts, after which the assembly of brake shoes, return springs, pivot pin and operating cam can be removed from the cover plate by light blows with a hammer and drift on the ends of the pivot pin and the operating cam. The return springs can then be unhooked from the spring posts in the brake shoes thus allowing the whole assembly to fall apart.

4. Replacing Brake Linings

Brake linings are supplied either in pairs ready drilled complete with rivets (Part No. 37786BX) or ready fitted to service replacement brake shoes (Part No. 38042). When riveting linings to shoes secure the two centre rivets first so as to ensure that the lining lies flat against the shoe. Standard linings are Ferodo MR41, which are drilled to receive cheese headed rivets.

5. Removal of Hub Spindle and Bearings

To remove the hub spindle and bearings having first removed the brake cover plate, unscrew the retaining nut and remove the dust excluder from the non-brake side of the hub. Now remove the felt washers and the distance washer from the brake side and hit one end of the spindle with a copper hammer or mallet, thus driving it out of the hub bringing one bearing with it and leaving the other in position in the hub. Drive the

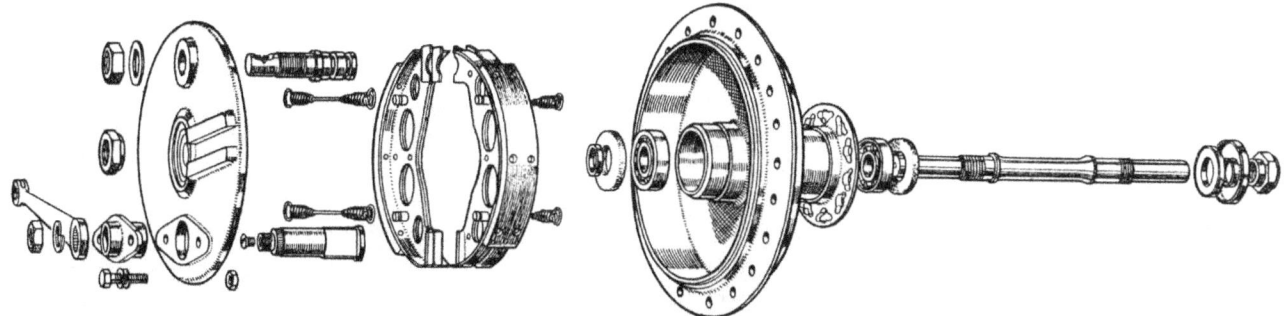

FRONT HUB
Fig. 1

7. Fitting Limits for Bearings

The fit of the bearings in the hub barrel is important. The bearings are locked on the spindle between shoulders and the distance pieces, 30528, which in turn are held up by the nuts on the spindle. In order to prevent endways pre-loading of the bearings it is essential that there is a small clearance between the inner edge of the outer race of the bearing and the back of the recess in either end of the hub barrel. To prevent any possibility of sideways movement of the hub barrel on the bearings it is, therefore, necessary for the bearings to be a tight fit in the barrel but this fit must not be so tight as to close down the outer race of the bearing and thus overload the balls. The following are the manufacturing tolerances which control the fit of the bearings. The figures for the bearings themselves are for SKF bearings but other manufacturers' tolerances are similar.

Bearing o/d	1·5622/1·5617 in.
Housing bore	1·5620/1·5616 in.
Bearing bore	·6252/·6247 in.
Shaft diameter	·6252/·6248 in.

8. Refitting Ball Bearings

Note that the two ends of the spindle are not identical. The end with the longer plain portion between the thread and the shoulder is fitted to the brake side of the wheel. To refit the bearings in the hub two hollow drifts are required, as shown in Fig. 3. One bearing is first fitted to one end of the spindle by means of the hollow drift; the spindle and bearing are then entered into one end of the hub barrel which is then supported on one of the hollow drifts. The other bearing is then threaded over the upper end of the spindle and driven home by means of the second hollow drift either under a press, or by means of a hammer, which will thus drive both bearings into position simultaneously. In order to make quite sure that there is clearance between the inner faces of the outer bearing races and the bottom of the recesses, fit the distance washer, cover plate, dust excluder and the nuts on the spindle. Tightening

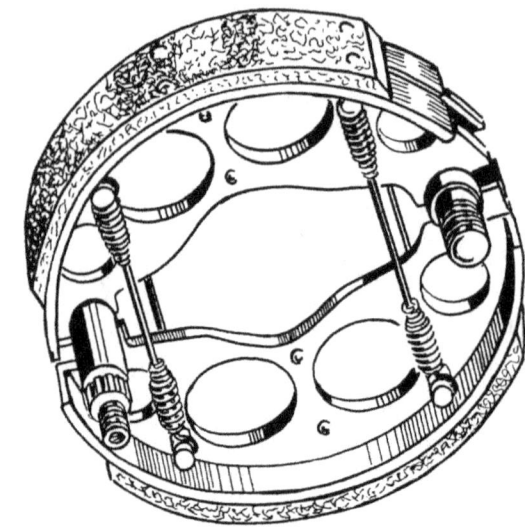

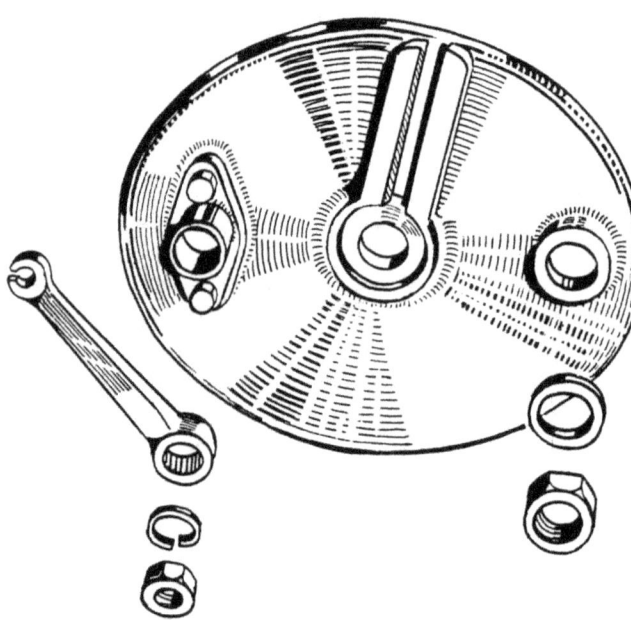

REMOVAL OF BRAKE SHOE ASSEMBLY
Fig. 2

bearing off the spindle and insert the latter once more in the hub at the end from which it was removed. Now drive the spindle through the hub the other way, when it will bring out the remaining bearing.

6. Hub Bearings

These are deep groove single row journal ball bearings, $\frac{5}{8}$ in. i/d by $1\frac{9}{16}$ in. o/d by $\frac{7}{16}$ in. wide. The Skefko Part No. is RLS5. Equivalent bearings of other makes are Hoffmann LS7, Ransome and Marles LJ$\frac{5}{8}$ in., Fischer LS7.

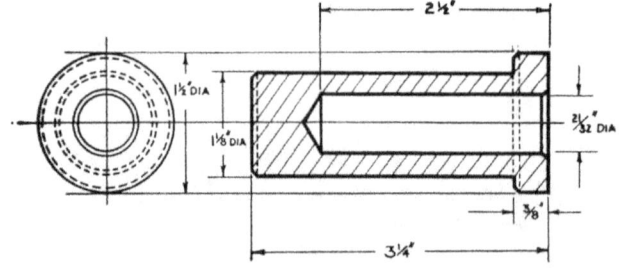

DRIFT FOR REFITTING BEARINGS
Fig. 3

the nuts should not have any effect on the ease with which the spindle can be turned. If tightening the nuts makes the spindle hard to turn this may be taken as proof that the bearings are bottoming in the recesses in the hub barrel before they are solid against the shoulders on the spindle. In this case the bearing should be removed and a thin packing shim fitted between the inner race and the shoulder on the spindle.

9. Reassembly of Brake Shoes to Cover Plate

Assemble the shoes with their return springs on to the pivot pin and operating cam, putting a smear of grease in the grooves of the pivot pin and on the operating faces of the cam. Now fit the assembly into the cover plate, putting a smear of grease on to the cylindrical bearing surface of the operating cam and secure with the pivot pin locknut and washer. Fit the operating lever on its spline in a position to suit the extent of wear on the linings and secure with the nut and washer. Note that the position of the operating lever may have to be corrected when adjusting the brake after refitting the wheel. The range of adjustment can be extended by moving this lever on to a different spline. Limit of wear is reached when the cam is turned through nearly 90° with the brake hard on so that there is a danger that the operating springs cannot return the brake to the off position.

10. Floating Cam Housing

Note that the cam housing is intended to be left free to float. The bolt holes in the cam housing are slotted and the securing pins are provided with double coil spring washers beneath their heads to enable them to be tightened sufficiently to prevent the cam housing moving under the influence of road shocks, while at the same time it can be, and should be, left free enough to be capable of being moved by hand in the direction of the slots. The pins are secured by locknuts which are centre punched as an additional precaution.

The leading shoe (i.e. the one towards the rear of the machine) has a servo action which renders it more effective than the trailing shoe. This servo action causes the lining on the leading shoe to wear more quickly than that on the trailing shoe and at the same time tends to lift the leading shoe off the cam and press the trailing shoe harder on to the cam. With a fixed cam housing the result is that the majority of the cam pressure is applied to the less efficient trailing shoe. By leaving the housing free to float the cam can follow up the leading shoe thus maintaining equal pressure between the cam and the two shoes and so making full use of the more efficient leading shoe. Owing to the servo action the wear on the leading shoe with a floating cam housing is greater than that of the trailing shoe and in time the limit of float of the cam housing will be reached, after which the brake will continue to function as a fixed cam brake with some loss of efficiency. This can be restored by removing the shoes and fitting them in the opposite positions. Floating cam brakes are self-centering and there is no need to take any special precautions to see that the two linings are of equal thickness, or that the brake shoe assembly is centered in the drum.

11. Refitting Brake Cover Plate

After assembling the brake shoe pivot pin and operating cam into the cover plate repack the hub bearings with grease. The recommended greases are Castrolease (Heavy), Mobilgrease (No. 4), Esso Grease, Energrease C3 or Shell Retinax A. These are all medium heavy lime soap or aluminium soap greases. The use of H.M.P. greases which have a soda soap base is not recommended as these tend to be slightly corrosive if any damp finds its way in to the hubs.

Before fitting the distance washer and felt washer make sure that the inside of the brake drum is quite clean and free from oil or grease, damp, etc. and replace the brake cover plate assembly. Securely tighten the cover plate nut.

12. Wheel Rims

The rim used on the "250 Clipper" and Model "S" is type WM1—19 in., internal width 1.60 in. The rim used on the other models is type WM2-19 in., internal width 1·580 in.

The rim diameter after building is the same in each case, i.e. 19·062 in., the tolerances on the circumference of the rim shoulders where the tyre fits being 59·930/59·870 in. The standard steel measuring tape for checking rims is $\frac{5}{16}$ in. wide, ·011 in. thick and its length is 59·964/59·904 in. All rims are pierced with forty holes for spoke nipples.

Note that two makes of rim are used— "Dunlop" and "Palmer Jointless." These differ in the positions of the pierced spoke holes. The Dunlop rims have a group of three holes on one side of the centre line, then a single hole on the other side, a further group of three and a single hole and so on. Palmer rims have the holes alternately spaced either side of the centre line. Both rims are interchangeable and both use the same length spokes but the method of lacing the wheel is different (see Subsection 14). Neither type of rim is symmetrical and care must be taken

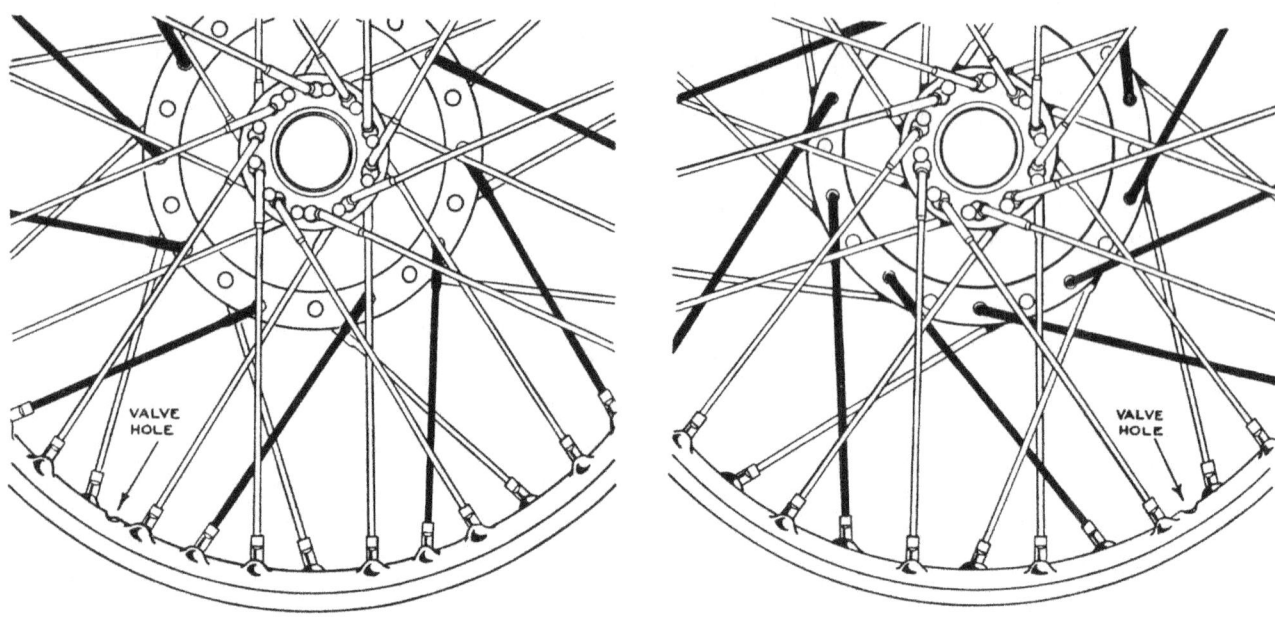

WHEEL LACING

Fig. 4A Dunlop Rim   Fig. 4B Palmer Rim

that they are built the right way round into the wheel.

13. Spokes

The spokes are of the single butted type 8—10 gauge with 90° countersunk heads, angle of bend 95°—100°, length $6\frac{5}{8}$ in. brake drum side, $8\frac{1}{2}$ in. spoke flange side, thread diameter ·144 in., 40 threads per inch, thread form British Standard Cycle.

14. Wheel Building and Truing

The spokes are laced one over two on the brake side and one over three on the spoke flange side of the wheel. The wheel must be built central in relation to the faces of the nuts on the spindle. The rim should be trued as accurately as possible, the maximum permissible run-out both sideways and radially being plus or minus $\frac{1}{32}$ in.

Figs. 4A and 4B show the difference between the lacing when using Dunlop and Palmer rims. The key to correct lacing is the inside spokes to the large flange on the brake drum side which must slope in the direction shown in Fig. 4. With the Dunlop rim this spoke goes to the middle hole of one of the groups of three (see Subsection 12) and the rim must be built into the wheel so that these groups of three holes are on the right of the centre line when the brake drum is on the left, i.e. the inside spokes to the large flange cross from the left to the right of the centre line.

With the Palmer rim the spokes from the large flange on the brake drum side go to the more steeply angled holes in the rim which must be on the left of the centre line when the brake drum is on the left, i.e. none of the spokes crosses from left to right of the centre line.

15. Tyres

Standard tyres on the "250 Clipper" and "Model S" are Dunlop 3·00—19 in. Lightweight Reinforced and on the other models Dunlop 3·25—19 in. Ribbed.

When removing the tyre always start close to the valve and see that the edge of the cover at the other side of the wheel is pushed down into the well in the rim.

When replacing the tyre fit the part by the valve last, also with the edge of the cover at the other side of the wheel pushed down into the well.

If the correct method of fitting and removal of the tyre is adopted it will be found that the covers can be manipulated quite easily with the small levers supplied in the toolkit. The use of long levers and/or excessive force is liable to damage the walls of the tyre. After inflation make sure that the tyre is fitting evenly all the way round the rim. A line moulded on the wall of the tyre indicates whether or not the tyre is correctly fitted. If the tyre has a white mark, indicating a balance point, this should be fitted near the valve.

16. Tyre Pressures

The load which the tyre will carry at different inflation pressures is shown below:—

Tyre Section Inches	Inflation Pressure—lb. per sq. in.		
	18	20	24
	Load per tyre—lb.		
3·00	180	200	240
3·25	240	280	300

17. Lubrication

A greasing point is provided in the centre of the hub barrel. Unless the barrel is packed full with grease on assembly (which is apt to lead to trouble through grease finding its way past the felt seals on to the brake linings) this greasing point is of little value and the best way to grease the bearings is by packing them with grease after dismantling the hub as described above.

Note that the brake cam is drilled for a grease passage but the end of this is stopped up with a countersunk screw instead of being fitted with a grease nipple. This is done to prevent excessive greasing by over-enthusiastic owners. If the cam is smeared with grease on assembly it should require no further attention but in case of necessity it is possible to remove the screw, fit a grease nipple in its place and grease the cam by this means.

NOTES

SECTION L1

Rear Wheel (Detachable Type)

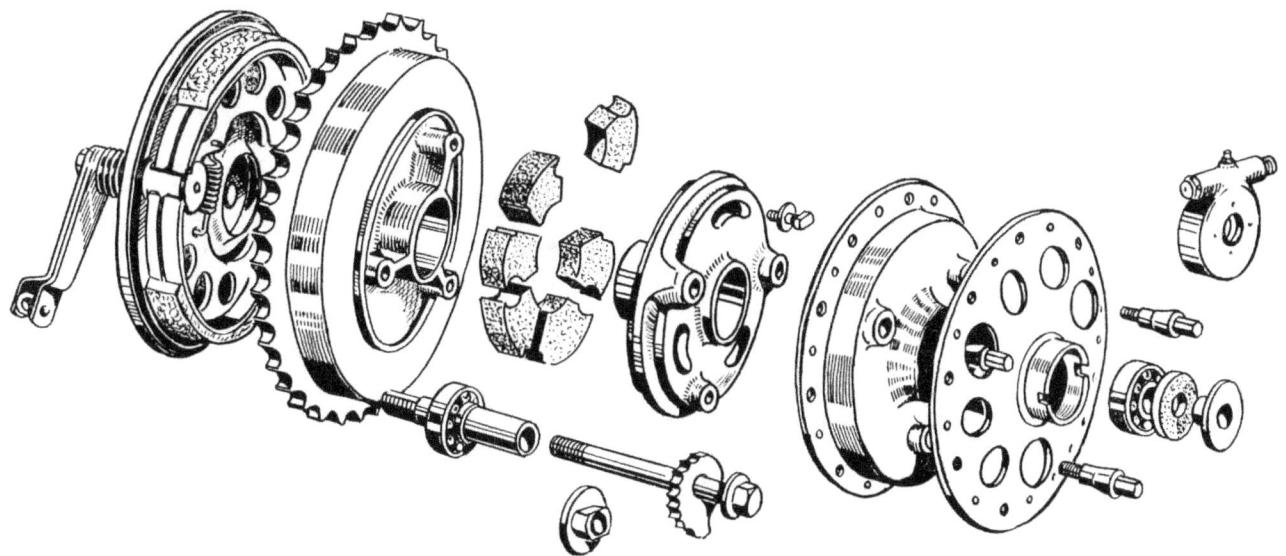

DETACHABLE REAR WHEEL
Fig. 1

1. Description

This wheel is of the "detachable" type which enables the main portion of the wheel to be removed from the machine without disturbing the chain or brake. The wheel incorporates the well known Enfield cush drive and also a 7 in. internal expanding brake.

2. Removal and Replacement of Main Portion of Wheel for Tyre Repairs, etc.

Place the machine on the centre stand, if necessary putting packing pieces beneath the legs of the stand to lift the wheel clear of the ground. Remove the dual seat (if fitted) and the detachable portion of the rear mudguard. Unscrew the three attachment bolts, 39316. Unscrew the loose section of the spindle, 39336, and withdraw this together with the chain adjuster cam, 36649, preferably marking this to ensure that it is replaced in the same position. Now slide the distance collar, 39323, out of the fork end and lift away the speedometer drive gearbox which can be left attached to the driving cable. The spacing collar, 39321, and the felt washer behind it may now be removed to prevent risk of them falling out when manipulating the tyre. If, however, these are too tight a fit in the hub to come out easily they may be left in place. The main body of the wheel can now be pulled across to the right hand side of the machine, thus disengaging it from the fixed section of the hub barrel and the cush drive shell and enabling the wheel to be lifted out of the machine.

When replacing the main portion of the wheel reverse the foregoing procedure, locating the wheel by the loose section of the spindle with the speedometer drive gearbox and distance collar in position before replacing the three attachment bolts, 39316. The cush drive shell can be prevented from rotating when turning the wheel to line up the holes for the attachment bolts if the machine is placed in gear or the rear brake is operated. When replacing the speedometer drive gearbox care must be taken to ensure that the driving dogs inside the gearbox engage with the slots in the end of the hub barrel. Before tightening the centre spindle make sure that the speedometer drive gearbox is correctly positioned so that there is no sharp bend in the driving cable.

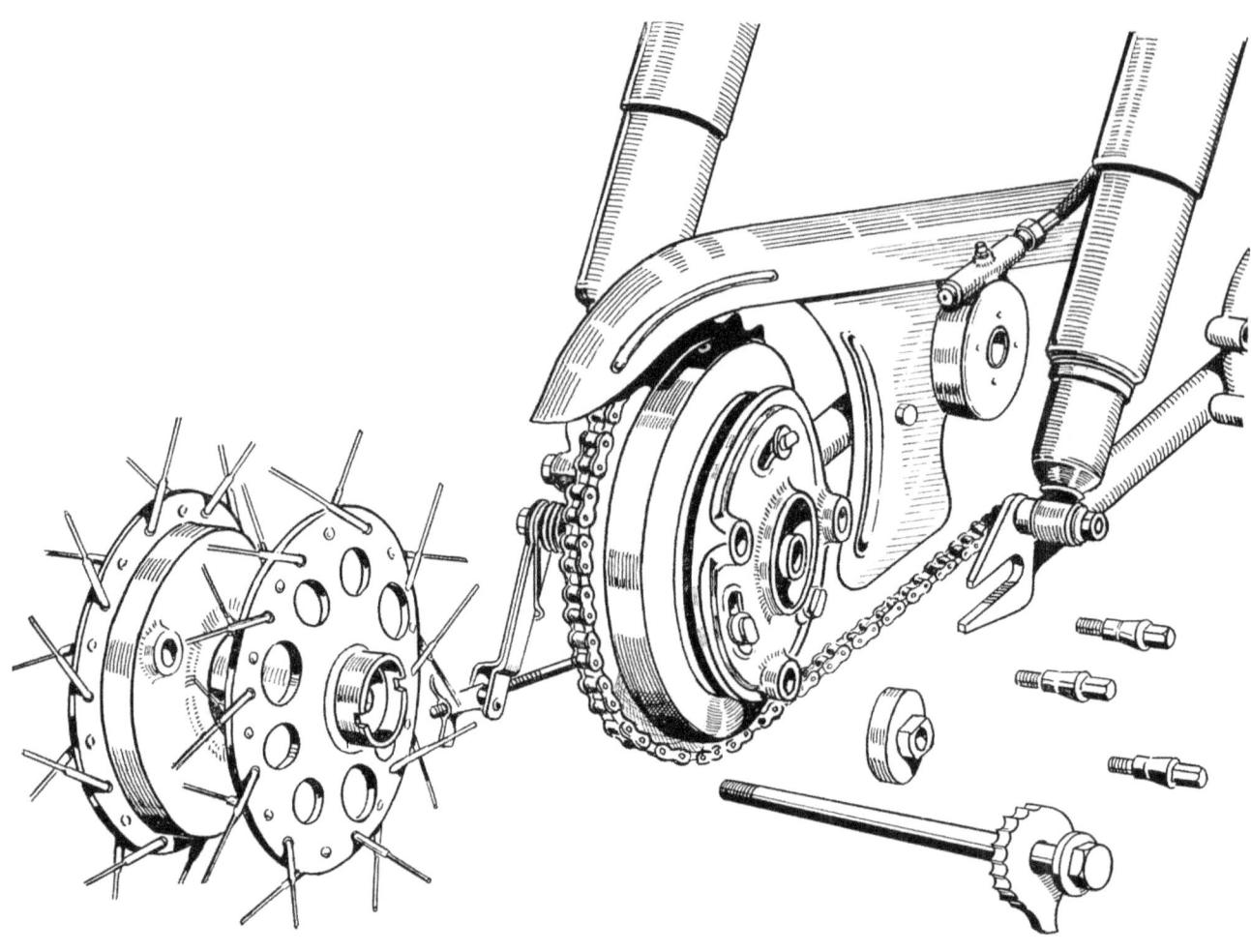

REMOVAL OF MAIN PORTION OF WHEEL
Fig. 2

3. Removal and Replacement of Complete Wheel for Access to Brake

Place the machine on the centre stand and remove the dual seat (if fitted) and detachable portion of the rear mudguard as if for removal of the main portion of the wheel only. Disconnect the rear driving chain at the spring link and remove the chain from the rear wheel sprocket leaving it in position on the gearbox countershaft sprocket. Unscrew the rear brake rod adjusting nut completely and depress the brake pedal so as to disengage the rod from the trunnion in the brake operating lever. Unscrew the brake cover plate anchor nut, 7598, and remove this together with the washer behind it. Unscrew the loose section of the spindle, 39336, two or three turns and the spindle nut, 36651, by a similar amount. Mark the chain adjuster cams to ensure replacing in the same position.* Disconnect the speedometer driving cable and slide the wheel out of the fork ends, tilting it so as to disengage the end of the brake shoe pivot pin from the slot in the fork end.

When replacing the wheel make sure that the dogs on the gear in the speedometer drive gearbox are engaged with the slots in the end of the hub barrel. Make sure also that the speedometer drive gearbox is correctly positioned so that there is no sudden bend in the driving cable. When

---

* Note that the wheel is not necessarily correctly lined up when the same notch position is used on both adjuster cams. Once the position of the cams which gives correct alignment has been found this alignment will, however, be maintained if both cams are moved the same number of notches.

replacing the connecting link in the driving chain make sure that the closed end of the spring link points in the direction of travel of the chain. Replace the chain adjuster cams in their original positions or, if necessary, turn each of them the same number of notches to tension the chain and maintain correct wheel alignment. Do not forget to refit the brake rod and adjust the brake so that the wheel turns freely when the brake is off, while at the same time only a small travel of the brake pedal is necessary to put the brake on.

4. Removal of Brake Shoes for Replacement, Fitting New Linings, etc.

Remove the complete wheel as described above, then remove the spindle nut, 36651, chain adjuster and the distance collar, 39315, thus permitting the complete brake cover plate with operating cam, pivot pin, shoes and return springs to be lifted off the hub spindle. The brake shoes can then be removed after detaching the return springs.

5. Replacing Brake Linings

Brake linings are supplied either in pairs ready drilled complete with rivets, 37787BX, or ready fitted to service replacement brake shoes, 38043. When riveting linings to shoes secure the two centre rivets first so as to ensure that the lining lies flat against the shoe. Standard linings are Ferodo MR41 which are drilled to receive cheese headed rivets.

6. Removal of Brake Operating Cam and Brake Shoe Pivot Pin

The pivot pin is threaded into the torque plate, from which it can be unscrewed after removing the locknut 39351. (Note the Part Number of the torque plate only is 36527 while the thin pressed steel cover plate is 36526. These two are riveted together and supplied as one unit Part Number 32525).

To remove the operating cam unscrew the nut, 10314, which secures the operating lever to the splines on the cam. A sharp tap on the end of the cam spindle will now free the lever after which the cam can be withdrawn from its housing.

7. Cush Drive

The sprocket/brake drum, 39301, is free to rotate on the hub barrel. Three radial vanes are formed on the back of the brake drum and three similar vanes are formed on the cush drive shell, 39302. Six rubber blocks are fitted between the vanes on the brake drum and those on the cush drive shell, thus permitting only a small amount of angular movement of the sprocket/

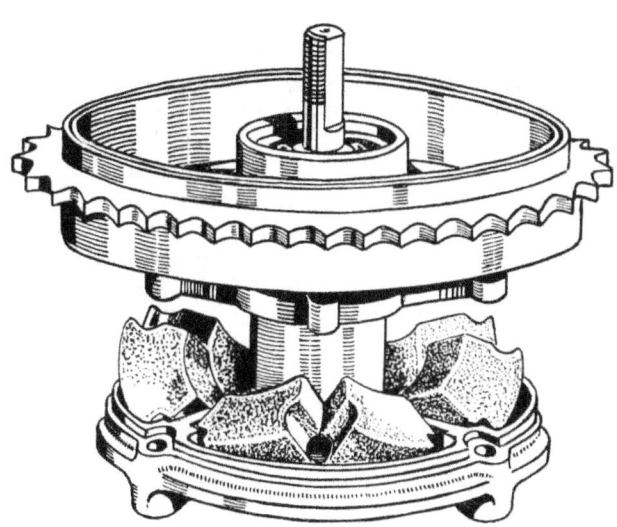

RE-ASSEMBLY OF CUSH DRIVE
Fig. 3

brake drum relative to the hub barrel and transmitting both driving and braking torques and smoothing out harshness and irregularity in the former.

If the cush drive rubbers become worn so that the amount of free movement measured at the tyre exceeds $\frac{1}{2}$ in. to 1 in., the rubbers should be replaced. To obtain access to them remove the complete wheel as described above, then unscrew the loose section of the spindle, 39336, completely and also the three attachment bolts, 39316. The main portion of the wheel can then be lifted away from the assembly consisting of the fixed section of the hub barrel, fixed portion of the spindle, sprocket/brake drum complete with brake and the cush drive shell. Now remove the brake cover plate complete with brake shoes as described above, thus giving access to the three cush drive pin locking pins, 8718. Unscrew these and then unscrew the cush drive pins, 39310, thus enabling the sprocket/brake drum to be separated from the cush drive shell, after which the six cush drive rubbers can be lifted out.

When reassembling the cush drive the entry of the vanes between the rubbers will be facilitated if the latter are fitted into the driving shell first and then tilted. The rubbers should be liberally painted with soapsuds to facilitate entry of the vanes. The three cush drive pins, 39310, should be tightened as far as possible and then slackened back half to one turn to enable the locking pins, 8718, to be fitted.

When reassembling the cush drive, coat the inside of the bore of the sprocket/brake drum liberally with grease where it fits over the hub barrel. Put grease also behind the washers on the three cush drive pins, 39310.

8. Removal of Ball Bearings

To remove the ball bearings take the complete wheel out of the machine and separate the main portion of the wheel from the sprocket/brake drum, cush drive shell assembly as described above. To remove the bearing from the fixed section of the hub barrel first remove the brake cover plate complete with brake shoe assembly; then remove the felt washer, 9484, and distance collar, 11203. Now screw the loose section of the spindle into the fixed section and drive out the bearing by hitting the hexagon headed end of the loose section of the spindle.

To remove the bearing from the loose half of the hub barrel first lift away the distance collar, 39323, speedometer drive gearbox, the spacing collar, 39321, and the felt washer, 9484. Now enter the loose section of the spindle into the distance tube, 39312, from the driving sprocket end and drive out the distance tube with the two distance tube washers, 39313, and the bearing by means of a hammer and drift applied to the hexagon headed end of the loose section of the spindle.

9. Hub Bearings

These are deep groove single row journal ball bearings $\frac{5}{8}$ in. i/d by $1\frac{13}{16}$ in. o/d by $\frac{5}{8}$ in. wide. The Skefko Part Number is RMS5. Equivalent bearings of other makes are Hoffmann MS7, Ransome and Marles MJ$\frac{5}{8}$ in., Fischer MS7.

10. Fitting Limits for Bearings

The fit of the bearings in the hub barrel is important. The bearings are locked on to the spindle by the various distance pieces. In order to prevent endways pre-loading of the bearings it is essential that, when everything is locked up, there is a small clearance between the inner edge of the outer race of the bearing and the back of the recess in each half of the hub barrel. To prevent any possibility of sideways movement of the hub barrel on the bearings it is, therefore, necessary for the bearings to be a tight fit in the barrel but this fit must not be so tight as to close down the outer race of the bearing and thus overload the balls. The following are the manufacturing tolerances which control the fit of the bearings. The figures for the bearings themselves are for SKF bearings but other manufacturers' tolerances are similar.

Bearing o/d	1·8122/1·8117 in.
Housing bore	1·8115/1·8110 in.
Bearing bore	·6252/·6247 in.
Shaft diameter (Loose side)	·624/·622 in.
Shaft diameter (Fixed side)	·6252/·6248 in.

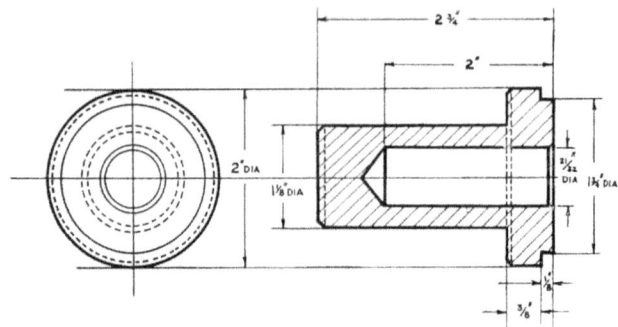

DRIFT FOR REFITTING BEARING (FIXED SECTION)
Fig. 4

11. Refitting Ball Bearings

In order to prevent the possibility of endways pre-loading of the bearings the following procedure should be followed carefully when fitting new bearings or refitting old ones—

(a) The bearing in the fixed section of the hub barrel should be fitted first together with the fixed section of the spindle using a special drift, as shown in Fig. 4, preferably under a press, if necessary using light hammer blows. This drift prevents the bearing being pushed right down to the bottom of its recess.

(b) The bearing in the loose half of the barrel is pressed in using either the drift part of E.4823,* or a suitable piece of tube $1\frac{3}{4}$ in. diameter with the end ground square so as to put pressure on the outer race of the bearing only. This bearing should be pressed or knocked only about half way into its recess at the present stage.

(c) The two parts of the wheel are put together and the three attachment bolts, 39316, are fitted and tightened.

(d) The bearing in the loose half of the barrel is now driven home by means of the same drift until further movement is prevented by the inner face of the inner race coming against the end of the distance tube, 39312.

As a check that the bearings are fitted correctly the loose section of the spindle and the spindle nut, 36651, can be fitted with suitable distance pieces beneath them so that, when the spindle and spindle nut are tightened, pressure is put on to the inner races of the bearings. When tightened solid the spindle should still be quite free to turn with the fingers. If the spindle is free before the nuts are tightened but not free afterwards, it is evident that there is end load on the bearings due to the bearing in the loose half of the hub not having been fitted deep enough in its recess. In this

---
* See Motor Cycle Service Tools Manual.

12. Reassembly of Brake Shoes, Pivot Pin and Operating Cam into Cover Plate

No difficulty should be experienced in carrying out these operations. Make sure that the pivot pin is really tight in the cover plate and put a smear of grease in the grooves of the pivot pin and on the operating face of the cam; also on to the cylindrical bearing surface of the operating cam if this has been removed. Fit the operating lever and trunnion, 23371, on its splines in a position to suit the extent of wear on the linings and secure with the nut. The range of adjustment can be extended by moving the lever on to a different spline.

13. Centering Cam Housing

Note that the bolt holes in the cam housing, 26347, are slotted, thus enabling the brake shoe assembly to be centered in the drum. It is not intended that on rear brakes the cam housing should be left free to float but the shoes should be centered by leaving the screws, 26309 and 35140, just short of dead tight. The brake cover plate assembly with the shoes should then be fitted over the spindle into the brake drum and the brake applied as hard as possible by means of the operating lever. This will centre the shoes in the drum. The screws should then be tightened dead tight and secured with the locknuts. If the shoes are not correctly centered the brake will be either ineffective or too fierce, depending on whether the trailing or leading shoe first makes contact with the drum. With the brake assembly correctly centered and the screws securing the cam housing correctly tightened wear on both linings should be approximately equal.

14. Final Reassembly of Hub before Replacing Wheel

Before replacing the felt washers which form the grease seals, pack both bearings with grease. Recommended greases are Castrolease (Heavy), Mobilgrease (No. 4), Esso Grease, Energrease C3 or Shell Retinax A. These are all medium heavy lime soap or aluminium soap greases. The use of H.M.P. greases which have a soda soap base is not recommended as these tend to be slightly corrosive if any damp finds its way into the hubs.

Make sure that the inside of the brake drum is quite free from oil or grease, damp, etc. Replace the felt washers, distance collars, the brake cover plate assembly, speedometer drive gearbox, distance collars, 39315 and 39323, chain adjuster cams, the loose section of the spindle and the spindle nut 36651. The wheel is then ready for reassembly into the machine.

15. Wheel Rim

The wheel rim is type WM2—19 in. plunged and pierced with forty holes for spoke nipples. The spoke holes are symmetrical, i.e. the rim can be assembled to the hub either way round. The rim diameter after building is 19·062 in., the tolerances on the circumference of the rim shoulders where the tyre fits being 59·930/59·870 in. The standard steel measuring tape for checking rims is $\frac{5}{16}$ in. wide, ·011 in. thick and its length is 59·964/59·904 in.

16. Spokes

The spokes are of the single butted type 8—10 gauge with 90° countersunk heads, angle of bend 95°—100°, length $6\frac{5}{8}$ in., thread diameter ·144 in., 40 threads per inch, thread form British Standard Cycle.

17. Wheel Building and Truing

The spokes are laced one over two and the wheel rim must be built central in relation to the outer faces of the distance collars 39315 and 39323. The rim should be trued as accurately as possible, the maximum permissible run-out both sideways and radially being plus or minus $\frac{1}{32}$ in.

18. Tyre

The standard tyre is Dunlop 3·50—19 in. Universal tread.

When removing the tyre always start close to the valve and see that the edge of the cover at the other side of the wheel is pushed down into the well in the rim.

When replacing the tyre fit the part by the valve last, also with the edge of the cover at the other side of the wheel pushed down into the well.

If the correct method of fitting and removal of the tyre is adopted it will be found that the covers can be manipulated quite easily with the small levers supplied in the toolkit. The use of long levers and/or excessive force is liable to damage the walls of the tyre. After inflation make sure that the tyre is fitting evenly all the way round the rim. A line moulded on the wall of the tyre indicates whether or not the tyre is correctly fitted. If the tyre has a white mark indicating a balance point, this should be fitted near the valve.

19. Tyre Pressures

The recommended pressures for the rear tyre are 16 lb. per square inch for wheel loads not exceeding 280 lb., 18 lb. per square inch for loads up to 320 lb., 20 lb. per square inch for loads up to 350 lb., 24 lb. per square inch for loads up to 400 lb., 28 lb. per square inch up to 450 lbs. and 32 lb. per square inch up to 500 lb.

20. Lubrication

A greasing point is provided in the centre of the hub barrel. Unless the barrel is packed full with grease on assembly (which is apt to lead to trouble through grease finding its way past the felt seals on to the brake linings) this greasing point is of little value and the best way to grease the bearings is by packing them with grease after dismantling the hub as described above.

Note that the brake cam is drilled for a grease passage but the end of this is stopped up with a countersunk screw instead of being fitted with a grease nipple. This is done to prevent excessive greasing by over-enthusiastic owners. If the cam is smeared with grease on assembly it should require no further attention but in case of necessity it is possible to remove the screw, fit a grease nipple in its place and grease the cam by this means.

SECTION L2

Rear Wheel (Non-Detachable Type)

Part No. 36788 for "500 Twin" and "350 Bullet"; Part No. 37278 for "Meteor 700" and "500 Bullet."

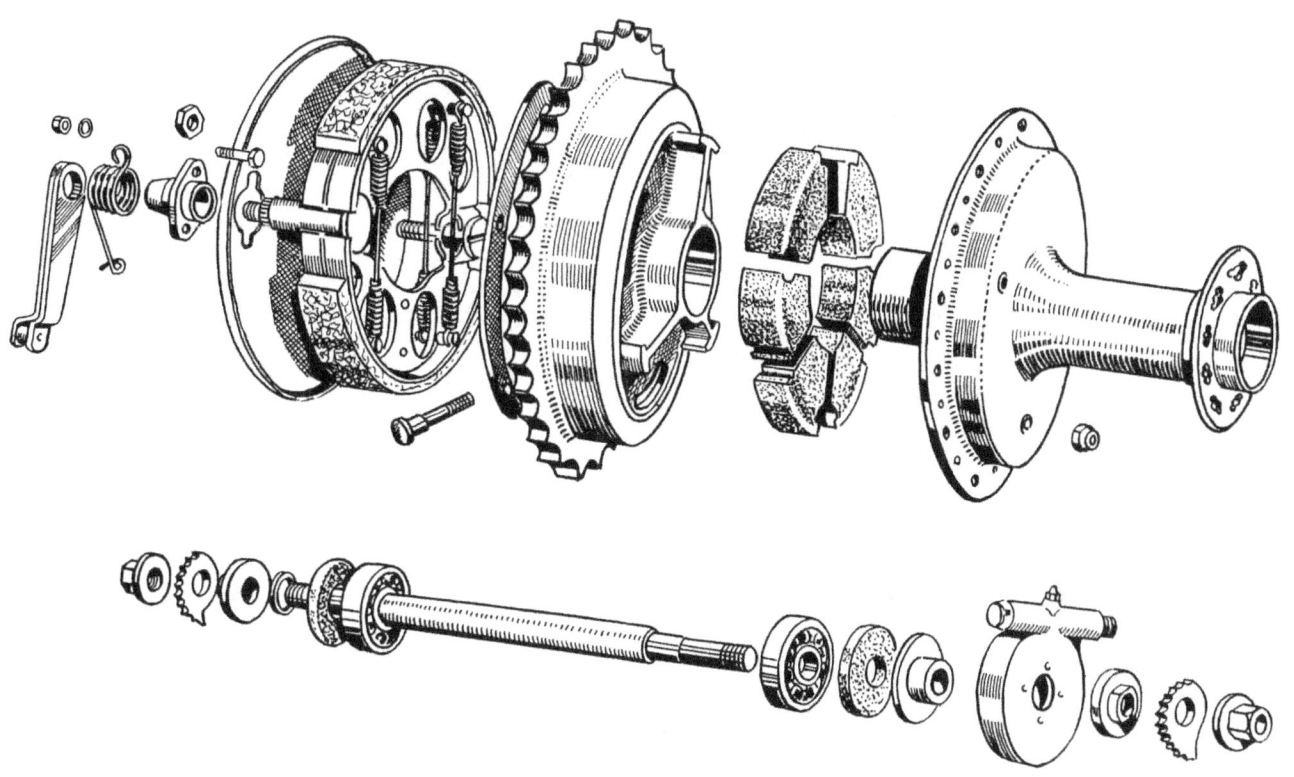

REAR HUB
Fig. 1

1. Description

These instructions cover the servicing of two different rear wheels, both of the non-detachable type incorporating a rubber cush drive and an internal expanding brake. Both types have a solid spindle and give a 3 in. chain line.

The heavier type used on the "Meteor 700" and "500 Twin" has a 7 in. diameter brake drum while the lighter type used on the "500 Twin" and "350 Bullet" has a 6 in. diameter brake.

2. Removal and Replacement of Wheel

Place machine on the centre stand, if necessary putting packing pieces beneath the legs of the stand to lift the wheel clear of the ground. Remove the dual seat, if fitted, and the detachable portion of the rear mudguard. Disconnect the rear driving chain at the spring link and remove the chain from the rear wheel sprocket, leaving it in position on the gearbox countershaft sprocket. Unscrew the rear brake rod adjusting nut completely and depress the brake pedal so as to disengage the rod from the trunnion in the brake operating lever. Unscrew the brake cover plate anchor nut and remove this together with the washer behind it. Disconnect the speedometer driving cable, loosen the spindle nuts and mark the chain adjuster cams to ensure replacing in the same position. Slide the wheel out of the fork ends, tilting it so as to disengage the end of the brake shoe pivot pin from the slot in the fork end.

When replacing the wheel make sure that the dogs on the speedometer drive gearbox are engaged with the slots in the end of the hub barrel. Make sure also that the speedometer drive gearbox is correctly positioned so that there is no sudden bend in the driving cable. Make sure that the closed end of the spring link points in the direction of travel of the chain. Replace the chain adjuster cams in their original positions or, if necessary, turn each of them the same number of notches to tension the chain and maintain correct wheel alignment. Do not forget to refit the brake rod and adjust the brake so that the wheel turns freely while the brake is off, while at the same time only a small travel of the brake pedal is necessary to put the brake on.

3. Removal of Brake Shoes for Replacement, Fitting New Linings, etc.

Remove the complete wheel as described above, then remove the left hand spindle nut, chain adjuster and distance collar, thus permitting the complete brake cover plate with operating cam, pivot pin, shoes and return springs to be lifted off the hub spindle.

In the case of the 7 in. brake fitted to the "Meteor 700" and "500 Bullet" Models the brake shoes can then be removed, after detaching the return springs.

In the case of the 6 in. brake fitted to the "500 Twin" and "350 Bullet" Models, unscrew the pivot pin locknut and the operating lever nut, after which the assembly of the brake shoes, return springs, pivot pin and operating cam can be removed from the cover plate by unscrewing the pivot pin and applying light blows with a hammer and drift on the end of the operating cam. The return springs can then be unhooked from the spring posts in the brake shoes, thus allowing the whole assembly to fall apart.

4. Replacing Brake Linings

Brake linings are supplied either in pairs ready drilled complete with rivets, Part No. 37786BX (6 in. shoes) or 37787BX (7 in. shoes), or ready fitted to service replacement brake shoes, Part No. 38042 (6 in. shoes) or 38043 (7 in. shoes). When riveting linings to shoes secure the two centre rivets first so as to ensure that the lining lies flat against the shoe. Standard linings are Ferodo MR41 which are drilled to receive cheese headed rivets.

5. Removal of Hub Spindle and Bearings

To remove the hub spindle and bearings, having already removed the brake cover plate assembly and speedometer drive gearbox, lift out the felt washers and distance pieces then hit one end of the spindle with a copper hammer or mallet thus driving it out of the hub, bringing one bearing with it and leaving the other in position in the hub. Drive the bearing off the spindle and insert the latter once more in the hub at the end from which it was removed. Now drive the spindle through the hub in the opposite direction, when it will bring out the remaining bearing.

6. Hub Bearings

These are deep groove single row journal ball bearings. The lighter bearings used in the "350 Bullet" and "500 Twin" hubs are $\frac{5}{8}$ in. i/d by $1\frac{9}{16}$ in. o/d by $\frac{7}{16}$ in. wide. The Skefko Part No. is RLS5. Equivalent bearings of other makes are Hoffmann LS7, Ransome and Marles LJ $\frac{5}{8}$ in., Fischer LS7.

The heavier bearings used in the "Meteor 700" and "500 Bullet" Models are $\frac{5}{8}$ in. i/d by $1\frac{13}{16}$ in. o/d by $\frac{5}{8}$ in. wide. The Skefko Part No. is RMS5. Equivalent bearings of other makes are Hoffmann MS7, Ransome and Marles MJ $\frac{5}{8}$ in., Fischer MS7.

7. Fitting Limits for Bearings

The fit of the bearings in the hub barrel is important. The bearings are locked on the spindle between shoulders and the distance pieces, which in turn are held up by the cover plate nuts. In order to prevent endways pre-loading of the bearings it is essential that there is a small clearance between the inner edge of the outer race of the bearing and the back of the recess in either end of the hub barrel. To prevent any possibility of sideways movement of the hub barrel on the bearings it is, therefore, necessary for the bearings to be a tight fit in the barrel but this fit must not be so tight as to close down the outer race of the bearing and thus overload the balls. The following are the manufacturing tolerances which control the fit of the bearings. The figures for the bearings themselves are for SKF bearings but other manufacturers' tolerances are similar.

	"350 Bullet" and "500 Twin"	"Meteor 700" and "500 Bullet"
Bearing o/d	1·5622/1·5617 in.	1·8122/1·8117 in.
Housing bore	1·5620/1·5615 in.	1·8115/1·8110 in.
Bearing bore	·6252/·6247 in.	·6252/·6247 in.
Shaft diameter	·6252/·6248 in.	·6252/·6248 in.

8. Refitting Ball Bearings

To refit the bearings in the hub two hollow drifts are required, as shown in Figs. 2 and 3. One bearing is first fitted to one end of the spindle by means of the hollow drift; the spindle and bearing are then entered into one end of the hub barrel which is then supported on one of the hollow drifts. The other bearing is then threaded over the upper end of the spindle and driven home by means of the second hollow drift either under a press or by means of a hammer which will thus drive both bearings into position simultaneously.

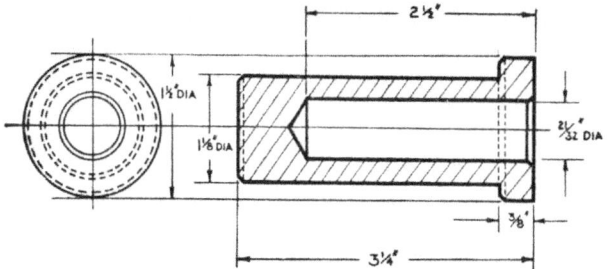

DRIFT FOR REFITTING BEARINGS
"350 Bullet"   "500 Twin"
Fig. 2

In order to make quite sure that there is clearance between the inner faces of the outer bearings and the bottom of the recesses fit the distance washers against the inner races of the bearings and either fit the assembly of brake cover plate, speedometer gearbox, etc., or make up this distance with tubular distance pieces. Fit and tighten the spindle nuts. Tightening the nuts

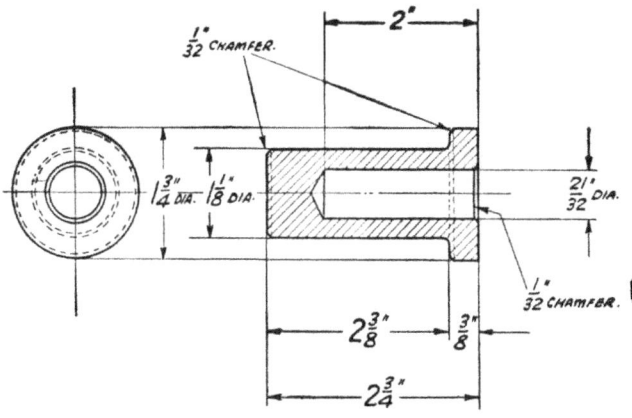

DRIFT FOR REFITTING BEARINGS
"Meteor 700"   "500 Bullet"
Fig. 3

should not have any effect on the ease with which the spindle can be turned. If tightening the nuts makes the spindle hard to turn this may be taken as proof that the bearings are bottoming in the recesses in the hub barrel before they are solid against the shoulders on the spindle. In this case the bearing should be removed and a thin packing shim fitted between the inner race and the shoulder on the spindle.

9. Removal of Brake Operating Cam and Brake Shoe Pivot Pin

The method of doing this has already been described in Paragraph 3 dealing with the 6 in. brake. The method is precisely the same for the 7 in. brake except that, owing to the different type of return springs used, it is, in this case, possible to remove the shoes from the pivot pin and operating cam before the latter are removed from the cover plate.

10. Cush Drive

The sprocket/brake drum is free to rotate on the hub barrel. Three radial vanes are formed on the back of the brake drum and three similar vanes are formed on the cush drive shell. Six rubber blocks are fitted between the vanes on the brake drum and those on the cush drive shell, thus permitting only a small amount of angular movement of the sprocket/brake drum relative to the hub barrel and transmitting both driving and braking torque and smoothing out harshness and irregularity in the former.

If the cush drive rubbers become worn so that the amount of free movement measured at the tyre exceeds $\frac{1}{2}$ in. to 1 in., the rubbers should be replaced. To obtain access to them remove the complete wheel as described above, remove the brake cover plate complete with the brake shoe assembly, unscrew the three Simmonds nuts at the back of the cush drive shell—if necessary holding the studs, 32431, by means of the flats on the heads inside the brake drum. Drive out the three studs into the brake drum after which the sprocket/brake drum can be separated from

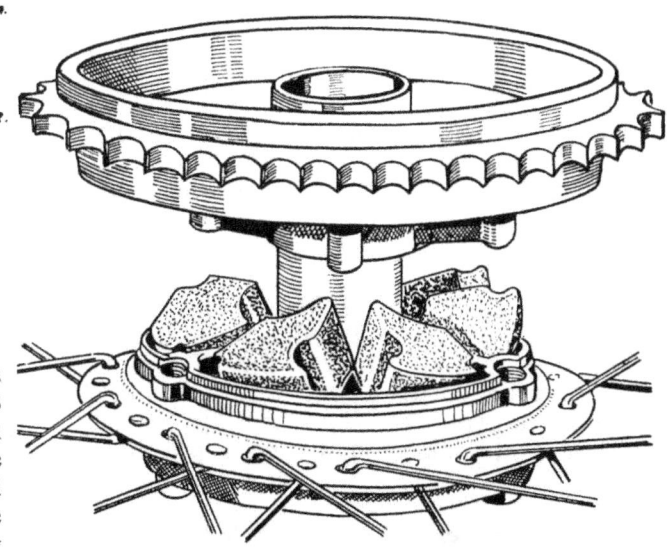

REASSEMBLY OF CUSH DRIVE
Fig. 4

the cush drive shell and the six cush drive rubbers can be lifted out.

When reassembling the cush drive the entry of the vanes between the rubbers will be facilitated if the latter are fitted into the driving shell first and then tilted. The rubbers should be liberally painted with soapsuds to faciliate entry of the vanes.

When reassembling the cush drive coat the inside of the bore of the sprocket/brake drum liberally with grease where it fits over the hub barrel and also put grease on the inner face of the lockring, 10097. The three Simmonds nuts should be tightened down solid as there is a shoulder on the stud which prevents tightening of the nuts from locking the operation of the cush drive.

11. Reassembly of Brake Shoes, Pivot Pin and Operating Cam into Cover Plate

No difficulty should be experienced in carrying out these operations. Make sure that the pivot pin is really tight in the cover plate and put a smear of grease in the grooves of the pivot pin and on the operating face of the cam; also on the cylindrical bearing surface of the operating cam if this has been removed. Fit the operating lever and trunnion on its splines in a position to suit the extent of wear on the linings and secure with the nut. The range of adjustment can be extended by moving the lever on to a different spline.

12. Centering Cam Housing

Note that the bolt holes in the cam housing are slotted, thus enabling the brake shoe assembly to be centered in the drum. It is not intended that on rear brakes the cam housing should be left free to float but the shoes should be centered by leaving the screws just short of dead tight. The brake cover plate assembly with the shoes should then be fitted over the spindle into the brake drum and the brake applied as hard as possible by means of the operating lever. This will centre the shoes in the drum. The screws should then be tightened dead tight and secured with the locknuts. If the shoes are not correctly centered the brake will be either ineffective or too fierce, depending on whether the trailing or leading shoe first makes contact with the drum. With the brake assembly correctly centered and the screws securing the cam housing correctly tightened wear on both linings should be approximately equal.

13. Final Reassembly of Hub before Replacing Wheel

Before replacing the felt washers which form the grease seals, pack both bearings with grease. Recommended greases are Castrolease (Heavy), Mobilgrease (No. 4), Esso Grease, Energrease C3 or Shell Retinax A. These are all medium heavy lime soap or aluminium soap greases. The use of H.M.P. greases which have a soda soap base is not recommended as these tend to be slightly corrosive if any damp finds its way into the hubs.

Make sure that the inside of the brake drum is quite free from oil or grease, damp, etc. Replace the felt washers, distance collars, the brake cover plate assembly, speedometer drive gearbox, distance collars, chain adjuster cams, the loose section of the spindle and the spindle nut. The wheel is then ready for reassembly into the machine.

14. Wheel Rims

The rim fitted to both types of wheel is WM2—19 in. pierced with 40 holes for spoke nipples. The internal width is 1·580 in. and the diameter after building 19·062 in., the tolerance on the circumference of the rim shoulders where the tyre fits being 59·930/59·870 in. The standard steel measuring tape for checking rims is $\frac{5}{16}$ in. wide, ·011 in. thick and its length is 59·964/59·904 in.

Note that two makes of rim are used — "Dunlop" and "Palmer Jointless." These differ in the positions of the pierced spoke holes. The Dunlop rims have a group of three holes on one side of the centre line, then a single hole on the other side, a further group of three and a single hole and so on. Palmer rims have the holes alternately spaced either side of the centre line. Both rims are interchangeable and both use the same length spokes but the method of lacing the wheel is different (see paragraph 16). Neither type of rim is symmetrical and care must be taken that they are built the right way round into the wheel.

15. Spokes

The spokes are of the single butted type 8—10 gauge with 90° countersunk heads, angle of bend 95°—100°, thread diameter ·144 in., 40 threads per inch, thread form British Standard Cycle. Spoke lengths are as follow :—
 "Meteor 700," and "500 Bullet,"
  Cush drive side, $7\frac{3}{4}$ in.
  Spoke flange side $8\frac{1}{4}$ in.
 "500 Twin" and "350 Bullet,"
  Cush drive side, $7\frac{7}{8}$ in.
  Spoke flange side $8\frac{5}{8}$ in.

16. Wheel Building and Truing

The spokes are laced one over three and the wheel must be built central in relation to the outer faces of the distance collars which fit between the

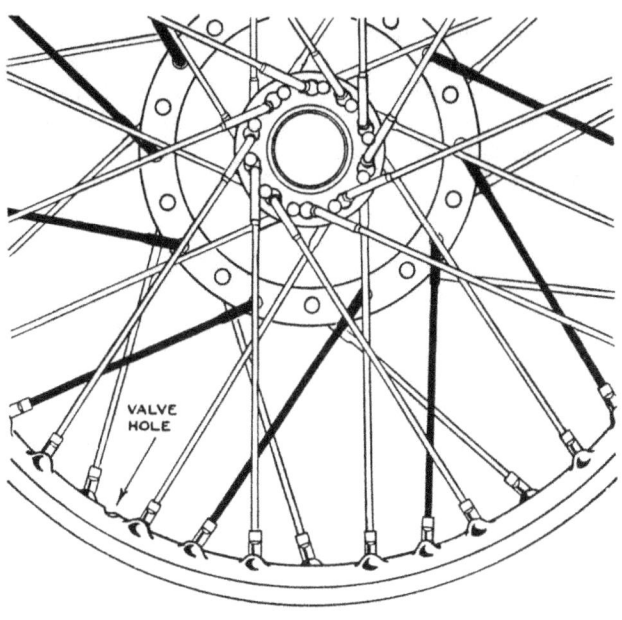

DUNLOP RIM
Fig. 5A

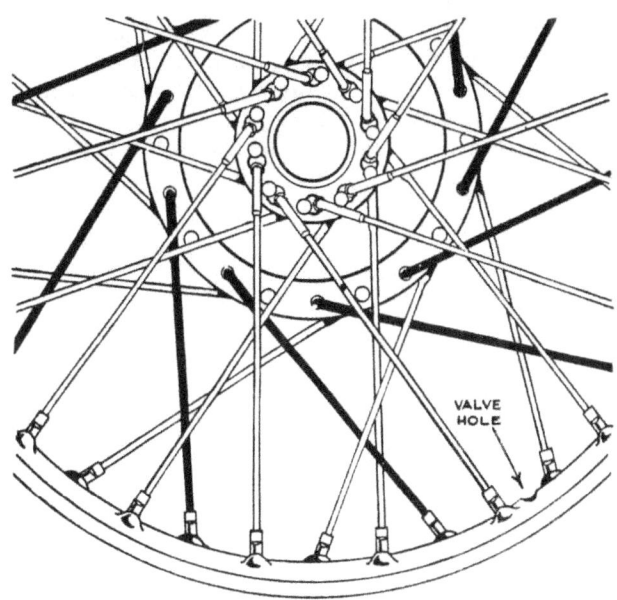

PALMER RIM
Fig. 5B

fork ends. The rim should be trued as accurately as possible, the maximum permissible run-out both sideways and radially being plus or minus $\frac{1}{32}$ in.

Fig. 5 shows the difference between the lacing when using Dunlop and Palmer rims. The key to correct lacing is the inside spokes to the large flange on the cush drive shell which must slope in the direction shown in Fig. 5. With the Dunlop rim this spoke goes to the middle hole of one of the groups of three (see paragraph 14) and the rim must be built into the wheel so that these groups of three holes are on the right of the centre line when the cush drive is on the left, i.e. the inside spokes to the large flange cross from the left to the right of the centre line.

With the Palmer rim the spokes from the large flange on the cush drive shell go to the more steeply angled holes in the rim which must be on the left of the centre line when the cush drive is on the left, i.e. none of the spokes crosses from left to right of the centre line.

17. Tyres

Standard tyres are Dunlop 3·50—19 in. Universal tread except on the "350 Bullet" where a 3·25—19 in. Universal tyre is used.

When removing the tyre always start close to the valve and see that the edge of the cover at the other side of the wheel is pushed down into the well in the rim.

When replacing the tyre fit the part by the valve last, also with the edge of the cover at the other side of the wheel pushed down into the well.

cover at the other side of the wheel pushed down into the well.

If the correct method of fitting and removal of the tyre is adopted it will be found that the covers can be manipulated quite easily with the small levers supplied in the toolkit. The use of long levers and/or excessive force is liable to damage the walls of the tyre. After inflation make sure that the tyre is fitting evenly all the way round the rim. A line moulded on the wall of the tyre indicates whether or not the tyre is correctly fitted. If the tyre has a white mark, indicating a balance point, this should be fitted near the valve.

18. Tyre Pressures

The load which the tyre will carry at different inflation pressures is shown below:—

Tyre Section Inches	Inflation Pressures—lb. per sq. in.					
	16	18	20	24	28	32
	Load per tyre—lb.					
3·25	200	240	280	350	400	440
3·50	280	320	350	400	450	500

19. Lubrication

A greasing point is provided in the centre of the hub barrel. Unless the barrel is packed full with grease on assembly (which is apt to lead to trouble through grease finding its way past the felt seals on to the brake linings) this greasing point is of little value and the best way to grease the bearings is by packing them with grease after dismantling the hub as described above.

Note that the brake cam is drilled for a grease passage but the end of this is stopped up with a countersunk screw instead of being fitted with a grease nipple. This is done to prevent excessive greasing by over-enthusiastic owners. If the cam is smeared with grease on assembly it should require no further attention but in case of necessity it is possible to remove the screw, fit a grease nipple in its place and grease the cam by this means.

WORKSHOP MAINTENANCE MANUAL

for the

Royal Enfield

CONSTELLATION
1958-1963
and
SUPER METEOR
1955-1962
MOTOR CYCLES

**A Floyd Clymer Publication
This edition published in 2023 by
www.VelocePress.com**

All rights reserved. This work may not be reproduced or transmitted in any form without the express written consent of the publisher.

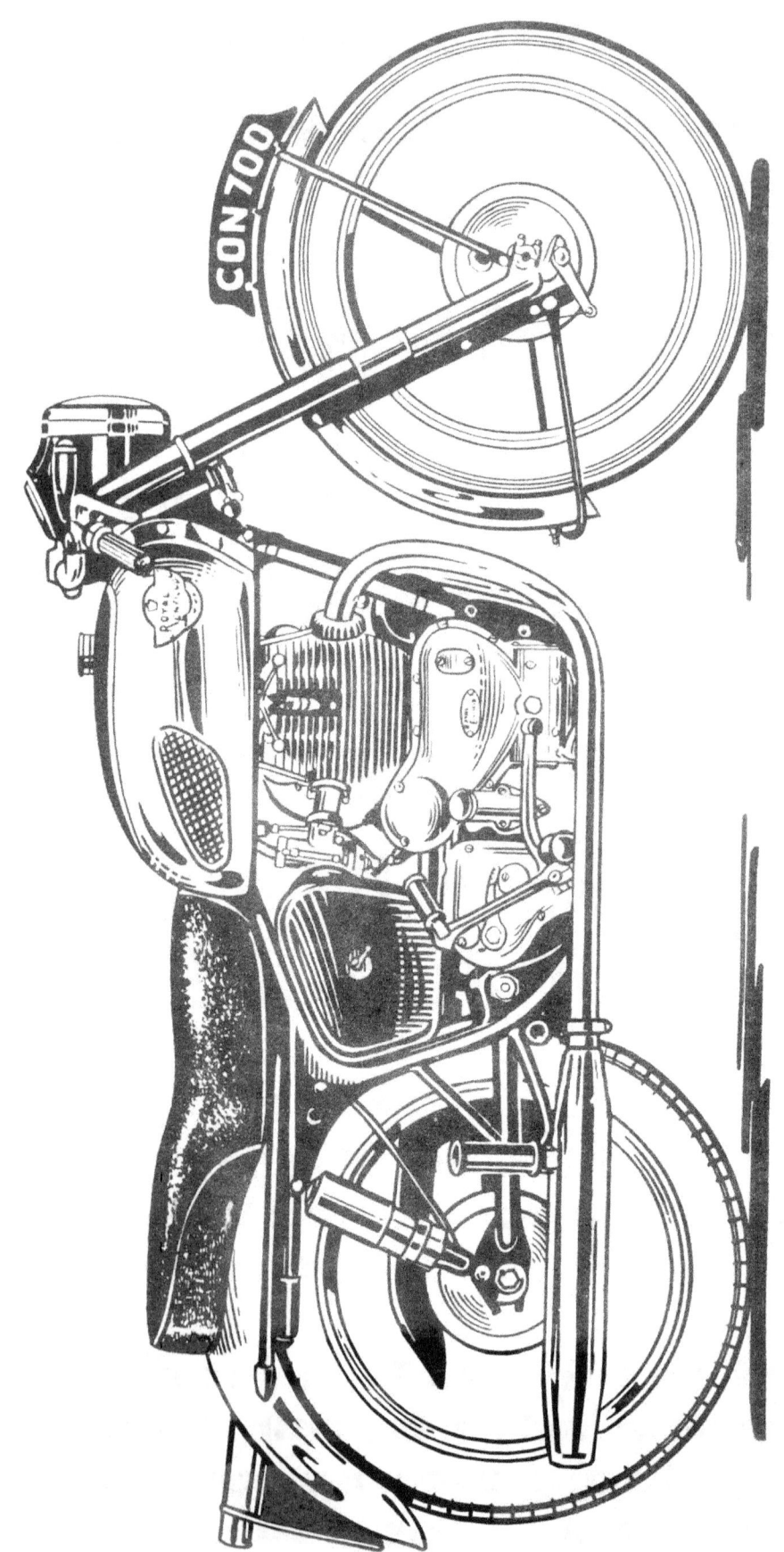

692 c.c. "CONSTELLATION"
(Frontispiece)

ROYAL ENFIELD WORKSHOP MANUAL

Contents
Constellation and Super Meteor

SECTION A11	CONSTELLATION ENGINE DATA
SECTION A12	SUPER METEOR ENGINE DATA
SECTION B11	CONSTELLATION ENGINE SPECIFICATION
SECTION B12	SUPER METEOR ENGINE SPECIFICATION
SECTION C11	CONSTELLATION SERVICE OPERATIONS WITH ENGINE IN FRAME
SECTION C12	SUPER METEOR SERVICE OPERATIONS WITH ENGINE IN FRAME
SECTION D10	SERVICE OPERATIONS WITH ENGINE REMOVED
SECTION E7	GEARBOX AND CLUTCH
SECTION F3	T.T. CARBURETTOR
SECTION F4	MONOBLOC CARBURETTORS
SECTION G1f	MAGNETO
SECTION G2h	GENERATOR/RECTIFIER CHARGING SET
SECTION G4a	BATTERY
SECTION G4c	BATTERY MODEL MLZ9E
SECTION G5d	HEAD AND TAIL LAMPS
SECTION H5	FRAME
SECTION J1	FRONT FORK
SECTION K6	FRONT WHEEL
SECTION L9	REAR WHEEL (QUICKLY DETACHABLE), FULL WIDTH HUB
SECTION M6	SPECIAL TOOLS

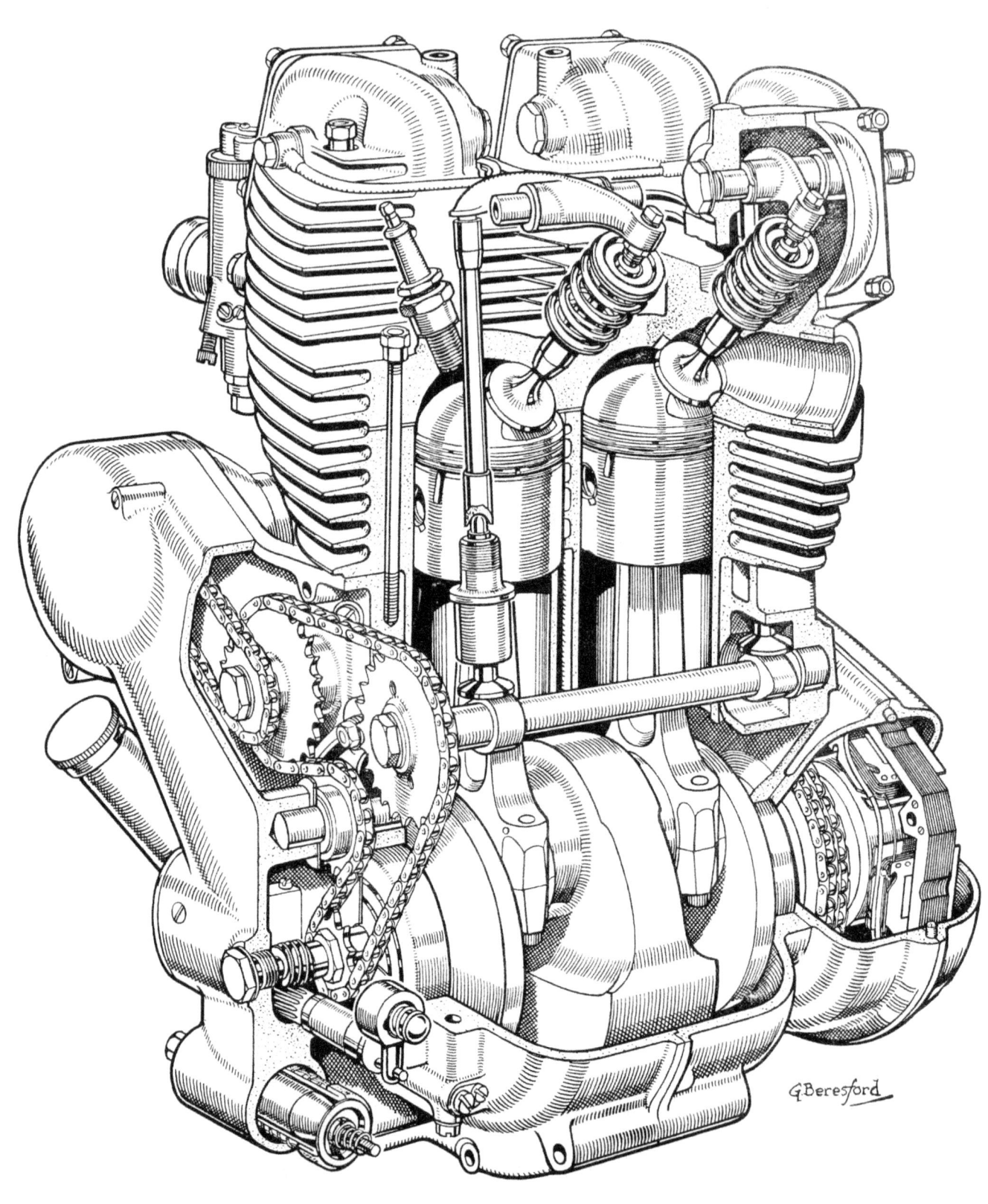

SECTIONAL VIEW OF TYPICAL TWIN CYLINDER ENGINE (EARLY TYPE)

SECTION A11

Technical Data

"Constellation" Engine

Cubic Capacity ... ... 692 c.c.
Stroke ... ... Nominal 90 mm.
Bore ... ... Nominal 70 mm.
                  Actual 69·877 mm./2·752 in.
Rebore to ·020 in. oversize when wear exceeds ·0065 in. and again to ·040 in. oversize after further ·0065 in. wear.
Compression Ratio ... ... 8 to 1
Piston Diameter—
  Bottom of Skirt—
    Fore and Aft ... ... 69·811 mm.
    Top Lands (early type) ... 69·40/69·35 mm.
    Top Lands (later type) ... 69·31/69·26 mm.
    Skirt is tapered and oval turned.
Piston Rings—
  Width—Plain Rings ... ... ·0625/·0635 in.
         Single Scraper Ring ... ·1550/·1560 in.
         Double Scraper Rings ·0781/·0776 in.
  Radial Thickness ... ... 2·883/3·085 mm.
  Gap when in unworn Cylinder ... ·011/·015 in.
  Clearance in grooves ... ... ·001/·003 in.
Renew Piston Rings when gap exceeds $\frac{1}{16}$ in.
Oversize Pistons and Rings available +·020 and +·040 in.

Piston Boss Internal Diameter ... ·7499/·7501 in.
Gudgeon Pin Diameter ... ... ·7499/·7501 in.
Con. Rod Small End Internal Diameter ·7507/·7505 in.
Big End Internal Diameter Con. Rod 2·0190/2·0185 in.
Big End Internal Dia. Bearing Shells 1·8760/1·8755 in.
Crank Pin Diameter ... ... 1·8750/1·8745 in.

Driving Side Main Ball Bearing—
  Type ... ... Hoffman 145 or
                        R and M—LJ45
  Outside Diameter ... ... 85 mm.
  Inside Diameter ... ... 45 mm.
  Width ... ... 19 mm.

Timing Side Main Roller Bearing—
  Type ... ... Hoffman R145 or
                        R and M—LR45
  Outside Diameter ... ... 85 mm.
  Inside Diameter ... ... 45 mm.
  Width ... ... 19 mm.

Rocker Inside Diameter ... ... ·5627/·5622 in.
Rocker Bearing Inside Diameter ... ·5622/·5617 in.
Rocker Spindle Diameter ... ... ·5617/·5615 in.

Inlet Valve Stem Diameter ... ... ·3430/·3425 in.
Exhaust Valve Stem Diameter ... ·3410/·3405 in.
Valve Guide Internal Diameter ... ·3437/·3447 in.
Valve Guide External Diameter ... ·6275/·6270 in.
Valve Guide Hole in Cylinder Head Dia. ·625/·626 in.

Tappet Stem Diameter ... ... ·3743/·3740 in.
Tappet Guide Internal Diameter ... ·3755/·3745 in.
Tappet Guide External Diameter ... 1·0125/1·0130 in.
Tappet Guide Hole in Crankcase Dia. 1·011/1·010 in.
Tappet Clearance with cold engine—
  Inlet ... ... Nil } Normal
  Exhaust ... ... Nil } running
  Inlet ... ... Nil } Continuous
  Exhaust ... ... ·005" } high-speed running

Valve Spring Free Length—
  Inner ... ... $1\frac{3}{8}$ in.
  Outer ... ... $1\frac{11}{16}$ in.
(Renew when reduced by $\frac{1}{16}$ in.)
Valve Timing with ·012 in. clearance—
  Exhaust Opens ... ... 83° before B.D.C.
  Exhaust Closes ... ... 35° after T.D.C.
  Inlet Opens ... ... 24° before T.D.C.
  Inlet Closes ... ... 73° after B.D.C.
Camshaft Bearing External Diameter ·9095/·9085 in.
Camshaft Bearing Internal Diameter ·7505/·7495 in.
(Bored in position in crankcase.)
Cam Lift—
  Exhaust ... ... ·328 in.
  Inlet ... ... ·344 in.
Valve Lift (approx.)—
  Exhaust ... ... ·328 in.
  Inlet ... ... ·344 in.
Timing Sprocket ... ... 12 Teeth
Camshaft Sprockets ... ... 24 Teeth
Magneto Sprocket ... ... 19 Teeth
Timing Chain—Type ... Single No. 110038 endless
              Length ... ... 66 Pitches
              Width ... ... ·225 in.
              Pitch ... ... ·375 in.
              Roller ... ... ·250 in.
Magneto Chain—Type ... Duplex No. 114500 endless
                Length ... ... 44 pitches
              Width ... ... 8·64 mm.
              Pitch ... ... 8 mm.
              Roller ... ... 5 mm.
Magneto Speed ... ... Half Engine Speed
  Points ... ... ·015 in.
  Timing—Retarded ... ... $\frac{1}{32}$ in. before T.D.C.
  Timing—Advanced ... $\frac{3}{8}$ in.–$\frac{7}{16}$ in. before T.D.C.
Engine Sprocket ... ... 29 Teeth
Clutch Sprocket ... ... 56 Teeth
Final Drive Sprocket ... ... 20 Teeth
Primary Chain—Type ... Duplex No. 114038 endless
             Length ... ... 92 Pitches
             Width ... ... ·628 in.
             Pitch ... ... ·375 in.
             Roller ... ... ·250 in.
Feed Oil Pump—Speed ... 1/6 Engine Speed
          Piston Diameter ... ·24975/·24950 in.
          Stroke length ... ·5 in.
Return Oil Pump—Speed ... 1/6 Engine Speed
          Stroke length ... ·5 in.
          Piston Diameter
            (Earlier type)... ·375/·3755 in.
            (Later type) ... ·500/·4997 in.
Sparking Plug—(1) Engines Nos. SMSA 6751–6795 (short reach plugs), Lodge 3HN, Champion L5 or L11S, or KLG F.100.
            (2) Engines Nos. SMSA 6796 onwards (long reach plugs), Lodge 2HLN. Champion N5 or NA8, or KLG FE.75. For high speed running over long distances, use Lodge 3HLN, Champion N3 or NA10, or KLG FE.100
  Diameter ... ... 14 mm.

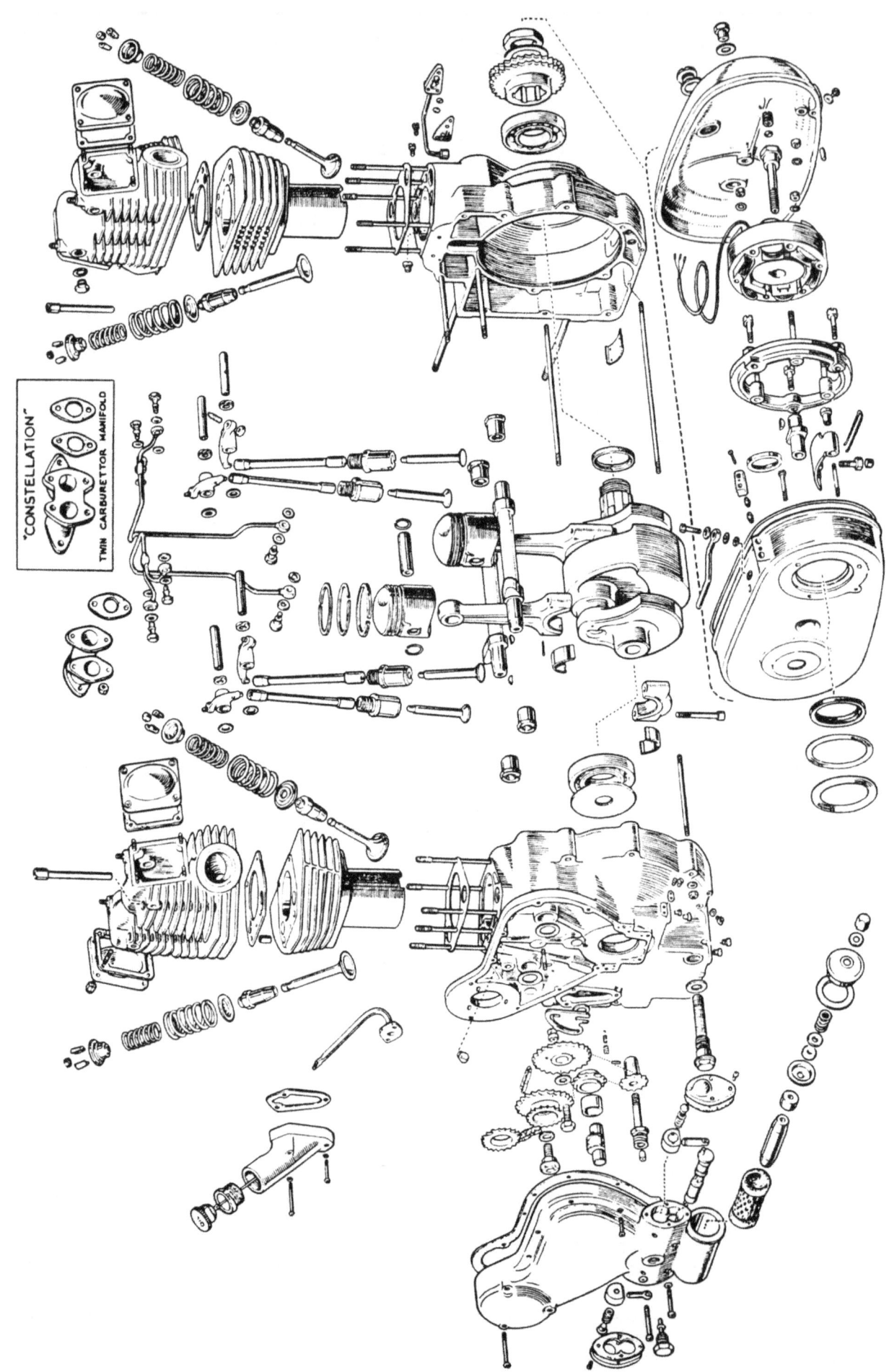

EXPLODED VIEW OF TYPICAL TWIN CYLINDER ENGINE
Fig. 1

SECTION A12

Technical Data

"Super Meteor" Engine

Cubic Capacity	692 c.c.
Stroke ... Nominal	90 m.m.
Bore ... Nominal	70 m.m.
Actual	69·874 m.m./2·751 in.

(Rebore to ·020 in. when wear exceeds ·0065 in. and again to ·040 in. after further ·0065 in. wear.)

Compression Ratio	7¼ to 1
Piston Diameter—	
Bottom of Skirt—Fore and Aft.	69·811 m.m.
Top Lands	69·40/69·35 m.m.

Skirt is tapered and oval-turned.

Piston Rings—	
Width—Plain Rings	·0625/·0635 in.
Scraper Ring	·1550/·1560 in.
Radial Thickness	2·883/3·085 m.m.
Gap when in unworn Cylinder	·011/·015 in.
Clearance in grooves	·001/·003 in.

Renew Piston Rings when gap exceeds $\frac{1}{16}$ in.
Oversize Pistons and Rings available ·020 and ·040 in.

Piston Boss Internal Diameter	·7499/·7501 in.
Gudgeon Pin Diameter	·7499/·7501 in.
Con. Rod Small End Internal Diameter	·7507/·7505 in.
Big End Internal Diameter	1·8760/1·8755 in.
Crank Pin Diameter	1·875/1·8795 in.
Driving Side Main Ball Bearing—	
Type	Hoffman—145 or R and M—LJ 45
Outside Diameter	85 m.m.
Inside Diameter	45 m.m.
Width	19 m.m.
Timing Side Main Roller Bearing—	
Type	Hoffman—R145 or R and M—LRJ54
Outside Diameter	85 m.m.
Inside Diameter	45 m.m.
Width	19 m.m.
Rocker Inside Diameter	·5627/·5622 in.
Rocker Bearing Inside Diameter	·5622/·5617 in.
Rocker Spindle Diameter	·5617/·5615 in.
Inlet Valve Stem Diameter	·3430/·3425 in.
Exhaust Valve Stem Diameter	·3410/·3405 in.
Valve Guide Internal Diameter	·3437/·3447 in.
Valve Guide External Diameter	·6275/·6270 in.
Valve Guide Hole in Cylinder Head Dia.	·625/·626 in.
Tappet Stem Diameter	·3743/·3740 in.
Tappet Guide Internal Diameter	·3755/·3745 in.
Tappet Guide External Diameter	1·0125/1·0130 in.
Tappet Guide Hole in Crankcase Dia.	1·011/1·010 in.
Tappet Clearance with cold engine—	
Normal Running:	
Inlet	Nil
Exhaust	Nil
Continuous High Speed Running:	
Inlet	Nil
Exhaust	·005 in.
Valve Spring Free Length—	
Inner	$2\frac{1}{32}$ in.
Outer	$2\frac{3}{32}$ in.

(Renew when reduced by $\frac{1}{16}$ in.)

Valve Timing with ·012 in. clearance—	
Exhaust Opens	75° before B.D.C.
Exhaust Closes	35° after T.D.C.
Inlet Opens	30° before T.D.C.
Inlet Closes	60° after B.D.C.
Camshaft Bearing External Diameter	·9095/·9085 in.
Camshaft Bearing Internal Diameter	·7505/·7495 in.
(Bored in position in crankcase)	
Cam Lift	·3125 in.
Valve Lift (approx.)	·3125 in.
Timing Sprocket	12 Teeth
Camshaft Sprocket	24 Teeth
Magneto Sprocket	19 Teeth
Timing Chain—Type	Single No. 110038 endless
Length	66 pitches
Width	·225 in.
Pitch	·375 in.
Roller	·250 in.
Magneto Chain—Type	Duplex No. 114500 endless
Length	44 pitches
Width	8·64 m.m.
Pitch	8 m.m.
Roller	5 m.m.
Magneto Speed	Half Engine Speed
Points	·015 in.
Timing Retarded	$\frac{1}{32}$ in. before T.D.C.
Timing Advanced	$\frac{3}{8}$ in.—$\frac{7}{16}$ in. before T.D.C.
Distributor Chain—Type	Single No. 110500 endless
Length	40 pitches
Width	8·64 m.m.
Pitch	8 m.m.
Roller Diameter	5 m.m.
Distributor Speed	Half Engine Speed
Points Gap	·015 in.
Timing Retarded	$\frac{1}{32}$ in. before T.D.C.
Timing Advanced	$\frac{3}{8}$ in.—$\frac{7}{16}$ in. before T.D.C.
Engine Sprocket	33 Teeth
Clutch Sprocket	56 Teeth
Final Drive Sprocket (Solo)	18 Teeth
Final Drive Sprocket (Sidecar)	16 Teeth
Primary Chain Type	Duplex No. 114038 endless
Length	94 pitches
Width	·628 in.
Pitch	·375 in.
Roller	·250 in.
Feed Oil Pump—Speed	1/6 Engine Speed.
Piston Diameter	·24975/·24950
Stroke	·5 in.
Return Oil Pump—Speed	1/6 Engine Speed.
Piston Diameter	·375/·3755 in.
Stroke	·5 in.
Sparking Plug. Type (i) Engines Nos. up to SMQA 4687 (Short Reach): Lodge H14, KLG F70 or Champion L7 (formerly L10S).	
(ii) Engines Nos. SMQA 4688 onwards (Long Reach): Lodge HLN, KLG FE70 or Champion N5 (formerly NA8).	
Diameter	14 m.m.

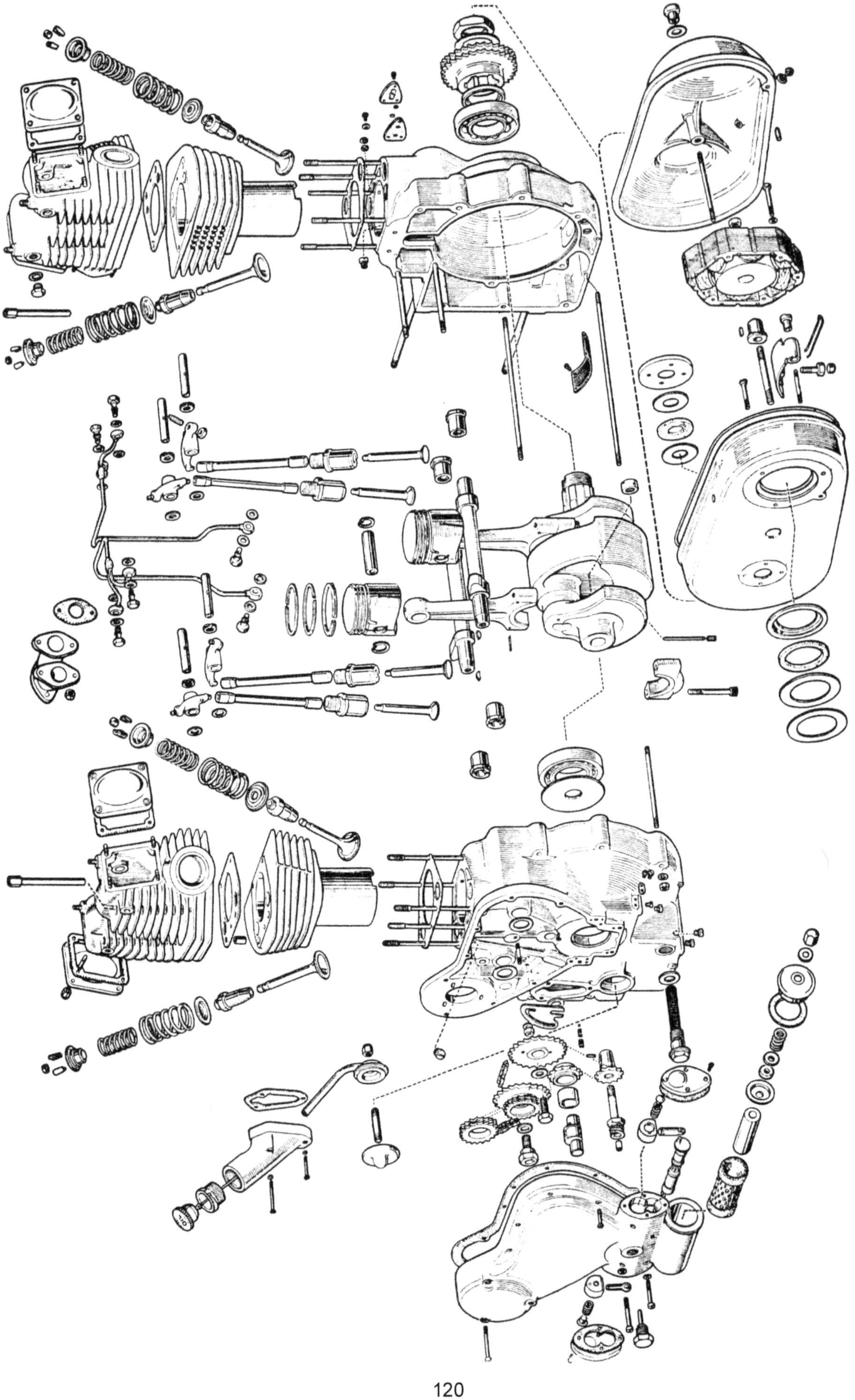

EXPLODED VIEW OF "SUPER METEOR" ENGINE
Fig. 1

SECTION B11

Engine Specification

"Constellation"

1. Engine

The engine is an even-firing vertical twin-cylinder, having separate cylinders and heads and fully enclosed pressure-lubricated overhead valve gear. It has a dry sump lubrication with the oil tank integral with the crankcase and a massive one-piece high-strength spheroidal graphite cast iron crankshaft.

2. Cylinder Heads

The cylinder heads are die-cast from light aluminium alloy with ample finning to ensure adequate cooling. The exhaust pipe inserts are cast-in and the valve inserts are of austenitic iron and are shrunk in so that they are replaceable. The large capacity induction ports are streamlined and blended to the valve seatings.

3. Cylinders

The separate cast-iron cylinders have a nominal bore of 70 m.m., the stroke being 90 m.m. The cubic capacity of the engine is 692 c.c. The cylinder heads are located on the cylinders by hollow dowels.

4. Pistons

The high compression pistons are of low expansion aluminium alloy, heat treated and form-turned oval. The compression ratio is 8 to 1.

Early models have three piston rings, the top two being compression rings, the bottom one a single slotted scraper. Later models have pistons of lighter weight than earlier types, and whilst retaining similar compression rings, the bottom piston ring groove contains two separate oil control rings (see Fig. 7, Section C). All compression rings are taper ground, the top one being chromium plated.

5. Connecting Rods

The connecting rods are produced from stampings of Hiduminium RR56 light alloy. The little end bearings are of alloy direct on to the gudgeon pin. In case of wear after long service the little end can be bored out and fitted with a bush, but this is rarely necessary.

The big end bearings consist of white-metalled steel liners which are renewable. The detachable bearing caps are bolted to the connecting rods by means of high tensile socket screws, secured by cotter pins.

6. Crankcase

The combined crankcase and oil tank is die-cast from light alloy in two halves, being split vertically.

7. Crankshaft and Flywheel

The crankshaft is cast in one piece, integral with the massive central flywheel, from high quality spheroidal graphitic cast iron. The total weight is approximately 24 lbs., and except in some of the earlier engines the crankshafts are dynamically balanced.

The main journals are ground, and the big end journals are ground and hand lapped. The main journal on the drive side of the later type crankshaft is drilled through its centre for the situation and operation of the crankcase breather.

8. Main Bearings

Heavy duty bearings are provided for the crankshaft, the driving side being ball and the timing side roller.

9. Camshafts

The camshafts are machined from drop forged steel stampings with the cams and bearings hardened and ground. The cam profiles are produced to give racing performance and, in order to obtain the maximum efficiency, the usual silencing ramps are omitted.

The camshafts are located in the crankcase and run in bronze bushes. The bushes on the nearside are pressed into detachable housings which are bolted to the driving side crankcase. This enables the camshafts to be changed, if so desired for tuning purposes, without the necessity of dismantling the crankcase.

10. Valves

The inlet valves are machined from stampings of special Silicon-Chrome Valve Steel and the exhaust valves are of High-Nickel-Chromium-Tungsten Valve Steel with the stems Stellite-faced.

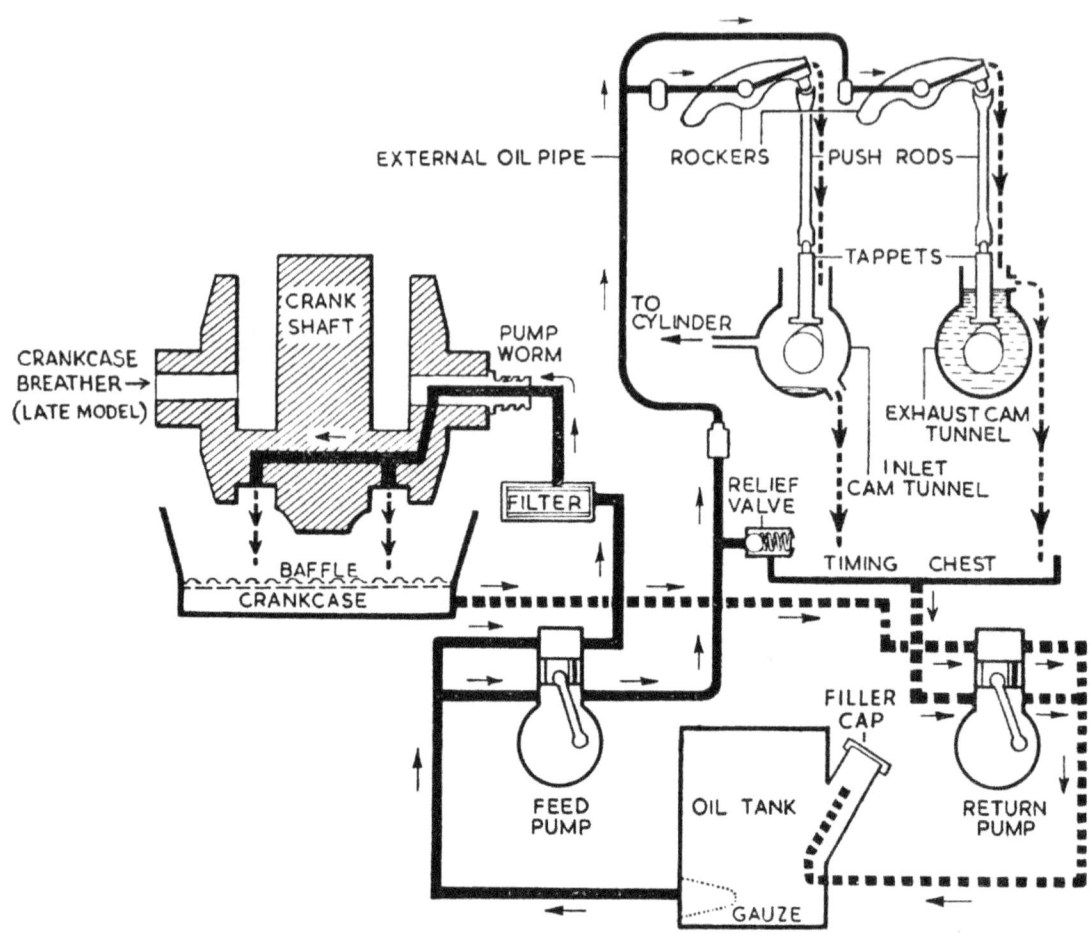

LUBRICATION SYSTEM. Diagrammatic Arrangement
Fig. 2

11. Valve Gear

The valves are operated from the camshaft by means of large, flat-based, guided tappets, tubular alloy push rods with induction hardened steel ends and overhead rockers. Two compression springs are fitted to each valve secured by Bullock Type split collets locking in Timinium collars. The springs are specially designed to give a variable rate on compression.

12. Timing Drive

The camshafts are located in the crankcase, running in bronze bushes. They are driven by a common endless chain from the timing sprocket on the crankshaft and the tightness of the chain can be adjusted by means of the chain tensioner in the timing chest.

The magneto is driven by a separate endless chain from the rear camshaft sprocket in the timing chest. The tension of this chain is adjusted by moving the magneto fixing bolts in their slotted holes.

A special slotted bolt securing the front camshaft sprocket provides a drive to a tachometer if this is required. This drive can be fixed to an aperture provided in the timing cover, which is otherwise covered by a small plate.

13. Ignition and Lighting System (See Section G)

The ignition is supplied from a Lucas K2F magneto and the lighting and other electrical circuits from a 6-volt battery which is charged through a rectifier from a Lucas alternator.

The alternator is housed in the primary chaincase, the permanent magnet rotor being mounted on the end of the crankshaft and the six coil stator fixed to the back of the chaincase.

The magneto is chain-driven from the inlet camshaft at half engine speed and the timing is hand controlled from a lever on the handlebar.

14. Single Carburettor (see Section F)

The carburettor is an Amal Type T10.TT9, with a bore of $1\frac{3}{16}$ inches.

For very high speeds it is essential to have an independent float chamber flexibly mounted as near the centre-line of the machine as possible.

There is, however, a tendency to flood, and for normal use a conventional float chamber fixed to the carburettor is more satisfactory.

    Main Jet   480
    Needle Jet   109
    Throttle Valve   ...   ...   No. 5
    Needle Clip in third groove from top.

Twin Carburettors (see Section F)

Both carburettors are identical in all respects but for the float chamber arrangement, which is as follows:

Carburettor type 376/242 supplies the left-hand cylinder, and has an integral float chamber which also controls the fuel supply via a connecting pipe to the right-hand instrument type 376/243. This does not have a float chamber in unit with it.

    Main Jet   320
    Needle Jet   106
    Throttle Valve 376/4
    Pilot Jet   ...   .   22 c.c.
    Needle Position   3

15. Air Filter

Provision is made for housing a 5 in. diameter Vokes Micro-Vee felt and gauze dry filter in a compartment of the toolbox, but the use of this may reduce the maximum speed slightly.

Owing to the positions of the twin carburettors in relation to the toolbox, it is not possible to attach air filters in this instance.

16. Lubrication System

Lubrication is by the Royal Enfield Dry Sump system which is entirely automatic and positive in action. The oil tank is integral with the crankcase, ensuring the full rate of circulation immediately the engine is started and rapid heating of the oil in cold weather.

There are two positively driven piston type oil pumps running at $\frac{1}{8}$ engine speed, one at the rear of the timing cover for pumping oil to the bearings under pressure and the other at the front for returning the oil from the crankcase to the tank. The return pump has a capacity approximately double that of the feed pump which ensures that oil does not accumulate in the crankcase.

The oil from the big ends drains into the bottom of the crankcase and is prevented by a baffle from being drawn up by the flywheel.

The oil from the rocker bearings is squirted through a small hole in the rocker on to the top end of the push rod. It flows down the push rod into the cam tunnel where it lubricates the cams and tappets and thence into the timing chest, lubricating the timing chains. There are small holes from the inlet cam tunnel through the cylinder walls for the purpose of lubricating the skirts of the pistons and a hole from the inlet cam tunnel into the timing chest through which surplus oil from the inlet rockers passes.

The exhaust cam tunnel, however, has no holes but is kept full of oil to ensure adequate lubrication of the exhaust cams and prevent wear. The oil level is maintained to a height in the groove in the tappet guide where a hole is drilled into the timing chest, through which surplus oil from the exhaust rockers passes.

Both pumps are double acting, one side of the feed pump supplying the big ends only and the other side the rockers and valve gear. In a similar manner one side of the return pump pumps the big end oil back to the tank from the crankcase and the other side the valve gear oil back to the tank from the timing chest.

A spring loaded relief valve controls the pressure of the oil to the valve rocker gear which is through external pipes.

A gauze strainer is provided for the feed oil leaving the tank and there is a large capacity felt filter in the feed to the big ends. An aluminium cylinder is fitted over the fixing stud inside the filter element to reduce the volume of oil required to fill the filter after it has been dismantled for cleaning and to ensure the rapid flow of oil to the big ends.

A small circular magnet is also fitted over the fixing stud inside the oil filter for the purpose of collecting any ferrous particles which may be suspended in the oil.

An oil cooler specially designed for the "Constellation" is available. This is a great asset when full power is used for long periods, particularly in the case of competition work.

It is attached by two plates to the bottom and middle front crankcase studs, which secure the front engine mounting plates. A feed pipe connects the scavenge pump to the bottom right-hand side of the cooler and a pipe on the top left-hand side of the cooler returns oil to the bottom of the oil tank. It is necessary to ensure that an unobstructed flow of cool air flows over the cooler. (See Fig. 4.)

17. Breather

The efficient operation of the breather is of paramount importance to the performance of the engine as it acts as a non-return valve between the crankcase and the outside atmosphere, causing a partial vacuum in the crankcase and rocker boxes which prevents the passage of oil into the cylinders and consequent smoking and oiling of the plugs.

The breather is located on the driving side of the crankcase and consists of a small housing attached to the crankcase by three screws. This housing contains two pen-steel discs covering two holes drilled into the crankcase. Accurate seating

Section **B11** *ROYAL ENFIELD WORKSHOP MANUAL* Page 4

OIL PUMP DIAGRAMS

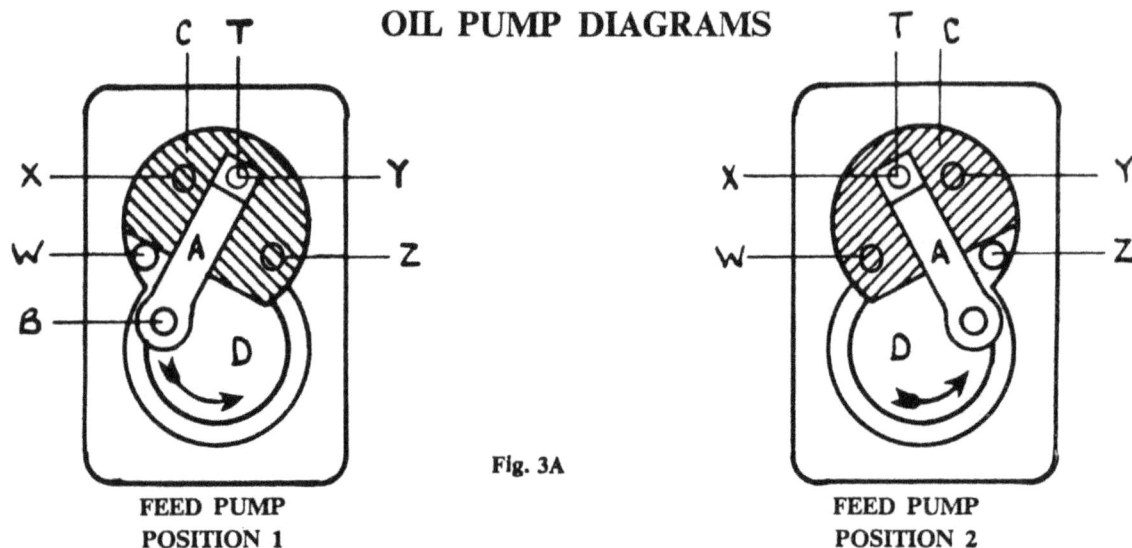

Fig. 3A

FEED PUMP POSITION 1 **FEED PUMP POSITION 2**

The ports in the housing are connected as follows :—
W — delivery to rocker gear.
X — delivery to big ends.
Y — suction from oil tank.
Z — suction from oil tank.

Position 1. The plunger A is being drawn out of the cylinder hole in the disc C by the action of the peg B on the shaft D. The port T in the disc C registers with the suction port Y in the housing, so that oil is drawn into the cylinder from the oil tank. At the same time the delivery port W in the housing is uncovered and oil below the disc in the housing is forced through W to the rocker Gear.

Position 2. The plunger A is being pushed into the cylinder hole in the disc C. The port T in the disc now registers with the delivery port X in the housing, so that oil is forced out of the cylinder to the big ends. At the same time the suction port Z in the housing is uncovered and oil is drawn into the housing below the disc from the oil tank.

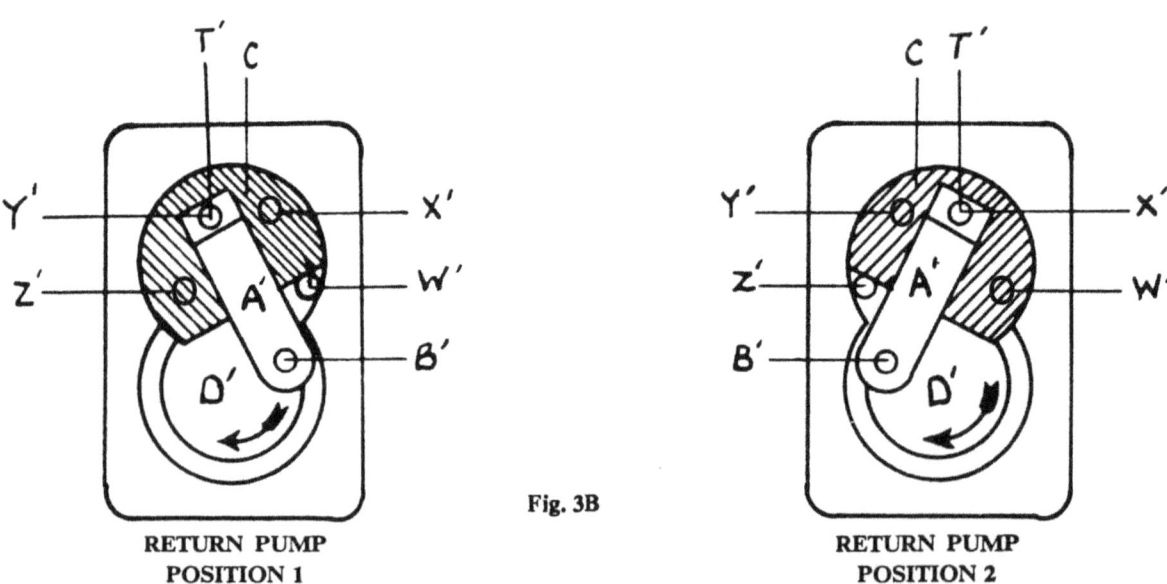

Fig. 3B

RETURN PUMP POSITION 1 **RETURN PUMP POSITION 2**

The ports in the housing are connected as follows :—
W' — delivery to oil tank.
X' — delivery to oil tank.
Y' — suction from crankcase.
Z' — suction from timing chest.

Position 1. The plunger A' is being drawn out of the cylinder hole in the disc C' by the action of the peg B' on the shaft D'. The port T' in the disc C' registers with the suction port Y' in the housing, so that oil is drawn into the cylinder from the crankcase sump. At the same time the delivery port W' in the housing is uncovered and oil below the disc in the housing is forced through W' back to the oil tank.

Position 2. The plunger A' is being pushed into the cylinder hole in the disc C'. The port T' in the disc now registers with the delivery port X' in the housing, so that oil is forced out of the cylinder back to the oil tank. At the same time the suction port Z' in the housing is uncovered and oil is drawn into the housing below the disc from the timing chest.

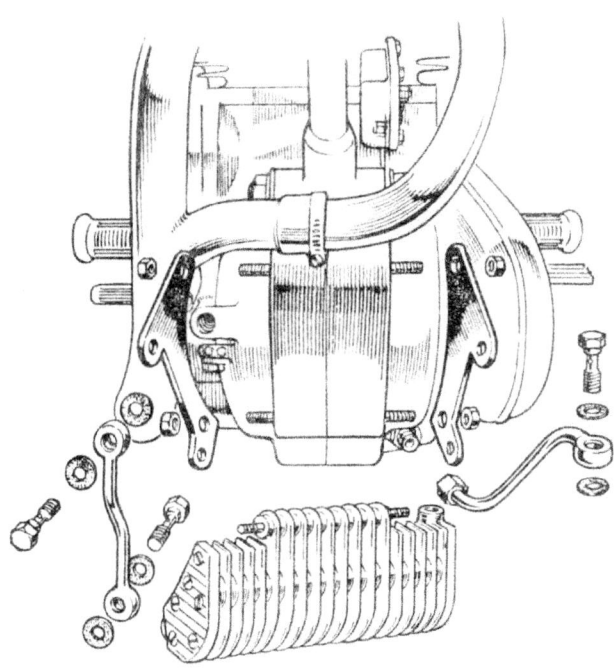

OIL COOLER, PIPES AND MOUNTING PLATES
Fig. 4

of the discs is ensured by a pen-steel plate held between the breather body and the crankcase.

The Neoprene pipe, found on early models, which breathes directly into the atmosphere from the breather housing, has been replaced on later models by a metal pipe running from the breather housing to the top of the oil tank.

In addition a breather, in the form of a pen-steel disc, is situated in a recess in the head of the special bolt, which secures the alternator rotor on to the end of the crankshaft. This bolt is drilled throughout its length, and communicates crankcase pressure to the breather via the hole drilled through the drive side main journal.

A plug screwed into the head of the bolt retains the disc, and a hole drilled in its centre allows the crankcase to breathe into the primary chaincase.

A vent pipe fitted to the top of the primary chain case has its aperture inside the case shielded by a baffle from oil flung from the chain. (See Fig. 9, Section C.)

18. Gearbox

The gearbox is bolted on to the back of the crankcase and has four speeds, which are foot controlled, and a patented neutral finder. All gears are in constant mesh, changes being effected by robust dog clutches. (See Section E).

The standard gear ratios are as follows :—

Bottom Gear	12·35
Second Gear	8·19
Third Gear	6·05
Top Gear	4·44

19. Clutch

The earlier type clutch has five pressure plates and four friction plates, including the sprocket, which is lined on both sides with friction material. All the other friction plates have Klingerite inserts.

The later version of this clutch employs a different friction material on the friction plate, which is first in order of assembly, to the following two plates. These have a friction material of a corky texture.

The clutch from 1961 models onwards has six pressure plates and five friction plates, including the sprocket, which is lined on both sides with friction material.

This assembly gives smooth operation and eliminates clutch slip under the most arduous conditions.

A description of the operating mechanism is given in Section E, Sub-section 1.

NOTES

SECTION B12

Engine Specification

"Super Meteor"

1. Engine

The engine is an even-firing vertical twin-cylinder, having separate cylinders and heads and fully enclosed pressure-fed overhead valve gear. It has dry sump lubrication with the oil tank integral with the crankcase and a massive one-piece high-strength cast iron crankshaft.

2. Cylinder Heads

The cylinder heads are die-cast from light aluminium alloy with ample finning to ensure adequate cooling. The exhaust pipe inserts are cast in and the valve inserts are of austenitic iron and are shrunk in so that they are replaceable. Steel wire thread inserts which are easily renewable are provided for the sparking plugs to prevent damage to the threads in the heads. The large capacity induction ports are streamlined and blended to the valve seatings.

3. Cylinders

The separate cast iron cylinders have a nominal bore of 70 m.m., the stroke being 90 m.m. The cubic capacity of the engine is 692 c.c. The cylinder heads are located on the cylinders by hollow dowels.

4. Pistons

The high compression pistons are of low expansion aluminium alloy, heat treated and form-turned oval and having split skirts. The compression ratio is $7\frac{1}{4}$ to 1. There are three piston rings, the top two of which are compression rings. Both are taper ground and the top one is chromium plated. The third ring is for oil control and is slotted.

5. Connecting Rods

The connecting rods are produced from stampings of Hiduminium RR 56 light alloy. The little end bearings are of alloy direct on to the gudgeon pin. In case of wear after long service the little end can be bored out and fitted with a bush, but this is rarely necessary.

The big end bearings are of alloy direct to the crankshaft. The detachable bearing caps are bolted to the connecting rods by means of high tensile socket screws, secured by cotter pins.

6. Crankcase

The combined crankcase and oil tank is die-cast from light alloy in two halves, being split vertically.

7. Crankshaft and Flywheel

The crankshaft is cast in one piece, integral with the massive central flywheel, from high quality meehanite cast iron. The total weight is 26 lbs. and it is carefully balanced.

The main journals are ground and the big end journals are ground and hand-lapped.

8. Main Bearings

Heavy duty bearings are provided for the crankshaft, the driving side being ball and the timing side roller.

9. Camshafts

The camshafts are machined from drop forged steel stampings with the cams and bearings hardened and ground. The cam profiles are produced with silencing ramps to ensure quiet running.

10. Valves

The inlet valves are machined from stampings of special Silicon-Chrome Valve Steel and the exhaust valves are of austenitic steel.

11. Valve Gear

The valves are operated from the camshafts by means of large flat based guided tappets, tubular alloy push rods and overhead rockers. Two compression rings are fitted to each valve.

12. Timing Drive

The camshafts are located in the crankcase, running in bronze bushes. They are driven by a common, endless chain from the timing sprocket on the crankshaft and the tightness of the chain can be adjusted by means of the chain tensioner in the timing chest.

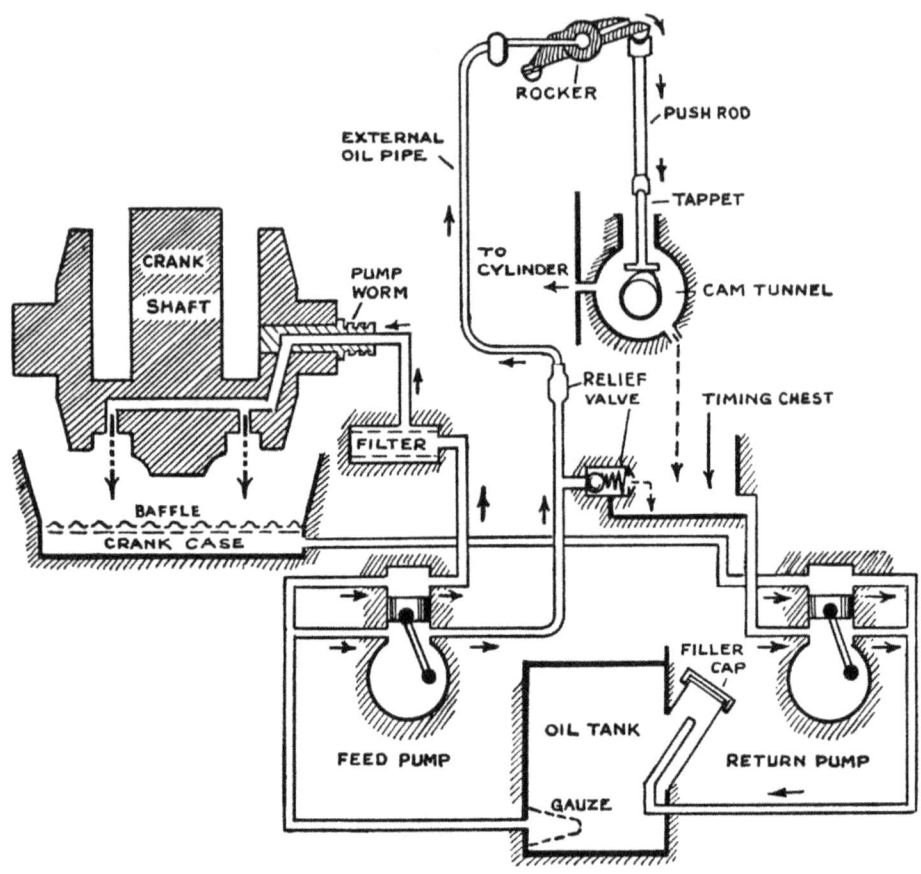

"SUPER METEOR" LUBRICATION SYSTEM. Diagrammatic Arrangement
Fig. 2

The magneto is driven by a separate endless chain from the rear camshaft sprocket in the timing chest. The tension of this chain is adjusted by moving the magneto fixing bolts in their slotted holes.

13(a). Ignition and Lighting System; early "Super Meteors." (See Section G).

Separate systems are provided for ignition and lighting. The former is by the latest type of Lucas brushless Magneto with rotating magnet and stationary contact breaker. The magneto runs at half engine speed and has a built-in distributor and double cam.

Lighting current is supplied by the battery which is charged through a rectifier from an alternator consisting of a rotating magnet mounted on the crankshaft and running in a six-coil stator in the primary chaincase.

13(b). Ignition and Lighting System; later models. (See Section G)

The ignition and lighting are provided by means of Lucas alternator, coil and distributor.

The alternator is housed in the primary chaincase, the permanent magent rotor being mounted on the end of the crankshaft and the six-coil stator fixed to the back of the chaincase.

The distributor is chain-driven from the inlet camshaft at half-engine speed and has a built-in automatic advance mechanism.

Lighting current is supplied by the battery which is charged through a rectifier from the alternator.

For normal running the ignition current is also supplied from the battery but, if the battery should be run down, starting can be effected by turning the ignition switch to the "Emergency" position which permits the distributor to be supplied direct from the alternator.

14. Carburettor. (See Section F)

Amal Monobloc, Type 376/36. Bore $1\frac{1}{16}$ in.
- Main Jet 240
- Needle Jet ... ... Standard
- Pilot Jet ... ... 30 c.c.
- Throttle Valve ... No. $3\frac{1}{2}$
- Needle Position ... No. 3
- Pilot Outlet ... ·025 in.

15. Air Filter

The air filter is a Vokes Micro-Vee felt and gauze dry filter, 5 in. diameter and housed in a compartment of the toolbox.

16. Lubrication System

Lubrication is by the Royal Enfield Dry Sump system which is entirely automatic and positive in action. The oil tank is integral with the crankcase, ensuring the full rate of circulation immediately the engine is started and rapid heating of the oil in cold weather.

There are two positively driven piston type oil pumps running at $\frac{1}{8}$ engine speed, one at the rear of the timing cover for pumping oil to the bearings under pressure and the other at the front for returning the oil from the crankcase to the tank. The return pump has a capacity approximately double that of the feed pump which ensures that oil does not accumulate in the crankcase.

The oil from the big ends drains into the bottom of the crankcase and is prevented by a baffle from being drawn up by the flywheel.

The oil from the rocker bearings is squirted through a small hole in the rocker on to the top end of the pushrod. It flows down the pushrod into the cam tunnel where it lubricates the cams and tappets and thence into the timing chest, lubricating the timing chains. There are small holes from the cam tunnels through the cylinder walls for the purpose of lubricating the skirts of the pistons.

Both pumps are double acting, one side of the feed pump supplying the big ends only and the other side the rockers and valve gear. In a similar manner one side of the return pump pumps the big end oil back to the tank from the crankcase and the other side the valve gear oil back to the tank from the timing chest.

A spring loaded relief valve controls the pressure of the oil to the valve rocker gear which is through external pipes.

A gauze strainer is provided (on models prior to 1960) for the feed oil leaving the tank and there is a large capacity felt filter in the feed to the big ends. An aluminium cylinder is fitted over the fixing stud inside the filter element to reduce the volume of oil required to fill the filter after it has been dismantled for cleaning and to ensure the rapid flow of oil to the big ends.

17. Breather

The efficient operation of the breather is of paramount importance to the performance of the engine as it acts as a non-return valve between the crankcase and the outside atmosphere, causing a partial vacuum in the crankcase and rocker boxes which prevents the passage of oil into the cylinders and consequent smoking and oiling of the plugs.

The breather is located on the driving side of the crankcase and consists of a small housing attached to the crankcase by three screws and having a short rubber tube with flattened end, which acts as a non-return valve.

On some models the housing contains two pen-steel discs covering two holes drilled in the crankcase. Accurate seating of the discs is ensured by a pen-steel plate held between the breather body and the crankcase.

For 1960 a new disc-type crankcase breather, built into the drive-side end of the crankshaft assembly, disposes of unwanted pressure. The previous breather mechanism now drains unwanted oil from the base of the cylinders back to the oil reservoir.

18. Gearbox

The gearbox is bolted on to the back of the crankcase and has four speeds, which are foot controlled, and a patented neutral finder. All gears are in constant mesh, changes being effected by robust dog clutches. (See Section E.)

The standard gear ratios are as follows:—

	Solo	Sidecar
Bottom Gear	12·35	13·75
Second Gear	8·19	8·87
Third Gear	6·05	6·4
Top Gear	4·44	4·93

19. Clutch

The clutch has five pressure plates and four friction plates, including the sprocket which is lined on both sides with friction material. Klinger and special linings for the other friction plates give smooth operation and freedom from slipping in the presence of oil.

The operating mechanism of the clutch is of the latest Enfield design which enables stronger clutch springs to be used without increasing the force required to operate it, thus giving increased load carrying capacity to the clutch.

A description of the operating mechanism is given in Section E, Subsection 1.

Section **B12**   *ROYAL ENFIELD WORKSHOP MANUAL*   Page 4

"SUPER METEOR" OIL PUMP DIAGRAMS

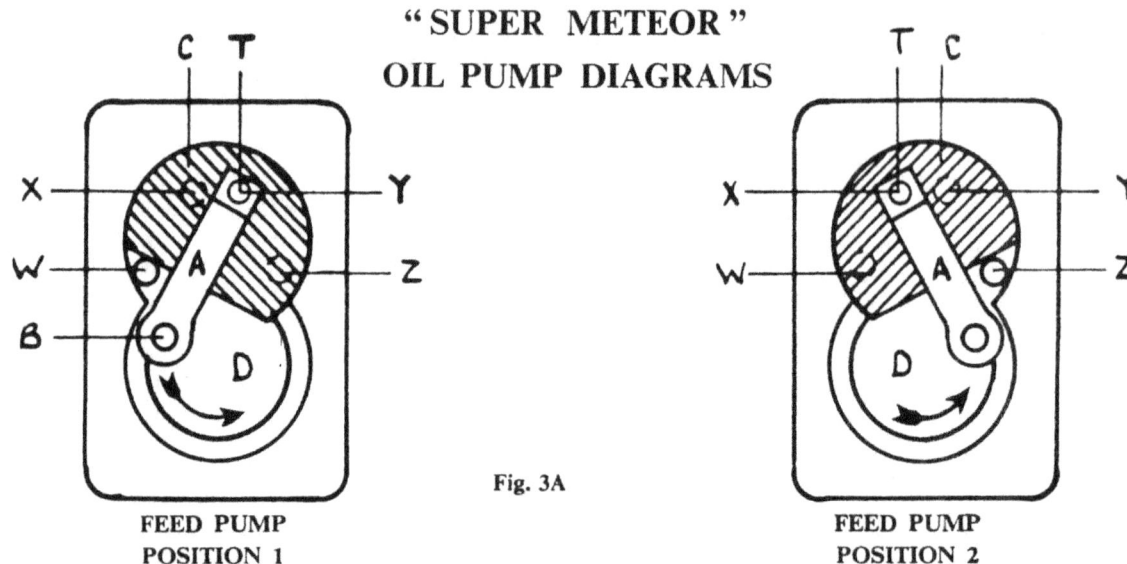

Fig. 3A

FEED PUMP POSITION 1

FEED PUMP POSITION 2

The ports in the housing are connected as follows:—

W — delivery to rocker gear.
X — delivery to big ends.
Y — suction from oil tank.
Z — suction from oil tank.

Position 1. The plunger A is being drawn out of the cylinder hole in the disc C by the action of the peg B on the shaft D. The port T in the disc C registers with the suction port Y in the housing, so that oil is drawn into the cylinder from the oil tank. At the same time the delivery port W in the housing is uncovered and oil below the disc in the housing is forced through W to the rocker Gear.

Position 2. The plunger A is being pushed into the cylinder hole in the disc C. The port T in the disc now registers with the delivery port X in the housing, so that oil is forced out of the cylinder to the big ends. At the same time the suction port Z in the housing is uncovered and oil is drawn into the housing below the disc from the oil tank.

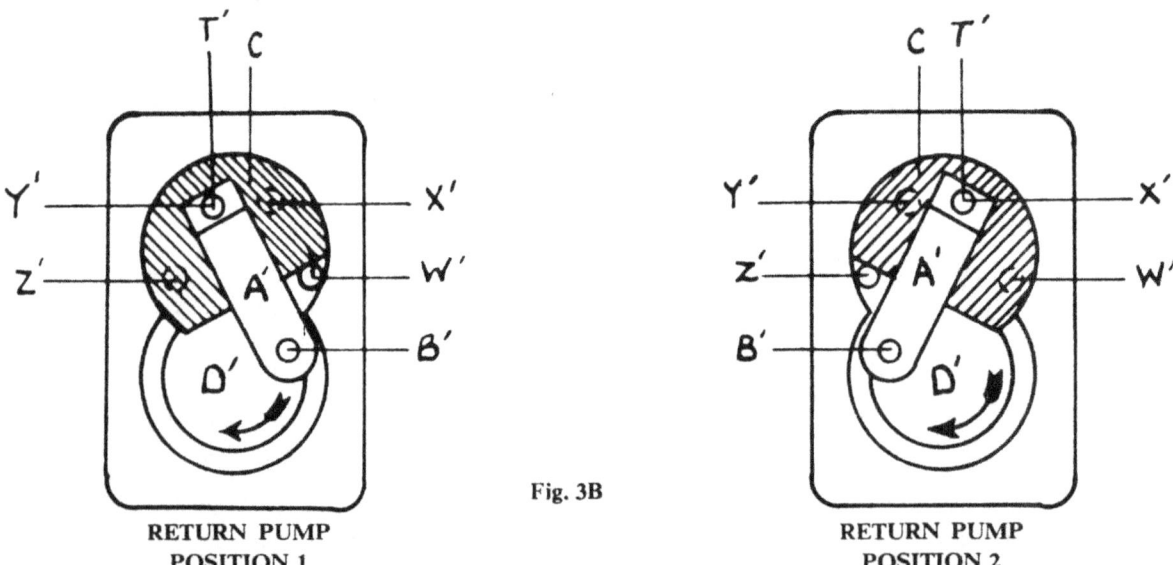

Fig. 3B

RETURN PUMP POSITION 1

RETURN PUMP POSITION 2

The ports in the housing are connected as follows:—

W' — delivery to oil tank.
X' — delivery to oil tank.
Y' — suction from crankcase.
Z' — suction from timing chest.

Position 1. The plunger A' is being drawn out of the cylinder hole in the disc C' by the action of the peg B' on the shaft D'. The port T' in the disc C' registers with the suction port Y' in the housing, so that oil is drawn into the cylinder from the crankcase sump. At the same time the delivery port W' in the housing is uncovered and oil below the disc in the housing is forced through W' back to the oil tank.

Position 2. The plunger A' is being pushed into the cylinder hole in the disc C'. The port T' in the disc now registers with the delivery port X' in the housing, so that oil is forced out of the cylinder back to the oil tank. At the same time the suction port Z' in the housing is uncovered and oil is drawn into the housing below the disc from the timing chest.

SECTION C11

Service Operations with Engine in Frame

"Constellation"

1. Removal of the Timing Cover

First place a tray under the engine to catch the oil which will escape when the cover is removed. Remove the timing side exhaust pipe. Remove the oil filler neck by taking out the three screws fixing it to the crankcase. Remove the timing cover fixing screws. Draw off the timing cover, tapping it lightly if necessary.

In refitting the cover, insert the two long screws through the cover to locate the gasket. See that the thrust washer is on the chain tensioner sprocket spindle and that the neoprene seal is in position on the oil feed plug. If the seal or plug is damaged a new one of either should be fitted. The seal is Part No. 42114 and the plug is Part No. 42113.

The refitting of the cover will be facilitated if the engine is turned gently forwards while the cover is being put into place. This will help the engagement of the pump worm with the pump spindle and prevent damage to the gears.

Always fill the filter with clean oil before refitting the timing cover and always take great care not to damage the gasket where the section is narrow.

To verify that the oil pumps are working after replacing the timing cover, start the engine and slacken the feed plug between the oil pumps. The return oil pump can be checked by removing the oil filler cap so that the oil return pipe can be seen. It may take several minutes for all the oil passages to fill and the oil to commence circulating. The feed to the rockers can be observed by removing the rocker-box covers, when oil will be seen flowing down the surface of the push rods.

2. Valve Timing

The camshaft sprockets are keyed to the camshafts so that the valve timing can only be incorrect if the timing chain is incorrectly fitted.

The correct setting is obtained with the marks stamped on the camshaft sprockets facing each other inwards on the centre line and the mark on the crankshaft sprocket pointing vertically downwards. If it is necessary to remove the sprockets see Subsections 23 and 24.

Remember that all three timing sprocket fixing bolts have **Left Hand Threads**. While tightening the camshaft bolts the sprockets should be held.

The correct valve timing at ·012 in. tappet clearance is as follows:—
Exhaust opens 83° before bottom dead centre.
Exhaust closes 35° after top dead centre.
Inlet opens 24° before top dead centre.
Inlet closes 73° after bottom dead centre.

3. Tappet Adjustment

The tappet clearance is adjusted by means of a screw in the outer end of the rocker. Access to the adjusting screws is obtained by removing the covers of the rocker boxes.

The clearance between the end of the screw and the valve stem should be nil or as little as possible with the engine **COLD**.

To adjust the clearance, loosen the locknut beneath the rocker arm, turn the screw with a small spanner and re-tighten the locknut.

The adjustment of each valve should be made with the corresponding valve of the other cylinder fully open. This ensures that the tappet is well clear of the cam.

If, after long service, the rocker adjusting screws are found to be worn, they should be renewed, as uneven thrust due to the screw being in a different position after adjustment may cause lateral movement of the rocker, giving rise to a sharp tapping noise.

3A. Removal of the Camshafts

Remove the timing cover (Subsection 1).
Remove the camshaft sprockets (Subsection 24).
Remove the three screws holding each of the camshaft bearing housings.
Compress the valve springs and withdraw the camshafts. It is necessary to rotate the camshafts slightly while withdrawing them in order that the cams will pass through the shaped hole in the crankcase.

When replacing the camshafts compress the valve springs and hold the tappets clear of the cams. If the rocker adjusting screws are screwed right back, it is not necessary to compress the valve springs.

4. Ignition Timing

To set the ignition timing, first remove the timing cover (subsection 1) and then remove the magneto sprocket nut and withdraw the sprocket, using Special Tool No. 14835.

Set the contact points to ·012 in., fully opened, but if they are worn or pitted refer to Section G.

Remove the sparking plugs and set the piston in the left-hand cylinder to $\frac{3}{8}$ in. before top dead centre on the compression stroke (i.e., with both valves closed).

Set the contacts to be just breaking with the ignition control fully advanced.

Replace the driving sprocket and tighten the nut.

Replace the timing cover.

(To determine the point at which the contacts are just breaking, insert a piece of tissue paper between them and rotate the contact-breaker in an anti-clockwise direction until the paper can just be pulled out.)

5. Primary Chain Adjustment

The tension of the primary chain can be checked through the inspection cover in the primary chain case and, should it require adjustment, access to the adjuster is gained by removing the chain case cover, which is held in position by a single nut. Before removing the nut, place a tray under the engine to catch the oil from the chaincase.

Beneath the bottom run of the chain is a curved slipper on which the chain rests and which may be raised or lowered by turning the adjusting screw after having first slackened the locknut.

A rubber button is fitted to the end of the adjusting screw to prevent the transmission of chain noise to the chaincase and this is held against the chaincase by a hairpin spring, which prevents it from bouncing.

Do not adjust the chain to be dead tight but rotate the engine slowly and, while doing so, test the tension of the top run of the chain by pressing it up and down with the fingers. Adjust the tension so that there is $\frac{1}{4}$ in. up and down movement at the tightest spot.

Re-tighten the locknut on the adjusting screw, replace the chain cover and replenish with oil.

6. Timing Chain Adjustment

Before adjusting the tension of the timing chain, turn the engine until the chain is in its tightest position, checking the chain between all sprockets.

Adjust the tension so that there is $\frac{1}{4}$ in. movement of the chain.

The tension of the timing chain is altered by moving the quadrant after slackening the nut A which secures it (see Fig. 2). This rotates the eccentric spindle on which the chain tensioner jockey sprocket is mounted. Tightening of the chain is effected by moving the quadrant to the left.

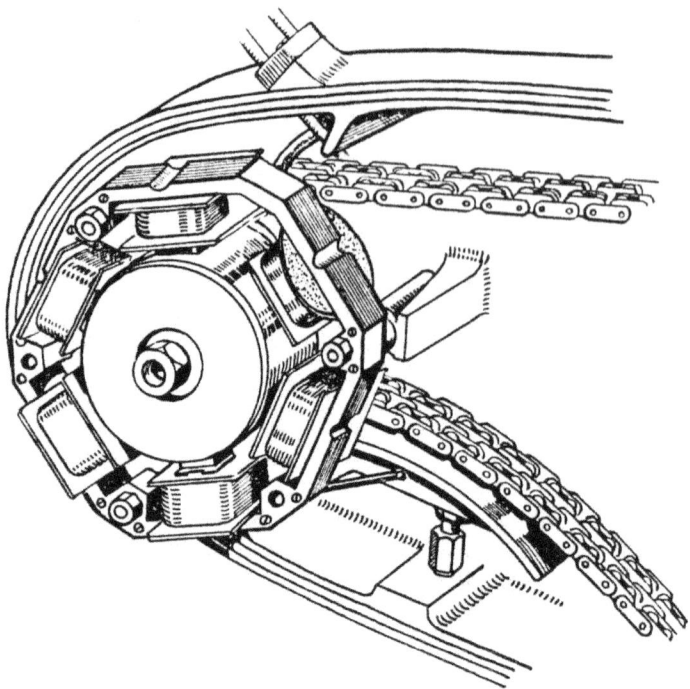

PRIMARY CHAIN ADJUSTMENT

Fig. 1

It is imperative that the quadrant is fitted the right way round and that the eccentric spindle is fitted correctly in the quadrant fork. If the chain tightens when the quadrant is moved to the right, the tensioner has been wrongly assembled and may cause damage to the quadrant (see Fig. 3).

In making the adjustment, care must be taken to see that any backlash in the quadrant is taken up in the "tightening" direction, i.e. do not make the chain too tight and then move the quadrant back slightly, but tighten the chain progressively until the correct tension is obtained and then lock the quadrant. If the chain becomes too tight during adjustment, slacken it right back and make the adjustment again.

If the chain is too slack it may give rise to a loud noise which can be mistaken for a faulty bearing. If it is too tight the result will be a high pitched howl. If such noises are heard, therefore, first check the adjustment of the timing chain.

7. Magneto Chain Adjustment

To adjust the magneto chain tension, remove the timing cover (see Subsection 1), slacken the three magneto fixing nuts, slide the magneto back until the chain has about $\frac{3}{16}$ in. up and down movement, then tighten the fixing nuts.

8. Removal of the Dual Seat and Rear Mudguard

Disconnect the leads to the rear lamp by pulling out the plugs in the connectors near the tool box.

Loosen the two nuts on either side of the seat attaching the mudguard carrier to the frame and lift the seat, mudguard and carrier off together. (See Section H, paragraph 9, and Fig. 3, for dismantling.)

The metal valances, situated on either side of the frame immediately below the rear mudguard of models from 1961 onwards, are detached when necessary by removing the $\tfrac{5}{16}$ in. bolts in the back of the tool box (two for each valance), and the small screw in the top of each suspension unit bracket. (See Section H, Fig. 2.)

9. Removal of the Petrol Tank

Remove the petrol tank by detaching the petrol pipe and removing the rubber mounted stud which secures the front of the tank to the frame. With early models release the bottom section of the rear clip by unscrewing the two $\tfrac{1}{4}$ in. attachment nuts. Tap out the two studs and raise the rear of the tank to release the clip. The tank may then be removed.

With later models the rear tank attachment is in the form of a laterally situated bracket with a rubber block fixed to it, this bears against the

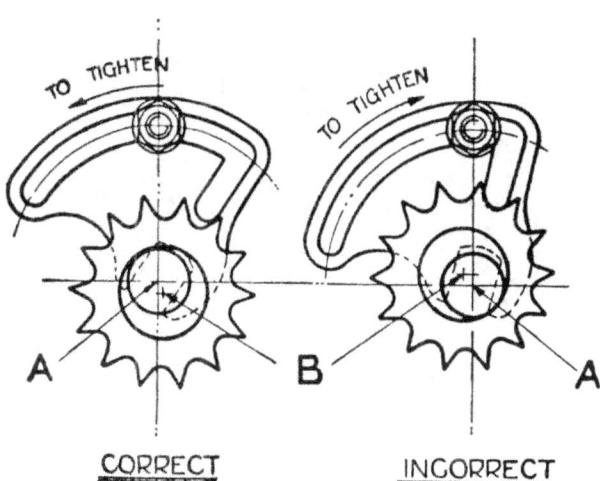

CORRECT   **INCORRECT**

TIMING CHAIN ADJUSTMENT

Fig. 3

underside of the frame top tube, drawing the tank down on to the rubber covering of the top tube.

To remove, unscrew the two bolts securing the bracket and lift the tank clear.

10. Removal of the Cylinder Head

First remove the petrol tank and petrol pipe. (Subsection 9.)

The dual seat may also be removed if desired. (Subsection 8.)

Disconnect the head steady link (early models).
Remove head steady brackets (later models).
Disconnect the oil pipes and plug leads.
Remove the exhaust pipes and carburettor(s) and induction manifold.
Remove the rocker box covers.
Turn the engine until both valves are closed.
Remove the five cylinder head nuts from each head and lift off.

In replacing the heads, see that the dowels are in position in the cylinder barrels and that the push rods are the right way up (shallow cups upwards).

Apply a thin coat of jointing compound to both sides of the gasket and place it in position.

Lower the cylinder heads over the push rods, making sure that the rockers locate in the push rod cups.

Fit the head nuts and washers and partially tighten down.

When both heads have reached this stage, fit the induction pipe and tighten the nuts. The cylinder head nuts can now be finally tightened down progressively and diagonally from one side to the other to prevent distortion. After the engine has been run long enough to get thoroughly hot, the tightness of the nuts should be re-checked.

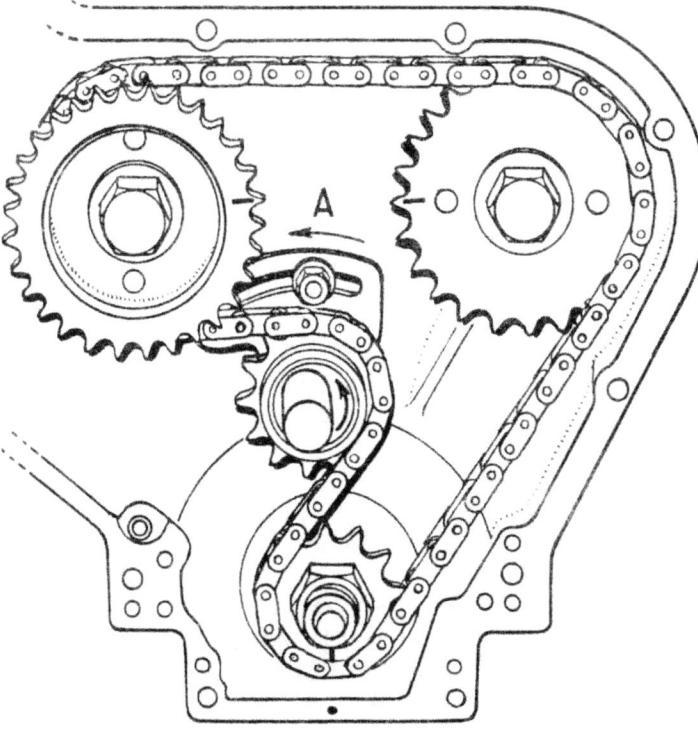

TIMING CHAIN ADJUSTMENT SHOWING TIMING MARKS

Fig. 2

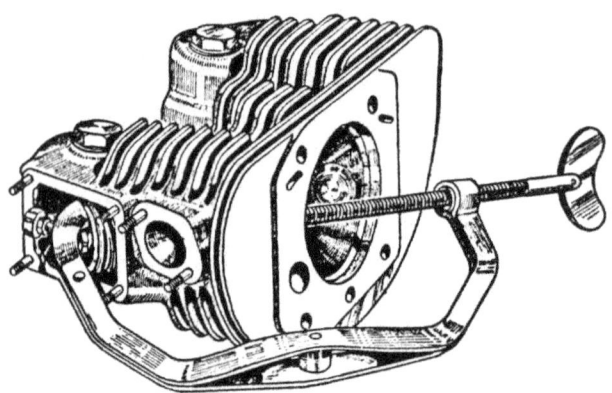

REMOVAL OF VALVES
Fig. 4

11. Removal of the Valves

Having removed the cylinder head, remove the rocker-box covers, each held by four nuts, and swing the rocker clear of the valve. Using a suitable valve spring compressing tool, compress the valve springs and remove the split collets from the end of the valve stem. Slacken back the compressing tool and release the springs. Withdraw the valve and place its springs, top spring collar (and bottom collar if it is loose) and split collets together in order that they may be re-assembled with the valve from which they were removed.

Deal similarly with the other valves in the heads.

If the valve will not slide easily through the valve guide, remove any slight burrs on the end of the valve stem with a carborundum stone. If the burrs are not removed and the valve is forced out, the guide may be damaged.

12. Removal of the Rockers

To remove the rocker, first take off the cylinder head. Remove the hexagon plug on the inner side and the rocker spindle may be drawn out by means of a bolt screwed into the rocker spindle, which is tapped $\frac{5}{16}''$ B.S.F.

On re-assembling make sure that the spring washers are fitted on the sides of the rockers nearest the centre of the engine and the plain thrust washers on the outer sides.

13. Removal of the Valve Guides

To remove the valve guides from the heads two special tools are required which can easily be made.

The first is a piece of tube with an internal bore of not less than $\frac{7}{8}$ in.

The second is a mandrel about 4 in. long made from $\frac{9}{16}$ in. diameter bar with the end turned down to about $\frac{6}{16}$ in. diameter for $\frac{1}{2}$ in.

Support the cylinder head on the tube which fits over the collar of the valve guide. Using the mandrel force the guide out of the head with a hand press or by using a hammer.

To fit a new guide, support the head at the correct angle and use a hand press and the same mandrel. If a hand press is not available and the guide is replaced by a hammer, use a piece of tube of $\frac{9}{16}$ in. internal diameter to prevent damage to the bore of the guide. If a valve guide is removed for any reason, an oversize one should be fitted in order to maintain the interference. It is necessary to re-cut the valve seat and grind in the valve after a guide has been replaced. (See Subsection 18.)

A worn exhaust valve guide may give rise to slight smoking from the exhaust pipe due to oil passing down the valve stem on to the hot valve head. This may also be caused or increased by faulty operation of the breather.

14. Removal of the Sparking Plugs

Care must be taken when removing and replacing the sparking plugs not to damage the threads in the cylinder heads.

If the threads do become damaged, they can be tapped out to a larger size and steel wire inserts fitted.

Special tools are available for tapping and inserting the steel wire inserts. The latter tool consists of a piece of $\frac{7}{16}$ in. diameter tube or rod with a slot cut in the end.

The insert is placed over the tool with the tag engaging in the slot and it is screwed into the plug hole in the cylinder head from the outside until the last coil is 1 to $1\frac{1}{2}$ threads below the top face. A reverse twist of the tool will then break off the tag.

If the cylinder head has been removed, the fitting of the insert will be facilitated if the tool is put through the hole from the inside and the insert screwed back from the outside.

If the cylinder head has not been removed, care must be taken not to drop the end of the tag into the cylinder and in such a case it is better to break off the tag with a pair of long-nosed pliers.

Note: Engines with a Number prior to SMSA 6800 have short reach plugs, in which case wire inserts are fitted as standard.

15. Removal of the Cylinders

When the cylinder heads have been removed the cylinders can be lifted clear of the studs. This should be done with the pistons at top dead centre.

It is advisable to put a clean cloth over the mouth of the crankcase to prevent anything, such as a piece of broken piston ring, from falling in.

When replacing the cylinders, clean off the joint faces and fit new paper joints, two to each cylinder.

16. Removal of Pistons

Remove the cylinder heads and cylinders.

With a tang of a file remove the two outer circlips retaining the gudgeon pins. Remove the long central cylinder studs which come opposite the gudgeon pins.

Use Special Tool No. E.5477 to extract the gudgeon pin or using a rod about $\frac{1}{4}$ in. in diameter insert this right through one gudgeon pin and drive the other pin out of its piston, supporting the connecting rod substantially meanwhile to prevent distortion.

Having lifted the first piston away, the other one may be readily removed in the same manner. Mark the pistons and gudgeon pins so that they go back into the same pistons the same way round and so that the pistons go back into the same barrels the same way round.

Take care not to drop the gudgeon pin circlip into the crankcase. A clean cloth should be put over the mouths of the crankcase to prevent this.

17. Decarbonising

Having removed the cylinder heads as described in Subsection 10, scrape away all carbon, bearing in mind that you are dealing with aluminium which is easily damaged. Scrape gently and avoid scoring the combustion chamber or the valve seats which are of austenitic iron shrunk into the head. Be careful while performing this work not to injure the joint faces which bed down on to the head gaskets.

Do not, in any circumstances, use caustic soda or potash for the removal of carbon from aluminium alloy.

Scrape away all carbon from the valve heads and beneath the heads, being very careful not to cause any damage to the valve faces.

If the piston rings are removed the grooves should be cleaned out and new rings fitted. For cleaning the grooves, a piece of discarded ring thrust into a wooden handle and filed to a chisel point is a useful tool.

If the piston ring gaps exceed $\frac{1}{16}$ in. when the rings are in position in the barrel, new rings should be fitted. The correct gap for new rings is ·011—·015 in. The gap should be measured in the least worn part of the cylinder, which will be found to be the extreme top or bottom of the bore.

While the cylinders and pistons are not in position on the engine, cover the crankcase with a clean cloth to prevent the ingress of dust and dirt of all kinds. Do not, of course, attempt to

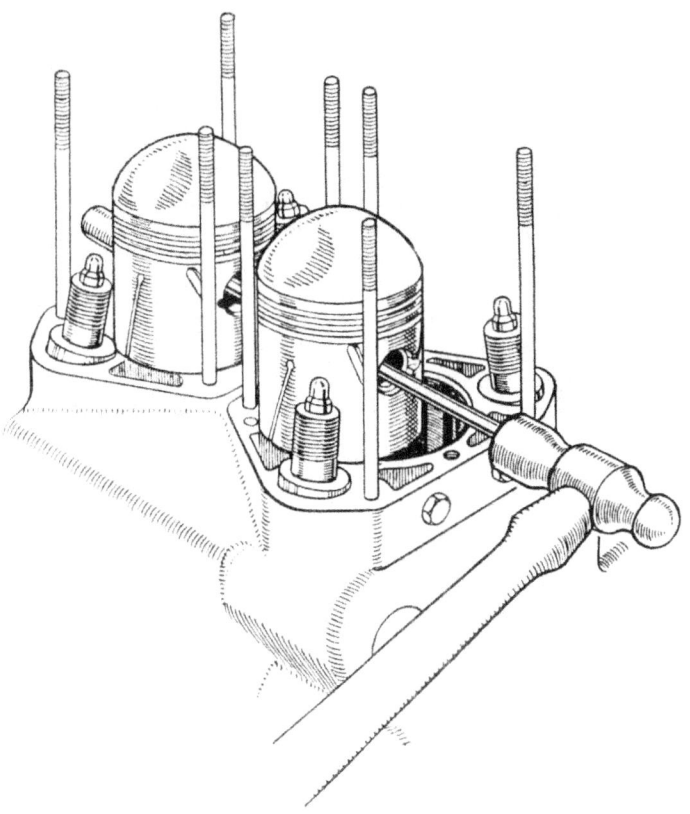

REMOVAL OF PISTONS
Fig. 5

scrape the carbon from the pistons when the mouths of the crankcase are open.

18. Grinding-in Valves

To grind a valve, smear the seating with a little grinding-in compound, place a light, short coil spring over the valve stem and beneath the head, insert the valve into its appropriate guide, press it on to the seat using a tool with a suction cup and with a backwards and forwards rotary motion, grind it on to its seat. Alternatively, a tool which pulls on the valve stem can be used. Frequently lift the valve and move it round so that an even and true seating is obtained. If no light spring is available, the lifting will have to be done by hand. Continue grinding until a bright ring is visible on both valve and seating.

The faces and seats of the exhaust valves are cut at 45 degrees but the profiles of the inlet seats are of a special streamlined design which eliminates pockets and sharp edges and allows a smooth flow of gas without eddies.

If the inlet valves or their seats are pitted and require re-cutting, care must be taken to reproduce the correct profile as shown in Fig. 6.

The cylinder heads should preferably be returned to the Works for the inlet valve seats to be re-cut, but, if this is not possible, a special tool consisting of an arbor No. T 2053 and cutter No. T2054 is available. Great care must be exercised in using this tool, as it is located off the valve guides and these may be damaged if suitable apparatus is not employed.

The inlet valve faces and seats can be cut at 45 degrees in cases of expediency but this may have a deleterious effect on the performance of the engine.

19. Re-Assembly after Decarbonising

Before building up the engine, see that all parts are scrupulously clean and place them conveniently to hand on a clean sheet of brown paper.

Check the piston ring gaps to find out whether excessive wear has taken place (see Subsection 17).

It is advisable to fit new gaskets to the cylinder base and cylinder head. Two paper gaskets are fitted to the base of each cylinder.

Smear clean oil over the pistons, having replaced the rings if these have been removed, lower the piston over the connecting rod and insert the gudgeon pin from the outer side. Fit the circlip and then fit the second piston in a similar manner.

Oil the cylinder bores and lower the barrels over the pistons and seat them gently on their gaskets.

Drop the push rods down their tunnels on to the tappet heads, shallow cups upwards.

Fit the copper cylinder head gaskets and see that the dowels are in position.

Replace the cylinder heads as described in Subsection 10.

After the engine has been assembled, run it for a brief period at a speed which will ensure that the ignition has been advanced by the automatic advance device. If it is run too slowly "blueing" of the exhaust pipes may take place.

After the engine has been run for some time and has become thoroughly hot, go over **all** the cylinder head and other nuts to ensure that they are tight.

The silencer fitted to 1961 models onwards, may be dismantled for cleaning before being refitted to the machine.

After removing the $\frac{5}{16}$ in. nut and tab washer in the tail, the tail piece and central body may be drawn off the long central stud located in the front portion of the silencer. (See Fig. 8.)

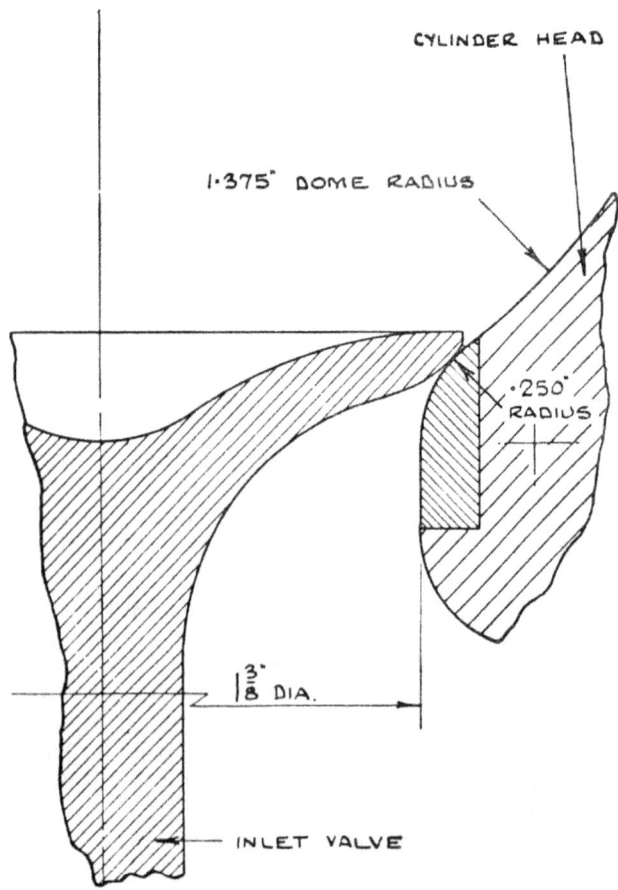

INLET VALVE SEAT PROFILE

Fig. 6

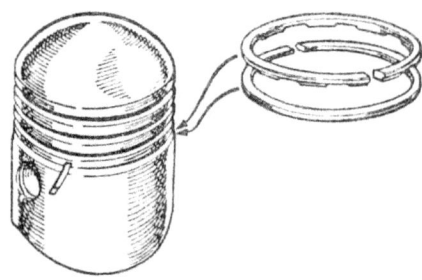

CORRECT RELATIVE POSITIONS OF DUAL SCRAPER RINGS (LATER MODELS)

Fig. 7

20. Cleaning the Oil Filters

The oil filter is located in the timing cover immediately below the oil pumps and is in the feed circuit to the big ends.

The filter element is removed by unscrewing the nut holding the end cap in position. When re-assembling the filter after cleaning, take care that no grit or other foreign matter is sticking to it.

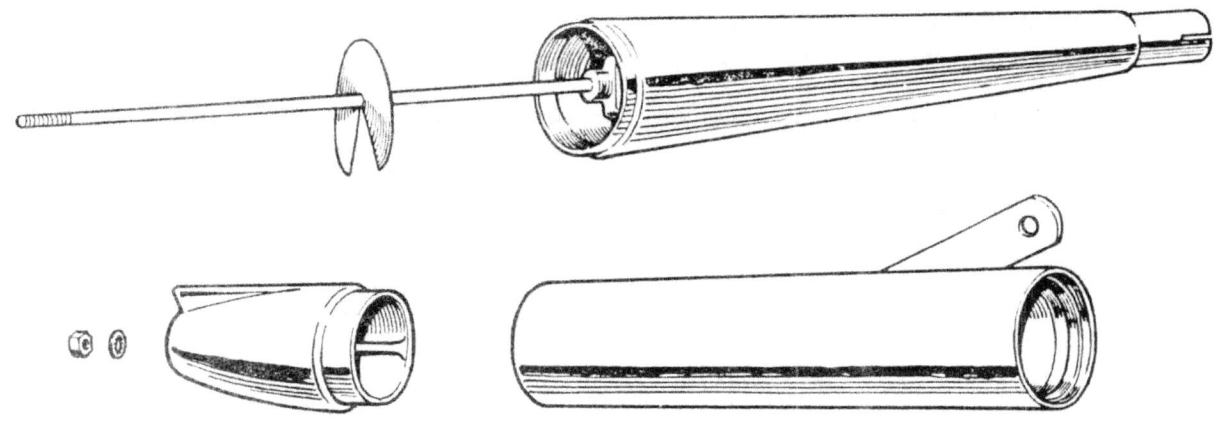
SILENCER FOR 1961 MODELS ONWARDS, DISMANTLED
Fig. 8

The aluminium cylinder fitted over the rod inside the filter element is to reduce the free space which has to be filled after cleaning before oil reaches the big ends. After emptying the filter chamber it is essential to run the engine slowly for about five minutes to ensure that oil is reaching the big ends.

The felt element should be taken out and washed in petrol after the first 500 miles and after every subsequent 2,000 miles. Fit a new element every 5,000 miles.

21. Overhaul of Oil Pumps

Remove the timing cover as described in Subsection 1.

Remove the end plates from both pumps.

Remove the pump discs and plungers.

Remove the pump spindle which can be pulled out from the front or return pump end.

Check the fit of the plungers in the pump discs which should have a minimum of clearance but should be able to be moved in and out by hand.

If, when fitting a new disc or plunger, the plunger is found to be too tight a fit, carefully lap with metal polish until it is just free. If the pump disc is not seating properly or if a new pump disc is being fitted, it should be lapped to the seating with Special Tool No. E.5425, using Carborundum 360 Fine Paste or liquid metal polish until an even grey surface is obtained.

Wash all passages, etc., thoroughly with petrol after lapping to remove all traces of grinding paste.

Check the pump disc springs for fatigue by assembling in the timing cover and placing the pump covers in position. If the springs are correct, the pump cover should be held $\frac{1}{4}$ in. off the timing cover by the feed pump spring and $\frac{1}{8}$ in. off by the return pump spring.

The pump spindle should be renewed if excessive wear has taken place on the teeth.

Re-assemble the oil pumps, replacing the paper cover gaskets if necessary. Before fitting each cover fill the pump chamber with clean oil.

Having assembled the pumps, lay the timing cover flat and fill the oil ports by means of an oilcan. Turn the pump spindle with a screw driver in a clockwise direction looking on the front and it can then be seen whether the pumps are operating correctly.

Fill the filter chamber with clean oil and replace the timing cover, taking great care not to damage the gasket where the section is narrow.

When the timing cover has been refitted on the engine, the oil feed to the big ends can be checked by partially unscrewing the feed plug in the timing cover between the oil pumps. The oil return to the tank can be checked by removing the oil filler cap. The feed to the rockers can be observed by removing the rocker-box covers, when oil will be seen flowing down the surface of the push rods.

22. Removal of the Timing Chains

Remove the magneto and chain (Subsection 25).

Loosen the chain tensioner locknut and stud.

Lift the adjusting plate clear of the chain tensioner spindle.

Remove the chain tensioner spindle and sprocket.

Lift the chain off the sprockets.

23. Removal of Pump Worm and Timing Sprocket

Remove the timing chains (Subsection 22).

Unscrew the oil pump worm by means of the hexagon head behind it. This is a **Left Hand Thread.**

Withdraw the timing sprocket using Special Tool No. E.4869.

24. Removal of the Camshaft Sprockets

Remove the timing chains (Subsection 22).

Unscrew the camshaft sprocket fixing bolt, **which has a Left Hand Thread,** at the same time holding the sprocket.

Withdraw the sprocket by means of a suitable extractor.

25. Removal of the Magneto

Remove the timing cover (Subsection 1).
Remove three fixing nuts.
Lift the chain off the sprocket and withdraw the magneto and sprocket complete.

26. Removal of the Engine and Clutch Sprockets

The primary chain is endless so that it is necessary to remove both the engine and clutch sprockets simultaneously.

On early models the alternator stator is removed by undoing the three fixing screws, but in the case of later types, the smaller diameter stator must be withdrawn from the adaptor ring after removing three nuts. The adaptor ring can then be removed from the primary chain case when the three screws have been taken out.

Remove the central hexagon bolt securing the alternator rotor, which can then be drawn off, taking care not to lose the key.

Unscrew the engine sprocket nut, using Special Tool No. E.4877. The engine sprocket is mounted on splines and can then be removed with the clutch sprocket.

To remove the clutch sprocket, disconnect the clutch cable, unscrew three pressure plate pins and remove the pressure plate assembly, the centre retaining ring and the assembly of driving and driven clutch plates. The clutch sprocket can then be withdrawn from the centre after the removal of the large circlip which secures it.

When replacing the engine sprocket, take care that the felt washer, fitted to earlier models, is not nipped behind the sprocket. This would make the engine very stiff to turn over, and would damage the washer, allowing leakage from the crankcase. The Neoprene washer of later engines cannot be caught in this manner. (See Subsection 31.)

27. Removal of the Tappets and Guides

It is only necessary to remove the tappets and guides if they have become worn.

Remove the cylinder heads and barrels. (Subsections 10 and 15.)

Extract the tappet guides, using Special Tool No. E.5790, having heated the case first.

The guides are made from Nickel Chrome Alloy Iron and if a guide should break while removing it, it can be withdrawn with a pair of pliers if the crankcase is heated locally with a blowlamp. Otherwise it is necessary to dismantle the crankcase and drive the tappet and guide out from underneath using a heavy bar in the cam tunnel.

The guide should have an interference of ·0015 to ·0025 in. in the crankcase and can be driven in with a bronze drift, care being taken when the guide is nearly home to avoid breaking the collar.

When replacing the exhaust valve tappet guides care must be taken to ensure that the groove in the timing side exhaust guide comes opposite the hole to the timing chest otherwise flooding of the push rod hole in the cylinder will occur causing over-oiling.

If a tappet guide is taken out it should be replaced by an oversize one.

28. Dismantling the Breathers

If the breathers are not operating efficiently, they may cause pressure in the crankcase, instead of a partial vacuum, giving rise to smoking or over-oiling.

See that the discs and backplate of the breather on the crankcase immediately below the left-hand cylinder are clean and undamaged, and that the discs are seating properly.

When reassembling the breather, apply jointing compound sparingly to the back of the steel plate, taking great care to keep the compound away from the discs and seatings.

Where fitted, the breather which operates through the end of the crankshaft, may be inspected by removing the slotted plug from the head of the rotor retaining bolt. (See Fig. 9.)

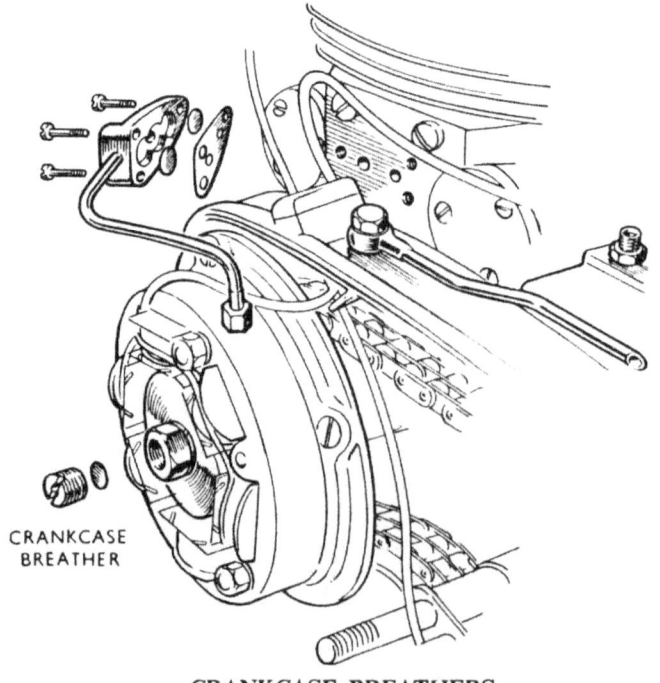

CRANKCASE BREATHERS
Fig. 9

29. Removal of the Clutch

Remove the engine sprocket and clutch sprocket together as described in Subsection 26.

To remove the clutch hub, hold the clutch with Special Tool No. E 4871 and remove the centre retaining nut and washer with a box spanner.

The hub can then be withdrawn from the shaft with Special Tool No. E.5414.

30. Removal of the Final Drive Sprocket

Remove the clutch as described in Subsection 29.

Remove the primary chain tensioner.

Remove the rear half of the primary chain case by taking out three socket screws.

Remove the grub screw locking the final drive sprocket nut.

Hold the sprocket and remove the nut (**Right Hand Thread**). The sprocket can then be withdrawn.

31. Removal of the Engine Bearing Housing Felt Washer (Engines prior to SMSA 6964)

Remove the engine sprocket, clutch and rear half of the primary chain case.

The felt washer is located in the steel housing at the back of the chain case.

Great care must be taken not to nip the felt washer behind the sprocket on re-assembly as this would make the engine very stiff to turn over and would damage the washer and allow leakage from the crankcase.

On Engine SMSA 6964 *et seq* a neoprene oil seal is fitted and the above does not apply.

32. Oil Pipe Unions

The oil feed to the rocker gear is through pipes from unions at the back of the crankcase below the cylinder base to unions on the cylinder heads.

The tapped holes into which the unions screw into the aluminium are fitted with steel wire inserts to prevent the threads in the aluminium from stripping.

The method of fitting the thread inserts is the same as that used for the sparking plug inserts described in Subsection 14.

33. Rocker Oil Feed Relief Valve

There is a pressure relief valve in the oil supply to the rocker gear, whose function is to prevent excessive pressure and whose setting is not critical.

The valve is located in the crankcase face behind the timing cover and consists of a $\frac{3}{16}$ in. diameter steel ball held in position by a spring and a brass plug.

The valve is set before leaving the Works and should not normally require to be disturbed but, if it is found necessary to dismantle it, it can be reset by screwing the plug in until it is flush with the face of the crankcase, which will cause the pressure to be relieved at approximately 10 lbs. per square inch. The plug is prevented from moving by peening over the aluminium **into** the screwdriver slot with a small centre punch.

34. Fitting the Alternator

The alternator consists of two parts, the stator and the rotor. The stator of 1960 models and onwards, is mounted on to the three studs of the adaptor ring, which in turn is secured to the back half of the primary chaincase by three screws.

On earlier models the stator is of greater diameter and mounted on to the primary chaincase with three studs and distance pieces.

The rotor, which contains the permanent magnet, is mounted on the end of the crankshaft and is located by a key and secured by a special bolt and spring washer on later models, and by a nut and tab washer on earlier models.

The radial air gap between the rotor and the poles of the stator should be ·020 in. in all positions and care must be taken when refitting to see that it is not less than ·010 in. at any point.

Fit the rotor first, making sure that it is located concentrically on the end of the crankshaft. Attention must be given to the seating of the key because a badly-fitting key may cause the rotor to run unevenly. Finally secure the rotor with the appropriate bolt or nut and washer.

Having fitted the rotor, secure the adaptor ring of later models with the three cheese-headed screws and shakeproof washers, or, in the case of earlier models, place the three distance pieces over the three chaincase studs. The stator may then be fitted, with the coil connections facing outwards.

Replace the nuts and shakeproof washers only finger-tight, and insert six strips (preferably of non-magnetic material) ·015 in. thick and about $\frac{1}{8}$ in. wide between the rotor and each pole piece.

Tighten the stator nuts and withdraw the strips.

Check the air gap with narrow feelers and, if less than ·010 in. at any point, remove the stator and file or grind the pole piece carefully until the correct gap is obtained.

An alternative, and more satisfactory, method of assembling the alternator requires the use of Special Tool No. T2055.

This is a gauge ·015 in. greater in radius than the rotor and fits over the adaptor on the end of the crankshaft in the rotor's place.

The stator is then put in position on the studs in the chaincase and the nuts tightened up.

Remove the gauge and fit the rotor, then check the air gap.

NOTES

SECTION C12

Service Operations with Engine in Frame

"Super Meteor"

1. Removal of Timing Cover

First place a tray under the engine to catch the oil which will escape when the cover is removed. Remove the timing side exhaust pipe and the oil filler neck, by taking out the three screws fixing it to the crankcase. Remove the timing cover fixing screws. Draw off the timing cover, tapping it lightly if necessary.

In refitting the cover, insert the two long screws through the cover to locate the gasket. See that the thrust washer is on the chain tensioner sprocket spindle and that the neoprene seal is in position on the oil feed plug. If the seal is split or otherwise damaged, a new one should be fitted, of the latest type, which is captive on the feed plug. The feed plug is Part No. 42113; seal is Part No. 42114. If the plug is damaged it should be renewed to ensure oil pressure to the big end bearings.

The refitting of the cover will be facilitated if the engine is turned gently forwards while the cover is being put into place. This will help the engagement of the pump worm with the pump spindle and prevent damage to the gears.

Always fill the filter with clean oil before refitting the timing cover and always take great care not to damage the gasket where the section is narrow.

To verify that the oil pumps are working after replacing the timing cover, start the engine and remove the oil filler cap so that the oil return pipe can be seen. It may take several minutes for all the oil passages to fill and the oil to commence to circulate.

2. Valve Timing

The camshaft sprockets are keyed to the camshafts so that the valve timing can only be incorrect if the timing chain is incorrectly fitted.

The correct setting is obtained with the marks stamped on the camshaft sprockets facing each other inwards on the centre line and the mark on the crankshaft sprockets pointing vertically downwards. If it is necessary to remove the sprockets see Subsections 23 and 24.

Remember that all three timing sprockets fixing bolts have **Left Hand Threads.** While tightening the camshaft bolts the sprockets should be held.

The correct valve timing at ·012 in. clearance is as follows:—
Exhaust opens 75° before bottom dead centre.
Exhaust closes 35° after top dead centre.
Inlet opens 30° before top dead centre.
Inlet closes 60° after bottom dead centre.

3. Tappet Adjustment

The tappet clearance is adjusted by means of a screw in the outer end of the rocker. Access to the adjusting screws is obtained by removing the covers of the rocker boxes.

The clearance between the end of the screw and the valve stem cap should be nil or as little as possible with the engine **COLD.**

To adjust the clearance, loosen the locknut beneath the rocker arm, turn the screw with a small spanner and re-tighten the locknut.

The adjustment for each valve should be made with the corresponding valve of the other cylinder fully open. This ensures that the tappet is well clear of the ramp which is located on either side of the cam to reduce valve noise.

If, after long service, the valve stem cap or the rocker adjusting screw are found to be worn, they should be renewed, as uneven thrust due to the screw being in a different position after adjustment may cause lateral movement of the rocker giving rise to a sharp tapping noise.

4(a). Ignition Timing (Magneto)

The setting of the ignition depends upon the position of the sprocket relative to the magneto shaft.

To obtain access to the magneto sprocket it is necessary to remove the timing cover (see Subsection 1).

The sprocket is built into the automatic advance device and is mounted on a smooth taper on the magneto shaft. It is held in position by a nut. **(Right Hand Thread.)**

To remove the sprocket and auto-advance device, unscrew the nut and this will draw the sprocket off.

Before setting the timing remove the rotor arm of the distributor and adjust the contact breaker points to a clearance of ·015 in. when fully opened.

Because of the auto-advance mechanism, the timing is normally in the "retard" position when the engine is stationary. Rotate the two halves

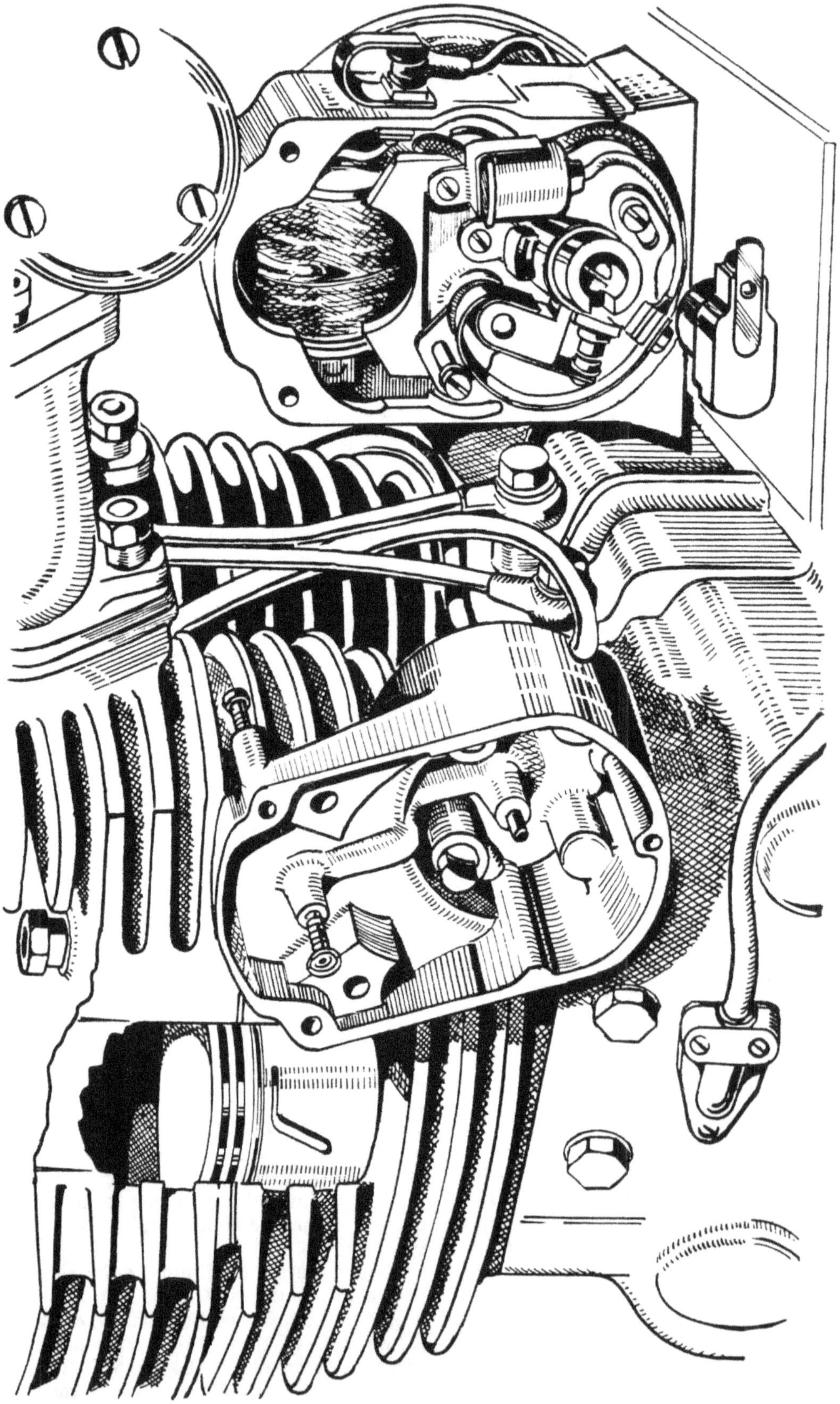

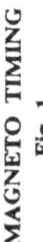

MAGNETO TIMING
Fig. 1

of the coupling relatively to each other against the springs, i.e. into the "advance" position, and hold it in this position with a piece of wire.

To set the timing, turn the engine until the pistons are $\frac{3}{8}-\frac{7}{16}$ in. before top dead centre on the compression stroke of the left hand cylinder, i.e. with both valves closed.

Insert a thin piece of tissue paper between the points of the contact breaker and turn the magneto forwards until the paper can just be pulled out, making sure that the rotor arm of the distributor when replaced will be pointing towards the segment connected to the left hand sparking plug lead.

Tighten the sprocket and auto-advance device on to the magneto shaft, taking care that it does not slip.

Remove the piece of wire holding the auto-advance mechanism.

The timing can be checked by removing the cap from the magneto and holding the rotor arm of the distributor in the advanced position, which is $\frac{3}{8}-\frac{7}{16}$ in. before top dead centre, without the necessity of taking off the timing cover.

On no account must the cam be altered from its original position on the rotor shaft or the efficiency of the magneto will be affected.

4(b). Ignition Timing (Coil)

On some models coil ignition is fitted instead of magneto.

Before setting the timing, remove the cover and rotor arm of the distributor and adjust the contact breaker points to a clearance of ·015 in. when fully opened. If the contacts are worn or pitted refer to Section G.

Because of the auto-advance mechanism, the timing is normally in the "retard" position when the engine is stationary, and the timing is set so that firing occurs when the piston is $\frac{1}{32}$ in. before top dead centre, which is equivalent to $\frac{3}{8}$ in. to $\frac{7}{16}$ in. when fully advanced.

To set the ignition timing, put the gearbox in top gear and turn the engine by means of the back wheel until the left-hand piston is $\frac{1}{32}$ in. before top dead centre on the compression stroke, i.e., with both valves closed. The position of the piston can be determined by means of a wire or rod inserted in the sparking plug hole. Slacken the clamp bolt which holds the distributor body to the housing at the back of the timing cover and turn the distributor body until the contact points are just opening, then re-tighten the clamp bolt.

Check the timing again and also the maximum opening of the points and check that the rotor arm, when replaced, points towards the segment connected to the left-hand sparking plug lead.

There are several methods of determining the point at which the contacts open:—

(1) Switch on the ignition. Looking on the left side of the engine, rotate the cam in a clockwise direction (or the housing in a counter-clockwise direction) until the warning light in the ammeter lights up or until the ammeter needle indicates a discharge. Continue to rotate the cam (or housing) slowly until the warning light goes out or until the ammeter needle returns to zero, indicating that the points have opened.

(2) Remove the sparking plug cap from the lead and tuck the lead between the fins of the cylinder. Rotate the cam (or housing) and a spark will be seen at the instant the points open.

(3) Insert a piece of thin tissue paper between the points of the contact breaker and turn the cam (or housing) until the paper can just be pulled out.

If the timing drive has been dismantled or the distributor removed for any reason, turn the engine until the left-hand piston is $\frac{1}{32}$ in. before top dead centre on the compression stroke, and clamp the distributor housing so that the name on it is roughly horizontal.

Replace the chain with the cam in such a position that the contacts are just opening (or as near as possible to this position), with the rotor arm, if replaced, pointing towards the lead to the left-hand sparking plug.

Make the final adjustment by slackening the clamp bolt and rotating the distributor body as described above.

5. Primary Chain Adjustment

The tension of the primary chain can be checked through the inspection cover in the primary

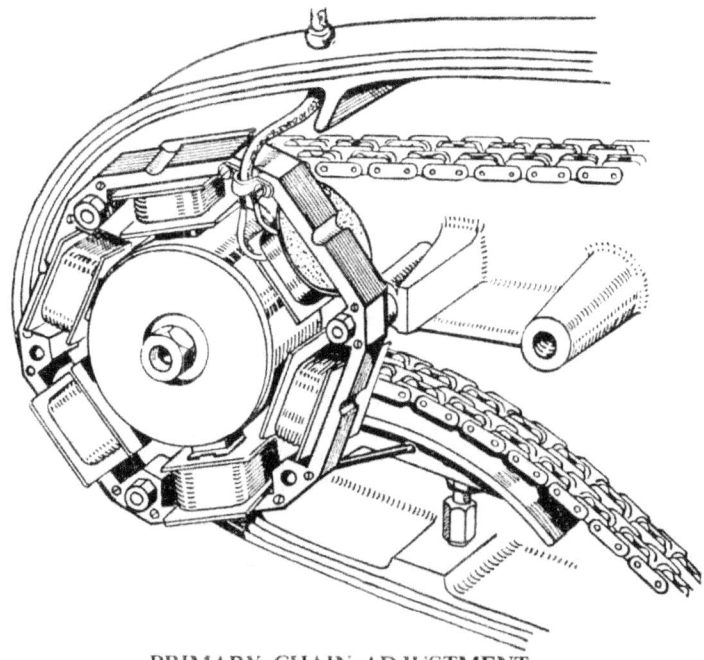

PRIMARY CHAIN ADJUSTMENT
Fig. 2

chain case and, should it require adjustment, access to the adjuster is gained by removing the chain case cover, which is held in position by a single nut. Before removing the nut, place a tray under the engine to catch the oil from the chaincase.

Beneath the bottom run of the chain is a curved slipper on which the chain rests and which may be raised or lowered by turning the adjusting screw after having first slackened the locknut.

A rubber button is fitted to the end of the adjusting screw to prevent the transmission of chain noise to the chaincase and this is held against the chaincase by a hairpin spring, which prevents it from bouncing.

After replacing the chain cover, remember to replenish the chaincase with oil.

Do not adjust the chain to be dead tight but rotate the engine slowly and, while doing so, test the tension of the top run of the chain by pressing it up and down with the fingers. Adjust the tension so that there is $\frac{1}{4}$ in. up and down movement at the tightest spot.

Re-tighten the locknut on the adjusting screw, replace the chain cover and replenish with oil.

6. Timing Chain Adjustment

Before adjusting the tension of the timing chain, turn the engine until the chain is in its tightest position and any slack is between the rear cam sprocket and the timing sprocket on the engine shaft.

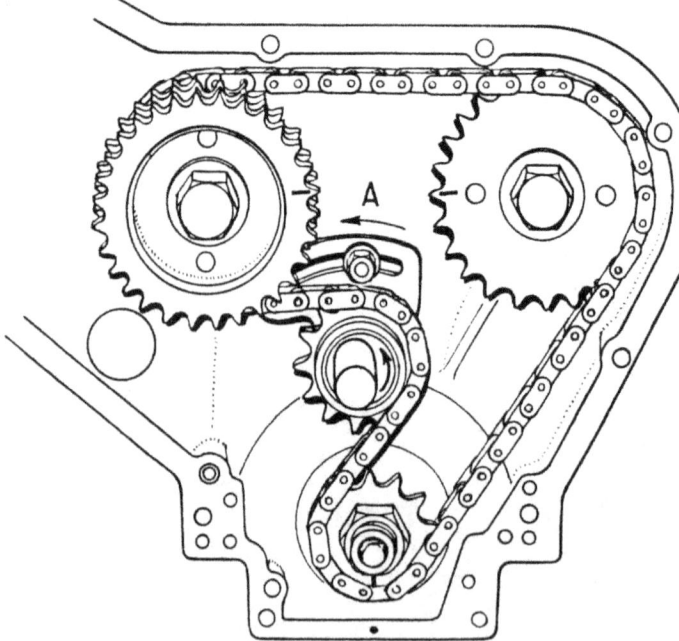

TIMING CHAIN ADJUSTMENT SHOWING TIMING MARKS
Fig. 3

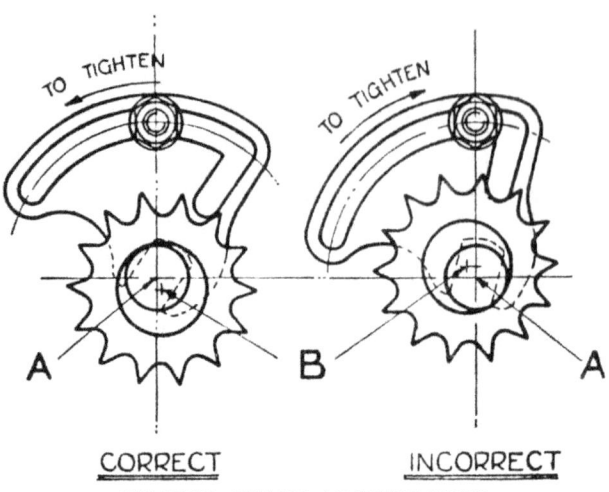

TIMING CHAIN ADJUSTMENT
Fig. 4

The tension of the timing chain is altered by moving the quadrant after slackening the nut A which secures it (see Fig. 3). This rotates the eccentric spindle on which the chain tensioner jockey sprocket is mounted. Tightening of the chain is effected by moving the quadrant to the left.

It is imperative that the quadrant is fitted the right way round and that the eccentric spindle is fitted correctly in the quadrant fork. If the chain tightens when the quadrant is moved to the right, the tensioner has been wrongly assembled and may cause damage to the quadrant (see Fig. 4).

In making the adjustment, care must be taken to see that any backlash in the quadrant is taken up in the "tightening" direction, i.e., do not make the chain too tight and then move the quadrant back slightly, but tighten the chain progressively until the correct tension is obtained and then lock the quadrant. If the chain becomes too tight during adjustment, slacken it right back and make the adjustment again.

If the chain is maladjusted, it may give rise to a loud noise which can be mistaken for a faulty bearing. If such a noise is heard, therefore, first check the adjustment of the timing chain.

7(a). Magneto Chain Adjustment

To adjust the magneto chain tension, remove the timing cover (see Subsection 1), slacken the three magneto fixing bolts, slide the magneto back until the chain has about $\frac{3}{16}$ in. up and down movement, then tighten the fixing bolts.

7(b). Distributor Chain Adjustment

To adjust the distributor chain tension, remove the timing cover (see Subsection 1), slacken the three distributor fixing bolts, slide the distributor back until the chain has about $\frac{3}{16}$ in. up and down movement, then tighten the fixing bolts.

8. Removal of Dual Seat and Rear Mudguard

Disconnect the leads to the rear lamp by pulling out the plugs in the connectors near the tool box.

Remove the two nuts on either side of the seat attaching it to the frame and lift the seat and mudguard off.

9. Removal of the Petrol Tank

Turn off the petrol tap.

The petrol tank is attached to the frame by a rubber mounted stud at the front, and is clipped at the rear to a rubber sleeve surrounding the top tube. To remove the tank, unscrew one front attachment nut, tap out the stud and, after disconnecting the petrol feed pipe, the rear of the tank can be pulled upwards to release the clip and then lifted clear of the frame.

10. Removal of Cylinder Head

First remove the petrol tank and petrol pipe (Subsection 9).

The dual seat may also be removed if desired (Subsection 8).

Disconnect the head steady link.

Disconnect the oil pipes and plug leads.

Remove the exhaust pipes and carburetter and induction pipe.

Remove the rocker box covers.

Turn the engine until both valves are closed.

Remove the five cylinder head nuts and lift off the head.

In replacing the head, see that the dowels are in position in the cylinder barrel and that the push rods are the right way up (shallow cups upwards).

Apply a thin coat of jointing compound to both sides of the gasket and place it in position.

Lower the cylinder head over the push rods, making sure that the rockers locate in the push rod cups.

Fit the head nuts and washers and partially tighten down.

When both heads have reached this stage, fit the induction pipe and tighten the nuts. The cylinder head nuts can now be finally tightened down progressively and diagonally from one side to the other to prevent distortion. After the engine has been run long enough to get thoroughly hot, the tightness of the nuts should be re-checked.

11. Removal of Valves

Remove the rocker-box covers, each held by four nuts, swing the rocker clear of the valve and lift or prise away the hardened steel thimble or end cap. If this has stuck, it can be removed by means of a screwdriver. Using a suitable valve spring compressing tool, compress the valve springs and remove the split conical collets from the end

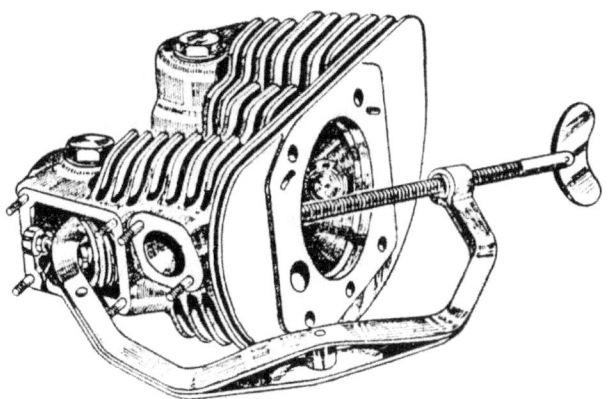

REMOVAL OF VALVES
Fig. 5

of the valve stem. Slacken back the compressing tool and release the springs. Withdraw the valve and place its springs, top spring collar (and bottom collar if it is loose) and split conical collets together in order that they may be re-assembled with the valve from which they were removed.

Deal similarly with the other valves in the heads.

If the valve will not slide easily through the valve guide, remove any slight burrs on the end of the valve stem with a carborundum stone. If the burrs are not removed and the valve is forced out, the guide may be damaged.

12. Removal of Rockers

To remove the rocker, first take off the cylinder head. Remove the hexagon plug on the inner side and the rocker spindle may be drawn out by means of a bolt screwed into the rocker spindle, which is tapped $\frac{5}{16}$ in. B.S.F.

On re-assembling make sure that the spring washers are fitted on the sides of the rockers nearest the centre of the engine and the plain thrust washers on the outer sides.

13. Removal of Valve Guides

To remove the valve guides from the heads two special tools are required which can easily be made.

The first is a piece of tube with an internal bore of not less than $\frac{7}{8}$ in.

The second is a mandrel about 4 in. long made from $\frac{9}{16}$ in. diameter bar with the end turned down to about $\frac{5}{16}$ in. diameter for $\frac{1}{2}$ in.

Support the cylinder head on the tube which fits over the collar of the valve guide. Using the mandrel force the guide out of the head with a hand press or by using a hammer.

To fit a new guide, support the head at the correct angle and use a hand press and the same mandrel. If a hand press is not available and the guide is replaced by a hammer, use a piece of tube of $\frac{9}{16}$ in. internal diameter to prevent damage

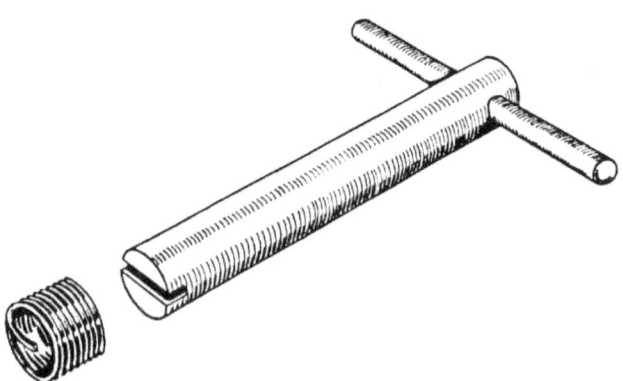

SPARKING PLUG INSERT
Fig. 6

to the bore of the guide. If a valve guide is removed for any reason, an oversize one should be fitted in order to maintain the interference. It is necessary to re-cut the valve seat and grind in the valve after a guide has been replaced. (See Subsection 18.)

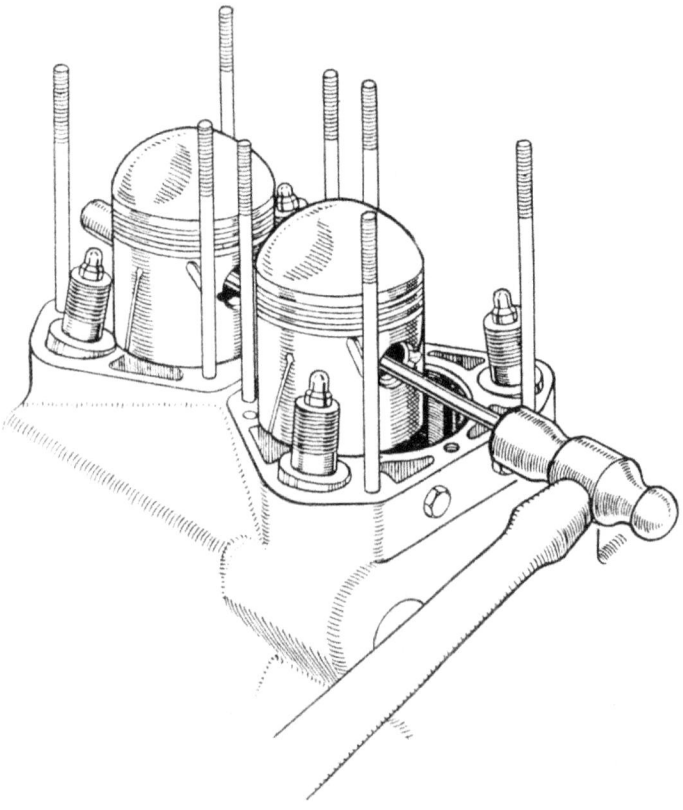

REMOVAL OF PISTONS
Fig. 7

A worn exhaust valve guide may give rise to slight smoking from the exhaust pipe due to oil passing down the valve stem on to the hot valve head. This may also be caused or increased by faulty operation of the breather.

14. Renewal of Sparking Plug Inserts

A steel thread insert is fitted into each sparking plug bore to prevent damage to the threads in the alloy cylinder heads.

This insert should not normally require renewal but if it does become damaged, for instance by a faulty plug, it can be pulled out with a pair of pliers and a new one fitted.

To fit a new insert a special tool T.2142, consisting of a piece of $\frac{7}{16}$ in. diameter tube or rod with a slot cut in the end is required.

The new insert is placed over the tool with the tag engaged in the slot and it is screwed into the plug hole in the cylinder head from the outside until the last coil is 1 to $1\frac{1}{2}$ threads below the top face. A reverse twist of the tool will then break off the tag.

If the cylinder head has not been removed from the engine, care must be taken not to drop the end of the tag into the cylinder and in such a case it is better to break off the tag with a pair of long-nosed pliers.

15. Removal of Cylinders

When the cylinder heads have been removed the cylinders can be lifted clear of the studs. This should be done with the pistons at bottom dead centre.

When replacing the cylinders, clean off the joint faces and fit new paper joints, two to each cylinder.

16. Removal of Pistons

Remove the cylinder heads and cylinders.

With a tang of a file remove one of the wire circlips retaining the gudgeon pins. If necessary rotate the engine slightly until the pistons are in such a position that the gudgeon pins will clear the long cylinder studs when being withdrawn.

Use Special Tool No. E.5477 to extract the gudgeon pin or using a rod about $\frac{1}{4}$ in. in diameter insert this right through one gudgeon pin and drive the other pin out of its piston, supporting the connecting rod substantially meanwhile to prevent distortion.

Having lifted the first piston away, the other one may be readily removed in the same manner. Mark the pistons and gudgeon pins so that they go back into the same pistons the same way round and so that the pistons go back into the same barrels the same way round.

Take care not to drop the gudgeon pin circlip into the crankcase. A clean cloth should be put over the mouths of the crankcase to prevent this.

17. Decarbonising

Having removed the cylinder heads as described in Subsection 10, scrape away all carbon, bearing in mind that you are dealing with aluminium which is easily damaged. Scrape gently and avoid scoring the combustion chamber of the valve seats which are of austenitic iron shrunk into the head. Be careful while performing this work not to injure the joint faces which bed down on to the head gaskets.

Do not, in any circumstances, use caustic soda or potash for the removal of carbon from aluminium alloy.

Scrape away all carbon from the valve heads and beneath the heads, being very careful not to cause any damage to the valve faces.

If the piston rings are removed the grooves should be cleaned out and new rings fitted. For cleaning the grooves a piece of discarded ring thrust into a wooden handle and filed to a chisel point is a useful tool.

If the piston ring gaps exceed $\frac{1}{16}$ in. when the rings are in position in the barrel, new rings should be fitted. The correct gap for new rings is ·011—·015 in. The gap should be measured in the least worn part of the cylinder, which will be found to be the extreme top or bottom of the bore.

While the cylinders and pistons are not in position on the engine, cover the crankcase with a clean cloth to prevent the ingress of dust and dirt of all kinds. Do not, of course, attempt to scrape the carbon from the pistons when the mouths of the crankcase are open.

18. Grinding-in Valves

To grind a valve, smear the seating with a little grinding-in compound, place a light, short coil spring over the valve stem and beneath the head, insert the valve into its appropriate guide, press it on to the seat using a tool with a suction cup and with a backwards and forwards rotary motion, grind it on to its seat. Alternatively, a tool which pulls on the valve stem can be used. Frequently lift the valve and move it round so that an even and true seating is obtained. If no light spring is available, the lifting will have to be done by hand. Continue grinding until a bright ring is visible on both valve and seating.

The faces and seats of the exhaust valves are cut at 45 degrees but the profiles of the inlet valves are of a special streamlined design which eliminates pockets and sharp edges and allows a smooth flow of gas without eddies.

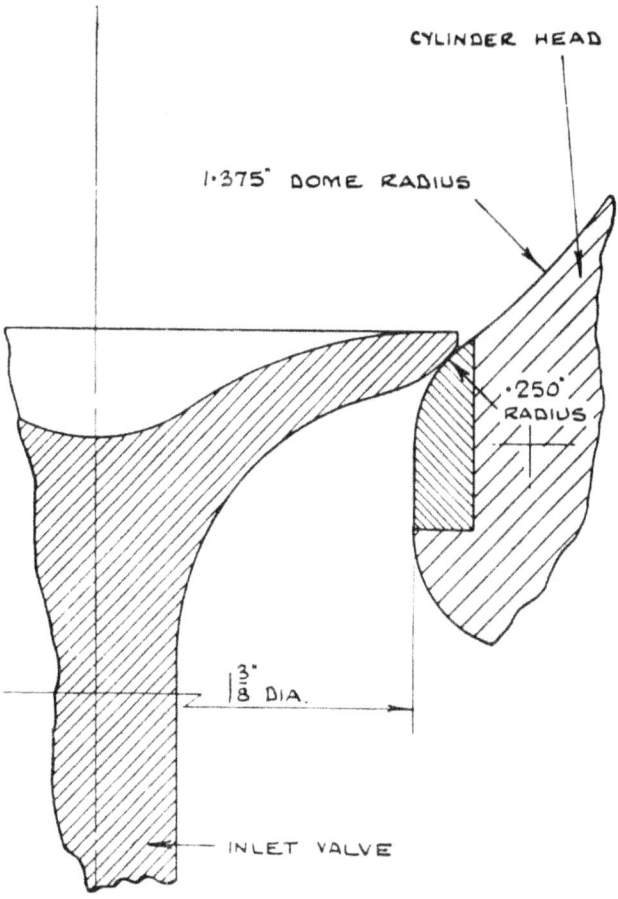

INLET VALVE SEAT PROFILE
Fig. 8

If the inlet valves or their seats are pitted and require re-cutting, care must be taken to reproduce the correct profile as shown in Fig. 8.

The cylinder heads should preferably be returned to the works for the inlet valve seats to be re-cut, but, if this is not possible, a special tool consisting of an arbor No. T.2053 and cutter No. T.2054 is available. Great care must be exercised in using this tool, as it is located off the valve guides and these may be damaged if suitable apparatus is not employed.

The inlet valve faces and seats can be cut at 45 degrees in cases of expediency but this may have a deleterious effect on the performance of the engine.

19. Re-assembly after Decarbonising

Before building up the engine, see that all parts are scrupulously clean and place them conveniently to hand on a clean sheet of brown paper.

It is advisable to fit new gaskets to the cylinder base and cylinder head. Two paper gaskets are fitted to the base of each cylinder.

Smear clean oil over the pistons, having replaced the rings if these have been removed, lower the piston over the connecting rod and insert the gudgeon pin from the outer side. Fit the circlip and then fit the second piston in a similar manner.

Check the piston ring gaps to find out whether excessive wear has taken place (see Subsection 17).

Oil the cylinder bores and lower the barrels over the pistons and seat them gently on their gaskets.

Drop the push rods down their tunnels on to the tappet heads, shallow cups upwards.

Fit the copper cylinder head gaskets and see that the dowels are in position.

Replace the cylinder heads as described in Subsection 10.

After the engine has been assembled, run it for a brief period at a speed which will ensure that the ignition has been advanced by the automatic advance device. If it is run too slowly "blueing" of the exhaust pipes may take place.

After the engine has been run for some time and has become thoroughly hot, go over **all** the cylinder head and other nuts to ensure that they are tight.

20. Cleaning the Oil Filters

The oil filter is located in the timing cover immediately below the oil pumps and is in the feed circuit to the big ends.

The filter element is removed by unscrewing the nut holding the end cap in position. When re-assembling the filter after cleaning, take care that no grit or other foreign matter is sticking to it. The aluminium cylinder fitted over the rod inside the filter element is to reduce the free space which has to be filled after cleaning before oil reaches the big ends. After emptying the filter chamber it is essential to run the engine slowly for about five minutes to ensure that oil is reaching the big ends.

The felt element should be taken out and washed in petrol after the first 500 miles and after every subsequent 2,000 miles. Fit a new element every 5,000 miles.

21. Overhaul of Oil Pumps

Remove the timing cover as described in Subsection 1.

Remove the end plates from both pumps.

Remove the pump discs and plungers.

Remove the pump spindle which can be pulled out from the front or return pump end.

Check the fit of the plungers in the pump discs which should have a minimum of clearance but should be able to be moved in and out by hand.

If, when fitting a new disc or plunger, the plunger is found to be too tight a fit, carefully lap with metal polish until it is just free. If the pump disc is not seating properly or if a new pump disc is being fitted, it should be lapped to the seating with Special Tool No. E.5425, using Carborundum 360 Fine Paste or liquid metal polish until an even grey surface is obtained.

Wash all passages, etc., thoroughly with petrol after lapping to remove all traces of grinding paste.

The feed pump spring is stronger than that in the return pump and care must be taken to see that they are not interchanged. The feed pump is at the rear or on the right-hand side looking on the timing cover.

Check the pump disc springs for fatigue by assembling in the timing cover and placing the pump covers in position. If the springs are correct, the pump cover should be held $\frac{1}{4}$ in. off the timing cover by the feed pump spring and $\frac{1}{8}$ in. off by the return pump spring.

The pump spindle should be renewed if excessive wear has taken place on the teeth.

Re-assemble the oil pumps, replacing the paper cover gaskets if necessary. Before fitting each cover fill the pump chamber with clean oil.

Having assembled the pumps, lay the timing cover flat and fill the oil ports by means of an oilcan. Turn the pump spindle with a screw driver in a clockwise direction looking on the front and it can then be seen whether the pumps are operating correctly.

Fill the filter chamber with clean oil and replace the timing cover, taking great care not to damage the gasket where the section is narrow.

When the timing cover has been fitted on the engine, the oil feed to the big ends can be checked by partially unscrewing the feed plug in the timing cover between the oil pumps. The oil return to the tank can be checked by removing the oil filler cap. The feed to the rockers can be observed by removing the rocker-box covers, when oil will be seen flowing down the surface of the push rods.

22. Removal of Timing Chains

Loosen the magneto fixing bolts.

Remove the magneto sprocket (Subsection 4).

Lift the magneto chain off the cam sprocket.

Loosen the chain tensioner locknut and stud.

Lift the adjusting plate clear of the chain tensioner spindle.

Remove the chain tensioner spindle and sprocket.

Lift the chain off the sprockets.

23. Removal of Pump Worm and Timing Sprocket

Remove the timing chains (Subsection 22).

Unscrew the oil pump worm by means of the

hexagon head behind it. This is a **Left Hand Thread.**

Withdraw the timing sprocket using Special Tool No. E.4869. **Do not attempt to withdraw the sprocket by tapping the worm as this will dislodge the locking nut in the crankshaft.** (See Section D, Subsection 6.)

24. Removal of Camshaft Sprockets

Remove the timing chains (Subsection 22).

Unscrew the camshaft sprocket fixing bolt, **which has a Left Hand Thread,** at the same time holding the sprocket.

Withdraw the sprocket by means of a suitable extractor.

25(a). Removal of Magneto Sprocket

Remove the timing cover and unscrew the nut securing the automatic advance mechanism. This will draw off the sprocket and auto-advance device from the magneto shaft.

25(b). Removal of the Distributor

Remove the timing cover (Subsection 1).

Remove three fixing screws.

Lift the chain off the sprocket and withdraw the distributor and sprocket complete.

Note that the sprocket is riveted to the shaft and cannot be drawn off in position.

26. Removal of Engine and Clutch Sprockets

The primary chain is endless so that it is necessary to remove both the engine and clutch sprockets simultaneously.

Remove the alternator stator by undoing three fixing screws.

Remove the central hexagon nut securing the alternator rotor, which can then be drawn off, taking care not to lose the key.

Unscrew the engine sprocket nut using Special Tool No. E.4877. The engine sprocket is mounted on splines and can then be removed with the clutch sprocket.

To remove the clutch sprocket unscrew the three clutch spring pins then lift away the spring cap, springs and distance pieces, clutch front plate, centre retaining ring and the assembly of driving and driven clutch plates. The clutch sprocket can then be withdrawn from the centre after removal of the large circlip which secures it.

When replacing the engine sprocket, take care that the felt washer is not nipped behind the sprocket. This would make the engine very stiff to turn over and would damage the washer and allow leakage from the crankcase.

27. Removal of Tappets and Guides

It is only necessary to remove the tappets and guides if they have become worn.

Remove the cylinder heads and barrels (Subsections 10 and 15).

Extract the tappet guides, using Special Tool No. E.5790, having heated the case first.

The guides are made from Nickel Chrome Alloy Iron and if a guide should break while removing it, it can be withdrawn with a pair of pliers if the crankcase is heated locally with a blowlamp. Otherwise it is necessary to dismantle the crankcase and drive the tappet and guide out from underneath using a heavy bar in the cam tunnel.

The guide should have an interference of ·0015 to ·0025 in. in the crankcase and can be driven in with a bronze drift, care being taken when the guide is nearly home to avoid breaking the collar.

If a tappet guide is taken out it should be replaced by an oversize one.

28. Dismantling the Breather

If the breather is not operating efficiently, it may cause pressure in the crankcase, instead of a partial vacuum, giving rise to smoking or overoiling.

See that the discs and backplate are clean and undamaged and that the discs are seating properly.

When re-assembling the breather, apply jointing compound sparingly to the back of the steel plate taking great care to keep it away from the discs or their seatings.

29. Removal of Clutch

Remove the engine sprocket and clutch sprocket together as described in Subsection 26.

To remove the clutch hub, hold the clutch with Special Tool No. E.4871 and remove the centre retaining nut and washer with a box spanner.

The hub can then be withdrawn from the shaft with Special Tool No. E.5414.

30. Removal of Final Drive Sprocket

Remove the clutch as described in Subsection 29.

Remove the primary chain tensioner.

Remove the rear half of the primary chain case by taking out three socket screws.

Remove the grub screw locking the final drive sprocket nut.

Hold the sprocket and remove the nut (**Right Hand Thread**). The sprocket can then be withdrawn.

31. Removal of Bearing Housing Felt Washer

Remove the engine sprocket, clutch and rear half of the primary chain case.

The felt washer is located in the steel housing at the back of the chain case.

Great care must be taken not to nip the felt washer behind the sprocket on re-assembly as this would make the engine very stiff to turn over and would damage the washer and allow leakage from the crankcase.

32. Oil Pipe Unions

The oil feed to the rocker gear is through pipes from unions at the back of the crankcase below the cylinder base to unions on the cylinder heads. The unions are fitted with steel wire thread inserts to prevent the threads in the aluminium from stripping.

The method of fitting the thread inserts is the same as that used for the sparking plug inserts described in Subsection 14.

33. Rocker Oil Feed Relief Valves

There is a pressure relief valve in the oil supply to the rocker gear, whose function is to prevent excessive pressure and whose setting is not critical.

The valve is located in the crankcase face behind the timing cover and consists of a $\frac{3}{16}$ in. diameter steel ball held in position by a spring and a brass plug.

The valve is set before leaving the Works and should not normally require to be disturbed but, if it is found necessary to dismantle it, it can be reset by screwing the plug in until it is flush with the face of the crankcase, which will cause the pressure to be relieved at approximately 10 lbs. per square inch. The plug is prevented from moving by peening over the aluminium into the screwdriver slot with a small centre punch.

34. Fitting the Alternator

The alternator consists of two parts, the stator and the rotor. The stator is mounted on the back half of the primary chaincase, being held in position by three studs and distance pieces. The rotor, which contains the permanent magnets is mounted by means of an adaptor on the end of the crankshaft and is secured by a stud and nut and located by a key.

The radial air gap between the rotor and the poles of the stator should be ·020 in. in all positions and care must be taken when re-fitting to see that it is not less than ·010 in. at any point.

Fit the rotor first, making sure that it is located concentrically on the end of the crankshaft. Attention must be given to the seating of the key because a badly-fitting key may cause the rotor to run unevenly. The nut holding the rotor in position is secured by a tab washer.

Having fitted the rotor, place the three distance collars over the three studs in the primary chaincase and put the stator in position with the coil connections facing outwards.

Replace the nuts and shakeproof washers only finger-tight and insert six strips (preferably of non-magnetic material) ·015 in. thick and about $\frac{1}{8}$ in. wide between the rotor and each pole piece.

Tighten the stator nuts and withdraw the strips.

Check the air gap with narrow feelers and, if less than ·010 in. at any point, remove the stator and file or grind the pole piece carefully until the correct gap is obtained.

An alternative, and more satisfactory, method of assembling the alternator requires the use of Special Tool No. T.2055.

This is a gauge ·015 in. greater in radius than the rotor and fits over the adaptor on the end of the crankshaft in the rotor's place.

The stator is then put in position on the studs in the chaincase and the nuts tightened up.

Remove the gauge and fit the rotor, then check the air gap.

35. Removal of Magneto

The magneto is bolted to the timing side crankcase by the hexagon-headed screws. Access to these is obtained by removing the timing cover (Subsection 1) and the magneto sprocket and automatic advance device (Subsection 25a).

SECTION D10

Service Operations with Engine Removed

"Constellation"

1. Removal of the Engine Gearbox Unit from the Frame

Disconnect the battery leads.
Remove the dual seat and petrol tank.
Remove the engine steady.
Remove the tool box cover and slide the flexible connection to the air cleaner off the induction pipe (where fitted).
Remove the exhaust pipe.
Disconnect the electric horn leads.
Loosen the rectifier bracket and swing the rectifier clear.
Remove contact breaker cover.
Remove carburettor fixing pins.
Remove the rear chain.

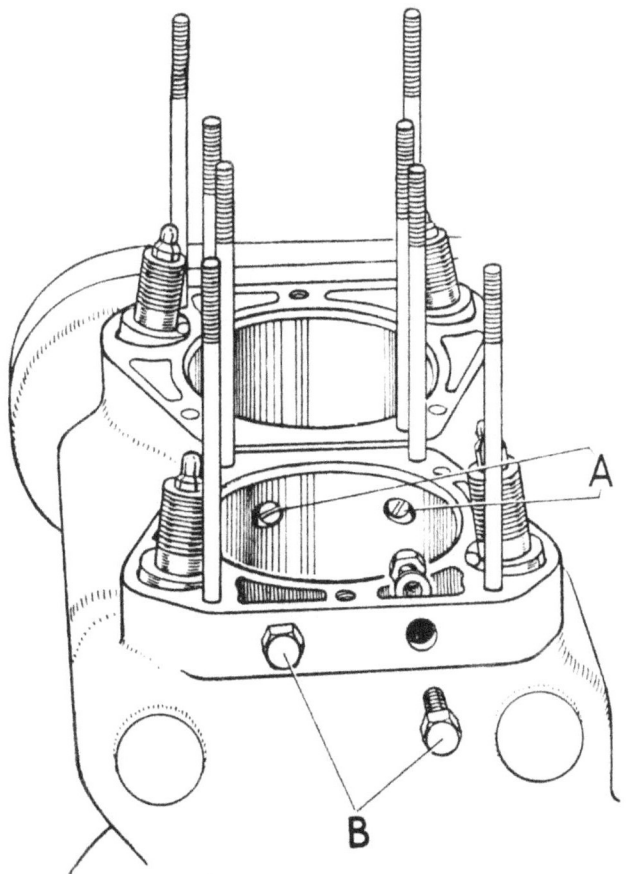

REMOVAL OF SCREWS IN CRANKCASE (EARLY MODELS)
Fig. 1

Disconnect the clutch cable.
Remove the footrest bar.
Remove the bottom rear engine bolt.
Support the engine on a suitable box or wood block.
Raise the centre stand and remove the spring.
Loosen the bottom gearbox nuts and swing the lower engine plates down.
Remove the front engine plates, horn and stand.
Lift the engine out of the frame.

2. Removal of the Gear Box

Remove the engine sprocket and clutch (Section C., Subsections 26 and 29).
Remove the rear half of the primary chaincase by removing three socket screws and the chain tensioner pivot.
The gearbox can now be withdrawn from the back of the crankcase after unscrewing the four nuts which secure it.

3. Dismantling the Crankcase

Drain the oil tank by removing the drain plug.
Having removed the engine from the frame as described in Subsection 1, dismantle the heads, barrels, pistons, timing gear, magneto, etc., as described in Section C.
Remove the gearbox as described in Subsection 2.
Remove the two hexagon-headed plugs on the driving side of the crankcase just below the cylinder base.
On no account must these plugs be disturbed on early models, unless the driving side cylinder has been, or is to be, lifted, because they cannot be tightened without holding the nuts inside. Later models do not have internal nuts, the holes in the crankcase being tapped and the plugs, which have slotted hexagon heads, screw into them.
Access can now be obtained through the plug holes to two screws holding the two halves of the crankcase together which must be removed.
Remove three nuts in the timing chest, two nuts on the driving side crankcase, two loose studs through the bottom of the crankcase and two loose studs through the back of the oil tank. (The other studs have already been removed to take the engine out of the frame.)

Turn the crankshaft until the connecting rods are at bottom dead centre and the two halves of the crankcase can then be separated, tapping the crankcase with a soft mallet.

The inner race of the roller bearings on the timing side will remain on the crankshaft bringing with it the cage and rollers and leaving the outer face fixed to the crankcase.

The inner race of the ball bearing on the driving side is a tight fit on the shaft and can be removed with Special Tool No. E.5121. If this is not available, the shaft can be driven out with a hide mallet or a soft metal drift.

To avoid damage to the ball bearing the case should be heated to about 100°C. before doing this.

4. Main Bearings

To remove the ball bearing from the driving side crankcase, heat the crankcase to about 100 degrees C. by immersion in hot water or in an oven after which the bearing can be driven out using a drift **which applies pressure to the outside race only.**

When refitting a new ball bearing, heat the crankcase in the same way and use the same drift taking great care to keep the bearing square with the bore.

To remove the outer roller race from the timing side crankcase, first heat the crankcase then drive the race out using a small punch through the three holes provided.

The inner race and rollers can be withdrawn from the crankshaft using a claw type extractor.

When refitting the inner race drive it on to the shaft until just flush with the end and no further.

5. Fitting the Connecting Rods

To remove the connecting rods from the crankshaft, first take out the cotter pins securing the socket screws in the connecting rods and then remove the socket screws themselves.

If the big end bearings caps are removed to examine the condition of the bearings, *make sure that the caps are refitted the same way round on the same rods and that the rods themselves are refitted the same way round on the same crank pins.*

In refitting the connecting rods, the socket screws should be tightened with a torque wrench set at 200—220 inch-lbs.

If the cotter pins do not come in line remove the socket screws and use a different thickness of washer. A difference of ·005 in. in the washer **alters the position of the screw approximately ⅛ of a turn.**

There is a recess in one side of the connecting rod for a cotter pin head and this side must face outwards when the connecting rod is assembled on the crankshaft to avoid fouling between the cotter and the crankshaft web.

If it is necessary to replace the big ends, a service crankshaft can be supplied with connecting rods fitted.

6. Re-assembly of the Crankcase

Fit the outer roller race in the timing side crankcase, the ball-bearing in the driving side crankcase and the inner roller race on the crankshaft as described in Subsection 4.

Be sure that the inner race is driven on just flush with the end of the crankshaft and no further.

There are several methods of assembling the crankcase. If the timing-side is fitted to the crankshaft first, care must be taken not to score the inside of the case. If the driving-side is fitted **first** it is possible, with some makes of roller bearing, though not probable, to drop one of the rollers into the crankcase and cause serious damage to the engine.

(*a*) *Timing-side First.* Heat the timing-side crankcase with the outer roller bearing race in position to about 100° C.

Lay the crankcase flat on the bench and insert the shaft, with the inner roller race in position, arranging the connecting rods so that they do not foul the crankcase.

Insert the camshafts in their correct position (exhaust front, inlet rear).

Put the distance piece in position on the driving side of the crankshaft.

Apply jointing compound to the timing side crankcase.

Heat the driving-side crankcase and bearing to 100° C. and drop it over the crankshaft, *making sure to lift the tappets clear of the cams.*

Bolt the two halves of the crankcase together. The crankshaft should now be drawn into its correct position by fitting the engine sprocket temporarily and tightening the nut whilst the crankcase is still hot.

(*b*) *Driving-side First.* Support the crankshaft with the driving end pointing upwards and place the distance piece in position. Heat the driving-side crankcase to about 100° C. and place it over the crankshaft. Fit the engine sprocket and tighten the nut while the crankcase is still hot.

Invert the crankshaft and crankcase and support it on two blocks of wood or a large block with a hole in it.

Insert the camshafts in their correct position (exhaust front, inlet rear).

Apply jointing compound to the driving-side crankcase.

Heat the timing-side crankcase (with the outer roller race) to about 100° C. and drop it over the crankshaft, *making sure to lift the tappets clear of the cams.*

Bolt the two halves of the crankcase together.

If so desired the heated timing-side crankcase can be supported on a block or blocks as above and the crankshaft dropped into it.

Alternatively, the crankshaft can be supported in a vertical position as above and the crankcase driven on to it (without heating) by means of a tubular drift applied to the inner race of the bearing or the crankcase may be drawn on to the shaft by means of the sprocket nut with a temporary distance piece in place of the sprocket.

7. Crankshaft Plugs

The oil passage through the big ends is sealed by two screwed aluminium plugs locked by centre punch.

If the crankshaft is taken out of the engine for any reason, the plugs should be removed and the oil passage cleared of sludge.

8. Pump Worm Threads

If the threads in the crankshaft, into which the pump worm screws, become damaged, a steel wire insert can be fitted. The crankshaft should preferably be returned to the Works for this to be done or, alternatively, the hole can be drilled out $\frac{7}{16}$ in. in dia., using the timing sprocket as a drill bush and new threads tapped with a special tool. **Note that the thread is left-hand.**

The method of fitting the wire insert is the same as described in Section C, Sub-section 14, for the sparking plugs.

NOTES

SECTION E7

Gearbox and Clutch

1. Description of the Clutch

Earlier Models:

The clutch is built into the clutch sprocket and is mounted on the gearbox mainshaft which projects through into the primary chaincase.

There are five driven plates which are plain and four driving plates, giving eight friction surfaces.

The driven plates comprise the clutch centre backplate, three plain plates on splines on the clutch centre and the clutch cover plate.

The driving plates comprise the clutch sprocket itself, which has a ring of friction material riveted to each side, and three plates which rotate with it. Early models have all three plates pierced and fitted with Klingerite inserts, but later models use a pierced plate with friction material inserts only on the plate nearest the clutch sprocket. The other two plates employ a material particularly resistent to slip, which is bonded on to both sides of each plate.

The clutch plates are held in contact, when driving, by six coil springs and are released when the springs are compressed by the clutch operating mechanism.

The clutch operating mechanism consists of a torque arm which is held stationary by a stud in the chaincase and an operating lever on the same centre is rotated relatively to the torque arm, with a scissor-like movement, by the clutch cable connected to the clutch lever on the handlebar. Between the operating lever and the torque arm are four $\frac{1}{4}$ in. diameter steel balls in recesses so that, when the levers are rotated relatively to each other, the balls are forced out of the recesses forcing the levers apart and thus compressing the clutch springs.

Clutch for 1961 onwards: Six pressure plates and five friction plates are fitted to this later type. The driving plates comprise the clutch sprocket, which has a ring of friction material riveted to each side, and four plates which rotate with it. The plate nearest to the sprocket is pierced for inserts, and the other three have bonded-on friction material.

The driven plates comprise the clutch centre backplate, four plain plates on splines on the clutch centre, and the clutch cover plate.

Six springs hold the plates in contact, and these are compressed by the push rod which runs through the centre of the gearbox main shaft and bears against the pressure plate when the pushrod is moved to the left by the clutch lever. This is operated through the central cable by the handle bar lever.

2. Description of the Gearbox

The operation of the gearbox is shown diagrammatically in Fig. 3.

The clutch sprocket A is mounted on the end of the mainshaft B which passes through the mainshaft sleeve C on the end of which is the final drive sprocket D.

At the other end of the mainshaft B is a pinion E which engages with a pinion F on the layshaft G. At the other end of the layshaft G is a pinion H engaging with a pinion J which runs free on the mainshaft sleeve C.

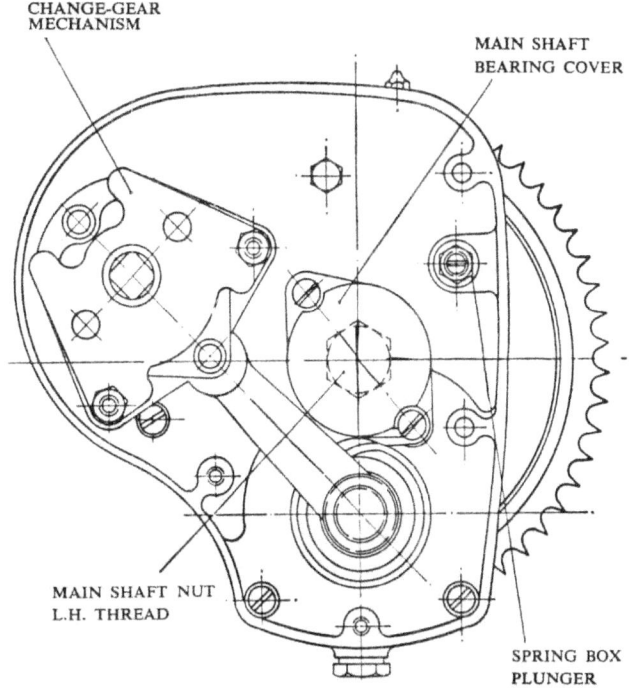

GEARBOX WITH OUTER COVER REMOVED

Fig. 1

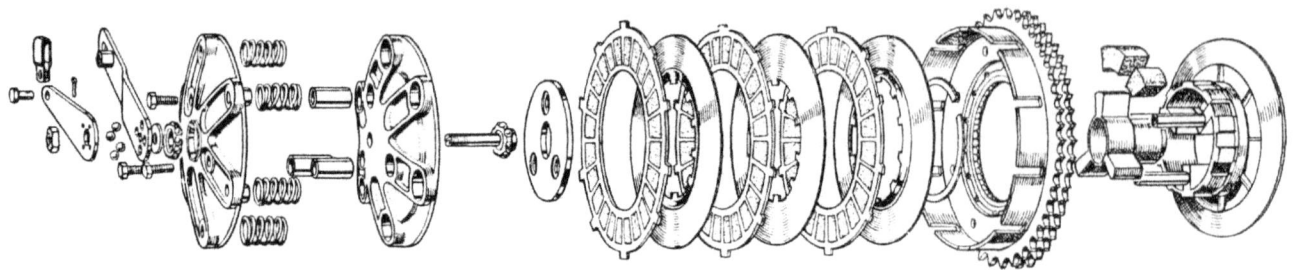

EXPLODED VIEW OF CLUTCH (EARLIER TYPE)
Fig. 2

The mainshaft sleeve C has splines on which slides a double pinion KL. This double pinion KL engages with two pinions M and N which are free to rotate or slide on the layshaft G.

The double pinion KL has dogs at each end which can engage with dogs on the pinion E or on the pinion J.

The pinions M and N have internal dogs which can engage or slide over projecting dogs P and Q on the layshaft G.

The double pinion KL and the pinions M and N all slide together and are moved by the operator fork R and are located by a spring plunger S which engages with a notched plate which is part of the operator arm R.

The kickstart lever is connected to the pinion F on the layshaft by a ratchet mechanism which automatically disengages when the lever is released.

3. Removal of the Gearbox

This is described in Section D, Subsection 2.

The gearbox can, however, be completely dismantled with the engine in the frame except for the removal of the inside operator and the bearings in the gearbox shell.

4. To Dismantle the Gearbox

First remove the kickstart crank, the change-gear lever and the neutral finder and pointer.

Remove four screws and the gearbox outer cover can then be detached.

Remove the change-gear mechanism, by taking off the two nuts securing it.

Remove the mainshaft bearing cover which is attached by two screws.

Remove four cheese-headed screws and one hexagon bolt.

Remove the spring box locating plunger nut and washer.

Remove the mainshaft nut **(left-hand thread)**.

The gearbox inner cover can then be removed.

The mainshaft can be drawn straight out if the clutch has been removed, which, however, should be done before taking off the gearbox inner cover. (See Section C.) The top gear pinion and dog will come away with the mainshaft.

The layshaft can then be removed and the 2nd and 3rd gears drawn off the final drive sleeve together with the operator fork.

To take out the final drive sleeve, the final drive sprocket must be removed and this is preferably done before removing the inner cover. (See Section C.)

5. Removal of the Ball Races

The mainshaft ball bearings can be removed by using a stepped drift $1\frac{7}{16}$—$1\frac{11}{64}$ in. diameter for

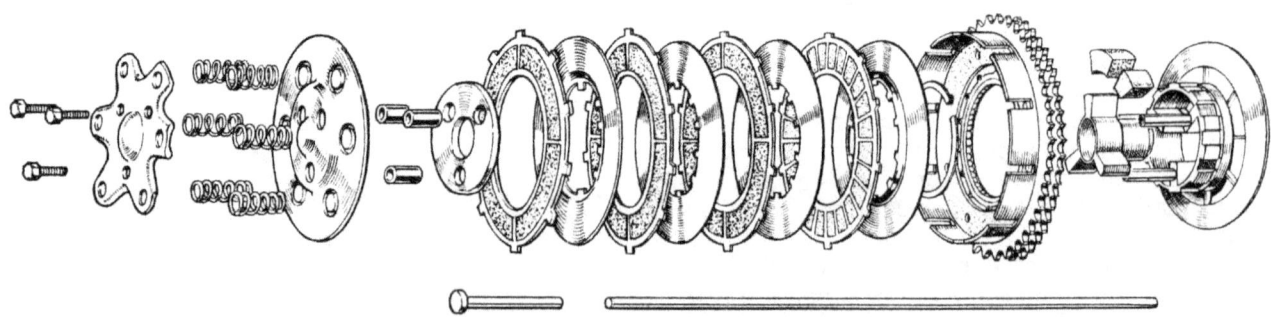

EXPLODED VIEW OF CLUTCH (LATER TYPE)
Fig. 2A

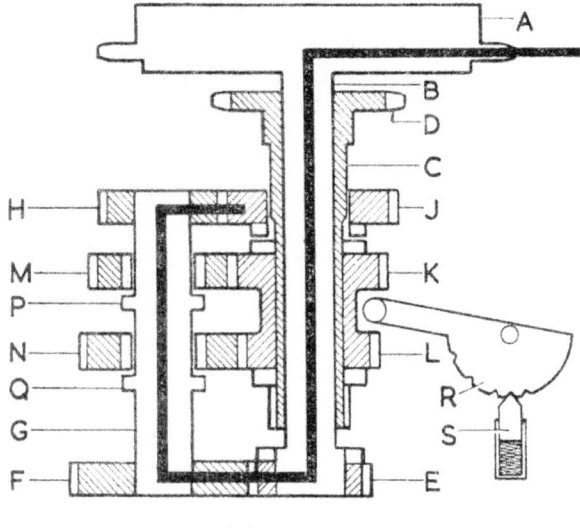
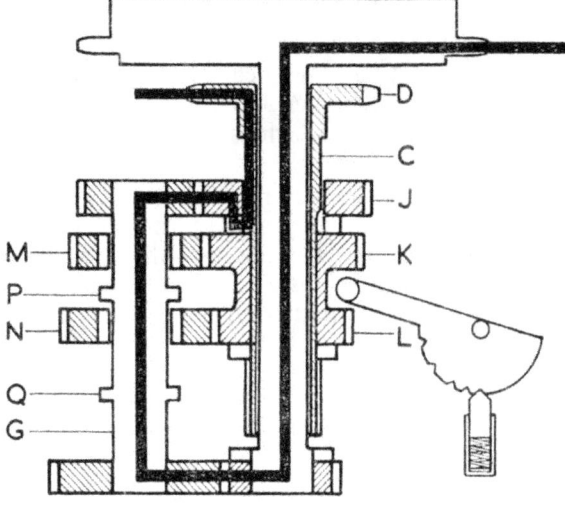
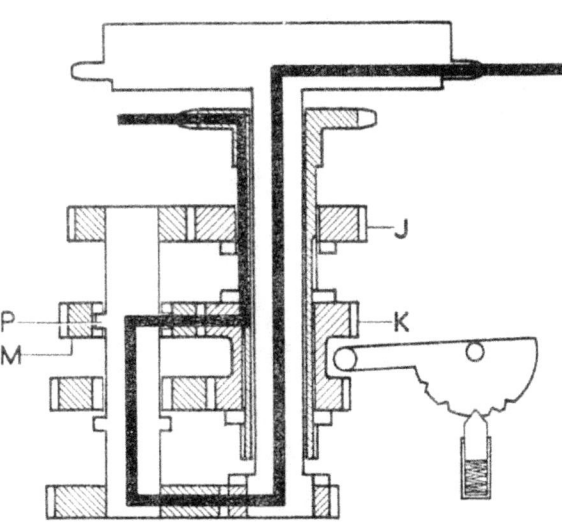
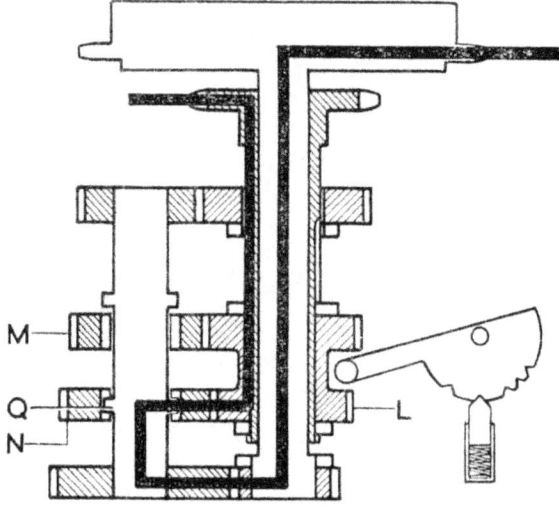
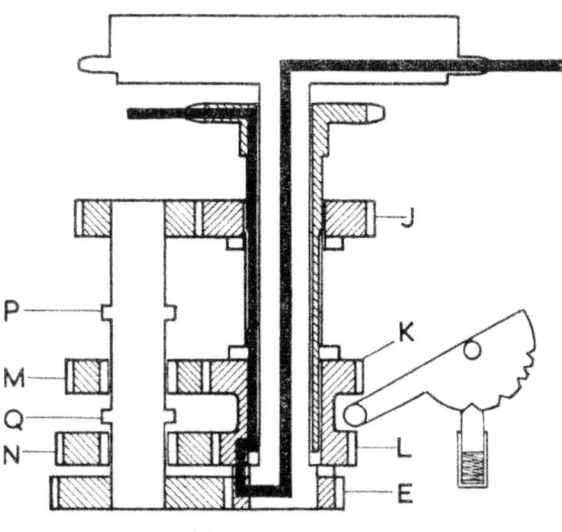

Fig. 3 OPERATION OF GEARS

Fig. 3A—Neutral. None of the dogs is engaged so that the mainshaft B and pinions E, F, H, J are rotating but the mainshaft sleeve C and the final drive sprocket are stationary.

Fig. 3B—Bottom Gear. The sliding pinions K, L, M, N have moved over so that the dogs on K engage with the dogs on the pinion J. This causes the double pinion KL, the mainshaft sleeve C and the sprocket D to rotate with the pinion J which is being driven from the mainshaft through the layshaft G. The dogs P and Q are not engaged.

Fig. 3C—Second Gear. The sliding pinions have moved so that the dogs on J are disengaged but the dogs P on the layshaft engage with the pinion M. The drive from the mainshaft and layshaft then passes through pinions M and K to the splines on the mainshaft sleeve and the pinion J is free on the sleeve.

Fig. 3D—Third Gear. The sliding pinions have moved further over so that the dogs Q on the layshaft engage with the pinion N which drives the pinion L and thus the mainshaft sleeve, the pinion M being free on the layshaft.

Fig. 3E—Top Gear. The sliding pinions have now moved right over so that both sets of dogs P and Q on the layshaft have disengaged but the dogs on the double pinion KL have engaged with those on the pinion E and the mainshaft and sleeve rotate together giving a one to one drive through the gearbox from the clutch sprocket to the output sprocket, the pinions M, N, J being free to rotate.

the bearing in the box and $\frac{13}{16}-\frac{39}{64}$ in. diameter for the bearing in the cover.

When refitting the bearings stepped drifts of $2\frac{5}{16}-1\frac{11}{64}$ in. diameter and $1\frac{11}{16}-\frac{39}{64}$ in. diameter must be used for the bearings in the box and cover respectively.

Note the felt washer in the recess behind the larger mainshaft bearing and the dished pen-steel washer between the bearing and the felt washer. The second dished pen-steel washer, if fitted, has a smaller central hole and is on the other side of the mainshaft bearing and is nipped between the inner face of the bearing and the shoulder on the final drive sleeve. See that both of the dished pen-steel washers have their raised portions facing towards the clutch and final drive sprockets.

6. Change-Gear Mechanism

If the two nuts securing the change-gear ratchet mechanism are slackened the adjuster plate can be set in the correct position. In this position the movement of the gear lever necessary to engage

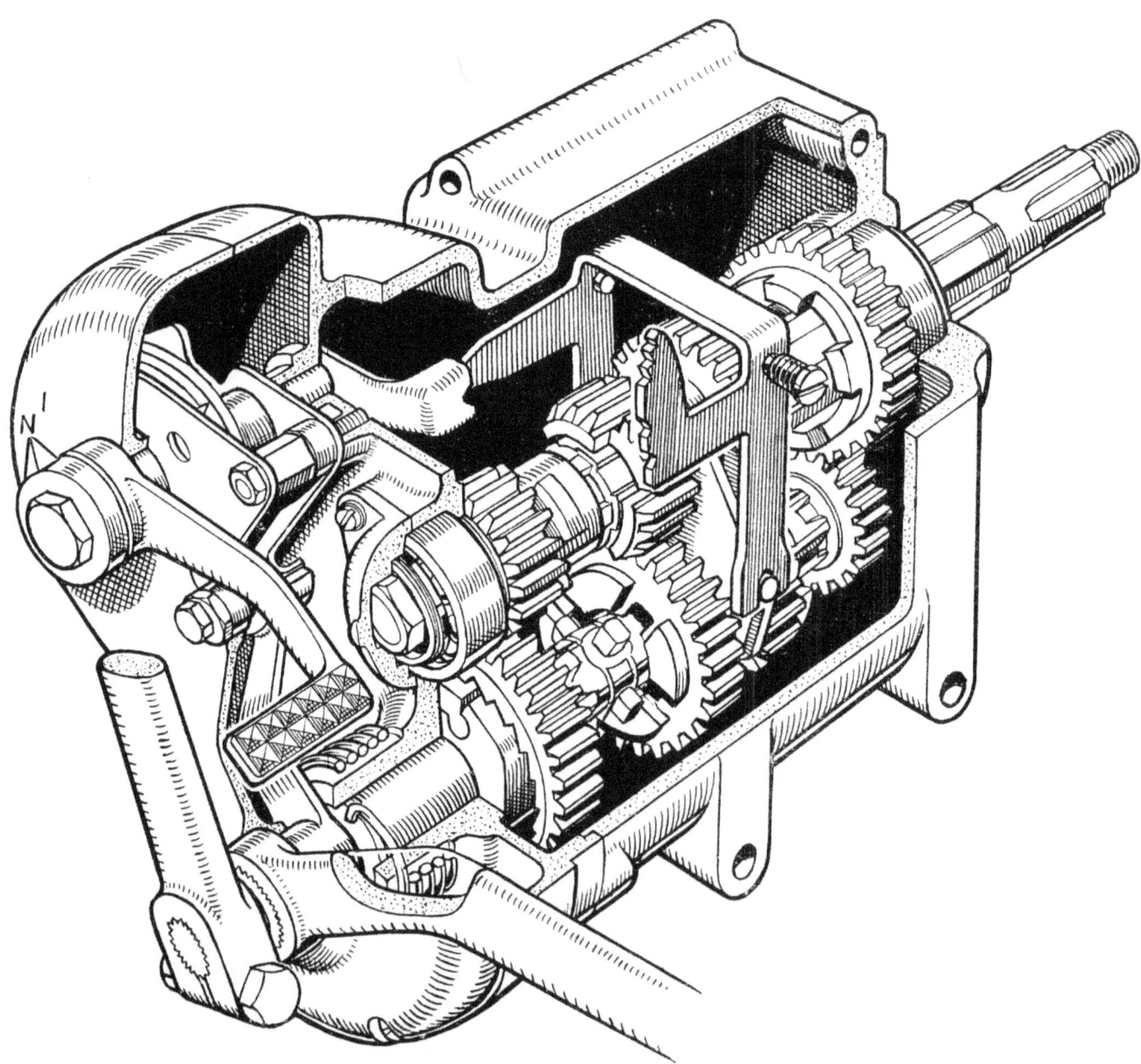

CUTAWAY SECTION OF GEARBOX

Fig. 4

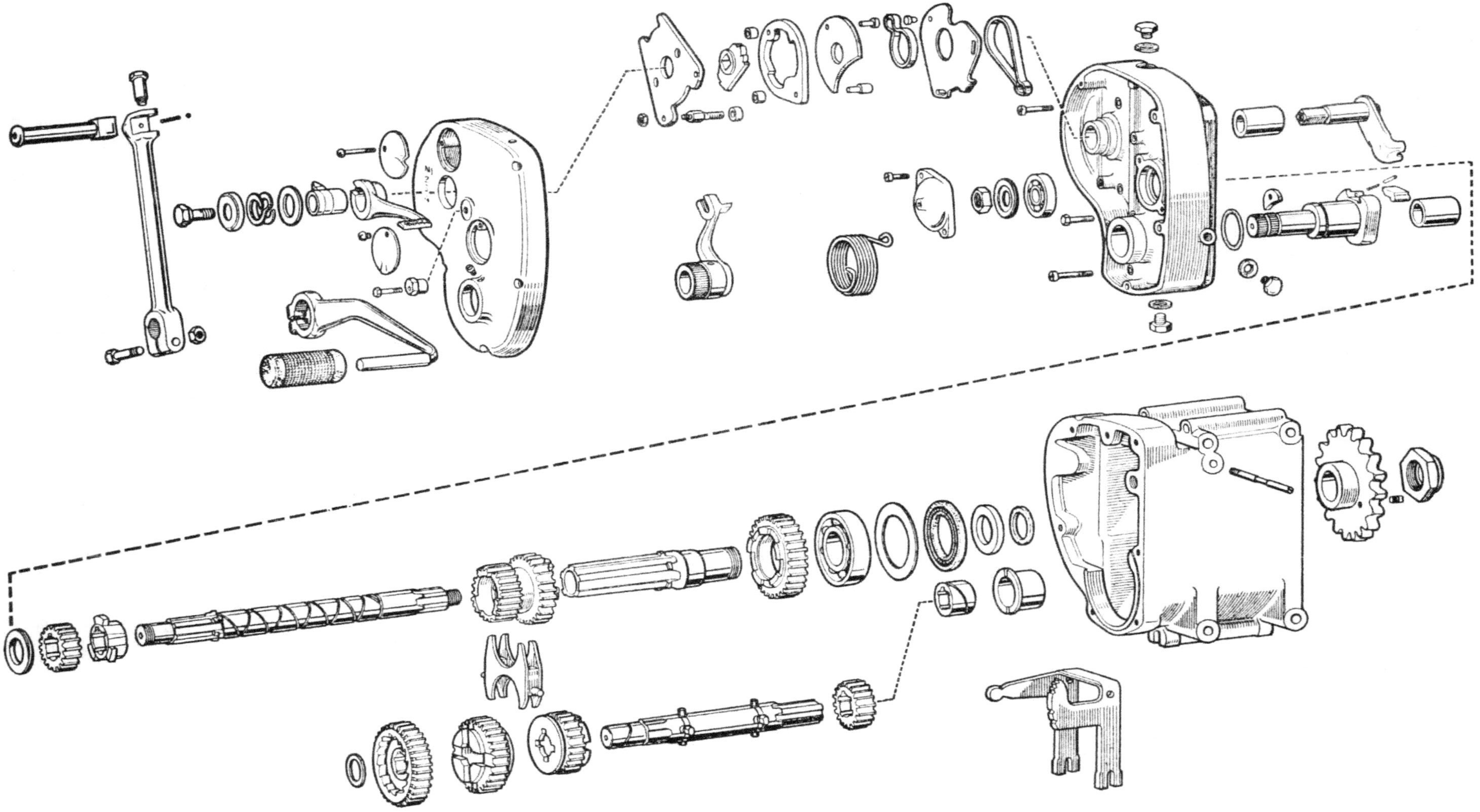

EXPLODED VIEW OF GEARBOX
Fig. 5

the ratchet teeth will be approximately the same in each direction.

If the plate is incorrectly adjusted, it may be found that, after moving from top to third or from bottom to second gear, the outer ratchets do not engage the teeth on the inner ratchets correctly.

If, when fitting new parts, it is found that the gears do not engage properly, ascertain whether a little more movement is required or whether there is too much movement so that the gear slips right through second or third gear into neutral. If more movement is required, this can be obtained by filing the adjuster plate very slightly at the points of contact with the pegs on the ratchet ring.

If too much movement is already present, a new adjuster plate giving less movement must be fitted.

7. Reassembling the Gearbox

The procedure is the reverse of that given in Subsection 4, but the following points should be noted:—

If the mainshaft top gear pinion and dog have been removed, make sure that the dog is replaced the right way round or third and top gears can be engaged simultaneously.

Make sure that the trunnions on the operator fork engage with the slots in the inside operator.

See that the mainshaft is pushed right home. It may tighten in the felt washer inside the final drive shaft nut.

The layshaft top gear and kickstarter pinion should be assembled on the layshaft and the kickstarter shaft and ratchet assembled on to it before fitting the end cover. Do not forget the washer on the layshaft between the kickstarter pinion and the kickstarter shaft.

The joint between the gearbox and the inner cover should be made with gold size, shellac or a similar jointing compound.

Make sure that all parts are clean before commencing assembly. In normal climates the recesses in the gearbox should be packed with soft grease and the box should be filled up to the correct level with engine oil. (See Subsection 11.) **On no account must heavy yellow grease be used.**

8. Dismantling and Reassembling the Clutch

The method of removing the clutch is described in Section C.

When reassembling the clutch, the following sequence must be adhered to, after first securing the clutch sprocket with the large circlip.

Fit the cush rubbers, retaining plates and three distance tubes, and follow the pressure plate assembly as follows:

    Plain dished plate. (Dish projecting outwards.)
    Friction plate. (24 inserts.)
    Plain flat plate.
    Friction plate. (Bonded $\frac{1}{4}$ segments.)
    Plain dished plate. (Dish projecting inwards.)
    Friction plate. (Bonded $\frac{1}{4}$ segments.)

When reassembling the pressure and outer plates, see that the three distance tubes are fitted over the pins securing the outer plate to the clutch centre and that the six springs are correctly positioned between the two plates.

Tighten the three pressure plate pins as far as they will go.

If the clutch lifts unevenly it is probably that one of the springs has taken a set, in which case new springs should be fitted.

In the case of the later clutch, the additional plain flat plate is fitted before the outer dished plate. The one pierced friction plate is fitted nearest to the sprocket, and the three bonded plates are as shown in Fig. 2A.

9. Adjustment of Clutch

As with any other type of friction clutch, correct adjustment of the control is essential if the clutch is to transmit torque without slip and to free correctly when lifted. Two points of adjustment are provided—one in the clutch operating mechanism itself and the other in the clutch control cable. The adjustment in the clutch control mechanism must be adjusted so that the end of the operating lever has about $\frac{1}{32}$ in. free movement. To do this first make sure that there is plenty of slack in the control cable (or disconnect it from the handlebar lever) then loosen the central locknut and rotate the pressure plate withdrawing pin by means of a screwdriver slot in its end. Turning this pin clockwise will increase the clearance in the operating mechanism; turning it anti-clockwise will take up the clearance. Lock up the locknut and check that there is still clearance in the operating mechanism. This can conveniently be done by means of a screwdriver in the slot in the end of the pressure plate withdrawing pin.

Surplus slack in the control cable can now be taken up by means of a mid-cable adjuster which should be adjusted so that there is about $\frac{1}{16}$ in. free movement on the cable and securely locked in this position.

(1) If the adjustment in the clutch operating mechanism is incorrectly adjusted so that there is no free movement of the pressure plate withdrawing pin, the clutch will slip even if plenty of clearance is given to the control cable.

(2) If excessive clearance is given either in the operating mechanism or in the control cable the clutch will drag when lifted.

(3) If excessive clearance is given in the operating mechanism and this is taken up by adjusting the control cable, it will be found that the top of the clutch operating lever knuckle will bear against the underside of the cable stop formed on the torque arm before the handlebar lever comes against the rubber grip. This will limit the movement of the clutch, which will drag when lifted.

Access to the adjustment on the clutch operating mechanism is obtained by removing the screwed plug from the centre of the primary chaincase cover.

10. Adjustment of the Neutral Finder

The neutral finder is adjusted by means of an eccentric stop secured to the front of the gearbox cover by a bolt which limits the travel of the operating pedal. Slacken the bolt and turn the eccentric until the correct movement of the pedal is obtained.

11. Gearbox Oil Level

The gearbox is filled with oil by removing a plug in the top and the correct level can be checked by removing a second plug lower down on the left-hand side looking at the cover.

The oil capacity is $\frac{3}{4}$ pint.

NOTES

SECTION F3
Amal 10TT9 Carburetter

1. General Description

This carburetter comprises two main parts, the mixing chamber and the float chamber. They are held together by the jet holder, which houses the main jet and the needle jet. Above these, and inside the mixing chamber, is the choke adaptor into which, from below, is screwed the jet choke tube. Sliding in the mixing chamber and surrounding the choke adaptor is the throttle valve (No. 5) and into this is clipped the jet needle by means of a sliding clip which will fit into any one of seven grooves. A tapered spring fits between the throttle valve and the mixing chamber top, which is secured by a screwed ring or cap.

At the side of the mixing chamber is a projecting boss having a narrow slot towards its lower end. Into the top of this boss a narrow slide is fitted, spring controlled and connected, through a cable, to the air lever on the handlebar.

Screwed into the mixing chamber body just below the inlet to the engine is the pilot jet which is spring loaded and controls the slow running or idling speed.

The mixing chamber is mounted on the cylinder head by a two-bolt flange and the air intake tube is screwed to the outer face of the mixing chamber. A spring clip embracing this tube is used to lock the top cap in position.

Screwed into the base of the float chamber is a base plug embodying a guide for the float. The float operates a needle valve seating in the float chamber top, which is secured to the float chamber by two screws. A float tickler is provided and a single banjo, connecting to the petrol feed, is secured by a large banjo nut.

2. Dismantling the Carburetter

By unscrewing the top cap from the mixing chamber, the top, spring, throttle slide and needle may be withdrawn. To remove the needle from the slide, pull the copper clip sideways from the needle groove.

To gain access to the main jet, remove the hexagon plug from beneath the float chamber connection; the hexagon bodied main jet may then be unscrewed. It fits into the jet holder, which is screwed into the mixing chamber. Unscrewing the jet holder releases the float chamber and also gives access to the needle jet, which is screwed into the top of the jet holder.

If you look up into the bottom of the mixing chamber when the jet holder has been removed, the jet choke tube will be seen. This is slotted to facilitate its removal, which should not be necessary, however, neither should it be necessary to remove the choke adaptor, but if it is removed, take note of the washer beneath it. Take note, also, of the two washers, one above and the other below the float chamber connection to the mixing chamber.

To dismantle the float chamber (it is assumed that the petrol feed connection has been broken), remove the float chamber banjo nut and the banjo, taking care of the washers on either side of the banjo. Unscrew the two hexagon headed screws which secure the float chamber top and remove the latter. This will release the float needle and give access to the float in the float chamber. The float guide may be removed by unscrewing it from below the float chamber; take care of its sealing washer.

3. Carburation

The "choke" or effective bore of the carburetter is of great importance for maximum speed. The design in this carburetter is such that the maximum volume of air may flow through to charge the cylinder, also causing the maximum depression or suction on the jet to supply the fuel and atomise it.

Needle Control to the Jet. Perfect carburation throughout the range of the opening of the throttle means ACCELERATION clean and snappy. This is where the needle control plays its part; you have a large main jet for power and for cooling the engine, and unless it is controlled it may give you a woolly rich mixture at small throttle openings —bad for acceleration and plugs. The needle reduces the flow of petrol above the main jet, and being taper, it reduces it most at small throttle openings, and as the throttle is opened, so the taper allows a bigger flow until the throttle is about three-quarters open, when the needle ceases to have any effect, and the main jet is fully in play.

The needle is attached to the throttle by a clip, the clip embracing one of seven grooves. This enables you to tune on the needle once you have set the main jet for power, by lowering the needle to get less petrol and *vice versa*, in its relation to the throttle opening. The needle is controlling the fuel flow in a needle jet, which has an accurately made bore, and this screws into the bolt that

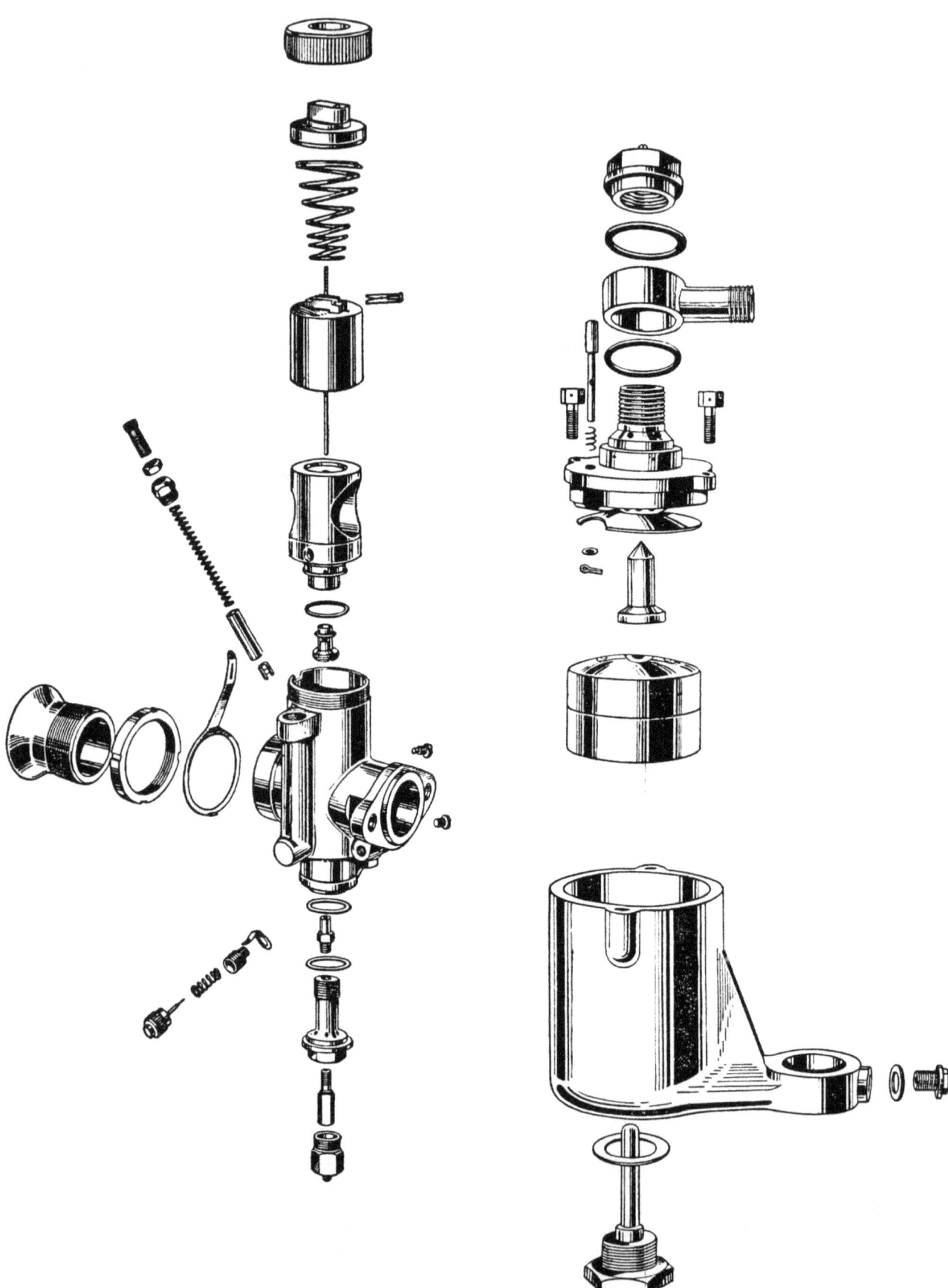

Fig. 1 AMAL 10TT9 CARBURETTER

holds the float chamber to the mixing chamber. The standard needle jet bore is numbered.

The Throttle Valve surrounds the choke block in the carburetter, and when it is open leaves a perfectly shaped passage. Apart from controlling the main jet outlet, it is also used to control the supply of air to the main jet supply at low throttle openings—this actual control is by means of the cut-away on the lower edge of the intake side of the throttle valve—a smaller cut-away increasing the mixture strength at smaller throttle openings and a larger cut-away a weakening effect.

Throttles with different cut-aways can be supplied, the number of the cut-away being the height of the cut-away from the bottom edge measured in sixteenths of an inch.

Jets. The pilot jet, for starting off with, is unlike the standard Amal touring pilot jet because the adjustment regulates the fuel flow and not the air. This adjustment gives a wider range for any fuel which is mixed with air coming through a small hole under the carburetter—this mixture for idling and "starting off" passes through into the carburetter outlet just behind the throttle, and is again mixed with air coming under the throttle through the main bore.

The main jet can be got at easily without disturbing the float chamber by removing the hexagon cap under the bolt that holds the float chamber to the mixing chamber. Main jets are numbered, the higher the number the larger the flow; various numbered main jets are available to suit requirements.

Float Chamber. The float chamber fitted to the current Model T.T. Carburetter is of a modified top-feed design incorporating a large-headed needle and seating, which ensures that the float chamber is capable of passing 10 gallons an hour, which is more than enough even when pure alcohol fuel is used. Consequently, the introduction of this float chamber has removed the necessity for a double float chamber as fitted previously.

Locking Devices. Vibration causes parts to come undone, so we have devised simple and quick-locking devices that are sure, viz. a leaf spring which is anchored on to the air funnel and engages the knurled mixing chamber cap, and a drilled boss for wiring up to hold the float chamber holding screw to prevent it from vibrating loose. For the petrol pipe union we leave you to make your own device.

Compensation and Air Control. The main jet does not spray directly into the choke bore of the mixing chamber. It first passes through the needle-jet and is there partially atomised by a blast of primary air, which can be seen at the base of the main choke. The richness of the mixture as it passes through the primary choke can be handlebar regulated by the air control at the side of the carburetter, less air being admitted to enrich the mixture for starting or atmosphere conditions demanding more liquid fuel to give the correct mixture strength. As the engine speed increases at a given throttle opening so the mixture would tend to get rich, but as the air flow through the primary choke above the main jet also increases, there is a damping effect on the flow of liquid and a compensated mixture is obtained.

Needle-Jet. Before tuning the carburetter, confirm that the correct size needle-jet is fitted.

Standard Carburetter Settings

Carburetter Type : Amal 10TT9.
Main Jet : 480.
Needle Jet : ·109.
Choke Bore : $1\frac{3}{16}$ in.
Throttle Valve : 5.
Needle Position : No. 3 Groove.
Float Chamber : 302/10 Single Banjo.

4. Tuning Instructions

To get carburation for any stated fuel when the choke bore is correct for the peak revs. of the engine and the correct needle jet for the fuel to be used, the procedure is simple. Start off with an assumed setting, and then tune as follows. There are four phases :

(i) Main jet for power at full throttle.
(ii) Pilot jet for idling.
(iii) Throttle cut-away for "take-off" from the pilot jet.
(iv) Needle position for "snappy" mixture at quarter to three-quarter throttle; then final idling adjustment of the pilot jet.

Always tune in this order, then any alteration will not upset a correct phase.

Sequence of tuning. (i) Main jet size. (ii) Pilot jet adjustment. (iii) Throttle valve cut-away. (iv) Needle attachment.

(i) Main Jet Size. This should be determined first : the smallest numbered jet which gives the greatest maximum speed should be selected, keeping in mind the safety factor for cooling. (The air lever should be fully open during these tests.)

(ii) Pilot Jet Adjustment. Before attempting to set the pilot adjuster the engine should be at its normal running temperature, otherwise a faulty adjustment is possible, which will upset the correct selection of the throttle valve. The pilot adjuster, which controls the amount of fuel passed, is rotated

clockwise, to weaken the mixture, and anti-clockwise to enrich it. Adjust this very gradually until a satisfactory tick-over is obtained, but take care that the achievement of too slow a tick-over—that is, slower than is actually necessary—does not lead to a "spot" which may cause stalling when the throttle is very slightly open.

(iii) *Throttle Cut-away.* Having set the pilot adjuster, open up the throttle progressively and note positions where, if at all, the exhaust note becomes irregular. If this is noticed, leave the throttle open at this position and close the air lever slightly ; this will indicate whether the spot is rich or weak. If it is a rich spot, fit a throttle valve with more cut-away on the air intake side (or *vice versa* if weak).

(iv) *Jet Needle Position.* Tuning sequence (ii) and (iii) will affect carburation up to somewhere over one-quarter throttle, after which the jet needle (which is suspended from the throttle valve) comes into action and when the throttle is opened further and tests are again made for rich or weak spots (as previously outlined) the needle can be raised to enrich or lowered to weaken the mixture, whichever may be found necessary. With these adjustments correctly made, and the main jet size settled, a perfectly progressive mixture will be obtainable from tick-over to full throttle.

SECTION F4

Amal Monobloc Carburetter

1. General Description

The Amal Monobloc Carburetter has been introduced as an improvement on the earlier standard needle type. In general it gives better petrol consumption, combined with improved starting and acceleration from low speeds and a small increase in maximum speed.

The float chamber is integral with the mixing chamber and contains a pivoted barrel-shaped float operating on a nylon fuel needle. There is a considerable leverage ratio between the float and the needle and, in consequence, flooding is rare unless there is dirt on the needle seating.

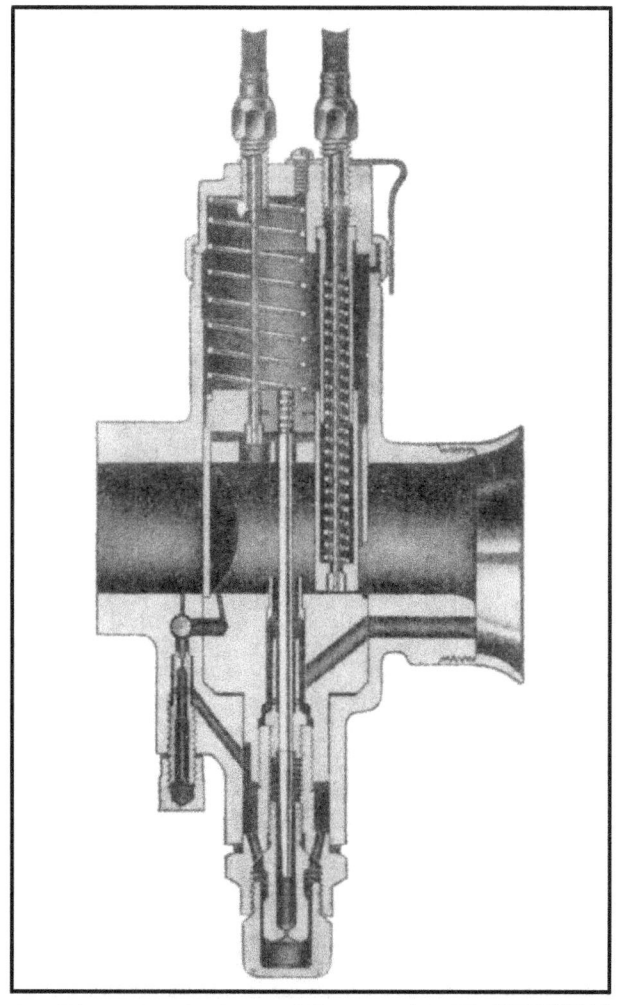

SECTION THROUGH MIXING CHAMBER, SHOWING AIR VALVE AND THROTTLE CLOSED

Fig. 1

The supply of air to the engine is controlled by a throttle slide which carries a taper needle operating in the needle jet. The needle is secured to the throttle slide by a spring clip fitting in one of five grooves and the mixture strength throughout a large proportion of the throttle range is controlled by the position of this needle in the slide and by the size of the jet in which it works. There is, however, a restricting or main jet at the bottom of the needle jet and the size of this controls the mixture strength at the largest throttle openings. At very small throttle openings petrol and air are fed to the engine through a separate pilot system, which has an outlet at the engine side of the throttle. The air supply to this pilot system is controlled by the pilot air screw and the slow running of the engine can be adjusted by means of this screw and a stop which holds the throttle open a very small amount. The throttle slide is cut away at the back and the shape of this cut-away controls the mixture at throttle openings slightly wider than that required for slow running. There is a compensating system to prevent undue enriching of the mixture with increasing engine speed, this system consisting of a primary choke surrounding the upper end of the needle jet through which air is drawn in increasing quantities as the depression in the main choke increases. This air supply and the supply to the pilot system are taken from two separate ducts in the main air intake to the carburetter so that all the air passing to the engine can be filtered by fitting an air cleaner to the main carburetter air intake.

Two small cross holes in the needle jet, at a level just below the static level in the float chamber, permit petrol to flow into the primary choke when the engine is not running or when it is running at very low speeds, thus forming a well of petrol which will be drawn into the engine on starting or accelerating from low speeds. At moderately high engine speeds the level of petrol in the float chamber falls slightly and in consequence no more fuel flows through the cross holes in the needle jet so that the petrol well remains empty until the engine slows down or stops.

A handlebar controlled air slide is provided to enrich the mixture temporarily when required.

2. Tuning the Carburetter(s)

The throttle opening at which each tuning point is most effective is shown in Fig. 2. It should be remembered, however, that a change of setting at any point will have some effect on the setting required at other points; for instance, a change of main jet will have some effect on the mixture strength at half throttle which, however, is mainly controlled by the needle position. Similarly an alteration to the throttle cut-away may affect both the needle position required and the adjustment of the pilot air screw. For this reason it is necessary to tune the carburetter in a definite sequence, which is as follows:

First—Main Jet. The size should be chosen which gives maximum speed at full throttle with the air control wide open. If two different sizes of jet give the same speed the larger should be chosen for safety as it is dangerous to run with too weak a mixture at full throttle.

Second—The pilot air screw should be set to give good idling. Note that the pilot jet is detachable and two sizes are available, 25 c.c. and 30 c.c. If the pilot air adjusting screw requires to be screwed out less than half a turn the larger size pilot jet should be used; if the air screw requires to be screwed out more than 2-3 turns fit the smaller size of pilot jet.

PHASES OF AMAL MONOBLOC CARBURETTER THROTTLE OPENINGS

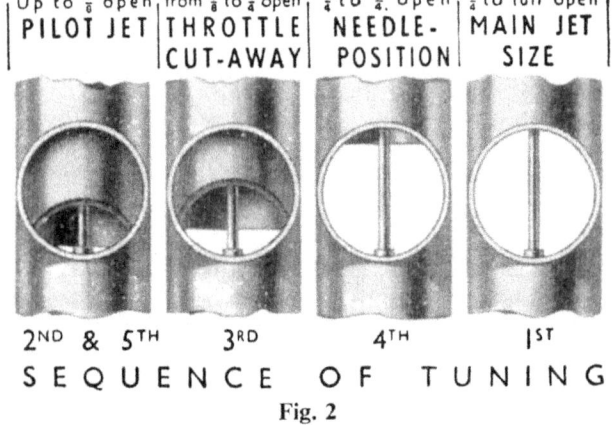

SEQUENCE OF TUNING
Fig. 2

Third—the throttle valve should be selected with the largest amount of cut-away which will prevent spitting or misfiring when opening the throttle slowly from the idling position.

Fourth—The lowest position of the taper needle should be found consistent with good acceleration with the air slide wide open.

Fifth—The pilot air screw should be checked to improve the idling if possible. When setting the adjustment of the pilot air screw this should be done in conjunction with the throttle stop. Note that the correct setting of the air screw is the one which gives the fastest idling speed for a given position of the throttle stop. If the idling speed is then undesirably fast it can be slowed down by unscrewing the throttle stop a fraction of a turn.

It will be noted that of the four points at which adjustments are normally made, i.e., pilot air screw, throttle cut-away, needle position and main jet size, the first and third do not require changing of any parts of the carburetter. Assuming that the carburetter has the standard setting to suit the particular type of engine any small adjustments occasioned by atmospheric conditions, changes in quality of fuel, etc., can usually be covered by adjustment of the pilot air screw and raising or lowering the taper needle one notch. If, however, the machine is used at very high altitudes or with a very restricted air cleaner a smaller main jet will be necessary. The following table gives the reduction in main jet size required at different altitudes:

Altitude, ft.	Reduction, %
3,000	5
6,000	9
9,000	13
12,000	17

In the case of carburetters for engine running on alcohol fuel considerably larger jets are needed. In most cases a No. 113 needle jet will be required and the main jet size will require to be increased by an amount varying from 50% to 150% according to the grade of fuel used.

If the engine is run on fuel containing a small proportion of alcohol added to the petrol, a rough and ready guide is that the main jet should be increased by 1% for every 1% of alcohol in the fuel. In most cases alcohol blends available from petrol pumps do not contain sufficient alcohol to require any alteration to the carburetter setting.

The range of adjustment of the taper needle and the pilot air screw are determined by the size of the needle jet and of the pilot outlet respectively. Standard needle jets have a bore at the smallest point of ·1065 in. and are marked 106. Alternative needle jets ·1055 in., ·1075 in., ·109 in. and ·113 in. bore are available and are marked 105, 107, 109 and 113 respectively.

The standard pilot outlet bore is ·025 in. but in some cases larger size pilot outlets are used. Since the pilot outlet is actually drilled in the body of the carburetter it is necessary to have a carburetter with the correct size pilot outlet if the best results are to be obtained.

The accompanying table shows the standard settings for Amal Monobloc Carburetters used on Royal Enfield motor cycles.

Both instruments used for the twin carburetter "Constellation" are identical in all respects but for the float chamber arrangement, which is as follows:

Carburetter type 376/242 supplies the left-hand cylinder and has an integral float chamber which

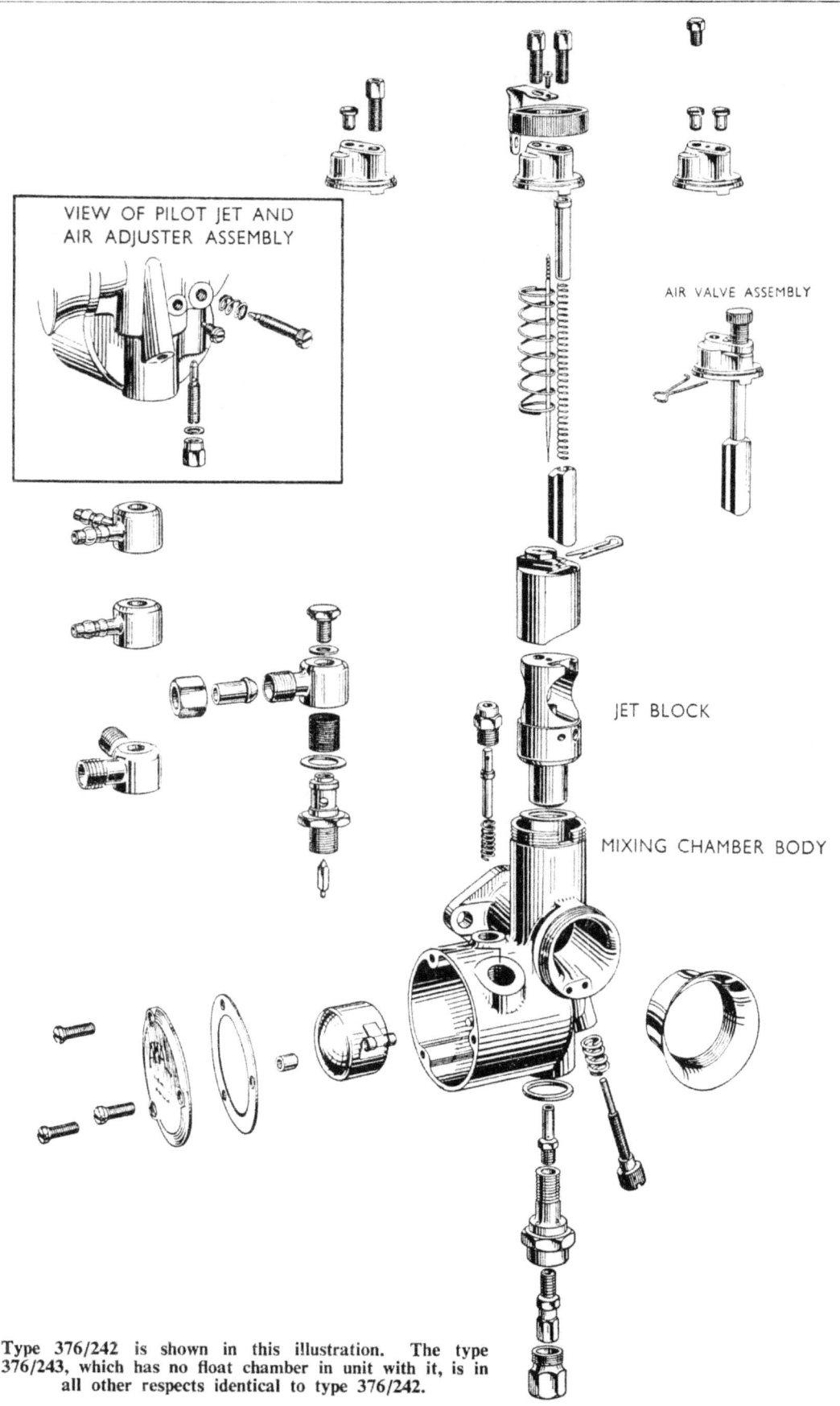

Type 376/242 is shown in this illustration. The type 376/243, which has no float chamber in unit with it, is in all other respects identical to type 376/242.

Fig. 3

also controls the fuel supply via a connecting pipe to the right-hand instrument type 376/243; this does not have a float chamber in unit with it.

It is important that the pilot air screws of both carburetters are in identical positions, relative to one another, the same applying to the throttle valves when seated on their stops. This is essential for an even smooth tickover and low-speed running. The speed of the tickover is regulated by these four adjuster screws. For an instant pick-up, both throttle valves must commence to rise from their stops simultaneously, when the twist grip is rotated. This is obtained by adjusting the twin control cables. Each main jet needle must be in the third groove.

Both air slides, operated from a single handlebar lever, must open and close identically, as failure to do this may result in one slide not opening fully, with a resultant loss of power.

It is most important that all of these adjustments are carried out in a thorough and careful manner if the maximum power and smoothness is to be obtained.

The "ears" to be found on the leading edges of the battery and toolbox lids are to shield the carburetter air intakes and so prevent misfiring at maximum revs.

3. Dismantling Carburetter

The construction of the carburetter is clearly shown in Fig. 3.

If the float chamber floods, first make sure that there is no dirt on the fuel needle seating. Owing to the use of a nylon needle and the leverage ratio between float and needle, flooding is very unlikely with this type of carburetter unless dirt is present or, of course, the float is punctured.

If it is necessary to remove the jet block note that this is withdrawn from the upper end of the mixing chamber after unscrewing the jet holder. Be careful not to damage the jet block when removing or refitting it. Note that the large diameter of the jet block pulls down on to a thin washer.

A single strand of an inner control cable is useful for clearing the small passages in the jet block and care must be taken not to enlarge these by forcing the wire through them. Compressed air from a pipe line or a tyre pump is preferable. A choked main jet should be cleared only by blowing through it.

4. Causes of High Petrol Consumption

If the petrol consumption is excessive first look for leaks either from the carburetter, petrol pipe, petrol tap(s) or tank. If coloured petrol is in use this will readily indicate the presence of any small leaks which otherwise might pass unnoticed. If the petrol system is free from leaks, carefully set the pilot adjusting screw as described in Subsection 2 to give the correct mixture when idling. Running with the pilot adjusting screw too far in is a common cause of excessive petrol consumption. If the consumption is still heavy try the effect of lowering the taper needle in the throttle slide by one notch. Do not fit a smaller main jet as this will not affect consumption except when driving on nearly full throttle and may make the mixture too weak at large throttle openings, thus causing overheating.

Settings for AMAL carburetters on ROYAL ENFIELD motor cycles

Machine	Carburetter Type No.	Choke Bore in.	Main Jet c.c.	Needle Jet	Needle Position	Throttle Valve	Pilot Jet c.c.
"250 Clipper" 1955 (late), 1956, 1957 and 1958 (early)	375/10	$\frac{29}{32}$	120	105	3	375/060/4	25
"Crusader 250" 1957 onwards "250 Clipper" 1958 (late) and 1959 onwards	375/16	$\frac{7}{8}$	120	105	3	375/060/3½	25
"Crusader Sports" 1959 onwards and "250 Trials" 1962 onwards	376/216	$\frac{15}{16}$	150	106	3	376/060/3½	25
"Crusader Super 5" 1962 onwards	376/283	1	170	106	3	376/3½	25
"350 Bullet" 1955 (late), 1956-7-8 and "350 Clipper" 1958 onwards	376/29	1	180	106	3	376/060/4	30
"350 Bullet" 1959 onwards	376/215	$1\frac{1}{16}$	190	106	3	376/060/4	30
"Works Replica" 1958 onwards	376/29	1	180	106	3	376/060/4	30
"500 Bullet" 1956-58	389/9	$1\frac{1}{8}$	200	106	2	389/060/3¼	30
"500 Bullet" 1959 onwards	389/34	$1\frac{3}{16}$	*220	106	3	389/060/3½	30
"Meteor Minor" 1958 onwards	376/92	$1\frac{1}{16}$	250	106	2	376/060/3½	30
"Meteor Minor Sports" 1960 onwards	376/92	$1\frac{1}{16}$	250	106	2	376/060/3½	30
"Super Meteor" 1956 onwards	376/41	$1\frac{1}{16}$	240	106	3	376/060/3½	30
"Constellation" 1960 onwards	L/hand 376/242 R/hand 376/243	$1\frac{1}{8}$	320	106	3	376/060/4	25

* With Air Cleaner. Main Jet 250 without Air Cleaner.

NOTES

SECTION G1f

Lucas Twin-Cylinder Magneto Models K2F (42369) and K2F (42369B)

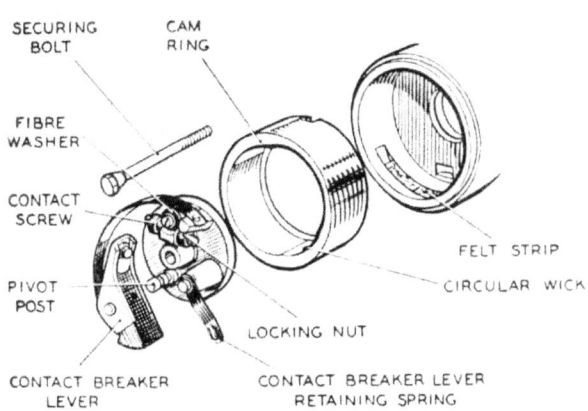

K2F (42369) MAGNETO CONTACT BREAKER
Fig. 1

1. General

This magneto incorporates a wound rotating armature and a high-energy permanent magnet field system, this latter being cast integral with the body. The unit is designed for 3-point flange fixing.

Small breathing holes are provided in the body of the magneto. These holes should not be allowed to become blocked.

Provision is made for altering the ignition timing by the manual control method, in which the cam ring is moved relatively to the armature. The lever controlling this movement is mounted conveniently on the handlebars and is connected by Bowden cable to the magneto.

2. Routine Maintenance

2 (a). Lubrication

To be carried out every 3,000 miles.

(i) Wipe out the outside of the magneto to remove dirt or grease, and then take off the contact breaker cover. Unscrew the hexagon-headed screw in the centre of the contact breaker and withdraw the contact breaker from its housing. Push aside the contact breaker arm retaining spring of the K2F (42369) type unit, and in the case of the later K2F (42369B) model, prise off the special locking plate from the contact breaker arm pivot pin, taking care not to lose the insulating washer beneath it.

Slacken the screw which retains the contact breaker arm spring. The contact breaker arm may then be lifted from its pivot.

Wipe away any dirt or grease from the contacts with a petrol-moistened cloth. If necessary, use a very fine carborundum stone to polish the contacts, recleaning afterwards with a petrol-moistened cloth. Smear the pivot pin with a little Mobilgrease No. 2 before refitting the contact breaker arm.

Remove the cam ring, which is a sliding fit in its housing, and lightly smear inside and outside surfaces with Mobilgrease No. 2. Both removal and refitting of the cam can be made easier if the handlebar control lever is half retarded, thus taking the cam away from its stop pin. Apply one or two drops of thin machine oil to the felt cam lubricator in the housing. Refit the cam, taking care that the stop peg in the housing and the plunger of the manual timing control engage with their respective slots.

Refit the contact breaker. This can be made easier if the contact breaker heel is away from the

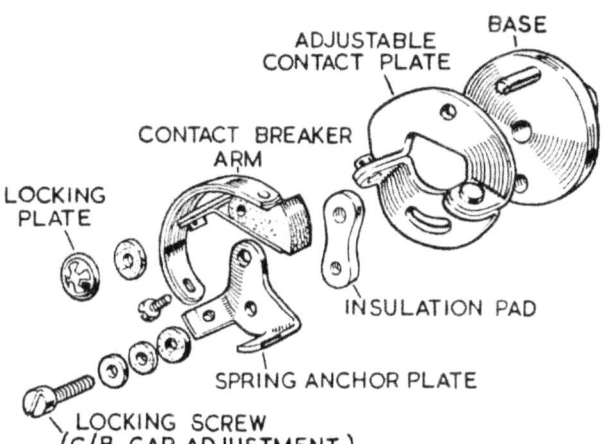

K2F (42369B) MAGNETO CONTACT BREAKER
Fig. 2

cam lobe; turn the engine until this is so. The key on the projecting part of the contact breaker base must engage with the keyway in the armature shaft. Refit the hexagon-headed screw and tighten with care. It must not be slack, nor must undue force be used.

(ii) *Bearings*. The main bearings of the magneto are packed with grease during manufacture and need no attention until a general overhaul is undertaken.

2 (b). Adjustments

Check every 3,000 miles.

(i) *Setting contact breaker gap.* The contact breaker gap must be set to 0·012–0·015 in. when the contacts are fully separated.

To adjust the gap, turn the engine until the contacts are fully opened. On K2F (42369) type magnetos the locking nut of the adjustable contact must first be slackened. Turn the contact by its hexagon head until a feeler gauge of appropriate thickness is a sliding fit in the gap. Tighten the locknut and recheck the gap. On K2F (42369B) type magnetos the cheese-headed screw which locates the spring anchor plate is slackened; the plate on which the contact is mounted may then be moved away from or towards the contact breaker arm, to give the required clearance.

(ii) *Adjusting the Timing Control Cable.* Slackness in the manual control timing can be taken up by sliding the waterproofing rubber shroud up the cable and turning the hexagon-headed cable adjuster. After adjusting, return the rubber shroud to its original position over the adjuster and control barrel.

2 (c). Cleaning

To be carried out every 6,000 miles.

Check the contact breaker contacts and, if necessary, clean them as described in Subsection 2 (a). Wipe the outside of the magneto to remove dirt or grease. Check the cable adjuster and control barrel for signs of water ingress.

Remove the high tension pick-ups and polish with a soft dry cloth. Each carbon brush must move freely in its holder and, if necessary, clean it with a petrol-moistened cloth. Should a brush be worn to within $\frac{1}{8}$ in. of the shoulder it must be renewed.

Whilst the pick-up moulding is removed, clean the slip ring track and flanges by holding a soft dry cloth against them with a suitably shaped piece of wood while the engine is slowly turned.

The high tension cables must be kept clean and dry.

2 (d). Renewing High Tension Cables

If, on inspection, the high tension cable shows signs of deterioration, it must be replaced, using 7 mm. rubber, P.V.C. or neoprene covered ignition cable. To fit a new high tension cable, bare the end for about $\frac{3}{8}$ in., thread the knurled moulded nut over the cable, and thread the bared cable through the washer removed from the old cable.

Bend back the strands radially, and screw the nut into the pick-up moulding.

2 (e). Renewing Timing Control Cable

The Bowden timing control cable should be renewed if it becomes frayed, otherwise moisture may enter the contact breaker housing.

To do this, slip back the rubber shroud and, by means of the hexagon at the base, unscrew the control barrel. If the cable and the plunger to which it is attached are now pulled upwards, the cable nipple can be disengaged from the plunger slot.

Soften the solder and remove the nipple.

Thread the new length of cable through the rubber shroud, cable adjuster, control barrel, sealing washer and restoring spring. Solder the nipple to the end of the cable. Engage the nipple with the slot in the plunger and screw the control barrel into the body, ensuring that the sealing washer is correctly fitted between the barrel and the body. Take up any slackness in the cable by means of the adjuster before refitting the rubber shroud in position.

2 (f). Contact Breaker Springs

Correct contact breaker spring pressure, measured at the contacts, is 18—24 oz.

3. Servicing

3 (a). Testing Magneto in Position on Engine

To locate cause of misfiring or failure of ignition, check as follows:

(i) Remove the sparking plugs from the engine. Hold the end of the H.T. cable about $\frac{1}{8}$ in. from the cylinder block and crank the engine. If strong and regular sparking is produced the fault lies with the sparking plug or plugs which must be cleaned and adjusted or renewed.

(ii) If no sparking is produced, examine the H.T. cable and, if necessary, renew it as described above in Subsection 2 (d).

(iii) Very occasionally, the fault may be due to a cracked or punctured pick-up moulding. This type of fault is not easily detected by inspection, and a check should therefore be made by substitution.

(iv) If the ignition cut out switch is suspected, disconnect the cable at the magneto and retest. If the magneto now functions normally, the fault is in either the cable or the cut out switch. Correct by replacement.

(v) If the magneto has recently been replaced or removed, it may be incorrectly timed. Refer to the engine makers' instructions, and check.

(vi) Check the contact breaker for cleanliness and correct contact setting as described under Maintenance.

If the cause of faulty operation cannot be traced from the foregoing checks, the cause may be an internal defect in the magneto. The magneto should therefore be removed from the engine for dismantling.

Further ignition particulars are given in a booklet issued by the makers, a copy of which we shall be pleased to forward upon request.

SECTION G2h

Generator/Rectifier Charging Set

1. General

(a) Constructional Notes

The alternator consists of a spigot mounted 6-coil laminated iron stator with a rotor carried on and driven by an extension of the crankshaft. The rotor has an hexagonal steel core, each face of which carries a high energy permanent magnet keyed to a laminated pole tip. The pole tips are riveted circumferentially to brass side plates, the assembly being cast in aluminium and machined to give a smooth external finish.

As shown in Figure 1, there are no rotating windings, commutator, brushgear, bearings or oil seals and consequently the alternator requires no maintenance apart from an occasional check of the three-way connector in the three output cables to see that this is clean and tight.

If removal of the rotor becomes necessary for any purpose, there will be no necessity to fit keepers to the rotor poles. When the rotor is removed, wipe off any metal swarf that may have been attracted to the pole tips and put the rotor in a clean place.

see that the connections are clean and tight. The nuts that clamp the rectifier plates together must never under any circumstances be slackened, as the clamping pressure has been carefully adjusted during manufacture to obtain the correct performance characteristics. A separate nut is used for securing the unit to the machine and this nut should be checked occasionally to see that it is tight.

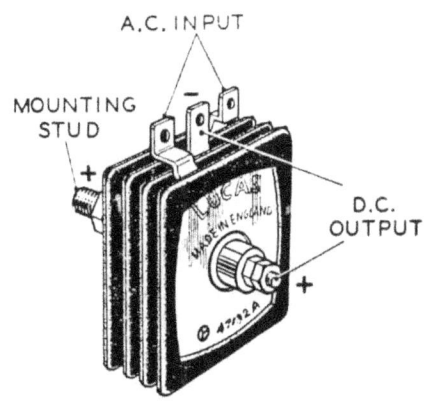

RECTIFIER
Fig. 2

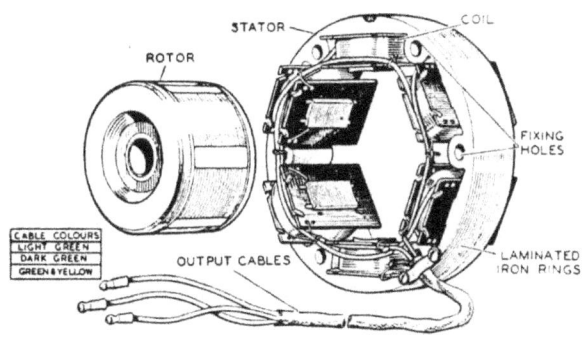

STATOR AND ROTOR OF ALTERNATOR RM15
Fig. 1

(b) Rectifier

A bridge-connected rectifier is fitted to convert the alternator output to a uni-directional battery charging current. The rectifier requires no maintenance apart from an occasional check to

(c) Operation

The alternator stator is wound with three pairs of series-connected coils, one pair being permanently connected across the rectifier. The purpose of this latter pair is to provide a small trickle charging current for the battery whenever the engine is running.

Connections to the remaining coils vary according to the demand on the battery and, as shown schematically in Figure 3, depend on the positions of the lighting switch. When no lights are in use, the coils are short-circuited and the alternator output is regulated to its minimum value by interaction of the rotor flux with the flux set up by the current flowing in the shorted coils. In the "Pilot" or parking lights position, the shorting link is disconnected and, the regulating fluxes being consequently reduced, the alternator output increases and compensates for the parking lights load. In the "Head" position of the lighting switch, the output is further increased by all three pairs of coils being connected in parallel.

2. Maintenance

(a) Check wiring occasionally to see that all connections are clean and tight.

(b) Check tightness of rectifier securing nut.

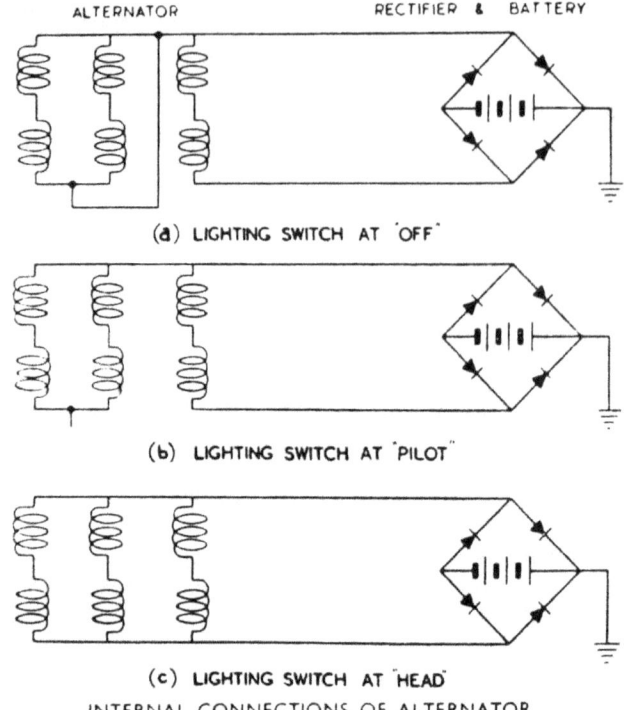

(a) LIGHTING SWITCH AT 'OFF'

(b) LIGHTING SWITCH AT 'PILOT'

(c) LIGHTING SWITCH AT 'HEAD'

INTERNAL CONNECTIONS OF ALTERNATOR

CIRCUIT DIAGRAMS FOR POSITIONS OF LIGHTING SWITCH Fig. 3

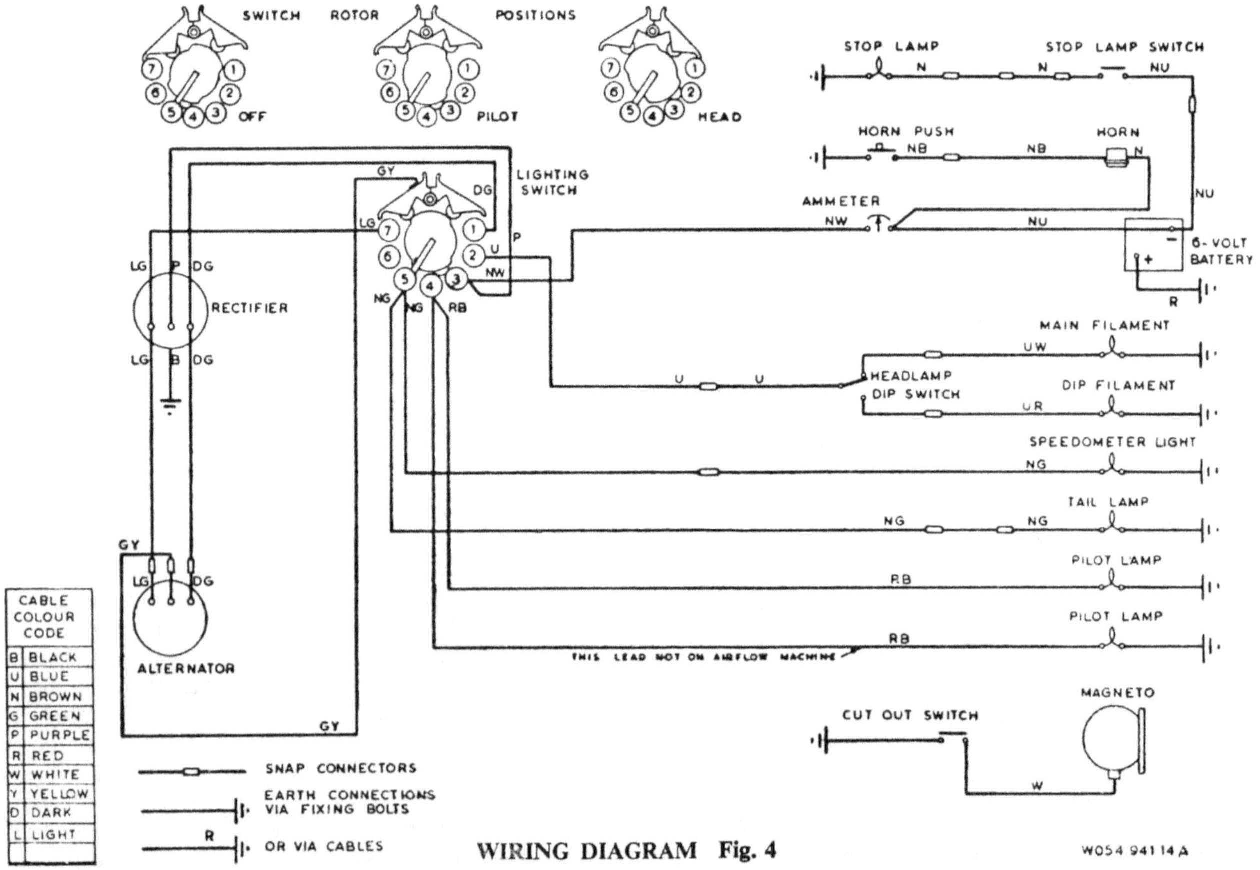

WIRING DIAGRAM Fig. 4

SECTION G4a
Battery Model PUZ7E

1. General

The model PUZ7E (see Fig. 1) is a "dry-charged" battery and is supplied without electrolyte but with its plates in a charged condition. When the battery is required for service it is only necessary to fill each cell with sulphuric acid of the correct specific gravity. No initial charging is required, but the battery must be left to stand at least one hour after filling before putting the machine into service and then adjusting the acid level if necessary.

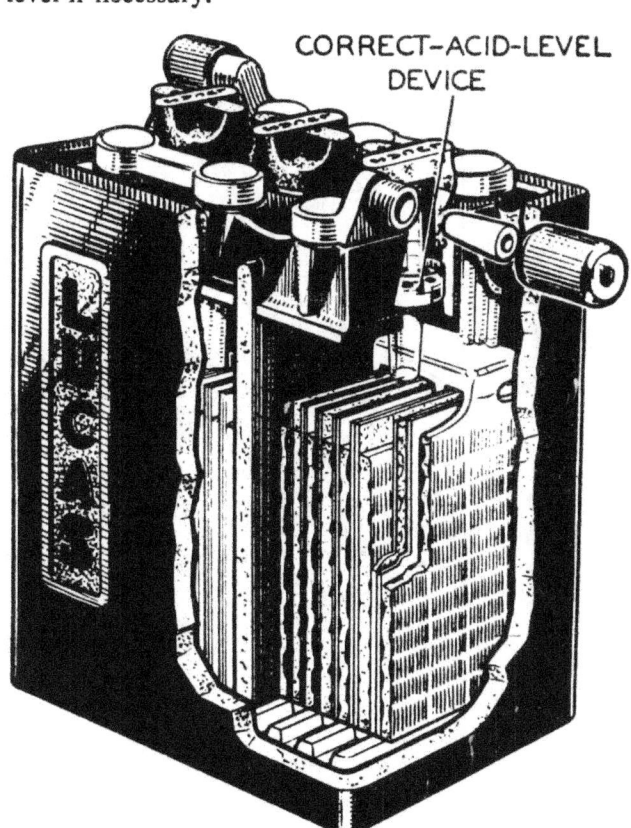

Fig. 1

2. Preparation for Service

The electrolyte is prepared by mixing together distilled water and concentrated sulphuric acid, using lead-lined tanks or suitable glass or earthenware vessels. Slowly add the acid to the water, stirring with a glass rod. Never add water to the acid, as this causes dangerous spurting of the concentrated acid. The specific gravity of the filling electrolyte depends on the climate in which the battery is to be used.

Specific gravity of electrolyte for filling "dry-charged" batteries:

Climates below 90°F. (32°C.)	Climates above 90°F. (32°C.)
Filling, 1·270	Filling, 1·210

The approximate proportions of acid and water to obtain these specific gravities:

To obtain specific gravity (corrected to 60°F.) of :	Add 1 vol. of 1·835 S.G. acid (corrected to 60°F.) to :
1·270	2·9 vols. of water.
1·210	4·0 vols. of water.

Heat is produced by the mixture of acid and water, the electrolyte should be allowed to cool before pouring it into the battery.

The specific gravity of the electrolyte varies with the temperature. For convenience in comparing specific gravities, they are always corrected to 60° F., which is adopted as a reference temperature.

The method of correction is as follows :—

For every 5°F. below 60°F., deduct ·002 from the observed reading to obtain the true specific gravity at 60°F. For every 5°F. above 60°F. add ·002 to the observed reading to obtain the true specific gravity at 60°F.

The temperature must be that indicated by a thermometer having its bulb actually immersed in the electrolyte and not the ambient temperature.

Fill the cells to the tops of the separators, *in one operation*. The battery filled in this way is 90% charged. When time permits, a short freshening charge for no more than four hours at the normal recharge rate of 1·5 amp. should be made.

3. Routine Maintenance

Fortnightly (or more frequently in hot climates) examine the level of electrolyte in the cells and if necessary add distilled water to bring the level up to the tops of the separators. The use of a Lucas Battery Filler will be found helpful, as it ensures that the correct electrolyte level is automatically maintained and also prevents distilled water from being spilled on the top of the battery (see Fig. 2).

Occasionally examine the terminals, clean and coat them with petroleum jelly. Wipe away all

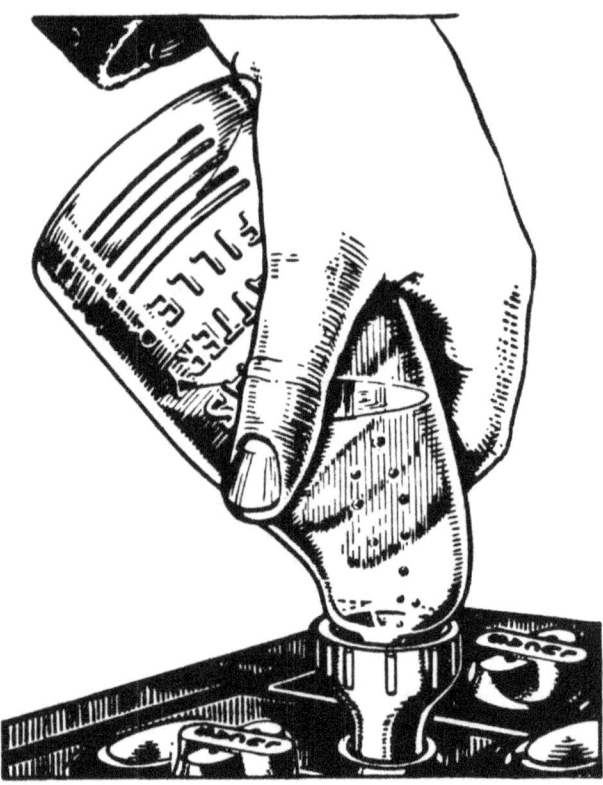

Fig. 2

dirt and moisture from the top of the battery and ensure that the connections are clean and tight.

4. Servicing

If the battery is subjected to long periods of night parking with the lights on, without suitable opportunities for recharging, a low state of charge is to be expected.

Measure the specific gravity of the acid of each cell in turn with a hydrometer (see Fig. 3).

The following table shows the state of charge at different values of specific gravities:

State of Charge	Temperature under 90°F.	Temperature over 90°F.
Battery fully charged ...	1·270—1·290	1·210—1·230
Battery about half charged ...	1·190—1·210	1·130—1·150
Battery fully discharged ...	1·110—1·130	1·050—1·070

If the battery is discharged, it must be recharged, either on the motor cycle by a period of daytime running or from an external D.C. supply at the normal recharge rate of 1·5 amp.

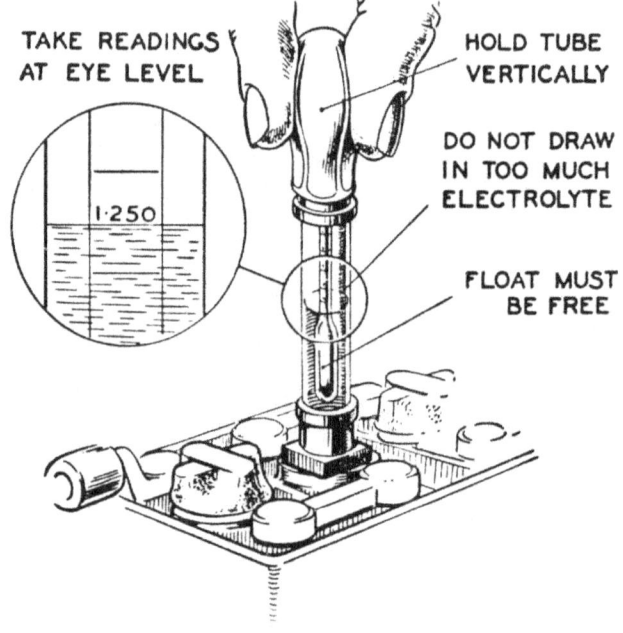

Fig. 3

SECTION G4c
Battery Model MLZ9E

Model MLZ9E is a 6-volt unit. The battery container is moulded in translucent polystyrene through which the acid can be seen. A coloured line denoting the maximum filling level is plainly marked on the outside of the container. When the battery is being charged, either on the machine or on the bench, the electrolyte level may rise above this line but will return to it during off-charge periods. During these latter periods, the upper surfaces of the plates are wetted by capillary attraction.

N.B. Unlike normal battery practice, the MLZ9E battery must not be topped up to the separator guard but only to the coloured line.

The top of the container is so designed that when the cover is in position the special anti-spill filler plugs are sealed in a common venting chamber. Gas from the filler plugs leaves this chamber through an elbow-shaped vent pipe union which can be inserted in one of four alternative sealed outlets. Polythene tubing may be attached to the vent pipe union to lead the corrosive fumes away from any parts of the machine where they might cause damage.

Heavy-duty, nut-and-bolt fixing terminals are isolated from the venting chamber.

Internally, the battery consists of three cell packs with separators formed from a dry inert micro-porous material. The use of this material means that a weaker filling acid can be used compared with the acid-diluting wet wood separators formerly employed.

Guards are fitted across the cell packs to protect the top edges of the separators from damage by battery filler nozzles, etc.

Model MLZ9E is supplied dry-charged, the filling and soaking instructions being given at the end of these notes.

Technical Data

(1) Nominal Voltage: 6
(2) Number of Plates: 9 per cell.
(3) Volume of Electrolyte: 125 c.c. per cell.
(4) Amp. hr. capacity: 12 at 10-hour rate: 13 at 20-hour rate
(5) Recharge current: 1·5 amperes.
(6) Specific gravity of electrolyte (corrected to 60°F., 15.5°C.) for filling the dry-charged battery:
 (a) In climates ordinarily below 80°F. (26·6°C.) use acid of 1·270 s.g. (corrected to 60°F.).
 (b) In climates ordinarily above 80°F., use acid of 1·210 s.g.
(7) Preparation of 1·270 and 1·210 s.g. electrolyte:
 (a) To prepare 1·270 s.g. electrolyte, slowly pour ONE PART by volume of 1·835 s.g. SULPHURIC ACID into 28 PARTS of DISTILLED WATER.
 (b) To prepare 1·210 s.g. electrolyte, the required ratio of acid to water is 1·4.

N.B. Always add the acid to the water and never vice versa or dangerous spurting may result.

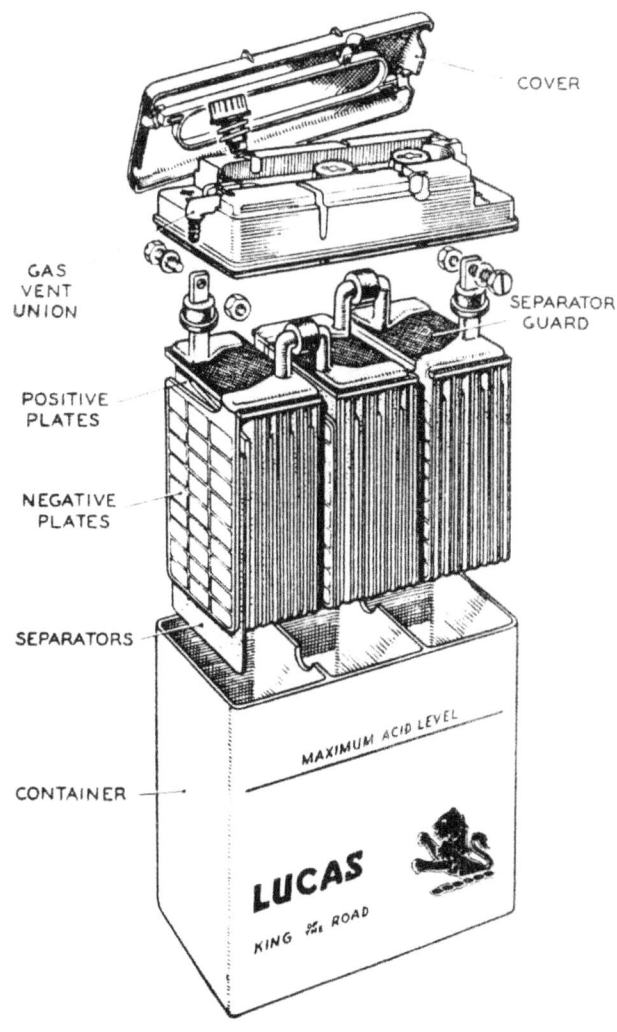

Fig. 1

Filling and Soaking the MLZ9E Battery

Discard the vent hole sealing tapes.

Pour into each cell pure dilute sulphuric acid of appropriate specific gravity to the coloured line denoting the maximum filling level and allow the battery to stand for one hour. Thereafter, keep the acid just level with the coloured line by topping up with distilled water.

A starting discharge can be taken from the battery one hour after it has been filled but, if time permits, it is advisable to first give the battery a four hour freshening charge at the normal recharge rate, i.e., 1·5 amperes.

SECTION G5d
Head and Tail Lamps

Used on "350 Bullet," "500 Bullet," "500 Twin," "Constellation" and "Super Meteor" 1956 onwards and "Meteor Minor" 1958 onwards

1. Headlamp

In all the above Models the headlamp incorporates the Lucas Light Unit MCF700. This is built into the Casquette fork head which contains twin parking lamps as well as the ammeter and switch.

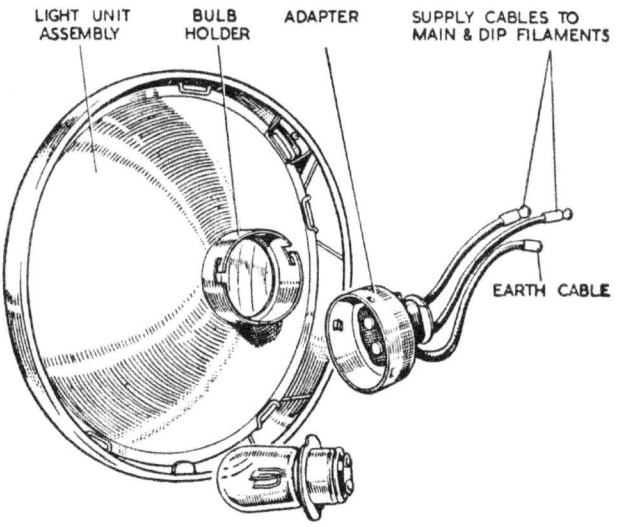

HEADLAMP MCF700
Fig. 1

2. Lucas Light Unit

The unit incorporates a combined reflector and front lens assembly (see Fig. 1). This construction ensures that the reflector and lenses are permanently protected, thus the unit keeps its high efficiency over a long period. A "prefocus" bulb is used, the filaments of which are accurately positioned with respect to the reflector, thus no focusing device is necessary.

The bulb has a large cap and a flange, which has been accurately positioned with relation to the bulb filaments during manufacture. A slot in the flange engages with a projection on the inside of the bulb holder positioned at the back of the reflector.

A bayonet-fitting adaptor with spring-loaded contacts secures the bulb firmly in position and carries the supply to the bulb contacts.

The outer surface of the lens is smooth to facilitate cleaning. The inner surface is formed of a series of lenses which determine the spread and pattern of the light beams.

In the event of damage to either the lens or reflector a replacement light unit must be fitted.

3. Replacing the Light Unit and Bulb

Slacken the securing screw at the top of the headlamp rim. Remove the front rim and Light Unit assembly.

Withdraw the adaptor from the Light Unit by twisting it in an anti-clockwise direction and pulling it off. Remove the bulb from its locating sleeve at the rear of the reflector.

Disengage the Light Unit securing springs from the rim and lift out the Light Unit.

Position the new unit in the rim so that the word "TOP" on the lens is correctly located when the assembly is mounted on the headlamp. Refit the securing springs ensuring that they are equally spaced around the rim.

Replace the bulb and adaptor. The bulb must be the Lucas "prefocus" type—6 v. 30/24 watt Lucas No. 312.

Locate the bottom of the Light Unit and front rim assembly in the headlamp shell or in the fixing rim attached to the Casquette fork head. Press the front on and tighten the securing screw at the top of the headlamp.

4. Parking Lights

Access to the parking bulbs is obtained by removing the parking lamp rim (see Fig. 2). This is forced over the edge of the rubber lamp body and is additionally secured by means of a small fixing

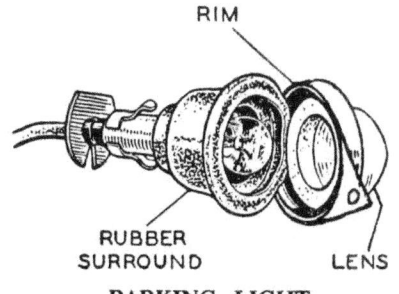

PARKING LIGHT
Fig. 2

screw. After removal of the lamp rim the parking lamp lens can be pulled out of the rubber body, after which the bulb will be accessible.

5. Tail Light

The Lucas lamp, Type 564 (Fig. 3) is a combined stop and tail light and also incorporates a reflector.

Access to the bulb is obtained by removing the two screws which secure the plastic cover.

The correct bulb is Lucas No. 384 6 volt 6/18 watt. The 6 watt filament provides the normal tail light, while the 18 watt filament is illuminated on movement of the brake pedal.

(**Note.**—6 watt bulbs are now required by law in Great Britain on machines of more than 250 c.c. capacity.)

Care must be taken that the leads to the stop tail lamp are correctly connected, as the use of the 18 watt filament on the normal tail light will not only discharge the battery but could cause trouble

STOP-TAIL LAMP L.564
Fig. 3

from excessive heat affecting the plastic cover. At the same time, the 6 watt filament, if used as a stop-tail light, will be ineffective in bright sunlight or at night when the tail light filament is illuminated.

SECTION H5

Frame

"Constellation" 1958-1961, "Super Meteor" 1956-61, "Meteor Minor" 1958-61, "Meteor Minor Sports" 1960-61, "350 and 500 Bullets" 1958-61, "350 Clipper" 1958-61, and "Works Replica" 1958-60

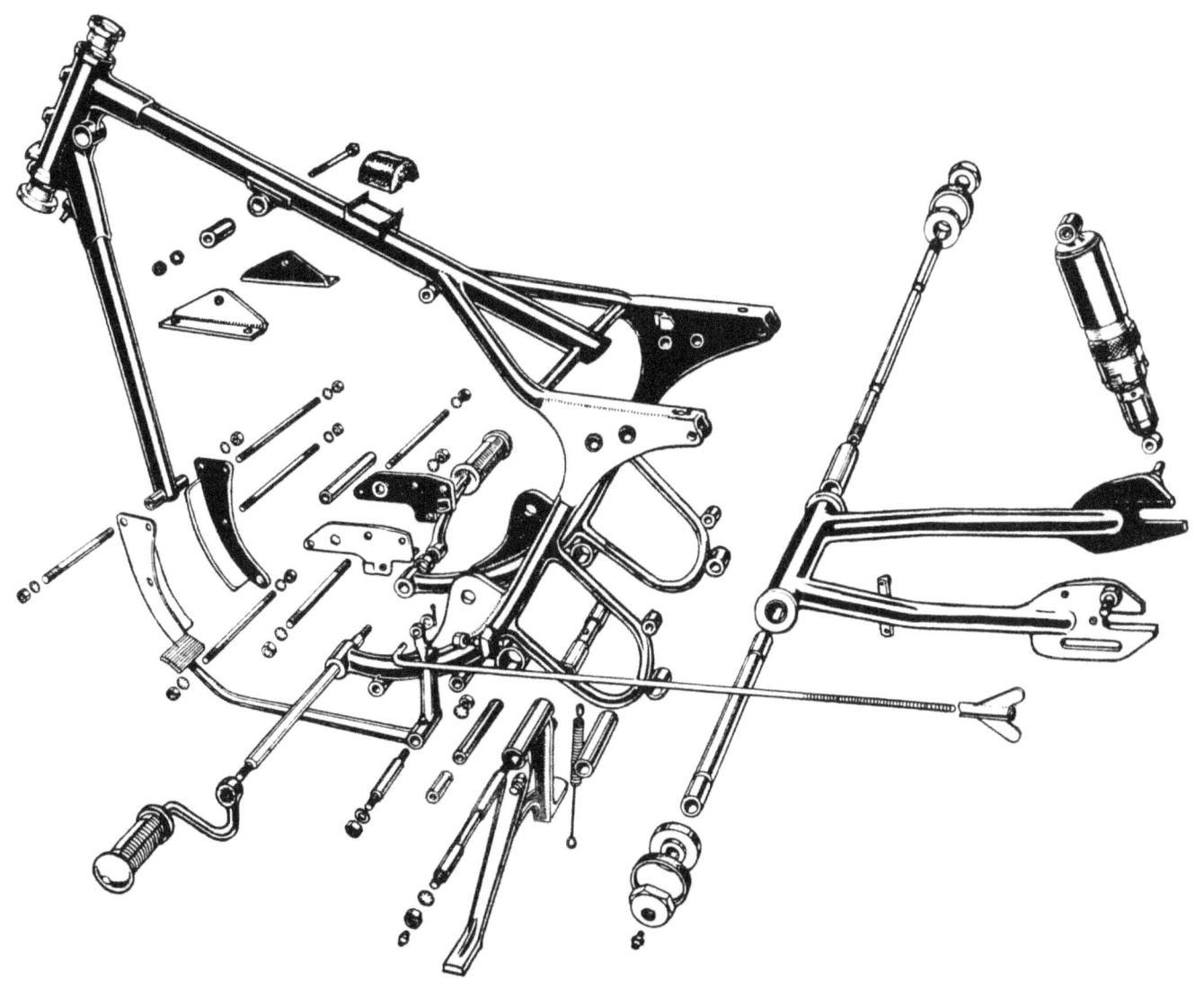

EXPLODED VIEW OF "CONSTELLATION" FRAME

Fig. 1

1. Description of Frame

The frame is built throughout of cold drawn weldless steel tubing with brazed or welded joints, liners being fitted where necessary for extra strength. All the main frame members are made of chrome-molybdenum alloy steel tubing which retains its strength and resistance to fatigue after brazing or welding.

The swinging arm unit which forms the chain stays is fitted with large diameter phosphor bronze bushes and pivots on a stout steel tube which is secured to the main frame by a long bolt passing through the pivot lugs. Hardened steel thrust washers are provided to deal with side thrust. The torsional rigidity of the swinging arm unit helps to maintain the rear wheel upright in the frame and thus relieves the wheel spindle of bending stresses to which it is subject with other types of rear suspension.

2. Steering Head Races

The steering head races, 34085, are the same at the top and bottom of the head lug and are the same for all models. They are easily removed by knocking them out with a hammer and drift and new races can be fitted either under a press or by means of a hammer and a wooden drift.

3. Removal of Rear Suspension Unit

On the "Constellation" and "Super Meteor" from 1961 onwards, the valances on either side of the frame must be removed to gain access to the top pivot pin. (See Section C, paragraph 8.)

The procedure for all models is then as follows. Remove the top pivot pin nut, drive out the pivot pin, then hinge the suspension unit back on the lower pivot pin. After removing the lower nut, the unit may be pushed off the pivot pin welded to the fork end.

4. Servicing Rear Suspension Units

The proprietary units fitted are sealed and servicing of the internal mechanism can be carried out only by the manufacturers.

The rubber bushes in the top and bottom eyes can easily be renewed and the spring can be removed by pushing down on the top spring cover so as to release the split collar above it. After removal of the split collar the top cover and spring can be lifted off. When reassembling, the spring should be greased to prevent rust and squeaking if it should come into contact with either of the covers.

The standard solo springs have a rate of 100—105 lb. per inch and it is not difficult to

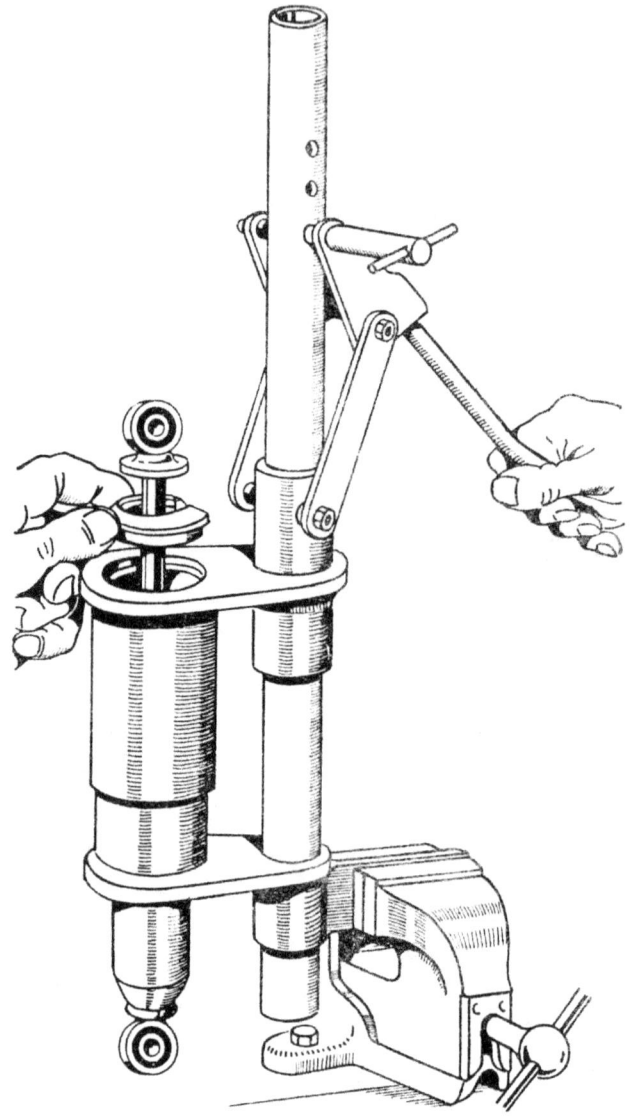

REAR SPRING COMPRESSOR
Fig. 2

compress these by hand. Heavier springs having a rate of 130 lb. per inch are available which may require the use of a spring compressor, as shown in Fig. 2.

5. Removal of Swinging Arm Chain Stays

First remove one of the pivot pin nuts and pull the pivot pin out from the other end. To release the pivot bearing it is necessary to spread the rear portion of the frame, using the frame expander E.5431, which will spread the frame sufficiently to enable the spigots on the thrust washers to clear the recesses in the pivot lugs forming part of the frame.

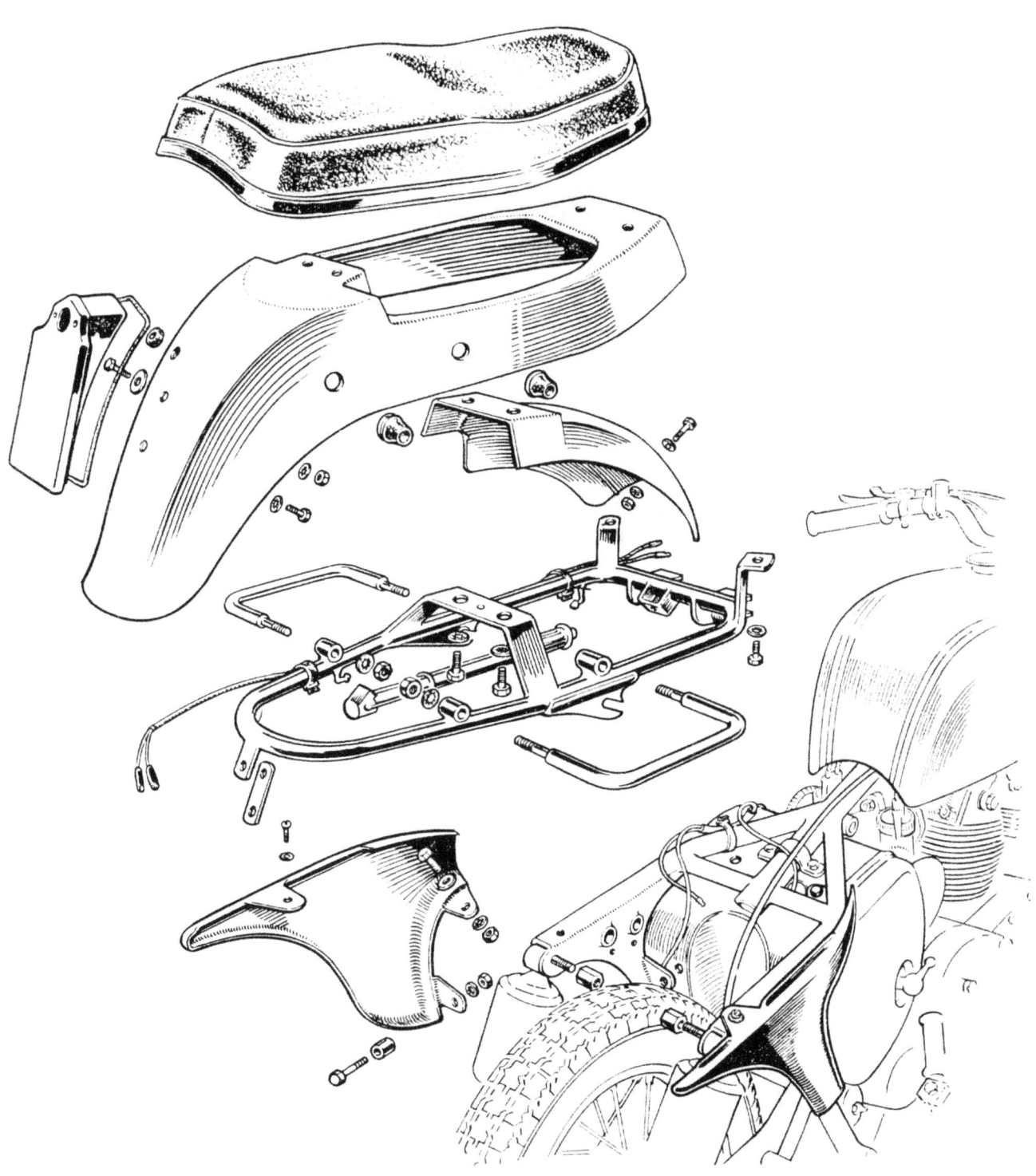

DUAL SEAT—MUDGUARD ASSEMBLY "CONSTELLATION" AND "SUPER METEOR," 1961 ONWARDS

Fig. 3

If it is necessary to remove the bronze bushes these can be driven out by means of a hammer and a suitable drift and new bushes can be fitted under a press without difficulty. After fitting the bushes they must be reamed to ·844/·843 in.

6. Centre Stand

To remove the centre stand unscrew the nut from one end of the stand spindle, knock out the latter and withdraw the stand complete with its bearing sleeve after disconnecting one end of the stand spring.

7. Wheel Alignment

Note that it is not possible to guarantee that the wheels are correctly aligned when the same notch position is used on both adjuster cams. It is therefore not sufficient to count the notches and use the same position on both sides of the machine. The only way to guarantee that the wheels are in line is to check the alignment from front wheel to back using either a straight edge or a piece of taut string. The alignment should be checked on both sides of the machine and if the front and rear tyres are of different section allowance must be made for this.

It is usual to check the alignment of the wheels at a point about six inches above the ground but, if the alignment is checked also towards the top of the wheels, it will be possible to ascertain whether or not the frame is twisted so as to cause one wheel to be leaning while the other is vertical. To do this it is always necessary to remove the mudguards and, unless a straight edge cut away in its centre portion is available, it will be necessary also to remove the cylinder, toolboxes, battery, etc., in order to allow an unbroken straight edge or a piece of taut string to contact the front and rear tyres.

8. Lubrication

The steering head races, swinging arm pivot bearing and stand pivot bearing should be well greased on assembly. The swinging arm pivot and stand pivot are provided with grease nipples but no nipples are provided for the steering head as experience has shown that the provision of nipples at this point causes trouble through chafing and cutting of control and lighting cables. If the steering head bearings are well packed they will last for several years or many thousands of miles.

Recommended greases are Castrolease (Heavy), Mobilgrease (No. 4), Esso Grease, Energrease C.3 or Shell Retinax A.

9. Dismantling the Rear Mudguard-dual Seat Assembly, 1961 onwards

Having removed the assembly from the frame, as described in Section C, paragraph 8, dismantling for repair or replacement is a simple matter.

First remove the single $\frac{3}{16}$ in. bolt securing the number plate, and disconnect the rear light wires at the junctions. The lifting handles are next pulled out, after undoing the two $\frac{5}{16}$ in. nuts on each handle. The grommets may be left in position in the mudguard.

Take out the two $\frac{3}{16}$ in. bolts in the nose of the mudguard. These screw into tapped holes in the dual seat. When replacing, the shakeproof washer must be next to the head of the bolt and the large plain washer must be against the underside of the mudguard.

Remove the single $\frac{3}{16}$ in. nut and bolt, attaching the rear of the mudguard to the carrier. Note the large plain washer, which must be under the bolt head, and bear against the top of the mudguard on assembly. Also the shakeproof washer and metal plate on the underside.

Lastly, the two $\frac{1}{4}$ in. bolts attaching the front of the carrier to the mudguard, and the two $\frac{5}{16}$ in. bolts in the carrier bridge piece, can be undone. They fit into tapped holes in the dual seat.

Note that shakeproof washers are fitted to all bolts and studs. Plain washers must be placed as described above and shown in Fig. 3.

On some early 1961 "Constellation" models, this mudguard is made from glass-fibre and in the event of damage small repair kits, consisting of a quantity of resin, catalyst and glass fibre, are available from our Service Department. Instructions for carrying out minor repairs are issued with this kit. All other models have the mudguard of pressed steel.

SECTION J1

Front Fork

With Casquette and Aluminium Alloy Bottom Tubes

1. Description

The telescopic fork consists of two legs each of which comprises a main tube of chrome molybdenum alloy steel tubing which is screwed into the Casquette fork head at the upper end and securely clamped to the fork crown. Fitted over the lower end of the main tube is the bottom tube made of high strength aluminium alloy with an integral lug which carries the wheel spindle. Fitted on the lower end of the main tube is a steel bush which is a close fit in the bore of the bottom tube. The upper end of the bottom tube carries a bronze bush which is a close fit over the outside diameter of the main tube. The bush is secured to the bottom tube by means of a threaded housing which contains an oil seal. A stud known as the "spring stud" is fitted in the lower end of the bottom tube and a valve port is secured to the lower end of the main tube. As the fork operates oil is forced between the spring stud and the bore of the valve port forming a hydraulic damping system. A compression spring is fitted inside the main tube between the upper end of the spring stud and the upper end of the main tube. The lower end of the main tube and upper end of the bottom tube are protected by a cover secured to the fork crown.

A special fork is available for sidecar machines. This has bottom tubes with extended wheel lugs giving less trail and is fitted with stronger springs and a steering damper.

2. Operation of the Fork

The fork provides a range of movement of 6 in. from the fully extended to the fully compressed position. The movement is controlled by the compression spring and by the hydraulic damping system. The hydraulic damping is light on the bump stroke and heavier on the rebound stroke, thus damping out any tendency to pitching or oscillation without interfering unduly with the free movement of the fork when the wheel encounters an obstacle.

The fork is filled with a light oil (S.A.E. 20) to a point above the lower end of the spring so that the damper chamber "B" is always kept

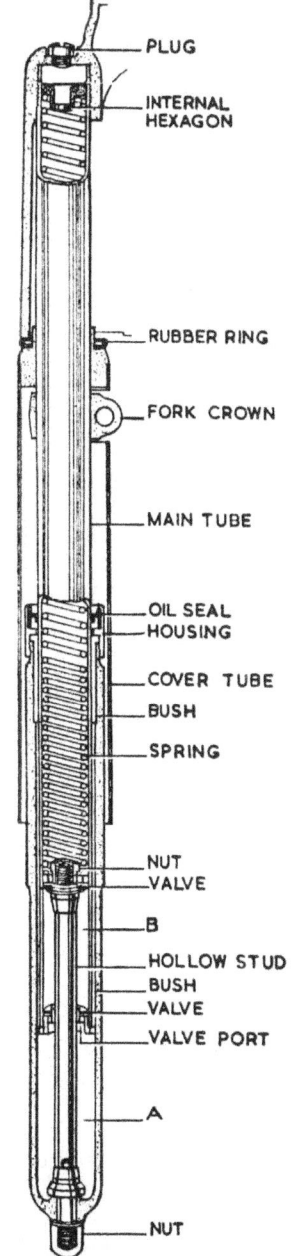

SECTION OF FORK LEG

Fig. 1

full of oil. Upward movement of the wheel spindle forces oil from the lower chamber "A" through the annular space between the spring stud (38067) and the bore of the main tube valve port (38138) into the damper chamber "B." During this stroke the pressure on the underside of the valve plate (38073) causes this to lift so that oil can also pass from "A" to "B" through the eight holes in the valve body. Since, however, the diameter of chamber "B" is less than that of chamber "A" there is not room in "B" to receive all the oil which must be displaced from "A" as the fork operates. The surplus oil passes through the cross hole in the spring stud and up the centre hole in the stud, spilling out through the nut (38076) which secures the upper end of the spring stud to the bronze guide at the lower end of the fork spring.

On the rebound stroke the oil in the damper chamber "B" is forced through the annular space between the spring stud and the bore of the main tube valve port. During this stroke pressure in chamber "B" closes the two disc valves at the upper and lower ends of the chamber so that the only path through which the oil can escape is the annular space between the spring stud and the port. Damping on the rebound stroke is therefore heavier than on the bump stroke. At the extreme end of either bump or rebound stroke a small taper portion on the spring stud enters the bore

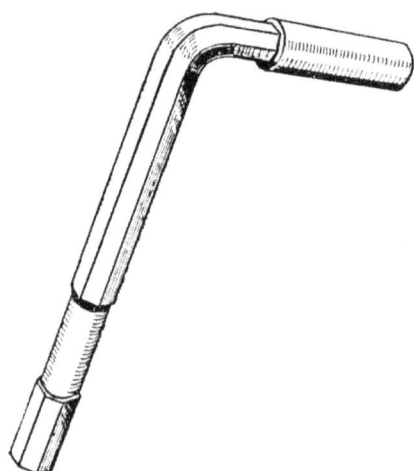

MAIN TUBE SPANNER

Fig. 2

of the valve port, thus restricting the annular space and increasing the amount of damping. At the extreme end of the bump stroke the larger diameter taper on the oil control collar (38075) enters the main counterbore of the valve port thus forming a hydraulic cushion to prevent metal to metal contact.

3. Dismantling the Fork to Replace Spring, Oil Seal or Bearing Bushes

Place the machine on the centre stand, disconnect the front brake control and remove the front wheel and mudguard complete with stays. Unscrew the bottom spring stud nut (38080) which will allow oil to run out of the fork down to

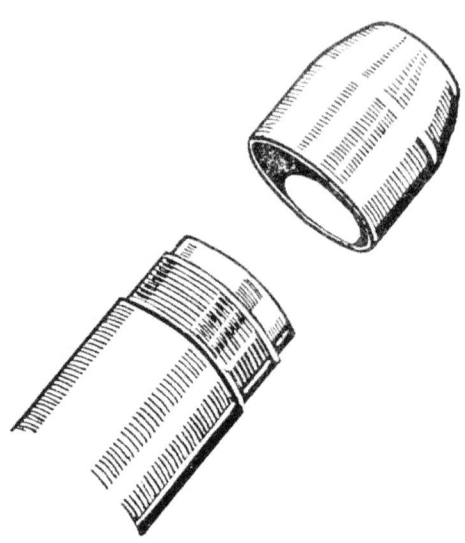

MAIN TUBE SEAL GUIDE

Fig. 3

the level of the cross hole in the spring stud. Now knock the spring stud upwards into the fork with a soft mallet, thus allowing the remainder of the oil to escape. Pull the fork bottom tube down as far as possible, thus exposing the oil seal housing (38157). Unscrew this housing either by means of a spanner on the flats with which it is provided or by using the gland nut hand grips (E.5417). The bottom tube can now be withdrawn completely from the main tube, leaving the bottom tube bush, oil seal housing and oil seal in position on the main tube.

Now unscrew the main tube valve port using "C" spanner (E5418). The spring stud and spring can now be withdrawn from the lower end of the main tube.

The steel main tube bush (38156) can now be tapped off the lower end of the tube, if necessary using the bottom tube bush for this purpose. Before doing this, however, it is advisable to mark the position of the bush with a pencil line so as to ensure reassembling it in the same position on the main tube. The reason for this is that these bushes are finish ground to size after fitting on to the tubes so as to ensure concentricity. After removal of the main tube bush the bottom tube bush, oil seal housing and oil seal can be removed.

In case of difficulty in removing the main tube bush it is possible to withdraw the oil seal housing after loosening the crown clip bolt 39038, removing the plug screw 38968 and unscrewing the main tube from the fork head by means of a hexagon bar ·500 in. across flats (Unbrako wrench W.11) or the special tool shown in Fig. 2.

4. Spring

Solo and Sidecar springs are available. The free length of each is 20½ ins. The spring should be replaced if it has closed by more than 1 inch.

5. Reassembly of Parts

When refitting the oil seal, or fitting a new one, great care must be exercised not to damage the synthetic rubber lip which forms the actual seal. If the seal has been removed from the upper end of the main tube and is refitted from this end a special nose piece (Fig. 3) must be fitted over the end of the tube to prevent the thread from damaging the oil seal.

The spring stud is a tight fit in the hole at the lower end of the bottom tube. Once the stud has been entered in the hole push the bottom tube up sharply against the spring until two or three threads on the stud project beneath the end of the bottom tube. Now fit the nut and washer and pull the stud into position by tightening the nut. If necessary fit the nut first without the washer until sufficient thread is projecting to enable the washer to be fitted.

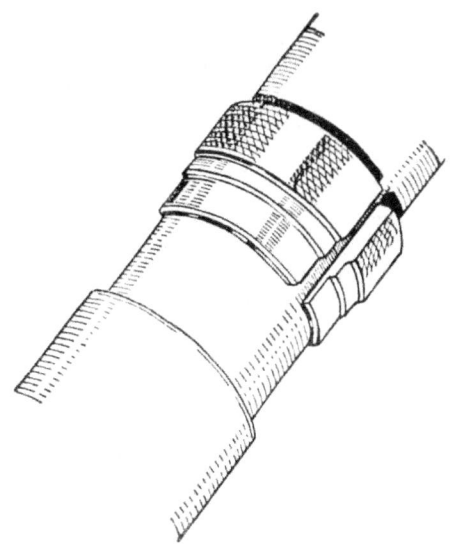

OUTER COVER CENTRALISING BUSHES

Fig. 5

6. Steering Head Races

The steering head bearing consists of two deep groove thrust races each containing nineteen ¼ in. diameter balls. The bearing is adjusted by tightening the steering stem locknut after loosening the ball head clip screw and both the fork crown clamp bolts. The head should be adjusted so that, when the front wheel is lifted clear of the ground, a light tap on the handlebars will cause the steering to swing to full lock in either direction, while at the same time there should be only the slightest trace of play in the bearings. When testing for freedom of movement the steering damper, if fitted, should be disconnected by unscrewing the anchor plate pin. Do not forget to tighten the ball head clip screw and fork crown clamp bolts. Before tightening the latter make sure that the cover tubes are located centrally round the main tubes so that the bottom tube does not rub inside the cover tube. A pair of split bushes (Fig. 5) is useful to ensure centralisation of the cover tubes.

7. Removal of Complete Fork

The fork complete with front wheel and mudguard can be removed from the machine if necessary by adopting the following procedure.

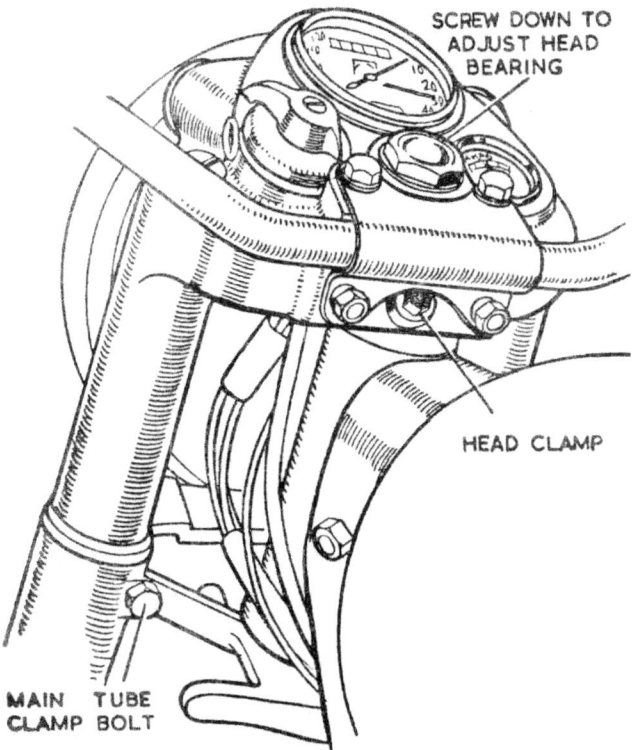

SHOWING THE POSITIONS OF THE CLAMP BOLTS SECURING THE STEERING STEM AND FORK TUBES

Fig. 4

The leads to the lighting switch and ammeter should be disconnected from the battery, regulator, tail lamp, etc. at their lower ends or by means of the plug and socket connectors when these are provided. The switch and ammeter are push fits into the rubber bushes in the fork head.

Disconnect the speedometer drive from the speedometer head and unscrew the steering damper knob and rod (on sidecar forks) after removal of the split pin through the lower end of the rod. Undo the steering damper anchor plate pin so as to disconnect the damper from the frame of the machine.

Remove the two plug screws (38968) and loosen the steering head clip bolt and the two fork crown clamp bolts.

Now unscrew the fork main tubes from the fork head and the steering stem locknut from the top of the steering stem, turning each tube and the nut a turn or two at a time. When the nut has been removed from the steering stem and the main tubes have been completely unscrewed from the fork head the complete fork and wheel with steering stem can be lifted out of the head lug of the frame.

8. Lubrication

The lubrication of the fork bearings is effected by the oil which forms the hydraulic damping medium. All that is necessary is to keep sufficient oil in the fork to ensure that the top end of the bottom spring stud is never uncovered even in the full rebound position. The level of oil in the fork can be gauged by removing the top plug screw and inserting a long rod about $\frac{3}{8}$ in. diameter. If slightly tilted this will ledge against the nut at the upper end of the bottom spring stud and indicate the level of oil above the stud. If the fork is empty to start with the quantity required is approximately $7\frac{1}{2}$ fluid ounces in each leg. Recommended grades of oil are Castrolite, Mobiloil Arctic, Essolube 20, B.P. Energol S.A.E. 20 and Shell X-100 20/20W.

9. Air Vents

The earlier forks of this type were provided with holes at the upper end of each main tube communicating with small vent holes in the Casquette head. Experience has shown that on rough roads oil may escape through these air vents which in consequence are now omitted. Escape of oil from the earlier forks can be largely eliminated by fitting specially long plug screws which are available. The Part Number is 40118. If these are fitted and the final vent hole is stopped up with a wooden plug leakage at this point is impossible. Fitting the special plug screws alone is sufficient in most instances.

SECTION K6

Front Wheel
With Dual 6in. Brake

1. Removal from Fork

To remove the front wheel from the fork place the machine on the centre stand and front stand, if fitted, or alternatively with sufficient packing (about 2 in.) beneath each side of the stand to lift the wheel clear of the ground when tilted back on to the rear wheel. Slacken brake cable adjustments and disconnect cables from handlebar lever and from operating cam levers on hub. Unscrew the four nuts securing the fork bottom tube lug caps (Part No. 38593) and allow the wheel to drop forwards out of the front fork. Make sure that the machine stands securely on the rear wheel and centre stand—if necessary place a weight on the saddle or a strut beneath the fork to ensure this.

2. Removal of Brake Cover Plate Assemblies

Lock the brake "on" by pressure on the operating lever, 38905 (R.H.) or 38906 (L.H.), and unscrew the cover plate nuts 31347. The right and left hand cover plate assemblies can then be withdrawn from the respective brake drums.

3. Removal of Brake Shoes and Springs

This is best done by unscrewing the pivot pin locknuts, 28715, and the operating lever nuts, 10314, after which the assembly of brake shoes, return springs, pivot pin and operating cam can be removed from the cover plate by light blows with a hammer and drift on the ends of the pivot pin and the operating cam, see Fig. 2. The return springs, 29236, can then be unhooked from the spring posts in the brake shoes thus allowing the whole assembly to fall apart.

4. Replacing Brake Linings

Brake linings are supplied either in pairs ready drilled complete with rivets (Part No. 37786BX) or ready fitted to service replacement brake shoes

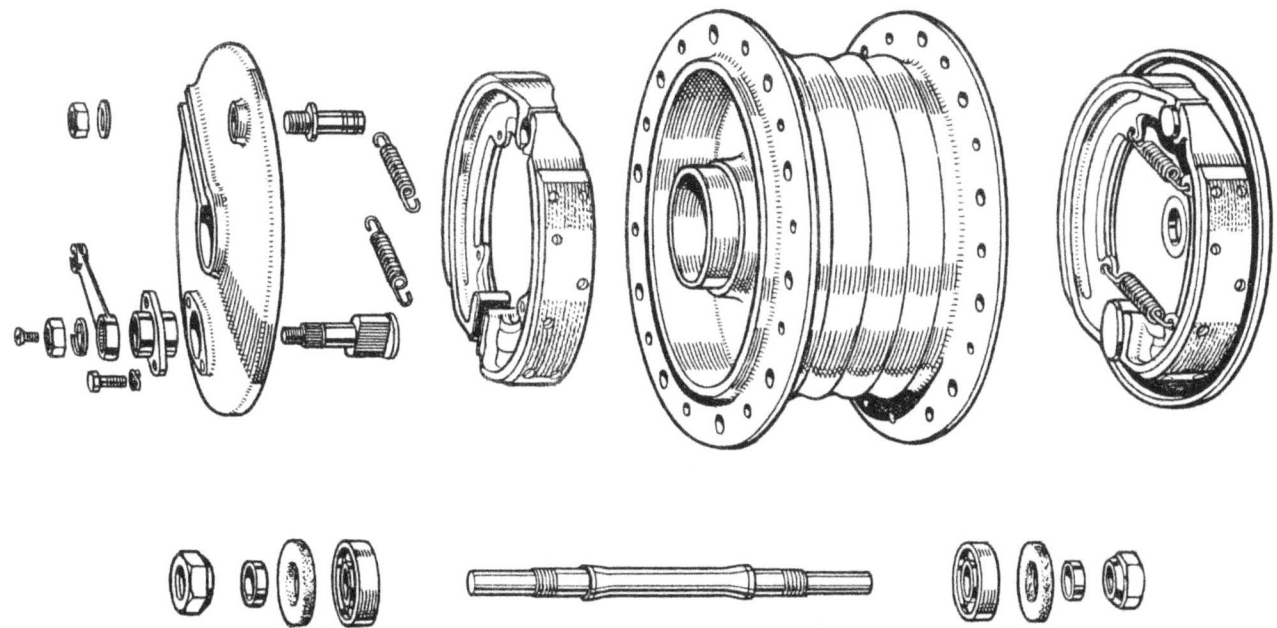

DUAL FRONT BRAKE
Fig. 1

(Part No. 38042). When riveting linings to shoes secure the two centre rivets first so as to ensure that the lining lies flat against the shoe. Standard linings are Ferodo MR41, which are drilled to receive cheese headed rivets.

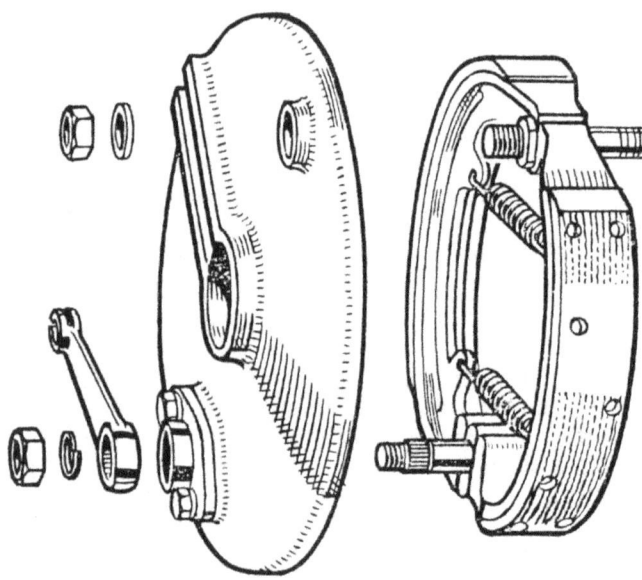

REMOVAL OF BRAKE SHOE ASSEMBLY
Fig. 2

5. Removal of Hub Spindle and Bearings

To remove the hub spindle and bearings having already removed the brake cover plate assemblies, lift out the felt washers, Part No. 21466, and distance washers, Part No. 30538. Now hit one end of the wheel spindle with a copper hammer or mallet, thus driving it out of the hub bringing one bearing with it and leaving the other in position in the hub. Drive the bearing off the spindle and insert the latter once more in the hub at the end from which it was removed. Now drive the spindle through the hub the other way, when it will bring out the remaining bearing.

6. Hub Bearings

These are deep groove single row journal ball bearings $\frac{5}{8}$ in. i/d by $1\frac{9}{16}$ in. o/d by $\frac{7}{16}$ in. wide. The Skefko Part No. is RLS5. Equivalent bearings of other makes are Hoffmann LS7, Ransome and Marles LJ$\frac{5}{8}$ in., Fischer LS7.

7. Fitting Limits for Bearings

The fit of the bearings in the hub barrel is important. The bearings are locked on the spindle between shoulders and the distance pieces, 30538, which in turn are held up by the cover plate nuts 31347. In order to prevent endways pre-loading of the bearings it is essential that there is a small clearance between the inner edge of the outer race of the bearing and the back of the recess in either end of the hub barrel. To prevent any possibility of sideways movement of the hub barrel on the bearings it is, therefore, necessary for the bearings to be a tight fit in the barrel but this fit must not be so tight as to close down the outer race of the bearing and thus overload the balls. The following are the manufacturing tolerances which control the fit of the bearings. The figures for the bearings themselves are for SKF bearings but other manufacturers' tolerances are similar.

Bearing o/d   1·5622/1·5617 in.
Housing bore   1·5620/1·5616 in.
Bearing bore   ·6252/·6247 in.
Shaft diameter   ·6252/·6248 in.

8. Refitting Ball Bearings

To refit the bearings in the hub two hollow drifts are required, as shown in Fig. 3. One bearing is first fitted to one end of the spindle by means of the hollow drift; the spindle and bearing are then entered into one end of the hub barrel which is then supported on one of the hollow drifts. The other bearing is then threaded over the upper end of the spindle and driven home by means of the second hollow drift either under a press or by means of a hammer which will thus drive both bearings into position simultaneously. In order to make quite sure that there is clearance between the inner faces of the outer bearing races and the bottom of the recesses, fit the distance washers, 30538, and the cover plate nuts, 31347, with either the cover plates themselves or additional packing washers behind the nuts. Tightening the nuts should not have any effect on the ease with which the spindle can be turned. If tightening the nuts makes the spindle hard to turn this may be taken as proof that the bearings are bottoming in the recesses in the hub barrel before they are solid against the shoulders on the spindle. In this case the bearing should be removed and a thin packing shim fitted between the inner race and the shoulder on the spindle.

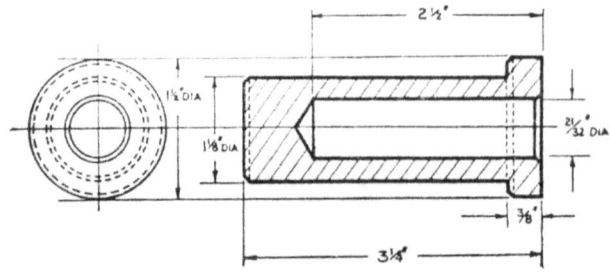

DRIFT FOR REFITTING BEARINGS
Fig. 3

9. Reassembly of Brake Shoes on to Cover Plates

Assemble each pair of shoes with their return springs on to the pivot pin and operating cam, putting a smear of grease in the grooves of the pivot pin and on the operating faces of the cam. Now fit the assembly into the cover plate, putting a smear of grease on to the cylindrical bearing surface of the operating cam and secure with the pivot pin locknut, 28715, and washer, 17551. Fit the operating lever, 38905 or 38906, on its splines in a position to suit the extent of wear on the linings and secure with the nut, 10314, and washer, 14613. Note that the position of the operating levers may have to be corrected when adjusting the brake after refitting the wheel. The range of adjustment can be extended by moving these levers on to different splines. Limit of wear is reached when the cam is turned through nearly 90° with the brake hard on so that there is a danger that the operating springs cannot return the brake to the off position.

10. Floating Cam Housings

Note that the cam housings, Part No. 26836, are intended to be left free to float. The bolt holes in the cam housings are slotted and the securing pins, Part No. 252, are provided with double coil spring washers beneath their heads to enable them to be tightened sufficiently to prevent the cam housings moving under the influence of road shocks, while at the same time they can be, and should be, left free enough to be capable of being moved by hand in the direction of the slots. The pins, 252, are secured by locknuts, 7916, which are centre punched as an additional precaution.

The leading shoes (i.e., those towards the rear of the machine) have a servo action which renders them more effective than the trailing shoes. This servo action causes the linings on the leading shoes to wear more quickly than those on the trailing shoes and at the same time tends to lift the leading shoes off the cams and press the trailing shoes harder on to the cams. With a fixed cam housing the result is that the majority of the cam pressure is applied to the less efficient trailing shoe. By leaving the housing free to float the cam can follow up the leading shoe thus maintaining equal pressure between the cam and the two shoes and so making full use of the more efficient leading shoe. Owing to the servo action the wear on the leading shoe with a floating cam housing is greater than that of the trailing shoe and in time the limit of float of the cam housing will be reached, after which the brake will continue to function as a fixed cam brake with some loss of efficiency. This can be restored by removing the shoes and fitting them in the opposite positions. Floating cam brakes are self-centering and there is no need to take any special precautions to see that the two linings are of equal thickness or that the brake shoe assembly is centred in the drum.

11. Refitting Brake Cover Plates

After assembling the brake shoe pivot pins and operating cams into the cover plates repack the hub bearings with grease. The recommended greases are Castrolease (Heavy), Mobilgrease (No. 4), Esso Grease, Energrease C3 or Shell Retinax A. These are all medium heavy lime soap or aluminium soap greases. The use of H.M.P. greases which have a soda soap base is not recommended as these tend to be slightly corrosive if any damp finds its way into the hubs.

Before fitting the distance washers and felt washers make sure that the inside of the brake drums are quite clean and free from oil or grease, damp, etc., and replace the brake cover plate assemblies. Securely tighten the cover plate nuts, 31347.

12. Wheel Rim

The rim is Type WM2—19 in. plunged and pierced with forty holes for spoke nipples. The spoke holes are symmetrical, i.e., the rim can be assembled to the hub either way round. Rim diameter after building is 19·062 in., tolerances on the circumference of the rim shoulders where the tyre fits being 59·930/59·870 in. The standard steel measuring tape for checking rims is $\frac{5}{16}$ in. wide, ·011 in. thick and its length is 59·964/59·904 in.

13. Spokes

The spokes are of the single butted type 8—10 gauge with 90° countersunk heads, angle of bend 95°—100°, length $6\frac{5}{8}$ in., thread diameter ·144 in., 40 threads per inch, thread form British Standard Cycle.

14. Wheel Building and Truing

The spokes are laced one over two and the wheel rim must be built central in relation to the nuts which secure the brake cover plates. The rim should be trued as accurately as possible, the maximum permissible run-out both sideways and radially being plus or minus $\frac{1}{32}$ in.

15. Tyre

The standard tyre is Dunlop 3·25—19 in. Ribbed tread.

When removing the tyre always start close to the valve and see that the edge of the cover at the other side of the wheel is pushed down into the well in the rim.

When replacing the tyre fit the part by the valve last, also with the edge of the cover at the other side of the wheel pushed down into the well.

If the correct method of fitting and removal of the tyre is adopted it will be found that the covers can be manipulated quite easily with the small levers supplied in the toolkit. The use of long levers and/or excessive force is liable to damage the walls of the tyre. After inflation make sure that the tyre is fitting evenly all the way round the rim. A line moulded on the wall of the tyre indicates whether or not the tyre is correctly fitted. If the tyre has a white mark, indicating a balance point, this should be fitted near the valve.

16. Tyre Pressure

The recommended pressure for the front tyre is 18 lb. per square inch for wheel loads up to 240 lb.

17. Lubrication

No grease nipple is provided on later hubs, due to the tendency to over-grease, resulting in grease finding its way past the felt seals on to the brake linings.

The correct method of lubrication is to pack the bearings with grease after dismantling the hub, as described above.

Note that the brake cams are drilled for grease passages but the ends of these are stopped up with countersunk screws instead of being fitted with grease nipples. This is done to prevent excessive greasing by over-enthusiastic owners. If the cams are smeared with grease on assembly they should require no further attention but in case of necessity it is possible to remove the screws, fit grease nipples in their place and grease the cams by this means.

SECTION L9

Rear Wheel

(Quickly Detachable Type with 7 in. diameter Brake and Full-Width Hub)

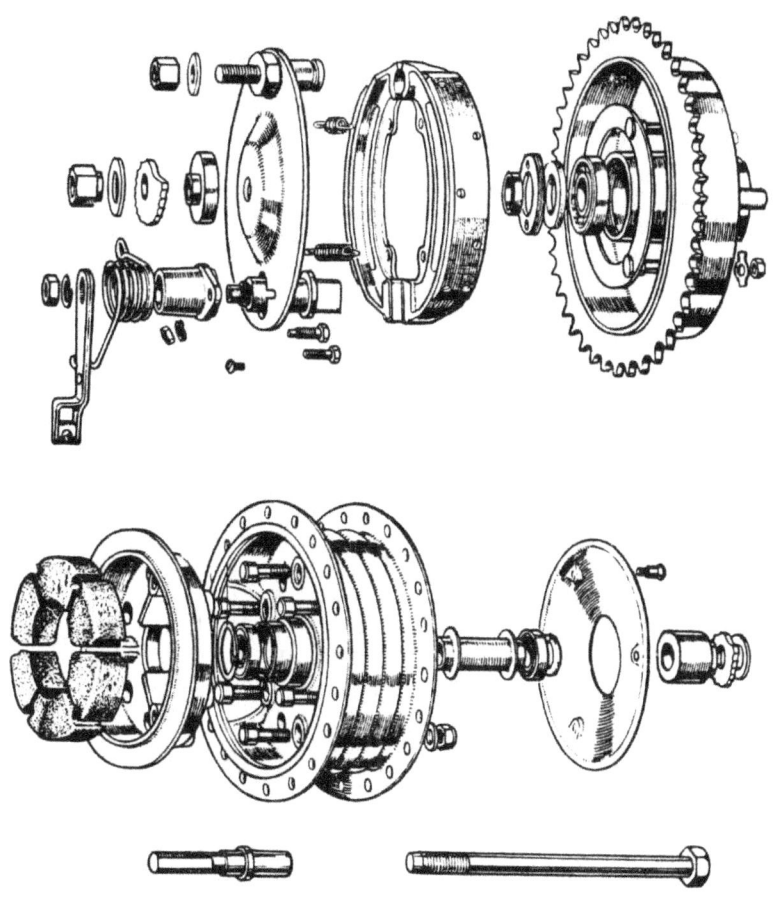

EXPLODED VIEW OF QUICKLY DETACHABLE REAR HUB

Fig. 1

1. Description

This wheel is of the "detachable" type, which enables the main portion of the wheel to be removed from the machine without disturbing the chain or brake. The wheel incorporates the well-known Enfield cush drive and also a 7-in. internal expanding brake.

2. Removal and Replacement of Main Portion of Wheel for Tyre Repairs, etc.

Place the machine on the centre stand, if necessary putting packing pieces beneath the legs of the stand to lift the wheel clear of the ground. Unscrew the loose section of the spindle and withdraw this, together with the chain adjuster cam, preferably marking it to ensure that it is replaced in the same position. Now slide the distance collar out of the fork end and lift away the speedometer drive gearbox, which can be left attached to the driving cable. The spacing collar and the felt washer behind it may now be removed to prevent risk of them falling out when manipulating the tyre. If, however, these are too tight a fit in the hub to come out easily they may be left in place. The main body of the wheel can now be pulled across to the right-hand side of the machine, thus disengaging the six driving pins from the cush drive shell and enabling the wheel to be removed from the machine.

When replacing the main portion of the wheel, reverse the foregoing procedure. The cush drive shell can be prevented from rotating when turning the wheel to engage the six driving pins, if the machine is placed in gear or the rear brake is operated, taking care, when replacing the speedometer drive gearbox, that the driving dogs inside the gearbox engage with the slots in the end of the hub barrel. Before tightening the centre spindle make sure that the speedometer drive gearbox is correctly positioned so that there is no sharp bend in the driving cable.

3. Removal and Replacement of Complete Wheel for Access to Brake

Place the machine on the centre stand and remove the rear mudguard unit. Disconnect the rear driving chain at the spring link and loop the top end of the chain over the tag provided at the top of the fixed portion of the chaincase. Pull on the other end of the chain and allow it to hang. Unscrew the rear brake rod adjusting nut completely and depress the brake pedal so as to disengage the rod from the trunnion in the brake operating lever. Unscrew the brake cover plate anchor nut and remove this together with the washer behind it. Unscrew the loose section of the spindle two or three turns and the spindle nut by a similar amount. Mark the chain adjuster cams to ensure replacing in the same position.* Disconnect the speedometer driving cable and slide the wheel out of the fork ends, tilting it so as to disengage the end of the brake shoe pivot pin from the slot in the fork end.

When replacing the wheel make sure that the dogs on the gear in the speedometer drive gearbox are engaged with the slots in the end of the hub barrel. Make sure also that the speedometer drive gearbox is correctly positioned so that there is no sudden bend in the driving cable. When replacing the connecting link in the driving chain, make sure that the closed end of the spring link points in the direction of travel of the chain. Replace the chain adjuster cams in their original positions or, if necessary, turn each of them the same number of notches to tension the chain and maintain correct wheel alignment. If the chain is adjusted it will be necessary to reposition the front part of the chaincase. This is easily done by slackening the two screws fastening it to the swinging arm chainstay before re-assembling the chaincase to the brake cover plate, then re-tightening the screws. Do not forget to refit the brake rod and adjust the brake so that the wheel turns freely when the brake is off, while at the same time only a small travel of the brake pedal is necessary to put the brake on.

4. Removal of Brake Shoes for Replacement, etc.

Remove the complete wheel as described above, then remove the spindle nut, chain adjuster and the distance collar, thus permitting the complete brake cover plate assembly, with operating cam, pivot pin, shoes and return springs, to be lifted off the hub spindle. The brake shoes can then be removed after detaching the return springs. Brake linings are supplied either in pairs ready drilled complete with rivets (Part No. 42469BX) or ready fitted to service replacement brake shoes (Part No. 41342SR). When riveting linings to shoes, secure the two centre rivets first so as to ensure that the lining lies flat against the shoe. Standard linings are Ferodo MS3, which are drilled to receive cheese-headed rivets.

5. Removal of Brake Operating Cam

To remove the operating cam unscrew the nut which secures the operating lever to the splines on the cam. A sharp tap on the end of the cam spindle will now free the lever, after which the cam can be withdrawn from its housing.

Do not try to remove the brake shoe pivot pin and nut, as these are brazed to the cover plate.

6. Cush Drive

The sprocket/brake drum is free to rotate on the hub barrel. Three radial vanes are formed on the back of the brake drum and three similar vanes are formed on the cush drive shell. Six rubber blocks are fitted between the vanes on the brake drum and those on the cush drive shell, thus permitting only a small amount of angular movement of the sprocket/brake drum relative

---

* Note that the wheel is not necessarily correctly lined up when the same notch position is used on both adjuster cams. Once the position of the cams which gives correct alignment has been found this alignment will, however, be maintained if both cams are moved the same number of notches.

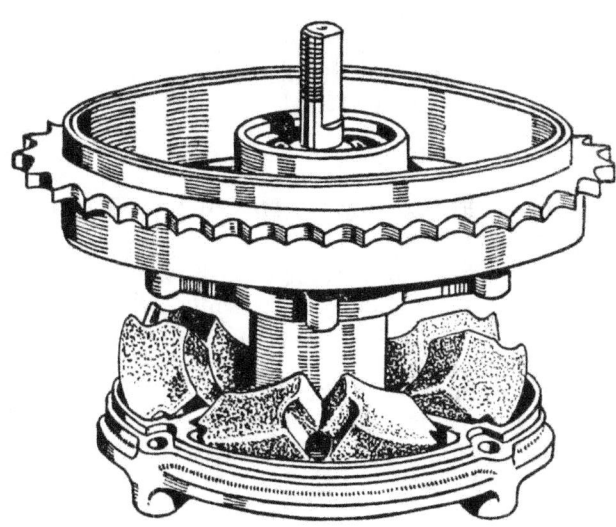

RE-ASSEMBLY OF CUSH DRIVE
Fig. 2

to the hub barrel and transmitting both driving and braking torques and smoothing out harshness and irregularity in the former.

If the cush drive rubbers become worn so that the amount of free movement measured at the tyre exceeds ½ in. to 1 in., the rubbers should be replaced. To obtain access to them remove the complete wheel as described above; then unscrew the loose section of the spindle completely. The main portion of the wheel can then be lifted away from the assembly consisting of the fixed portion of the spindle, sprocket/brake drum complete with brake and the cush drive shell. Now remove the brake cover plate complete with brake shoes as described above, and unscrew the three nuts at the back of the cush drive shell after bending back the locking washers. The three studs are brazed to the lockring and should be driven out of the cush drive shell, each a little at a time to avoid distorting the lockring or bending the studs. The sprocket/brake drum can now be separated from the cush drive shell, and the six cush drive rubbers lifted out.

When reassembling the cush drive the entry of the vanes between the rubbers will be facilitated if the latter are fitted into the driving shell first and then tilted. The rubbers should be liberally smeared with soapsuds to facilitate entry of the vanes. Grease the inner face of the lockring before assembling and tighten the three nuts down solid as there is a shoulder on the stud which prevents tightening of the nuts from locking the operation of the cush drive. Do not forget to bend up the tabs of the three locking washers.

When reassembling the cush drive, coat the inside of the bore of the sprocket/brake drum liberally with grease where it fits over the hub barrel.

7. Removal of Ball Bearings

To remove the ball bearings take the complete wheel out of the machine and separate the main portion of the wheel from the sprocket/brake drum, cush drive shell assembly, as described above. To remove the bearing from the sprocket/brake drum, first remove the brake cover plate complete with brake shoe assembly; then remove the distance collar and unscrew the bearing retaining ring with peg spanner. Now screw the loose section of the spindle into the fixed section and drive out the bearing by hitting the hexagon-headed end of the loose section of the spindle.

To remove the bearings from the loose half of the hub barrel, first lift away the distance collar, speedometer drive gearbox, the spacing collar and the felt washer. Remove the bearing retaining circlip from the driving sprocket end of the barrel. Between the two bearings is a spacer, slotted at one end to enable a drift to be used on the bearing at that end. Remove this bearing first, then enter the loose section of the spindle into the spacer and drive out the remaining bearing by means of a hammer and drift applied to the hexagon-headed end of the spindle.

8. Hub Bearings

These are deep-groove single-row journal ball bearings. The sprocket/brake drum bearing is a Skefko RLS7, $\frac{7}{8}$ in. i/d, by 2 in. o/d, by $\frac{9}{16}$ in. wide. Equivalent bearings of other makes are Hoffmann LS9, Ransome & Marles LJ $\frac{7}{8}$ in., and Fischer LS9. The two bearings in the hub barrel are Skefko RLS5, $\frac{5}{8}$ in. i/d, by $1\frac{9}{16}$ in. o/d, by $\frac{7}{16}$ in. wide. Equivalent bearings of other makes are Hoffmann LS7, Ransome & Marles LJ $\frac{5}{8}$ in., and Fischer LS7.

9. Removal of Hub Driving Pins

To remove the six driving pins from the aluminium full-width hub, first remove the hub cap after unscrewing the three screws attaching it to the hub. Unscrew the six Simmonds nuts and drive out the pins.

10. Refitting Ball Bearings

To refit the sprocket/brake drum bearing, use a hollow drift as shown in Fig. 3. The bearing is first fitted to the fixed section of the spindle; the spindle and bearing are then entered into the sprocket/brake drum and driven home, preferably under a press or using light hammer blows.

The two bearings in the hub barrel are pressed in, using the drift part of E.4823. First assemble the bearing into the circlip grooved end of the barrel and fit the circlip. Replace the bearing spacer, the slot in the spacer can be at either end of the hubs, and assemble the second bearing, supporting the hub on the inner race of the other

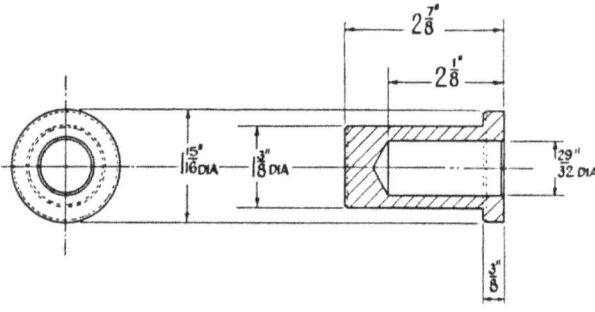

DRIFT FOR RE-FITTING BEARING

Fig. 3

bearing. If the drift part of E.4823 is not available it is essential that the last bearing is assembled by applying pressure to both inner and outer races simultaneously to avoid pre-loading the two hub barrel bearings.

11. Reassembly of Brake Shoes and Operating Cam into Cover Plate

No difficulty should be experienced in carrying out these operations. Put a smear of grease in the grooves of the pivot pin and on the operating face of the cam; also on to the cylindrical bearing surface of the operating cam if this has been removed. Fit the operating lever and trunnion on its splines in a position to suit the extent of wear on the linings and secure with the nut. The range of adjustment can be extended by moving the lever on to a different spline.

12. Centering Cam Housing

Note that the bolt holes in the cam housing are slotted, thus enabling the brake shoe assembly to be centred in the drum. It is not intended that on rear brakes the cam housing should be left free to float but the shoes should be centred by leaving the screws just short of dead tight. The brake cover plate assembly with the shoes should then be fitted over the spindle into the brake drum and the brake applied as hard as possible by means of the operating lever. This will centre the shoes in the drum. The screws should then be tightened dead tight and secured with the locknuts. If the shoes are not correctly centred the brake will be either ineffective or too fierce, depending on whether the trailing or leading shoe first makes contact with the drum. With the brake assembly correctly centred and the screws securing the cam housing correctly tightened wear on both linings should be approximately equal.

13. Final Reassembly of Hub Before Replacing Wheel

Before replacing the felt washers which form the grease seals, pack all bearings with grease. Recommended greases are Castrolease (Heavy), Mobilgrease (No. 4), Esso Grease, Energrease C3 or Shell Retinax A. These are all medium heavy lime soap or aluminium soap greases. The use of H.M.P. greases which have a soda soap base is not recommended as these tend to be slightly corrosive if any damp finds its way into the hubs.

Make sure that the inside of the brake drum is quite free from oil or grease, damp, etc. Replace the felt washers, distance collars, the brake cover plate assembly, speedometer drive gearbox, distance collars, chain adjuster cams, the loose section of the spindle and the spindle nut. The wheel is then ready for reassembly into the machine.

14. Wheel Rim

The wheel rim is type WM2-19 in. plunged and pierced with forty holes for spoke nipples. The spoke holes are symmetrical, i.e., the rim can be assembled to the hub either way round. The rim diameter after building is 19·062 in., the tolerances on the circumference of the rim shoulders where the tyre fits being 59·930/59·870 in. The standard steel measuring tape for checking rims is $\frac{5}{16}$ in. wide, ·011 in. thick, and its length is 59·964/59·904 in. Two security bolts are fitted.

15. Spokes

The spokes are of the single butted type, 8-10 gauge, with 90° countersunk heads, thread diameter ·144 in., 40 threads per inch, thread form British Standard Cycle. The inner spokes are $6\frac{5}{8}$ in. long with an angle of bend 100°, and the outer spokes $6\frac{3}{4}$ in. long with an angle of bend 80°. One security bolt is fitted. There is also a balance weight clipped to a spoke by means of a small screw.

16. Wheel Building and Truing

The spokes are laced one over two and the wheel rim must be built central in relation to the outer faces of the distance collars. The rim should be trued as accurately as possible, the maximum permissible run-out both sideways and radially being plus or minus $\frac{1}{32}$ in.

17. Tyre

The standard tyre is Dunlop 3·50—19 in. studded tread.

When removing the tyre always start close to the valve and see that the edge of the cover at the other side of the wheel is pushed down into the well in the rim.

When replacing the tyre fit the part by the valve last, also with the edge of the cover at the other side of the wheel pushed down into the well.

If the correct method of fitting and removal of the tyre is adopted it will be found that the covers can be manipulated quite easily with the small levers supplied in the tool-kit. The use of long levers and/or excessive force is liable to damage the walls of the tyre. After inflation make sure that the tyre is fitting evenly all the way round the rim. A line moulded on the wall of the tyre indicates whether or not the tyre is correctly fitted. If the tyre has a white mark indicating a balance point, this should be fitted near the valve.

18. Tyre Pressures

The recommended pressures for the rear tyre are 20 lb. per sq. in. for a solo rider and 32 lb. per sq. in when a pillion passenger is carried.

19. Lubrication

Grease the bearings by packing them with grease after dismantling the hub as described above.

Note that the brake cam is drilled for a grease passage but the end of this is stopped up with a countersunk screw instead of being fitted with a grease nipple. This is done to prevent excessive greasing by over-enthusiastic owners. If the cam is smeared with grease on assembly it should require no further attention but in case of necessity it is possible to remove the screw, fit a grease nipple in its place and grease the cam by this means.

NOTES

SECTION M6

Special Tools

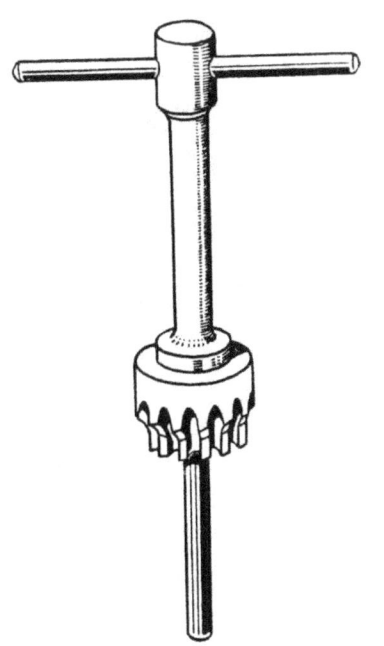

INLET VALVE SEAT ARBOR
T.2053 all models

INLET VALVE SEAT CUTTER
T.2054 Constellation, Super Meteor and Meteor Minor
T.2137 500 Twin
T.1892 500 Bullet
T.1891 350 Bullet

ASSEMBLY GAUGE IN USE TO CENTRALISE ROTOR

T.2055 Constellation, Super Meteor and Meteor Minor, also 1956 350 Bullet and 500 Bullet

T.2138 1955-56 250 Clipper

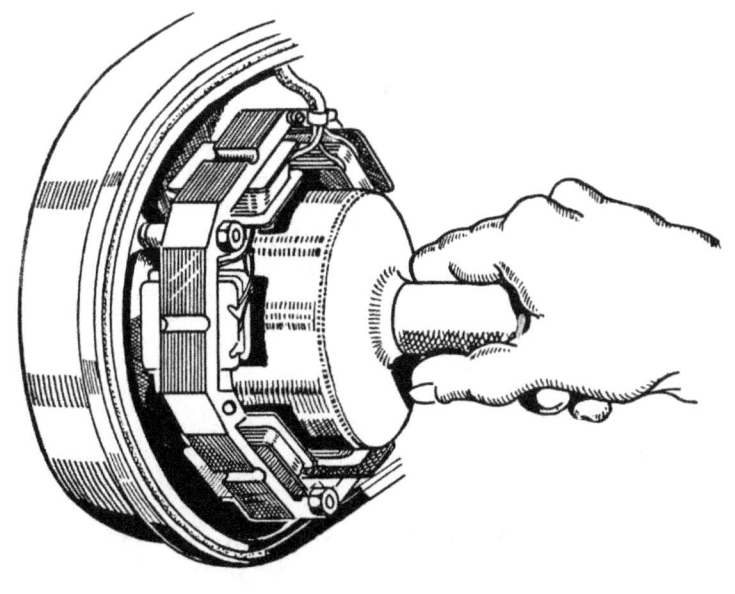

Special Tools for "Constellation"; "Super Meteor"; "Meteor 700"; "Meteor Minor" and "500 Twin"

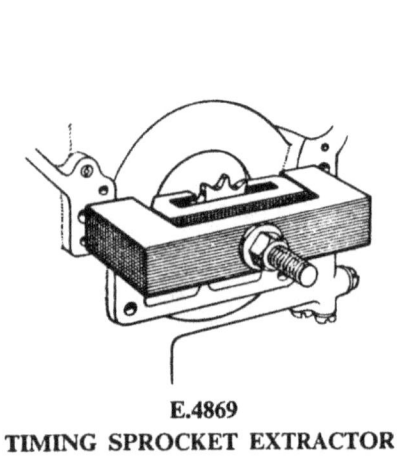

E.4869
TIMING SPROCKET EXTRACTOR

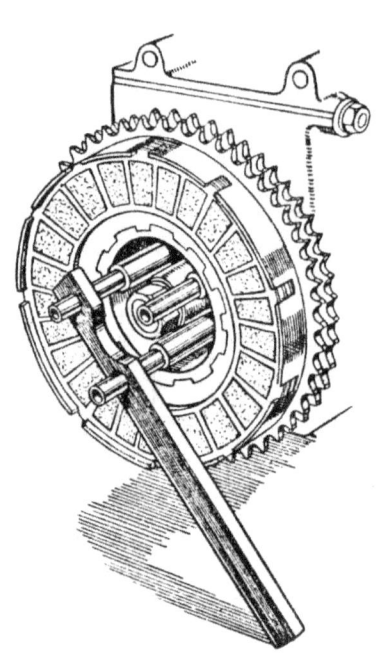

E.4871
CLUTCH HOLDING TOOL

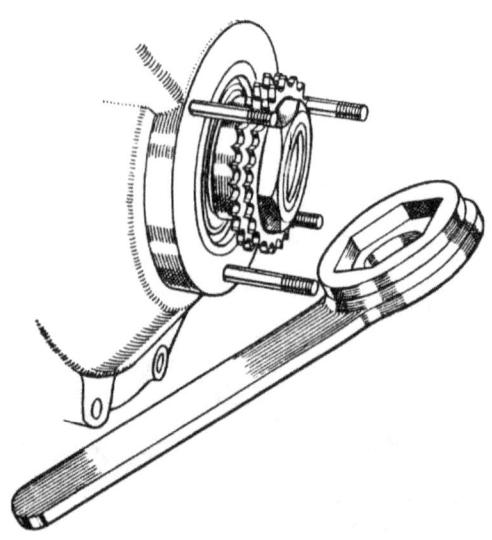

E.4877
ENGINE SPROCKET NUT SPANNER

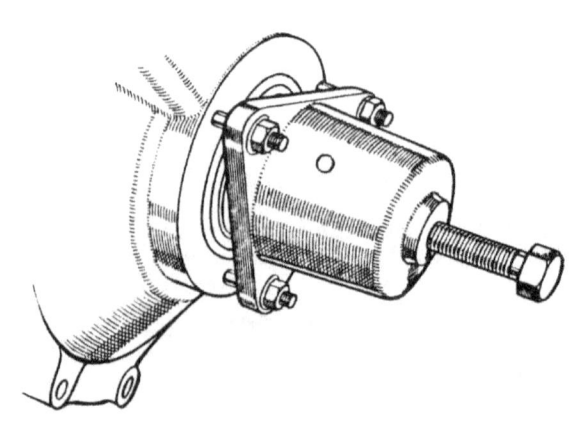

E.5121
CRANKSHAFT EXTRACTOR

Special Tools for "Constellation"; "Super Meteor"; "Meteor 700"; "Meteor Minor" and "500 Twin"

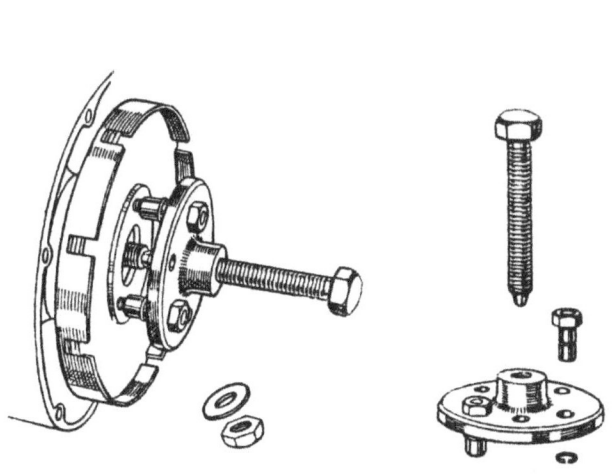

E.5414
CLUTCH HUB EXTRACTOR

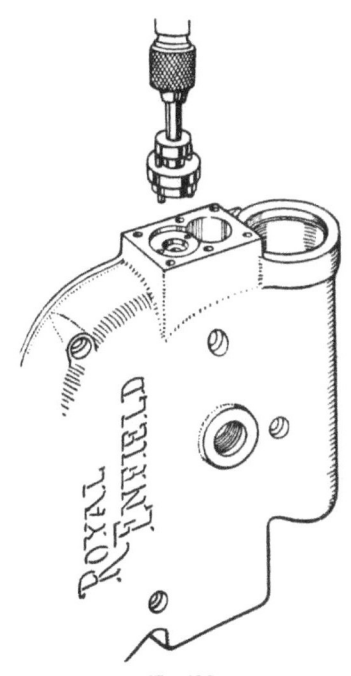

E.5425
PUMP DISC LAPPING TOOL

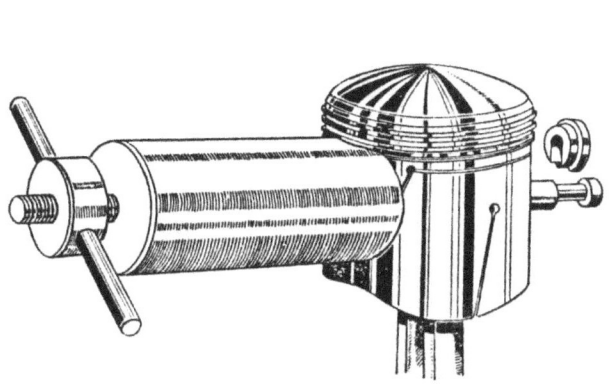

E.5477
GUDGEON PIN EXTRACTOR

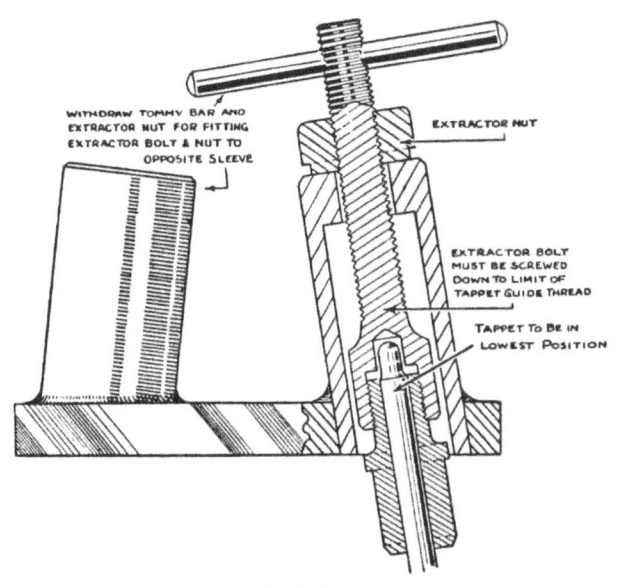

E.5790
TAPPET GUIDE EXTRACTOR

Special Tools for "Constellation"; "Super Meteor"; "Meteor 700"; "Meteor Minor" and "500 Twin"

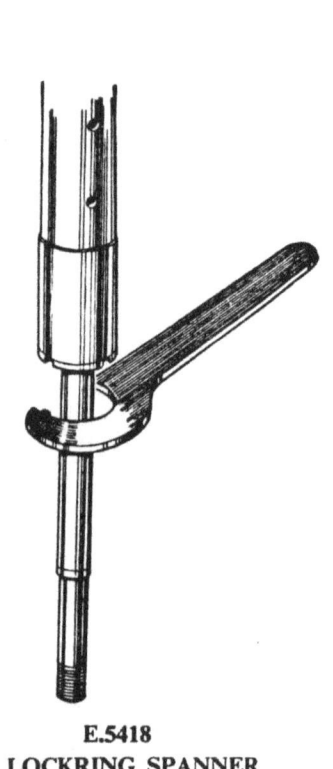

E.5418
LOCKRING SPANNER

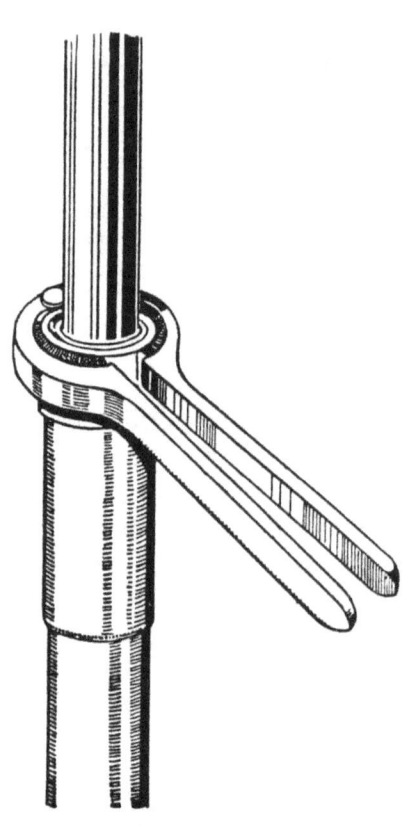

E.4912
OUTER TUBE HAND GRIPS

Special Tools for "Constellation"; "Super Meteor"; "Meteor 700"; "Meteor Minor" and "500 Twin"

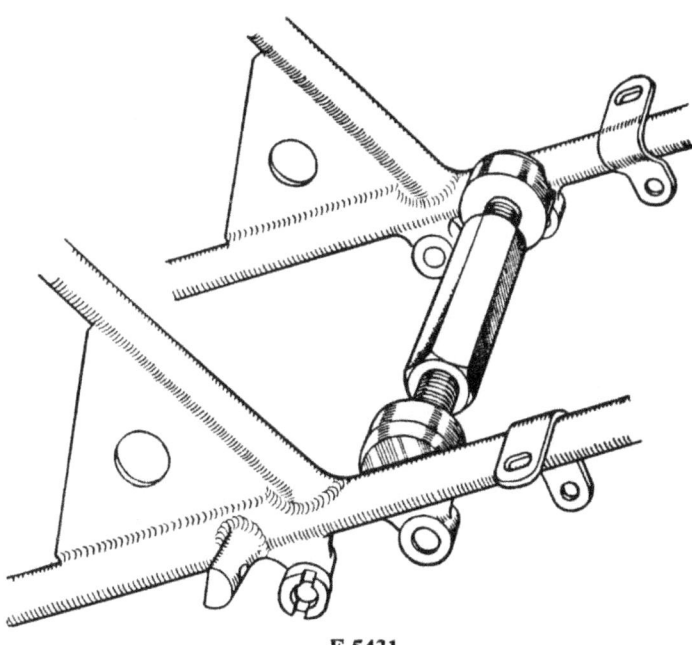

E.5431
FRAME EXPANDER

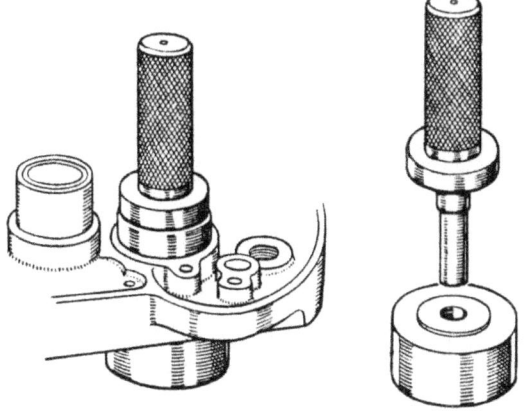

E.4823
GEARBOX COVER BALL BEARING

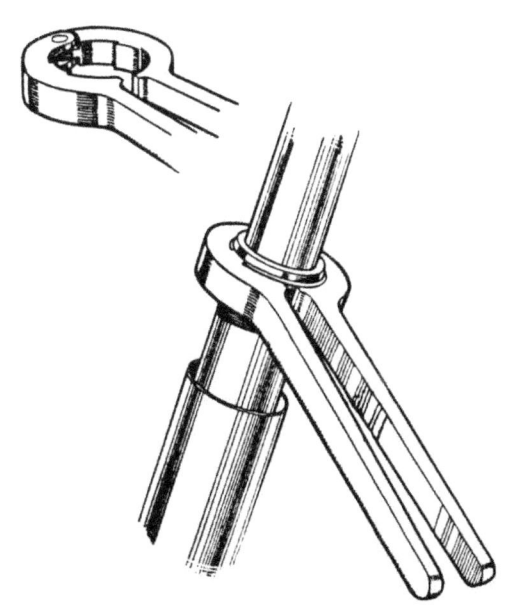

E.5417
GLAND NUT HAND GRIPS

VELOCEPRESS MANUALS – MOTORCYCLE BY MAKE

AJS 1932-1948 SINGLES & TWINS 250cc THRU 1000cc (BOOK OF)
AJS 1945-1960 SINGLES 350cc & 500cc MODELS 16 & 18 (BOOK OF)
AJS 1955-1965 SINGLES 350cc & 500cc (BOOK OF)
AJS 1957-1966 FACTORY WSM - ALL SINGLES & TWINS
ARIEL UP TO 1932 (BOOK OF)
ARIEL 1932-1939 PREWAR MODELS (BOOK OF)
ARIEL 1933-1951 (WORKSHOP MANUAL)
ARIEL 1939-1960 4 STROKE SINGLES (BOOK OF)
ARIEL 1958-1964 LEADER & ARROW FACTORY WSM & PARTS LIST
ARIEL 1958-1964 LEADER & ARROW (BOOK OF)
BMW R26 R27 (1956-1967) FACTORY WORKSHOP MANUAL
BMW R50 R50S R60 R69S (1955-1969) FACTORY WORKSHOP MANUAL
BRIDGESTONE 90 SERIES FACTORY WSM & PARTS CATALOGUE
BRIDGESTONE 175 SERIES FACTORY WSM & PARTS CATALOGUE
BRIDGESTONE 350 SERIES FACTORY WSM & PARTS CATALOGUES
BSA SERVICE SHEETS MASTER CATALOGUE ALL MODELS 1945-1967
BSA BANTAM D1 TO D7 1948-1966 FACTORY SERVICE SHEETS MANUAL
BSA BANTAM ALL MODELS FROM 1948 ONWARDS (BOOK OF)
BSA DANDY FACTORY WORKSHOP MANUAL (COMPILATION)
BSA SINGLES & V-TWINS UP TO 1927 (BOOK OF)
BSA SINGLES & V-TWINS UP TO 1930 (BOOK OF)
BSA SINGLES & V-TWINS UP TO 1935 (BOOK OF)
BSA SINGLES & V-TWINS 1936-1939 (BOOK OF)
BSA C10, C11 & C12 1945-1958 FACTORY SERVICE SHEETS MANUAL
BSA OHV & SV SINGLES 250-600cc 1945-1959 (BOOK OF)
BSA C15 & B40 1958-1967 FACTORY SERVICE SHEETS MANUAL
BSA OHV & SV SINGLES 250cc (ONLY) 1954-1970 (BOOK OF)
BSA B31, B32, B33 & B34 1945-60 FACTORY SERVICE SHEETS MANUAL
BSA OHV SINGLES 350 & 500cc 1955-1967 (BOOK OF)
BSA M20, M21 & M33 1945-1963 FACTORY SERVICE SHEETS MANUAL
BSA TWINS A7 & A10 1948-1962 FACTORY SERVICE SHEETS MANUAL
BSA TWINS A7 & A10 1948-1962 (BOOK OF)
BSA TWINS A50 & A65 1962-1965 FACTORY WORKSHOP MANUAL
BSA TWINS A50 & A65 1962-1969 (SECOND BOOK OF)
DOUGLAS 1929-1939 PREWAR ALL MODELS (BOOK OF)
DOUGLAS 1948-1957 POSTWAR ALL MODELS FACTORY SHOP MANUAL
DUCATI 160cc, 250cc & 350cc OHC MODELS FACTORY SHOP MANUAL
HONDA 50cc ALL MODELS UP TO 1970 INC MONKEY & TRAIL (BOOK OF)
HONDA 90cc ALL MODELS UP TO 1966 (BOOK OF)
HONDA 50-65-70-90cc OHC SINGLES 1959-1983 FACTORY WSM
HONDA 100-125cc SINGLES CB/CD/CL/SL/TL 1970-1984 FACTORY WSM
HONDA 125-150cc TWINS C/CS/CB/CA FACTORY WORKSHOP MANUAL
HONDA 125-160-175-200cc TWINS 1965-1978 FACTORY WORKSHOP MANUAL
HONDA 250-305cc TWINS C/CS/CB 1959-1967 FACTORY WSM
HOHDA 250-350cc TWINS CB/CL/SL 1968-1973 FACTORY WSM
HONDA 250-360cc TWINS CB/CL/CJ 1974-1977 FACTORY WSM
HONDA 450cc TWINS CB/CL 1965-1974 K0 TO K7 WORKSHOP MANUAL
HONDA 500cc & 550cc 4CYL 1971-1978 FACTORY WORKSHOP MANUAL
HONDA 750cc SHOC 4 CYL 1969-1978 K0~K8 WORKSHOP MANUAL
HONDA C100 SUPER CUB FACTORY WORKSHOP MANUAL
HONDA C110 SPORT CUB 1962-1969 FACTORY WORKSHOP MANUAL
HONDA TWINS & SINGLES 50cc THRU 305cc 1960-1966 (BOOK OF)
HONDA TWINS ALL MODELS 125cc THRU 450cc UP TO 1968 (BOOK OF)
INDIAN PONYBIKE, BOY RACER & PAPOOSE ILL PARTS LIST & SALES LIT
J.A.P. ENGINES 1927-1952 & MOTORCYCLES 1934-1952 (BOOK OF)
MATCHLESS 1931-1939 ALL MODELS 250cc THRU 990cc (BOOK OF)
MATCHLESS 1945-1956 350 & 500cc SINGLES (BOOK OF)
MATCHLESS 1955-1966 350 & 500cc SINGLES (BOOK OF)
MATCHLESS 1957-1966 FACTORY WSM - ALL SINGLES & TWINS
NEW IMPERIAL ALL SV & OHV FROM 1935 ONWARDS (BOOK OF)
NORTON 1932-1939 PREWAR MODELS (BOOK OF)
NORTON 1932-1947 (BOOK OF)
NORTON 1938-1956 (BOOK OF)
NORTON 1945-1963 MODELS 16H, Big4, ES2, 19 & 50 WSM'S & PARTS
NORTON 1955-1963 MODELS 19, 50 & ES2 (BOOK OF)
NORTON 1948-1970 DOMINATOR TWINS FACTORY WSM'S & PARTS
NORTON 1955-1965 DOMINATOR TWINS (BOOK OF)
NORTON 1960-1970 TWIN CYLINDER FACTORY WORKSHOP MANUAL
NORTON 1970-1975 COMMANDO 850 & 750cc FACTORY WSM
NORTON 1975-1978 MK 3 COMMANDO 850 cc FACTORY WSM
PANTHER 1932-1958 LIGHTWEIGHT MODELS 250 & 350cc (BOOK OF)
PANTHER 1938-1966 HEAVYWEIGHT MODELS 600 & 650cc (BOOK OF)
RALEIGH MOTORCYCLES 1919-1933 (BOOK OF)
ROYAL ENFIELD 1934-1946 SINGLES & V TWINS (BOOK OF)
ROYAL ENFIELD 1937-1953 SINGLES & V TWINS (BOOK OF)
ROYAL ENFIELD 1946-1962 SINGLES (BOOK OF)
ROYAL ENFIELD 1952-1963 700cc TWINS FACTORY WORKSHOP MANUAL
ROYAL ENFIELD 1958-1966 250cc & 350cc SINGLES (SECOND BOOK OF)
ROYAL ENFIELD 1962-1970 INTERCEPTOR WSM'S & PARTS (Compilation)
RUDGE 1933-1939 (BOOK OF)
SUNBEAM 1928-1939 (BOOK OF)
SUNBEAM 1946-1957 S7 & S8 (BOOK OF)
SUZUKI 50cc & 80cc UP TO 1966 (BOOK OF)
SUZUKI T10 1963-1967 FACTORY WORKSHOP MANUAL
SUZUKI T20 & T200 1965-1969 FACTORY WORKSHOP MANUAL
SUZUKI TWINS 1962 ONWARDS 125-500cc WORKSHOP MANUAL
TRIUMPH 1935-1949 SINGLES & TWINS (BOOK OF)
TRIUMPH 1937-1951 (WORKSHOP MANUAL)
TRIUMPH 1945-1955 FACTORY WORKSHOP MANUAL
TRIUMPH 1945-1959 TWINS (BOOK OF)
TRIUMPH 1956-1969 TWINS (BOOK OF)
TRIUMPH 1963-1970 UNIT CONSTRUCTION 650cc FACTORY WSM
TRIUMPH 1963-1974 UNIT CONSTRUCTION 350-500cc FACTORY WSM
TRIUMPH 1968-1974 TRIDENT T150 & T150V FACTORY WSM
VELOCETTE 1925-1970 ALL SINGLES & TWINS (BOOK OF)
VELOCETTE 1933-1952 MOV-MAC-MSS RIGID FRAME FACTORY WSM
VELOCETTE 1954-1971 MSS-VENOM-THRUXTON-VIPER FACTORY WSM
VILLIERS ENGINE UP TO 1959 INC. 3 WHEELERS (BOOK OF)
VILLIERS ENGINE UP TO 1969 (BOOK OF)
VINCENT 1935-1955 (WORKSHOP MANUAL)
YAMAHA 1961-1967 YA5 & YA6 (WORKSHOP MANUAL & ILL PARTS LIST)
YAMAHA 1971-1972 JT18 & JT2 (WORKSHOP MANUAL & ILL PARTS LIST)

VELOCEPRESS TECHNICAL BOOKS – MOTORCYCLE

1930'S BRITISH MOTORCYCLE CARBS & ELEC COMPONENTS (BOOK OF)
1930'S BRITISH MOTORCYCLE ENGINES (OVERHAUL & MAINTENANCE)
1930'S BRITISH MOTORCYCLE GEARBOXES & CLUTCHES (BOOK OF)
CATALOG OF BRITISH MOTORCYCLES (1951 MODELS)
LUCAS ELECTRONICS BRITISH M/CYCLES REPAIR & PARTS (1950-1977)
MOTORCYCLE ENGINEERING (P.E. Irving)
MOTORCYCLE ROAD TESTS 1949-1953 (Motor Cycle Magazine UK)
SPEED AND HOW TO OBTAIN IT (Motor Cycle Magazine UK)
TUNING FOR SPEED (P.E. Irving)
WIPAC (COMBO) MANUAL NUMBER 3 + M/CYCLE & SCOOTER MANUAL

VELOCEPRESS MANUALS – SCOOTERS BY MAKE

BSA SUNBEAM SCOOTER WORKSHOP MANUAL 1959-1965
BSA SUNBEAM SCOOTER 1959-1965 (BOOK OF)
LAMBRETTA 1947-1957 ALL 125 & 150cc MODELS (BOOK OF)
LAMBRETTA 1957-1970 LI & TV MODELS (SECOND BOOK OF)
NSU PRIMA 1956-1964 ALL MODELS (BOOK OF)
TRIUMPH TIGRESS SCOOTER WORKSHOP MANUAL 1959-1965
TRIUMPH TIGRESS SCOOTER (BOOK OF)
VESPA 1951-1961 (BOOK OF)
VESPA 1955-1963 125 & 150cc & GS MODELS (SECOND BOOK OF)
VESPA 1955-1968 GS & SS (BOOK OF)
VESPA 1963-1972 90, 125 & 150cc (THIRD BOOK OF)

VELOCEPRESS MANUALS – MOPEDS & MOTORIZED BICYCLES

CYCLEMOTOR (BOOK OF)
NSU QUICKLY 1953-1963 ALL MODELS (BOOK OF)
PUCH MAXI N & S MAINTENANCE & REPAIR (3 MANUAL COMPILATION)
RALEIGH MOPEDS 1960-1969 (BOOK OF)

VELOCEPRESS MANUALS - THREE WHEELER'S

BOND MINICAR THREE WHEELER 1948-1967 (BOOK OF)
BMW ISETTA FACTORY WORKSHOP MANUAL
BSA THREE WHEELER (BOOK OF)
RELIANT REGAL THREE WHEELER 1952-1973 (BOOK OF)
VINTAGE MORGAN THREE WHEELER (BOOK OF)

VELOCEPRESS MANUALS – AUTOMOBILE BY MAKE

ALFA ROMEO GIULIA WORKSHOP MANUAL 1300 TO 2000cc 1962-1975
ALFA ROMEO GIULIA TECH MANUAL CARBURETED CARS FROM 1962
ALFA ROMEO GIULIA TECH MANUAL FUEL INJECTED CARS FROM 1969
ALFA ROMEO GIULIETTA & GIULIA 750 & 101 SERIES 1955-1965 WSM
AUSTIN-HEALEY SPRITE & MG MIDGET WORKSHOP MANUAL 1958-1971
BMW 600 LIMOUSINE FACTORY WORKSHOP MANUAL
BMW 600 LIMOUSINE OWNERS HAND BOOK & SERVICE MANUAL
BMW 2000 & 2002 1966-1976 WORKSHOP MANUAL
CORVAIR 1960-1969 WORKSHOP MANUAL
CORVETTE V8 1955-1962 WORKSHOP MANUAL
FERRARI HANDBOOK ROAD & RACE CARS (SERVICE/SPECS) 1948-1958
FERRARI 250/GT SERVICE & MAINTENANCE MANUAL 1956-1965
FIAT 500 FACTORY WORKSHOP MANUAL 1957-1973
FIAT 600, 600D & MULTIPLA FACTORY WORKSHOP MANUAL 1955-1969
JAGUAR E-TYPE 3.8 & 4.2 SERIES 1 & 2 WORKSHOP MANUAL
JAGUAR MK 7, 8, 9 & XK120, 140, 150 WORKSHOP MANUAL 1948-1961
METROPOLITAN FACTORY WORKSHOP MANUAL
MGA & MGB OWNERS HANDBOOK & WORKSHOP MANUAL
MG MIDGET TC, TD, TF & TF1500 WORKSHOP MANUAL
PORSCHE 356 1948-1965 WORKSHOP MANUAL
PORSCHE 911 2.0, 2.2, 2.4 LITRE 1964-1973 WORKSHOP MANUAL
PORSCHE 911 2.7, 3.0, 3.2 LITRE 1973-1989 WORKSHOP MANUAL
PORSCHE 912 WORKSHOP MANUAL
PORSCHE 914/4 & 914/6 1.7, 1.8, 2.0 LITRE 1970-1976 WSM
TRIUMPH TR2, TR3, TR4 1953-1965 WORKSHOP MANUAL
VOLKSWAGEN TRANSPORTER, TRUCKS & WAGONS 1950-1979 WSM
VOLVO 1944-1968 ALL MODELS WORKSHOP MANUAL

VELOCEPRESS TECHNICAL BOOKS - AUTOMOBILE

HOW TO BUILD A FIBERGLASS CAR
HOW TO BUILD A RACING CAR
HOW TO RESTORE THE MODEL 'A' FORD
MASERATI OWNER'S HANDBOOK
PERFORMANCE TUNING THE SUNBEAM TIGER
SOUPING THE VOLKSWAGEN
SOLEX CARBURETORS (EMPHASIS ON UK & EU AUTOMOBILES)
SU CARBURETORS (EMPHASIS ON UK AUTOMOBILES)
WEBER CARBURETORS (EMPHASIS ON ALFA & FIAT)

VELOCEPRESS BOOKS & GUIDES - AUTOMOBILE

COMPLETE CATALOG OF JAPANESE MOTOR VEHICLES
FERRARI 308 SERIES BUYER'S AND OWNER'S GUIDE
FERRARI BROCHURES AND SALES LITERATURE 1968-1989
FERRARI SERIAL NUMBERS PART I - ODD NUMBERS TO 21399
FERRARI SERIAL NUMBERS PART II - EVEN NUMBERS TO 1050
HENRY'S FABULOUS MODEL "A" FORD
MASERATI BROCHURES AND SALES LITERATURE

VELOCEPRESS BOOKS – RACING

CARRERA PANAMERICANA - MEXICAN ROAD RACE (BOOK OF)
DIALED IN - THE JAN OPPERMAN STORY
VEDA ORR'S NEW REVISED HOT ROD PICTORIAL

********** www.VelocePress.com **********

Please check our website:

www.VelocePress.com

for a complete
up-to-date list of
available titles

www.ingramcontent.com/pod-product-compliance
Lightning Source LLC
Chambersburg PA
CBHW080734300426
44114CB00019B/2589